From Deleuze and Guattari to Posthumanism

Theory in the New Humanities

Series editor: Rosi Braidotti

Theory is back! The vitality of critical thinking in the world today is palpable, as is a spirit of insurgency that sustains it. Theoretical practice has exploded with renewed energy in media, society, the arts and the corporate world. New generations of critical 'studies' areas have grown alongside the classical radical epistemologies of the 1970s: gender, feminist, queer, race, postcolonial and subaltern studies, cultural studies, film, television and media studies.

This series aims to present cartographic accounts of emerging critical theories and to reflect the vitality and inspirational force of on-going theoretical debates.

Editorial board
Stacy Alaimo (University of Texas at Arlington, USA)
Simone Bignall (University of Technology Sydney, Australia)
Judith Butler (University of Berkeley, USA)
Christine Daigle (Brock University, Canada)
Rick Dolphijn (Utrecht University, The Netherlands)
Matthew Fuller (Goldsmiths, University of London, UK)
Engin Isin (Queen Mary University of London, UK, and University of London Institute in Paris, France)
Patricia MacCormack (Anglia Ruskin University, UK)
Achille Mbembe (University Witwatersrand, South Africa)
Henrietta Moore (University College London, UK)

Other titles in the series:
Posthuman Glossary, edited by Rosi Braidotti and Maria Hlavajova
Conflicting Humanities, edited by Rosi Braidotti and Paul Gilroy
General Ecology, edited by Erich Hörl with James Burton
Philosophical Posthumanism, Francesca Ferrando
The Philosophy of Matter, Rick Dolphijn
Materialist Phenomenology, Manuel DeLanda

From Deleuze and Guattari to Posthumanism

Philosophies of Immanence

Edited by
Christine Daigle and Terrance H. McDonald

BLOOMSBURY ACADEMIC
LONDON • NEW YORK • OXFORD • NEW DELHI • SYDNEY

BLOOMSBURY ACADEMIC
Bloomsbury Publishing Plc
50 Bedford Square, London, WC1B 3DP, UK
1385 Broadway, New York, NY 10018, USA
29 Earlsfort Terrace, Dublin 2, Ireland

BLOOMSBURY, BLOOMSBURY ACADEMIC and the Diana logo are trademarks
of Bloomsbury Publishing Plc

First published in Great Britain 2022
This paperback edition published 2023

Copyright © Christine Daigle, Terrance H. McDonald, and Contributors, 2022

Christine Daigle and Terrance H. McDonald have asserted their right under the Copyright,
Designs and Patents Act, 1988, to be identified as Editors of this work.

For legal purposes the Acknowledgements on p. x constitute an extension
of this copyright page.

Cover design by Ben Anslow
Cover images: George Berkeley (1685–1753) Anglo-Irish philosopher aka Bishop Berkeley
(© Pictorial Press Ltd / Alamy); George Berkeley (1685–1753), aka Bishop Berkeley (Bishop
of Cloyne). Anglo-Irish philosopher. Vanderbank (© Classic Image / Alamy); A vertical
oval ornate decorative hand carved natural wooden frame (© Image Farm Inc. / Alamy);
A vertical gold thin decorative ornate oval antique frame (© Image Farm Inc. / Alamy)

All rights reserved. No part of this publication may be reproduced or transmitted
in any form or by any means, electronic or mechanical, including photocopying,
recording, or any information storage or retrieval system, without prior permission
in writing from the publishers.

Bloomsbury Publishing Plc does not have any control over, or responsibility for, any
third-party websites referred to or in this book. All internet addresses given in this
book were correct at the time of going to press. The author and publisher regret any
inconvenience caused if addresses have changed or sites have ceased to exist, but
can accept no responsibility for any such changes.

A catalogue record for this book is available from the British Library.

Library of Congress Cataloging-in-Publication Data
Names: Daigle, Christine, 1967- editor. | McDonald, Terrance H., editor.
Title: From Deleuze and Guattari to posthumanism: philosophies of
immanence / edited by Christine Daigle and Terrance H. McDonald.
Description: London; New York: Bloomsbury Academic, 2022. | Series:
Theory in the new humanities | Includes bibliographical references and index.
Identifiers: LCCN 2021026016 (print) | LCCN 2021026017 (ebook) |
ISBN 9781350262225 (hardback) | ISBN 9781350262232 (ebook) |
ISBN 9781350262249 (epub)
Subjects: LCSH: Immanence (Philosophy) | Posthumanism. | Immanence
(Philosophy) in literature. | Posthumanism in literature.
Classification: LCC B823.F76 2022 (print) | LCC B823 (ebook) | DDC 141–dc23
LC record available at https://lccn.loc.gov/2021026016
LC ebook record available at https://lccn.loc.gov/2021026017

ISBN: HB: 978-1-3502-6222-5
PB: 978-1-3502-6226-3
ePDF: 978-1-3502-6223-2
eBook: 978-1-3502-6224-9

Series: Theory in the New Humanities

Typeset by Deanta Global Publishing Services, Chennai, India

To find out more about our authors and books visit www.bloomsbury.com
and sign up for our newsletters.

Contents

List of contributors	vii
Acknowledgements	x
Introduction: Posthumanisms through Deleuze and Guattari *Christine Daigle and Terrance H. McDonald*	1

Part One Philosophical genealogies – From Deleuze and Guattari to posthumanism

1	Posthuman neo-materialisms and affirmation *Rosi Braidotti*	23
2	Deleuzian traces: The self of the polyp *Christine Daigle*	41
3	The art of good encounters: Spinoza, Deleuze and Macherey on moving from passive to active joy *Bruce Baugh*	63
4	Symmetry and asymmetry in conceptual and morphological formations: The difference plant body growth can make to human thought *Karen L. F. Houle*	85
5	Back to earth! A comparative study between Husserl's and Deleuze's cosmologies *Alain Beaulieu*	106

Part Two From Deleuze and Guattari to posthuman aesthetics

6	Posthuman cinema: Terrence Malick and a Cinema of Life *Terrance H. McDonald*	129
7	Affect/face/close-up: Beyond the affection-image in postsecular cinema *Russell J. A. Kilbourn*	147
8	'Subaltern' imaginings of artificial intelligence: *Enthiran* and *CHAPPiE William Brown*	170
9	Becoming-squid, becoming-insect and the refrain of/from becoming-imperceptible in contemporary science fiction *David H. Fleming*	188

Part Three The politics of Deleuze, Guattari and posthumanism

10	The biopolitics of posthumanism in *Tears in Rain Sherryl Vint*	211
11	Dis/abled reflections on posthumanism and biotech *Martin Boucher*	226

12 Deleuze after Afro-pessimism *Claire Colebrook* 250
13 Incorporeal transformations in truth and reconciliation: A posthuman approach to transitional justice *Mickey Vallee* 268

Index 283

Contributors

Bruce Baugh is Professor Emeritus, philosophy, at Thompson Rivers University. He is the author of *French Hegel: From Surrealism to Postmodernism* (2003) and *Philosophers' Walks* (2021) and the editor and translator of Benjamin Fondane, *Existential Monday* (2016). He has authored many articles and essays on Fondane, Sartre, Derrida, Spinoza and Deleuze.

Alain Beaulieu is Professor of philosophy at Laurentian University. He is the author of *Gilles Deleuze et la phénoménologie* (2006) and *Gilles Deleuze et ses contemporains* (2011). He is the editor of *Gilles Deleuze: héritage philosophique* (2005), *Michel Foucault et le contrôle social* (2008) and *Abécédaire de Martin Heidegger* (2008). He has co-edited *Michel Foucault and Power Today* (2006) with David Gabbard. He has authored many articles and essays on Foucault and Deleuze.

Martin Boucher is a doctoral candidate in Human Studies at Laurentian University in Ontario, Canada. His research deals with the politics of abnormality in the social sciences and the philosophy of science more generally. He is also the Executive Director of a peer-led mental health organization, where he seeks to further the consumer/survivor movement and the role of peers in the mental health system.

Rosi Braidotti is Distinguished University Professor and Director of the Centre for Humanities at the University of Utrecht. She is the author of *Patterns of Dissonance* (1991), *Metamorphoses: Towards a Materialist Theory of Becoming* (2002), *Transpositions: On Nomadic Ethics* (2006), *Nomadic Subjects: Embodiment and Sexual Difference in Contemporary Feminist Theory* (2011) and *The Posthuman* (2013). She also edited *After Cosmopolitanism* (2013) with Patrick Hanafin and Bolette Blaagaard and *Revisiting Normativity with Deleuze* (2012) with Patricia Pisters.

William Brown is an assistant professor of Film at the University of British Columbia, as well as an Honorary Fellow for the School of Arts at the University of Roehampton, London. He is the author of *Non-Cinema: Global Digital Filmmaking and the Multitude* (2018) and, with David H Fleming, of *The Squid Cinema from Hell: Kinoteuthis Infernalis and the Emergence of Chthulumedia* (2020). Forthcoming works include *Navigating from the White Anthropocene to the Black Chthulucene* and *Infinite Ontology: Streaming Media in the Chthulucene* (with David H Fleming, under consideration). He is also a maker of no-budget films, including *This Is Cinema* (2018) and *Mantis* (forthcoming).

Claire Colebrook is Edwin Erle Sparks Professor of English at Penn State University. She is the author of *Deleuze: A Guide for the Perplexed* (1997), *Gilles Deleuze* (2002),

Understanding Deleuze (2002) and *Deleuze and the Meaning of Life* (2010). She is the co-editor, with Tom Cohen, of a series of monographs for Open Humanities Press: Critical Climate Change. She recently completed two books on Extinction for Open Humanities Press – *The Death of the Posthuman* and *Sex After Life* – and has co-authored (with Jason Maxwell) *Agamben* (2015) and (with Tom Cohen and J. Hillis Miller) *Twilight of the Anthropocene Idols* (2016).

Christine Daigle is a professor of philosophy at Brock University. She is the director of the Posthumanism Research Institute. She is the author of *Le nihilisme est-il un humanisme? Étude sur Nietzsche et Sartre* (2005), *Routledge Critical Thinkers: Jean-Paul Sartre* (2009), and *Nietzsche as Phenomenologist. Becoming What One Is* (2021). She is the editor of *Existentialist Thinkers and Ethics* (2006) in which she contributed a chapter on Simone de Beauvoir's ethics. She has also co-edited *Beauvoir and Sartre: The Riddle of Influence* (2009) with Jacob Golomb and *Nietzsche and Phenomenology. Life, Power, Subjectivity* with Élodie Boublil (2013). She is the author of a number of articles on Nietzsche, Sartre, Simone de Beauvoir and most recently on posthumanism.

David H. Fleming is Senior Lecturer in the Communication, Media and Culture division at the University of Stirling, Scotland. His research interests gravitate around the intersectionalities of technology, thought, philosophy and images. He is co-author of *The Squid Cinema from Hell: Kinoteuthis Infernalis and the Emergence of Chthulumedia* (with William Brown) (2020), *Chinese Urban Shi-nema: Cinematicity, Society and Millennial China* (with Simon Harrison) (2020), and the author of *Unbecoming Cinema: Unsettling Encounters with Ethical Event Films* (2017). He is currently working on projects exploring Infinite Ontology and racializing machines in the streaming era.

Karen L. F. Houle is a professor of philosophy at the University of Guelph. She has edited the volume *Minor Ethics: Deleuzian Variations* (2021) with Casey Ford and Suzanne McCullagh, and a second edited volume *Hegel and Deleuze: Together Again for the First Time* (2013) with Jim Vernon. Houle is the author of *Toward a New Image of Thought: Responsibility, Complexity and Abortion* (2013). Her academic articles build off the work of Spinoza, Derrida, Irigaray, Bataille, Foucault, Cixous, and Deleuze and Guattari. She is also the award-winning author of three books of poetry, *Ballast* (2000), *During* (2005) and *The Grand River Watershed: A Folk Ecology* (2019), which were nominated for the Canadian Governor General's Literary Award.

Russell J. A. Kilbourn is a professor in English and film studies at Wilfrid Laurier University. He publishes in memory studies, film theory, adaptation, and comparative literature. His books include *Cinema, Memory, Modernity: The Representation of Memory from the Art Film to Transnational Cinema* (2010) and *The Cinema of Paolo Sorrentino: Commitment to Style* (2020), and he is co-editor of *The Memory Effect: The Remediation of Memory in Literature and Film* (2013).

Terrance H. McDonald is a sessional lecturer II of cinema studies at the University of Toronto Mississauga. Film philosophy, film genre, posthumanism and feminist media studies are his main research areas, which include a primary focus on Hollywood cinema and secondary research on popular cinemas in a global context. His work is published in *Men and Masculinities*, *NORMA: International Journal for Masculinity Studies* and *Symposium*, among other venues. Currently, he is working towards the completion of a monograph: *Posthuman Cinema: Film Philosophy for Life Yet to Come*.

Mickey Vallee teaches in the Centre for Interdisciplinary Studies at Athabasca University, where he holds a Canada Research Chair (Tier II) in Community, Identity and Digital Media. He has co-edited *Demystifying Deleuze: An Introductory Assemblage of Crucial Concepts* (2013) with Rob Shields. He has authored essays and articles on Žižek, Deleuze and Glenn Gould published in such venues as *Deleuze Studies* and *Cultural Studies*. He is the author of *Sounding Bodies Sounding Worlds. An Exploration of Embodiments in Sound* (2019).

Sherryl Vint is Professor of English and media and cultural studies at the University of California, Riverside. She is the author of *Bodies of Tomorrow: Technology Subjectivity, Science Fiction* (2007), *Animal Alterity: Science Fiction and the Question of the Animal* (2010), *Science Fiction: A Guide for the Perplexed* (2014), *Science Fiction: The Essential Knowledge* (2020) and *Biopolitical Futures in Twenty-First Century Speculative Fiction* (2021). She has also edited or co-edited several books, including most recently *After the Human: Culture, Theory and Criticism in the Twenty-First Century* (2020).

Acknowledgements

Christine Daigle would like to thank her co-editor for inspiring this project and for the work he put into it.

Terrance McDonald would like to thank all the professors that sparked his interest in Deleuze, especially those who contributed to this volume, as well as his co-editor for all of her time and guidance on this and many other projects.

We are both thankful for our contributors' support of this project and are delighted that they entrusted their work to us. We thank Dominika Baczyńska Kimberley and Brett Robinson for their work on the manuscript and thank everyone at Bloomsbury, especially Liza Thompson, for their help in finalizing this publication. Thanks also go to anonymous reviewers whose comments and suggestions helped improve our volume.

Introduction

Posthumanisms through Deleuze and Guattari

Christine Daigle and Terrance H. McDonald

In their *What Is Philosophy?*, Deleuze and Guattari explicitly call for new humans: 'We lack creation. *We lack resistance to the present*. The creation of concepts in itself calls for a future form, for a new earth and people that do not yet exist.'[1] One is not born; one becomes a human.[2] This process is complex, as is the lengthy history and development of this process, through which humans have constructed the discourses that give rise to their assumed privilege. As soon as humans were thrown into existence with others, they have been working feverishly to remove themselves from any dependence on relations in order to take command of their world. But who are humans? The category is as elusive as it is exclusive. The categorical distinctions and the philosophies articulating them, which are used to answer this question, have generated real oppressions and limitations. As the borders and edges of the category 'human' continuously erode and expand, a growing number of thinkers are claiming that 'we have never been human'.[3] Moreover, we may recognize that the category of the human and, by extension, humanism functions as a set of transcendent ideas that are only ever construed as part of experience. 'The reversal of values had to go so far', state Deleuze and Guattari, 'making us think that immanence is a prison (solipsism) from which the Transcendent will save us'.[4] This reversal, which posits humans as transcending all other forms of life rather than entangled in multiple relations, seeks to save humanity at any given moment by privileging the few and sacrificing the many. However, this transcendent idea generates much more than an illusion as it provides the basis to inflict suffering on other people and non-human animals. Furthermore, it supports the destruction of other forms of organic and inorganic life through the claim that privileges whoever is considered to be human above all of us with the exception of, the transcendent idea par excellence, god. Thus, posthumanism emerges from Deleuze and Guattari's philosophy as a multiplicity of immanent ideas that seek to reset our perspectives in order for us to come to terms with our relations and our interconnections and thereby be more humble about ourselves. We are fortunate to start in the middle of this movement as there are many works that explore posthumanism and seek to define its potentialities. From the middle, our edited collection will move back and forth as the chapters collected here map pathways for reimagining life through posthumanism in relation to Deleuze, Deleuze and Guattari, as well as the thinkers that affected their ideas that explore philosophies of immanence and many theorists that have created concepts within this wake.[5]

Posthumanism and the posthuman

Posthumanism is a contemporary way of thinking that has been gaining increasing prominence since the turn of the century. The proliferation of work addressing posthumanism itself in an attempt to define it is a sign that a radical potentiality is emerging within the writings of those thinkers that can be grouped, sometimes loosely, under the label 'posthumanism'. What interests us in particular and forms the ground upon which this volume grew is the way in which Deleuze and Guattari's philosophy, as well as the philosophies of immanence that launched their thoughts, have been an inspirational force that gives life to posthumanism in many forms. How do these philosophies shape posthumanist thinking? What concepts and ideas are being put to work in this philosophical movement that seeks to undo centuries of humanist thinking perceived to be responsible for the chaotic state of the world? A mode of posthumanist thinking informed by philosophies of immanence seeks to move away from oppressive and alienating dualistic worldviews by providing a rather intense and harsh critique of classical philosophical understandings of the human as separate from nature and other beings, and of the human as superior to other beings in virtue of possessing reason. It is this human exceptionalism that is identified by posthumanist thinkers of immanence as the root cause of the problems we currently face such as racial oppression and violence, wild capitalism born of neoliberalism, environmental destruction and mass extinctions. Thinkers from various disciplinary positions came to the realization that such an understanding of the human was alienating and destructive in the end. A move away from humanism and its dire consequences is needed.

What are these consequences? A major one is that we destroy the planet we live in, and yet we are deeply connected to it. Another is that we fail globally to relate with others in a way that allows for all to flourish, and instead, we engage in multivalent forms of oppression and exploitation towards other humans and non-humans alike. The driving forces behind this logic of domination and exploitation are hegemonic humanistic systems of thought that permeate Western thinking. The powerful 'man of reason' that is the epitome of Enlightenment thinking and the pinnacle of centuries of philosophizing conceptualizes himself and the world using logical categories, dualistic distinctions, and neat classifications in order to gain control over what is really a dynamic and perpetually changing world of blurred lines and interconnectivity at the individual and collective level. Indeed, the human's rationalistic attempts to gain control over oneself and live ethically have failed since ethical theories have all understood the human in terms of false categories and formulas which frame the human as transcendent. This mode of thinking is in utter disregard of the being of the human that fails to fit these rational and logical ideals. Despite its illusory power and its continued attempt to do so, human reason is unable to rationalize the irrational or, better said, the a-rational. Life itself, in its overflowing dynamic state of flux, resists and subverts as it unfolds as an auto-poietic force. Our edited volume seeks to bring together many alternatives and directions that imagine and map non-hierarchical relations through posthumanist theory informed by philosophies of immanence – with lines running through Deleuze, Deleuze and Guattari, Spinoza, Nietzsche, Braidotti, and other thinkers that open up the capacities of monism for the creation of posthuman tools and concepts.

Our volume does not aim to outline a fixed definition of posthumanism or what a posthuman would look like. Cary Wolfe has already pointed out that there seems to be a clearer understanding of what humanism is about than there is about posthumanism.[6] Moreover, as Rosi Braidotti states, 'The posthuman is a work in progress. It is a working hypothesis about the kind of subjects we are becoming.'[7] In addition, our volume does not intend to serve as an introduction or survey of posthumanism. Anyone familiar with the literature knows that there are a number of strong introductions to posthumanism from a number of theoretical and foundational approaches. The topic itself has been burgeoning since the turn-of-the-millennium with considerations of technologies and their impact on humans as examined from a positive perspective by N. Katherine Hayles (1999) in *How We Became Posthuman* and from a negative perspective by Francis Fukuyama (2002) in *Our Posthuman Future*. More recently, in Pramod K. Nayar's (2014) *Posthumanism* and Stefan Herbrechter's (2013) *Posthumanism*, we find diverse considerations of posthumanism beyond the implications of technologies alone. Mapping of what posthumanism is or its capacities is taken up through lineages of deconstruction and Derrida by Cary Wolfe (2010) in *What Is Posthumanism?* and through lineages of immanence and Deleuze and Guattari by Rosi Braidotti in *The Posthuman* (2013) and, most recently, in *Posthuman Knowledge* (2019). Although Derrida and Deleuze are often inadequately defined as post-structuralist, postmodernist, or, pejoratively, *all too obtuse*, it is evident that the theoretical lineages of these thinkers spur two main posthuman outposts. It is from Deleuze and Guattari that we make our expedition in this collection. Our rationale for this methodological choice is delineated in the next section.

What emerges from a survey of the literature is that there is extent variety in the definitions offered of posthumanism or the posthuman.[8] Our preference is to refer to this variety as 'variations on the theme' of posthumanism. This does not mean that there are no core themes and ideas shared by thinkers engaged in this theoretical approach. It is often the case that positions are shared but expressed through different methodologies and conceptualizations. To start with, posthumanism positions itself against humanism. As Nayar defines it, critical posthumanism, in which our own project is grounded, operates a '*radical decentering of the traditional sovereign, coherent and autonomous human in order to demonstrate how the human is always already evolving with, constituted by and constitutive of multiple forms of life and machines*'.[9] It is a mode of thinking that conceives of the human as constituted by and engaged in dynamic relations, a becoming-human rather than a being-human, the 'becoming' pointing to the always already post of our current self, a beyond the self, a more-than-self that is always already inscribed in its being *qua* relational. For this theoretical approach, relationality is key as is the vitality of forces and the embodied grounding of experiences in its manifold intermingling.

The idea that we must overcome humanist thinking, its dualistic stance and concomitant human exceptionalism is at the core of critical posthumanism. Not always an anti-humanism, posthumanism seeks to radically rethink the human rather than do entirely without it.[10] First and foremost, posthumanism is literally a '*post*-humanism', a reconceptualization of ourselves, the beings we share life with, and that life itself. This conceptual shift entails rejecting binarism in order to think through beings and their life as interconnected, sharing in the same materiality, and conceiving of life as one in which no being takes precedence over any other. Posthumanism, in its varied iterations, emphasizes becoming over being, pointing to the fluctuating and dynamic encounters that constitute us. This conceptualization of continuous flux is what makes defining the posthuman difficult and obscures the possibility of giving it a fixed and stable image. This working hypothesis, to reference Braidotti, realizes a constant becoming that may appear to call for a negative definition: that we indicate what it is not, rather than what it is. The posthuman is *not* the rationalist, autarkic, free-willed, exceptional subject of humanism.

Just as there is variation in how posthumanism is explored, there is variation in the degree to which thinkers embrace any of the negative characterizations listed above. To be fair, there is also just as much variation in how humanist thinkers embrace any of the characteristics of the humanist subject: there is, for example, plenty of debate as to the degree of free will one may possess and exercise with a full range spanning from absolute freedom to absolute determinism. Nevertheless, humanist thinkers tend to emphasize subjectivity, consciousness, rationality as separate from, albeit related to, materiality. Mind and body exist in a relation where mind is conceived of as ultimately separate and transcendent to materiality and accordingly of more importance, as that which distinguishes us from other beings – sometimes conceived as machines without minds as in Descartes – thereby justifying the human exceptionalism that has been so detrimental to the beings with whom we share life but also to ourselves as interconnected beings. Human exceptionalism grounds regimes of oppression and violence where non-humans are systematically devalued and can be exploited without any concern, one of the dire consequences of humanist thinking referred to above. This issue is made worst when 'human' is understood as 'cis, heterosexual, white, able-bodied male', which is most often the case. The ontological stance of humanist thinking grounds a valuing system that is perceived to be problematic by posthumanist thinkers. The posthumanist enterprise seeks to establish a new ontology and thereby new grounds for valuing beings and their relations. Posthumanism forces us to rethink the limits of human perspectives and the inadequacy of a hierarchical and categorical world view that places the greatest importance on humans. Its fundamental transdisciplinary theoretical approach entails a rethinking of ontology, phenomenology, epistemology, ethics and politics. It demands radical new modes of thought that use different means of expression and exploration to challenge the humanist rationalist approach to ourselves, others, life and the world.

That critical posthumanism would emerge in large part from feminist and postcolonial discourses or should have any affinities with them should not come as a surprise. These discourses' challenge and rejection of the oppressive regime of patriarchy and colonialism is often expressed as a questioning of the notions of identity, subjectivity and agency upon which it rests. Who counts as a subject worthy of respect and equality and whose agency ought to be allowed to thrive? Asking the question means revisiting the humanist notion of the subject and subverting it. Feminism and postcolonialism emphasize embodiment as a means of reconnecting the mind to its body and pointing to how different bodies come to experience the world otherwise and how some bodies have taken and occupied an unjustified vantage point. This kind of approach begins to dismantle the binaries erected by humanism, such as mind/body, consciousness/world, self/other, and human/non-human, among others. The dismantling is further pushed by posthumanist thinkers, material feminists, and other new materialists whose inquiries in materiality and interconnectivity pervades a lot of the thinking in this book.[11] Both humanist and material feminism insist on the relationality of selves and the intersubjective construction of identities and thereby push away from humanist conceptions of a unified and singular self that relates to similarly unified and singular others. As Braidotti suggests, 'The theoretical premise of humanist feminism is a materialist notion of embodiment that spells the premises of new and more accurate analyses of power.'[12] While this mode of feminism remains humanist and may revert to identity politics, the feminist new materialism or material feminism, that emerges from it further emphasizes the materiality of bodies and their intertwining. Unitary self-sufficient selves are definitely out of the question for such feminism. This theoretical line informs our understanding of posthumanism and the project pursued in this volume. It has the potential to contribute to the ethical position of critical posthumanism as described by Nayar, namely one that is 'against hierarchization of life forms because such rankings have inevitably resulted in exclusionary practices directed at particular life forms, races and groups'.[13] It opposes the exclusionary mode of thinking embedded in humanism and instead proposes an inclusive approach in which all instances of life and matter have affirmative rather than transcendent moral value. The critical posthumanism engaged with in this volume will at times be of the material feminist or of the postcolonial kind.

Before concluding this section, it is important to address a rather common misunderstanding of posthumanism which identifies it as transhumanism. In fact, this may well be the most popular understanding of the term as it evokes images of cyborgs, artificial intelligence and human enhancement. Transhumanism, however, is a mode of thought that emphasizes the intermingling of the human with technological matter and advancements. It thereby explores how the human self is deeply impacted by these relations in a move, as Ray Kurzweil and others believe, from carbon- to silicon-based life. However, it seems to constitute an intensification of humanism as it moves towards the perfectibility of the human through technological enhancements. As Nayar states, 'Transhumanism continues to believe in the Enlightenment ideals of the human/animal divide' and 'This version of posthumanism is techno-deterministic, and techno-utopian, in its faith in technology's ability to ensure a certain kind of future'.[14] Moreover, transhumanism seems to reinforce human exceptionalism in focusing on how to enhance the human – especially, the mind – and reinforces instrumentalism in that it makes use of matter, technology and life in its pursuit of human purposes. Such a move further exaggerates the assumed superiority of mind over body, which remains a key component of Cartesian dualism. As such, it fails to undermine individualism and anthropocentrism in its reconceptualization of the human and perpetuates a dualistic logic of domination. Worse, through its technological pursuits of perfecting the abilities of the human mind, it risks the destruction of all organic life by providing humans with ever-more efficient tools to exercise their domination and exploitation of the natural world irremediably seen as a set of resources.[15]

Despite all this, a transhumanist discourse is still often understood as having the potential to offer modes of exploration that may serve the posthumanist project. Its pursuit of human enhancement is sometimes perceived as another way to criticize humanism by pointing to the insufficiencies of the humanist self. The problem that arises in some transhumanist approaches, however, is a misrepresentation of human intelligence as the solution to humanist problems. At its most radical, it champions a 'human' independent of most life systems on earth – with perhaps only the exception of the sun for energy. It is problematic precisely because it reverts to a championing of the unitary – self-sufficient if appropriately enhanced – individual. Transhumanism as a methodological stance can be a creative way to explore our human and anthropocentric selves, but any privileging of the mind and human intelligence cannot escape 'the contempt for the flesh and the trans-humanist fantasy of escape from the finite materiality of the enfleshed self'.[16] It is difficult, if not impossible, to imagine a transhumanist theorizing that does not embrace this fantasy of a transcendent realm or state of being that one may achieve by escaping materiality. With that said, there are many pathways for exploring the intersections of posthumanism and technologies that have the capacity to unfold new potentialities without reverting to a transhumanist privileging of mind over body. When considering the implications of technologies on humans, it is indeed more generative to approach the impact on all life instead of the mere enhancement of human beings, which often involves speculation foregrounded in dualism and explorations of how human and human-derived existence could be perfected. The contributions in this volume that explore technologies, and our interactions with them, offer instead a reflesion on posthuman/transhuman identities and relations as opposed to a transhumanism that privileges a mind/body dualism and which seeks to perfect the human only.

The critical posthumanism we embrace is a method, a critique, a thinking after humanism, and, often but not always, an anti-humanism. The posthuman is the human that is theorized by this mode of thinking, a being that differs greatly from the humanist subject, a non-humanist human. When we speak of the posthuman, however, we are also referring to the posthuman condition. We are thereby engaged in a theoretical approach that connects to a lineage of thinkers conceptualizing the postmodern condition in the last part of the last century. Faced with significant changes in all spheres of our existence, it is urgent to rethink our condition and reassess how we live our lives especially given the ongoing instability of our planet. In our current moment, which has continued to change at a frenzied and accelerating pace, and in an epoch now officially referred to as the Anthropocene – a geological epoch in which the human has radically altered the earth system – many problems call for new methodologies. These problems are dynamic and global, and include climate change and how it impacts humans and non-humans; the technologization of every aspect of our daily lives and the ethical problems this generates; a constant state of war and terror in many different forms and related issues such as the migrant crisis and racialized violence; and the rise of global crises such as the pandemic (or potential endemic) generated by COVID-19. All of these problems call for a new understanding of ourselves and the others with which we share the planet, and how this sharing takes shape. Our posthuman condition[17] is radically different in terms of its particularities than that of the postmodern or modern one, and, as such, requires new theorizations. Entries in this volume discuss this condition and offer ways to conceptualize it and offer suggestions for how these new conceptualizations may bring means to address the challenges with which we are faced.

Posthumanism, Deleuze and Guattari, and philosophies of immanence

In this volume, we choose to explore critical posthumanism as it emerges from the philosophical lineage grounded in a neo-Spinozist monistic ontology with interconnections with philosophies of immanence and thinkers that advance life and its manifold striving, including Nietzsche, Bergson, Deleuze and Guattari.[18] Taking these as pathways, that directly and indirectly work through his philosophy, Deleuze reads these thinkers as belonging to a lineage of immanence. In this sense, posthumanisms through Deleuze and Guattari map modes for rethinking the human subject and the tenets of humanism by relying on Deleuze and Guattari or on related thinkers that are embraced by methodologies intimately tied to Deleuze's reading of them as well as the modes of thought that emerge in their wake. We agree with Braidotti that there is a connection between a rejection of humanism as well as its anthropocentrism and a monistic ontology that Deleuze reads in Spinoza.[19] Spinoza and his monism have been generative for a diverse range of thinkers throughout the late twentieth and early twenty-first century who seek alternatives to dualistic modes of understanding.[20] Common to all the recent engagements with Spinoza's philosophy is a striving to break down the barriers, categories and hierarchies held in place by dualistic, dialectic and negative modes of thinking.

Spinoza's monism and its inherent vitalism resonate in Nietzsche's philosophy although Nietzsche's interest in Spinozist philosophy seems to have focused in particular on the rejection of free will and the ethics. Importantly for the pathways we investigate here, Nietzsche was highly sceptical of humanist philosophies that conceived of the human in dualistic terms and in opposition to its own embodied self and the world it lives in.[21] Instead, he argued that the world is will to power and offered that 'wherever I found a living creature, there I found will to power'.[22] For him, all creatures, human and non-human alike, are the embodiment of this creative and generative force that the will to power is. This, combined with his rejection of any transcendent realm, makes him an important precursor to posthumanism. Likewise, Bergson's philosophy focuses on life and its unfolding through 'élan vital'. The focus on biology and evolutionary processes, unpredictable and a-rational as they are and yet constitutive of the intellect, makes of Bergson a good precursor to critical posthumanism. Deleuze had a strong interest in these thinkers and devoted monographs to their philosophies. However, it would be mistaken to think that Deleuze's books on Spinoza, Nietzsche, Bergson, and any other, are simple scholarly commentaries on their works. In many ways, he explores their thinking and shapes his own by borrowing concepts and themes – such as life, immanence, affects, will to power, overcoming and élan vital – to take them in his own, different directions. These concepts and themes, and their Deleuzian expressions, are further developed and taken in yet other directions by thinkers inspired by his work as well as his methodology and those who inscribe themselves in this lineage of thought. In our volume, we invited our contributors to engage in similar modes of thinking: to take pathways through Deleuze, Deleuze and Guattari, or other philosophers of immanence, both those that were an inspirational force to them and those that read Deleuze and Guattari as an inspirational force for their thoughts, within their theoretical explorations of posthumanism. At times, these Deleuzian and Guattarian detours will take the form of commentary and interpretation, but at other times these will be more mischievous and creative. In our view, the latter move generates a becoming Deleuzoguattarian in relation to their invitation to philosophize as an enticement to create concepts and to engage in generative thinking. In our volume, Deleuze and Guattari are thereby vibrant nodes that are constantly taking new forms, new pathways, new lines.

Philosophies of immanence, such as the one Deleuze and Guattari map throughout their independent work and collaborations, not only propose key conceptual tools, but they also offer essential methodologies for developing posthumanist theory as they move us away from what has been a history of arborescent models of existence towards a rhizomatic approach to thinking and becoming. In the introduction to *A Thousand Plateaus*, Deleuze and Guattari state:

> Thought is not arborescent, and the brain is not a rooted or ramified matter. What are wrongly called 'dendrites' do not assure the connection of neurons in a continuous fabric. The discontinuity between cells, the role of the axons, the functioning of the synapses, the existence of synaptic microfissures, the leap each message makes across these fissures, make the brain a multiplicity immersed in its plane of consistency or neuroglia, a whole uncertain, probabilistic system ('the uncertain nervous system').[23]

Here Deleuze and Guattari gesture towards modes of thinking that are far less structured and organized than has hitherto been conceived, especially by those that uphold ideals of reason, logic and transcendence. According to Deleuze and Guattari, we are dealing with a play of forces, both internal and external, involving discontinuities and approximations, rather than straightforward communication and causation. Certainty is replaced by probability and causation by chance. A manner of thinking that is more appropriate for experiences as rhizomatic thinking that explores 'all manner of "becomings"'.[24] This mode of thinking, that breaks down dualisms and moves beyond them, has the capacity to explore the interconnectedness that posthumanism seeks to affirm. Life unfolds myriad relations that we cannot control just as we cannot control our thoughts, dependent as they are on a multiplicity of affects and percepts that spark thinking and the many more minuscule inclinations – such as biochemical reactions – that we could never perceive and yet make our thoughts possible.

Philosophies of immanence offer a pathway to confront the conditions of life as an auto-poietic force through which relations may increase one's power of acting. Deleuze and Guattari seek to map such philosophical pathways through thinkers that seek to disengage from transcendent ideas or rethink the relation between transcendence and immanence. Immanuel Kant's[25] notion that the world, as a knowable object, is an illusion provides an inspiration for Deleuze's thinking about immanence. 'Strictly speaking, the world is not an object of our experience', states Daniel W. Smith in a discussion of Kant's influence on Deleuze, 'what we actually know is the problematic of causality, a series of causal relations that we can extend indefinitely.'[26] Thus, as the Deleuze and Guattari quote in the opening section alludes to, transcendent ideas push us away from actual experience and into notions of imagined experience – that there are knowable objects such as the world. 'Hence, we are led into inevitable illusions', states Smith, 'when we ask questions about the world *as if* it were an object of experience.'[27] As a transcendent idea, the world is an object that exceeds any possible experience. Ideas such as god, the human soul, or even the human of humanism are of a similar nature because if we ask questions *as if* they were objects or subjects of experience, we fabricate illusions and are then led to such notions as the superiority of the human over all other forms of life. Therefore, we recognize, through philosophies of immanence as mapped by Deleuze, Guattari and others, that humanism takes us outside actual experiences of life and sets us on the wrong path, a path of transcendence. Conversely, posthumanism or at least posthumanism from Deleuze and Guattari, opens up a path of immanence or a path of life that seeks to map actual experiences and to come to terms with our interconnections in the world.

The emphasis on immanence put forward by Deleuze and Guattari is meant to dismiss the dualistic modes of thinking that have been dominant. In discussion with Deleuze, Claire Parnet remarks that the deleuzoguattarean rejection of dualistic thinking leads to a new set of dualisms. She questions whether the attempt to dismiss dualisms is successful if this is the case.[28] The theoretical move being made here, however, is not framed as from dualism to dualism, and instead an embracing of continuum. Primarily, within a theoretical posthumanism informed by a monistic ontology, we move away from dualisms and embrace a mind/body continuum as well as a nature/culture continuum which unfolds in immanence. It might be misinterpreted as a reverting to some other form of dualism, but this view fails to grasp this methodology as an ongoing process. Although, for example, a posthumanist thinker may criticize and reject the humanist agent but may also want to cling to some notion of agency and struggle with ways to refer to that posthuman agent. Using 'agent' carries a humanistic conceptual weight that they are seeking to dismantle, yet they read this agent as in flux as it relates to a mind/body continuum as opposed to assuming, as is conceptualized through a humanist agent, that the mind is privileged above the body. Different strategies are put to work to avoid this misinterpretation and to make visible this ongoing process, such as adopting the phrase 'agentic capacity', for example.[29] There are similar efforts being launched by posthuman theorists for a multiplicity of other concepts – some of which take shape in this volume. The method put to work by philosophies of immanence, monistic ontology and Deleuze and Guattari, in particular, seeks to overcome dualisms rather than embrace them. In place of dualisms, we embrace a perspective that explores the inspirational force of continuum.

This mode of thinking, mobilized by philosophies of immanence and monistic ontology, also foregrounds affects, intensities, haecceities, assemblages, and deterritorialization to 'Arrive at the magic formula we all seek – PLURALISM = MONISM – via all the dualisms that are the enemy, an entirely necessary enemy, the furniture we are forever rearranging'.[30] A playful use and creation of concepts, one that risks putting things, objects, ideas, and notions in unfamiliar situations or into uncharacteristic tasks in order to further explore the multiplicity and dynamism of being, is an approach that can open up our thinking and actualize new perspectives. A posthumanism theoretically and methodologically informed by philosophies of immanence and a monistic ontology asks not what posthumanism should do or what specifically a posthuman is, rather it investigates what posthumanism can do as a generative force that disrupts, fragments, escapes, overflows and deterritorializes old modes of thinking. We do recognize that not every reader of Deleuze embraces the generative and joyful interpretation of his philosophy. Some, like Andrew Culp, emphasize a 'dark Deleuze', one who champions a nihilistic approach that does away with the world and reality for good. 'This is where the Dark Deleuze', states Culp, 'parts ways with the joyful by inviting the death of this world.'[31] However, a nihilistic stance can be constructive and joyful, in fact, nihilism might be needed for joy to be possible.[32] Culp argues, 'It is in these moments of opacity, insufficiency, and breakdown that darkness most threatens the ties that bind us to this world.'[33] This world needs to be recognized as illusory, grounded in transcendent thinking, and thereby a harmful construct, one that keeps us away from immanence. A nihilism that rejects this generates possibilities and joy. It is itself joyous. 'A life is everywhere, in all the moments that a given living subject goes through and that are measured by given lived objects', maps Deleuze, 'an immanent life carrying with it the events or singularities that are merely actualized in subjects and objects.'[34] This may be recognized once the veil of transcendent thinking is lifted or ripped, a dark moment but one that is itself generative. In this sense, we move from Deleuze to posthumanism as a means of exploring life through methodologies that aim to avoid the inevitable illusions that arise when the world, god, the 'man' of reason, and, especially, the human are assumed to be transcendent in any and all manifestations. Life flows everywhere.

Posthumanism has the capacity to affirm new methods for the exploration and expression of life, a nomadology that operates through rhizomatic thinking, assemblages and subversion, through thinking that pursues lines of flight and mulls over plateaux. A generative force unfolds when thinking reflects the dynamic intermingling of beings, of matter, of which we are a part, the intermingling we ourselves are. Philosophies of immanence and ensuing posthumanisms subvert arborescent logical thinking and transcendent ideas. No longer the object of inquiry for a logically driven, positivistic mind, life awaits to be grappled and explored through its multiple facets. Deleuze and Guattari say:

Precisely because the plane of immanence is prephilosophical and does not immediately take effect with concepts, it implies a sort of groping experimentation and its layout resorts to measures that are not very respectable, rational, or reasonable. These measures belong to the other order of dreams, of pathological processes, esoteric experiences, drunkenness, and excess. We head for the horizon, on the plane of immanence, and we return with bloodshot eyes, yet they are the eyes of the mind.[35]

To speak of lineage in the way we have may sound as if we are conceiving of thinking as arborescent. 'Posthumanisms Through Deleuze and Guattari' or *From Deleuze and Guattari to Posthumanism* would thereby identify a sequence of thinking that culminates in posthumanism, namely posthumanism as it has been funnelled through the thought of Deleuze and Guattari, and Deleuze and Guattari only. This is not the case within this volume as Deleuze and Guattari form a vibrant node of immanence as opposed to a hierarchal, patriarchal symbol to which our posthumanisms obey. Instead, we see the many intricate connections between all the thinkers involved in the web, or rhizome, of immanentist thinking through which Deleuze and Guattari, and, by extension, posthumanism, takes shape. Indeed, philosophizing is rhizomatic. María Puig de la Bellacasa's discussion of her engagement with Donna J. Haraway's philosophy to think through the notion of care aligns with the methodological approach taken in this volume. She points to the necessity of *thinking-with* which does not amount to a commentary, an embrace, or a direct application of a theorist's views, but an engagement with the whole cluster of thinking that supports and permeates the thinking offered by any given theorist, refusing to encapsulate them in a taxonomy of theoretical positions and schools of thought.[36]

Thinking-with amounts to taking pathways from and, in our case, posthumanisms from Deleuze and Guattari. This approach is what we invited our contributors to do and this may sometimes even lead to a leaving behind of those safeguarded concepts or modes that hopeful disciples of Deleuze and Guattari celebrate in order to formulate new thoughts and visions and focuses our attention on immanence. These formulations, however, could not take the same shape more than once. Therefore, the possibility of taking the same pathway and undertaking the same thinking-with becomes the only impossibility. What we are interested in, ultimately, is how posthumanism takes shape through engaging with Deleuze, Guattari, and the thinkers that form a cluster of thought in relation to philosophies of immanence and monistic ontology. With this in mind, if the chapters included in this book are not read by some as explicitly Deleuzian or Guattarian in their content and theoretical stance, if they are not read as expressing a Deleuzoguattarian orthodoxy, whatever that might mean, they are Deleuzoguattarian in their methodological approach, provided we understand this method as a thinking-with, as generating concepts and embracing the multiple and potentialities for thought, as pathways from Deleuze and Guattari to posthumanisms. Posthumanisms that continually unfold through an engagement with this inspirational force that takes Deleuze and Guattari as a vibrant node – that which coalesces in their thinking and that which is thereafter generated by their thinking – may even have little to do with Deleuze and Guattari in the middle. Nonetheless, the chapters in this volume all take shape through the vitality of Deleuze and Guattari's insistence on what has yet to come.

Summary of contributions

The chapters contained within this volume flow through philosophy to aesthetics to politics. From Braidotti's through to Beaulieu's chapter, the pathways taken by contributors in the first section of the volume map philosophical engagements with questions pertaining to posthumanism as a theoretical force to deal with immanence, which seeks to reimagine life and the human subject amid the interconnections such a subject exists with despite humanist methodologies that take this subject to be primary and independent. The opening chapter 'Posthuman Neo-materialisms, Affirmation', is by Rosi Braidotti. As one of the most timely and cherished philosophers in this contemporary moment, Braidotti continues to challenge and increase the capacities of posthumanist theory by mapping the 'conceptual personae' of the posthuman rather than considering a set of substantive concepts. Her chapter unfolds nomadically with the position that Deleuze and Guattari are 'profoundly anti-humanist and post-anthropocentric thinkers'. By opening up the posthuman as conceptual personae, Braidotti's chapter flows into a rigorous encounter with the question of the posthuman in Deleuze. In the concluding sections, she maps the germinal intersections of affirmative ethics and neo-materialism with generative capacities for political subjectivities in the Anthropocene. We begin our volume with Braidotti's chapter because of the timely and necessary pathway that she affirms, which frames a posthumanist lineage of immanence and maps the vibrancy of materialism for new challenges and thinking to emerge. Furthermore, Braidotti's chapter gestures towards the importance of her work to the field of posthumanism in general, and many of the authors within this volume rely on her conceptualization of posthumanism as much as they rely on Deleuze.

The following chapter by Christine Daigle works through the philosophy of Nietzsche as a key interlocutor to Deleuze. She explores overcoming anthropocentrism and takes a position that is enmeshed within materialism and the potentiality that emerges from intermingling Deleuze and Guattari's philosophy with that of Ricœur's. By outlining the posthuman concept of transjectivity, Daigle argues for a more nuanced account of how the being of the human is formed by a multiplicity of encounters, both internal and external. Putting to work a Nietzschean metaphor on polyps, she pushes for a posthumanist feminism that retains traces of the self – as opposed to completely eradicating agency, a risk that emerges in Deleuze and Guattari's challenge to the humanist subject – which offers the possibility for a bolstered ethical flourishing.

Both Bruce Baugh and Karen L. F. Houle embrace pathways through Spinoza and Deleuze, which continues the philosophical pathways within this volume that seek modes for thinking through posthumanism and immanence without solely relying on Deleuze. In his chapter, 'The Art of Good Encounters: Spinoza, Deleuze and Macherey on moving from passive to active joy', Baugh identifies a disagreement between Deleuze and Macherey in their reading of Spinoza because they see the relation between mind and body differently. However, he points out that this is not merely an exegetical matter. Conceptualizing good encounters, this chapter navigates joy from Spinoza and Deleuze towards a discussion of active and passive joy. Baugh articulates how affects and emotions can help us have positive encounters and increase/improve our capacities. This shows the connection between mind and body – or mind and body as one in Spinoza – which is vital for grasping how joyful affects compose us as well as our entanglement in nature. While less explicitly championing a posthumanist position, as Daigle and Braidotti do in the previous chapters, Baugh's return to the human in a pathway that works back from Spinoza reminds us of the influential and prominent force that our subjective experiences have. Therefore, even in return to human experience, Baugh takes influence from immanence and concepts that are key to posthumanist theory in order to make this experience strange. We see this approach as a necessary endeavour in the field of posthumanism as it works to challenge and rethink how we conceive of ourselves as much as other posthumanist endeavours seek to uncover and engage with more than ourselves.

The following contribution by Houle offers an alternative approach that embraces creativity and demonstrates how similar influences – primarily Spinoza and Deleuze – can open up divergent pathways. Her work relies on similar philosophers found in Baugh's chapter, but this is precisely an example of making that which is beyond ourselves strange. Houle's chapter, through Spinoza, explores concepts as having form, which positions concepts as evolving as a result of new assemblages and new problems. She conceptualizes plant ethics as such a concept that operates in a realm different from that of animality. In a radical challenge to humanist modes of thinking, Houle explores how we can participate in this creation of new concepts that reveal our animal-thinking to be bound within binaries. This animal-thinking is always centred on the human, but to think about the moral status of plants, new concepts that take inspiration from sciences like botany, developmental biology and ecology are needed. This exposes the concepts of philosophy to unfold a multiplicity of becoming-plant, which forces us to question if our thinking contributes to 'a life of vitality, interconnectedness and resilience'.

Alain Beaulieu's contribution takes Husserl's philosophy as having the potential to enter into a conversation with Deleuze in order to move towards a rethinking of a cosmos and the role such a rethinking has for posthumanism. Again, similar to Baugh's chapter, Beaulieu is less interested in marking something as posthumanism or committing to a posthuman ethics – such as Houle's work does – but, nonetheless, we see this work as undertaking a strangification of something we have come to feel we know: the earth. Beaulieu's chapter undertakes an analysis of Husserl's notion of 'Ark-Earth' as a means to delve into Deleuze and Guattari's critique of Husserl in *What Is Philosophy?* This points to the counter-notion of cosmic earth. Beaulieu argues that Deleuze's cosmology remains underdeveloped as few works explore in depth his vibrant cosmological questions. Where Husserl's views are limited and do not allow for the experiences of the posthuman, this chapter maps how Deleuzian conceptualization of the cosmos opens up key pathways to develop our thinking towards posthuman futures. In addition, Beaulieu's work gestures towards the non-human turn in terms of incorporating other than human forces into our conception of the world.

In the second section of the volume, Terrance H. McDonald's contribution marks a shift within the volume towards posthuman aesthetics through which philosophical concepts can be thought as well as serving to spark the formation of new concepts. This chapter works through Deleuze's transcendental empiricism in relation to posthumanism in a philosophical mode and then moves to the forms that take shape in a reading of posthuman cinema. Also picking up, like Beaulieu, on aspects of the cosmic, McDonald's chapter turns to Terrence Malick's film *The Tree of Life* (2011), and the cosmos sequence of film as a means of interrogating the conditions of possible experience taken to be conditions of real experience. By foregrounding Deleuze's transcendental empiricism, McDonald maps the potentialities of a posthuman cinema through philosophies of immanence that expose human exceptionalism as an illusion. In a speculative encounter with cinematic forms, he argues that cinema can be embraced to reimagine and rethink our subjective views of the world to actively acknowledge the field of experience that makes these views possible. In a different approach to posthuman aesthetics, Russell J. A. Kilbourn analyses Deleuze's affection-image within postsecular cinema, specifically Xavier Beauvois's *Of Gods and Men* (2010). Like Baugh and Beaulieu, Kilbourn is also concerned more with an engagement with the human subject within this moment of posthumanist theory than in gestures towards posthuman subjectivities. In a similar mode to McDonald, he picks up on philosophical positions – primarily Levinas and Buber – to read cinematic images. In the chapter, he looks for methods within a posthuman, post-cinematic era that can be used to comprehend the subject that can be completely dissolved by posthumanist theory. Kilbourn insists that some form of the subject is necessary, despite more radical endeavours undertaken by Deleuzian posthumanists, because, through cinema, the affection-image and the close-up demonstrate it cannot simply be done away with. Combining the philosophies of Emmanual Levinas and Martin Buber, theories of affect and film theory with Deleuze's concepts, this chapter argues for a posthumanism that retains ethical aspects of the secular, which may not disintegrate the human subject but importantly reveals alternative pathways that challenge the preconceived notions of humanism. This contribution frames an important counterpoint to other works within the volume that embrace a more vigorous dismantling of the human subject, and, in this regard, Kilbourn's chapter demonstrates the vibrant potentialities for thinking through Deleuze and posthumanism by identifying pathways for making the human strange without entirely leaving core philosophical notions of humanism behind.

The subsequent chapters on posthuman aesthetics offer robust readings of specific films and subjects through posthumanist concepts in order to unpack the ways in which technology becomes a key interlocutor for posthumanisms that take their root in Deleuze. The following chapters by William Brown and David H. Fleming unfold this work by confronting technologies and the impact this modification can have on subjectivities. Brown's chapter focuses on the Global South and the appearances and uses of artificial intelligence in science fiction films. Specifically, he analyses *Enthiran/ The Robot* (Shankar, India, 2010) and *CHAPPiE* (Neill Blomkamp, USA/Mexico, 2015) because these films offer representations of 'subaltern' peoples, specifically South Asian/ Indian, who are often the source of labour for the computing industry. For Brown, posthumanism does not seem to function well with postcolonialism, despite a history of claims to the contrary because the former is often Eurocentric, but he speculates that Deleuze may help overcome this issue. Examining the work of Donna Haraway, N. Katherine Hayles, and Rosi Braidotti, Brown demonstrates aspects of incapability between the two positions as he questions whether the post- in posthumanism is the same post- in postcolonial. Here, posthumanism seems to be reserved for the privileged centre and not the periphery, but the availability of technology in the postcolonial periphery allows for the empowerment of filmmaking in such regions. In his analysis of *CHAPPiE*, he examines how transhumanist fantasy can be understood against posthumanism as a reminder of our bodily existence – in addition to readings mobilized by postcolonial theory – but Brown also points out that this transcendence of the body often assumes the normalized position of white, patriarchal privilege. In comparison, a hybrid movement/time-image *Enthiran* allows for posthumanism and postcolonialism to connect beyond Eurocentrism.

Where Brown focuses on technology in relation to the Global South, Fleming directs his focus to films starring Scarlet Johansson. Specifically, Fleming engages with science fiction film, which he argues may be considered the most philosophical of cinematic genres because its technophilic tendencies offer ways to think about issues pertaining to technologies and sociotechnical practices in the present. In this chapter, he explores the 'triangulated congress' that arises from the interconnections of the human, the cinema and the digital. For him, this interweaving can transform cinema, especially in the blockbusters featuring Scarlett Johansson where her roles allow us to see the emergence of the animal in the digital. This chapter also explores the role of technology within and beyond the frame. For Flemming, female and male bodies are represented differently by technologies and their resulting becomings vary greatly. Where films with male protagonists tend to be more nostalgic and resist a posthuman becoming, films with female protagonists explore the becoming-woman, becoming-animal and becoming-molecular.

In the third section of the volume, the chapters by Sherryl Vint, Martin Boucher, Claire Colebrook and Mickey Vallee explore the politics of Deleuze and posthumanism at diverse intersections. Vint's chapter turns to biopolitics and literature, specifically Rosa Montero's (2012) novel *Tears in Rain* in discussion with Philip K. Dick's *Do Androids Dream of Electric Sheep?* and Montero's (2016) novel *Weight of the Heart*. For her, the posthuman is situated in the tension between the transhuman – the posthuman as enhanced human – and the politically vulnerable groups seeking recognition as human. There is a need to consider, Vint argues, the biopolitical context of marginalized humans, such as migrant workers, the homeless, the underemployed, who are the 'inhuman'. Science fiction is a great tool to imagine the posthuman, as exemplified by *Tears in Rain* as a Deleuzian line of flight away from the human as superlative achievement. As a result, the vital posthumanism that is proposed not only dismisses hierarchies inherited from liberal humanism but also dismisses transhumanism as an exacerbation of such. Vint's engagement with literature through Deleuze and posthumanism opens up new ways to conceive of ourselves in the global order. Continuing an examination of technologies and posthumanism, Martin Boucher's chapter looks at the rise of technomedicine, in particular the impact on subjects and the negative effects it has on disability politics. While the work does not explore technologies through literature and cinema, as Vint and Brown do, it does gesture towards a shared concern with technologies and the impact this can have on humans. Boucher's careful analysis maps a long-standing history of difficult relationships between medicine and disability, which he notes Deleuze foresaw within his own work and how Deleuze's conceptualization of becoming has been put to work within the field of disability studies. He traces how medicine has evolved from a medicine of symptoms to molar medicine to molecular medicine, and how each phase has a different perspective on the body and life. This chapter puts to work a certain form of feminist posthumanism which takes into consideration the lived material embodiment of marginalized subjects. What emerges is a perspective that allows us to think the body and dis/ability in a fruitful way. Here the dis/human has potential to disrupt and point to different embodiments, but there is a need to resist normalization. Through Deleuzian becoming and a posthumanist framework that relies more on key figures embracing Deleuze within this particular field than Deleuze explicitly, Boucher relies on the work of Foucault to articulate a positive technological approach that opens up possibilities rather than aims to cure. Furthermore, as Brown and Vint also make apparent, the need for further interrogations of the relations between humans and technologies forms a key posthumanist endeavour, and much work in this area has yet to come.

The next two chapters, by Colebrook and Vallee, showcase further flows between politics, Deleuze and posthumanism as each work engages with social justice. Colebrook situates her chapter within a discussion of Afro-pessimism. Like Brown, a critique of posthumanist theory emerges within the contribution as a timely and important position that counters more enthusiastic embraces of Deleuze, immanence and posthumanism without considering potential threats or complications. For Colebrook, it is potentially problematic for privileged white male theorists, such as Deleuze and Guattari, to be employed in a discussion of race. Specifically, as she states, 'At first glance there would seem to be nothing at all worthy in reading Deleuze and Guattari in the aftermath or wake of Afro-pessimism.' Therefore, despite the affirmative capacities of posthumanism and *A Thousand Plateaus*, Colebrook cautions that there may be even more reasons now to oppose or to end a specific mode of posthumanism by mapping connections to a lineage of Afro-pessimism. She addresses this concern by noting the critique of humanism in the works of Deleuze and Guattari discovers a pathway for overcoming these concerns within artistic traditions composed by the very ideals they interrogate. By working through connections to Fanon and Baldwin, among others, Colebrook transitions to explore what *A Thousand Plateaus* looks like after the end of the world, or after the end of a specific mode of posthumanism. In this sense, pessimism becomes a vibrant mode for dismantling the human and for a new mode of posthumanism. Pessimism, like chaos, can be generative.

The final chapter is Mickey Vallee's, 'Incorporeal Transformations in Truth and Reconciliation: A posthuman approach to transitional justice', which explores whether truth commissions are better conceived as assemblages. Although less a philosophical parsing of a particular concept in relation to posthumanism than early chapters in the volume, Vallee's ability to bring a mobilization of posthumanist creativity and the spirit of Deleuze to think through a particular mode of justice illuminates the vibrant capacities of posthumanism. The chapter also demonstrates the transdisciplinary potentialities of posthumanism that motivate our volume because he brings a sociological methodology into conversation with posthumanist theory, which is glaringly unique in comparison to the approaches to philosophy and/or art in most other chapters. In their articulation of past, present and future, and their exploration of the relation between the victim and the accused, Vallee argues that truth commissions constitute assemblages that think co-agency in a novel way. In acknowledging historical trauma, truth commissions distribute affect and exercise a form of social control. However, Vallee demonstrates that they also serve as a platform for the performance of an apology and confession that is mediatized and uses technology. Therefore, this chapter maps how this process goes beyond the victim-accused direct relation. In doing so, Vallee opens up thinking in relation to truth commissions that allow for transition and repair of the collective in addition to the direct relation.

What follows are many, but far from exhaustive, pathways for thinking through posthumanism in relation to Deleuze, Guattari and other theorists of immanence. Each individual chapter charts a route, and we have assembled them around related pathways – from philosophical perspectives to posthuman aesthetics and the creative force that generates new concepts to political and social perspectives. By organizing the chapters in this way, we offer the readers one of many possible pathways. We imagine that a reader may read through the chapters in any number of pathways following their own curiosities, questionings and puzzlements. No matter how one chooses to navigate this edited volume, we anticipate that this engagement will open up new ideas through the creative force which takes shape between Deleuze and Guattari, philosophies of immanence and posthumanism. The structure we have mapped begins with a section that examines the building of concepts and the reimagining of the fundamental nature of existence in relation to immanent ideas before coming to the next section that explores the ways in which aesthetics can mobilize new concepts and reimaginings and, finally, a third section that investigates modes for applying posthumanist thought to politics and the issues taking shape around us. In this manner, readers will be delighted at the threads that materialize in expected and unexpected places because Deleuze, Guattari and immanence generate the spirit of each chapter, even if the references and methodologies remain distinct. We hope that the following chapters will spark new singularities in the pursuit of joy.

Notes

1 Gilles Deleuze and Félix Guattari, *What Is Philosophy?*, 108.
2 This is paraphrasing Simone de Beauvoir's famous sentence opening Book II of her *The Second Sex*: 'One is not born but rather becomes, woman'. There is debate on how to appropriately translate this sentence as evidenced in the edited volume edited by Bonnie Mann and Martina Ferrari, *On ne Naît pas Femme on le Devient: The Life of a Sentence*. However, we contend that the French original clearly invites the use of the

indefinite article 'a' and should read: 'One is not born but rather becomes, a woman'. We adopt this formulation here.

3 This is a paraphrase of Bruno Latour's famous claim, argued for in his book bearing the same claim as the title, *We Have Never Been Human*. We are not the first to offer this twist on it since an issue of *Angelaki* explores the paraphrase and what it may entail to think about the human in this way.

4 Gilles Deleuze and Félix Guattari, *What Is Philosophy?*, 47.

5 We title our work *From Deleuze and Guattari to Posthumanism* as opposed to *From Deleuze to Posthumanism* even though we recognize the early works of Deleuze – including the works on Spinoza as well as *Difference and Repetition* – as singularities that connect immanence and posthumanism. Guattari and Deleuze have generative collaborations that unfold key concepts for the development of posthumanism and our title reflects the affective intensity that runs through Deleuze's work in all directions as well as his shared thinking with Guattari. Furthermore, even when it is to the works of Deleuze only that contributors turn in this volume, there is no denying the important role played by Guattari in the development of Deleuze's later thinking. Thinking immanence and entangled relations together, it is indeed difficult to parse which idea is whose in works such as *Anti-Oedipus, A Thousand Plateaus*, and *What Is Philosophy?*

6 Cary Wolfe, *What Is Posthumanism?*, xi.

7 Rosi Braidotti, *Posthuman Knowledge*, 2.

8 Francesca Ferrando's *Philosophical Posthumanism* (2019) provides an insightful and detailed analysis of the various iterations of posthumanism and transhumanism. In another vein, the *Posthuman Glossary* (2018) offers a cartography of theoretical positions and themes that, as the editors put it, is open to potentially diverging conceptual and/or political views on 'the posthuman predicament'. (6). This openness allows for a presentation of the vibrancy of the field and the multiplicity of manifestations of the 'posthuman'.

9 Pramod K. Nayar, *Posthumanism*, 2.

10 We agree with Rosi Braidotti's stance according to which 'One needs at least *some* subject position: this need not be either unitary or exclusively anthropocentric, but it must be the site for political and ethical accountability, for collective imaginaries and shared aspirations' (*The Posthuman*, 102). Circumscribing what that subject position might be is a challenge and one that is undertaken by the contributors to this volume, as are the correlate questions of the location of that being and its relations with a multiplicity of human and non-human others.

11 As we will see with Boucher's chapter, disability studies is another field that challenges notions of embodiment and agency and its encounter with posthumanist thinking contributes to this sustained challenge of humanist assumptions. Rosi Braidotti has argued that the emergence of the studies – gender studies, postcolonial studies, etc. – has prepared the ground for the emergence of posthumanism and its critique and rejection of central tenets of humanism. See her 'Contested Humanities' (15–20). See also *Posthuman Knowledge*.

12 Rosi Braidotti, *The Posthuman*, 22.

13 Pramod K. Nayar, *Posthumanism*, 31.

14 Ibid. 7. In an essay on transhumanism, Nicolas Le Dévédec argues that transhumanism's embrace of human perfectibility is individualistic and, therefore, not grounded in Enlightenment thought that embraces the social and political goal of collective perfectibility ('Unfit for the Future').

15 For a discussion of the various types of transhumanism, see Ferrando, *Philosophical Posthumanism*.
16 Rosi Braidotti, *The Posthuman*, 91.
17 Braidotti discusses this in detail in her *Posthuman Knowledge* (2019). The posthuman condition 'is a way of reconstituting the human' (38). Our current convergence requires that we acknowledge ourselves as transversal subjectivities, that is, 'we-are-in -this-together-but-we-are-not-one-and-the-same' (161).
18 See Rosi Braidotti, 'A Theoretical Framework for the Critical Posthumanities', 31–61.
19 Braidotti, *The Posthuman*, 56–7.
20 These theoretical encounters with Spinoza include political writings, such as Antonio Negri's *Savage Anomaly: The Power of Spinoza's Metaphysics and Politics* (2000) and *Spinoza for Our Time: Politics and Postmodernity* (2013); material feminist writings, such as Moira Gatens's and Genevieve Lloyd's *Collective Imaginings: Spinoza, Past and Present* (1999) and Moira Gatens's edited collection *Feminist Interpretations of Benedict Spinoza* (2009); new materialist writings, such as Jane Bennett's *Vibrant Matter: A Political Ecology of Things* (2010); interdisciplinary inquiries, such as Dimitris Vardoulakis's edited collection *Spinoza Now* (2011); and theories of affect in relation to Deleuze and others, such as Eugenie Brinkema's *The Forms of the Affects* (2014), Elena del Rìo's *Deleuze and the Cinemas of Performance: Powers of Affection* (2008), and Brian Massumi's *Parables for the Virtual: Movement, Affect, Sensation* (2002).
21 Interestingly, Nietzsche is also a key figure in the other lineage feeding into posthumanist thinking through Derrida and deconstruction. Indeed, his philosophy was instrumental in the development of this movement of thought.
22 Friedrich Nietzsche, *Thus Spoke Zarathustra*, 'Of Self-overcoming'.
23 Gilles Deleuze and Félix Guattari, *A Thousand Plateaus*, 15.
24 Ibid. 21.
25 In addition to his reading of Kant (see *Kant's Critical Philosophy*, among other works), Deleuze also develops his conception of immanence and empiricism through the work of David Hume. While Spinoza and Nietzsche, for example, may be more closely aligned with philosophies of immanence, an interpretation of Kant and Hume are also key to Deleuze's understanding of immanence (see *Empiricism and Subjectivity: An Essay on Hume's Theory of Human Nature*).
26 Daniel W. Smith, 'The Theory of Immanent Ideas', 46.
27 Ibid. 46.
28 Gilles Deleuze and Claire Parnet, *Dialogues*, 42.
29 The concept has gained prominence among material feminists thanks to Diana Coole and Samantha Frost and their use of the concept in the introduction to the volume they co-edited, *New Materialisms: Ontology, Agency, and Politics* (2010) and material feminists who have adopted it in their work.
30 Gilles Deleuze and Félix Guattari, *A Thousand Plateaus*, 20–1.
31 Ibid. 68.
32 This is another way in which Nietzsche's philosophy of immanence influences Deleuze. Nietzsche advocates a nihilistic stance that serves to free humans from the yoke of the transcendent and the alienation it causes. Nihilism thereby opens to a joyful thriving.
33 Ibid. 70.
34 Gilles Deleuze, *Pure Immanence*, 29.
35 Ibid. 41.
36 María Puig de la Bellacasa, *Matters of Care*, 71–8.

Bibliography

Beauvoir, Simone de. *The Second Sex*. Translated by Constance Borde and Sheila Malovany-Chevallier. New York: Vintage Books, 2011.
Bennett, Jane. *Vibrant Matter: A Political Ecology of Things*. Durham, NC: Duke University Press, 2010.
Braidotti, Rosi. 'A Theoretical Framework for the Critical Posthumanities'. *Theory, Culture & Society* 36, no. 6 (2019): 31–61.
Braitotti, Rosi. 'The Contested Humanities'. In *Conflicting Humanities*, edited by Rosi Braidotti and Paul Gilroy, 9–45. London: Bloomsbury, 2016.
Braidotti, Rosi. *The Posthuman*. Cambridge: Polity Press, 2013.
Braidotti, Rosi. *Posthuman Knowledge*. Cambridge: Polity Press, 2019.
Braidotti, Rosi and Maria Hlavajova, eds. *Posthuman Glossary*. London: Bloomsbury, 2018.
Culp, Andrew. *Dark Deleuze*. Minneapolis, MN: University of Minnesota Press, 2016.
Deleuze, Gilles. *Empiricism and Subjectivity: An Essay on Hume's Theory of Human Nature*. 1953. Translated by Constantin V. Boundas. New York: Columbia University Press, 1991.
Deleuze, Gilles. *Kant's Critical Philosophy*. 1963. Translated by Hugh Tomlinson and Barbara Habberjam. London: Continuum, 2008.
Deleuze, Gilles. *Pure Immanence: Essays on A Life*. Translated by Anne Boyman. New York: Zone Books, 2005.
Deleuze, Gilles and Félix Guattari. *A Thousand Plateaus*. 1980. Translated by Brian Massumi. London: Continuum, 2004.
Deleuze, Gilles and Félix Guattari. *What is Philosophy?* 1991. Translated by Hugh Tomlinson and Graham Burchell. New York: Columbia University Press, 1994.
Deleuze, Gilles and Claire Parnet. *Dialogues*. Paris: Flammarion, 1996.
Ferrando, Franscesca. *Philosophical Posthumanism*. London: Bloomsbury, 2019.
Latour, Bruno. *We Have Never Been Modern*. Translated by Catherine Porter. Cambridge, MA: Harvard University Press, 1993.
Le Dévédec, Nicolas. 'Unfit for the Future? The Depoliticization of Human Perfectibility, from the Enlightenment to Transhumanism'. *European Journal of Social Theory* 21, no. 4 (2018): 488–507.
Morton, Timothy. *Hyperobjects: Philosophy and Ecology after the End of the World*. Minneapolis, MN: University of Minnesota Press, 2013.
Nayar, Pramod K. *Posthumanism*. Cambridge: Polity Press, 2014.
Nietzsche, Friedrich. *Human, All Too Human. A Book for Free Spirits*. Translated by R. J. Hollingdale. Introduction by Richard Schacht. Cambridge: Cambridge University Press, 1996.
Nietzsche, Friedrich. *Thus Spoke Zarathustra. A Book for Everyone and No One*. Translated by with introduction R. J. Hollingdale. London: Penguin Books, 1969.
Puig de la Bellacasa, María. *Matters of Care. Speculative Ethics in More Than Human Worlds*. Minneapolis, MN: University of Minnesota Press, 2017.
Smith, Daniel W. 'Deleuze, Kant, and the Theory of Immanent Ideas'. In *Deleuze and Philosophy*, edited by Constantin V. Boundas, 43–61. Edinburgh: Edinburgh University Press, 2006.
Wolfe, Cary. *What Is Posthumanism?* Minneapolis, MN: University of Minnesota Press, 2009.

Part One

Philosophical genealogies – From Deleuze and Guattari to posthumanism

1

Posthuman neo-materialisms and affirmation

Rosi Braidotti

Introduction

The outline of this chapter is as follows: I take as beginning assumptions, first, the twofold empirical-transcendental equation demonstrated by Deleuze and Guattari, namely that thinking is not the prerogative of humans or any other bound entity. Second, that the specific mode of thought promoted by philosophy is about the creation of new concepts. All along – nomadically speaking – I will uphold the conviction that both Deleuze and Guattari, as profoundly anti-humanist and post-anthropocentric thinkers, offer a significant new approach to the discussions on naturalism, the environment, ecological justice and the posthuman. And as the ever-shifting horizon for the thought processes dramatized within these pages, I will defend the ethics of affirmation and the politics of radical immanence. The working definition I have adopted in my rhizomatic, multidirectional argument is that the posthuman – and its multiple posthumanisms – are not substantive concepts, but rather navigational tools or *conceptual personae*. With this specific framing of the question of the posthuman in mind, let me then proceed to explore the steps of the argument, in a nomadic manner that offers the rigour of consistency, not the comfort of linearity.

The posthuman as *conceptual persona*

Posthuman thought in contemporary scholarship is a convergence phenomenon unfolding at the intersection between posthumanism on the one hand and post-anthropocentrism on the other. The former proposes the philosophical critique of the Western Humanist ideal of 'Man' as the allegedly universal measure of all things on the one hand, whereas the latter rests on the rejection of species hierarchy and human exceptionalism. They are equally powerful discourses, but they refer to different theoretical and philosophical genealogies and engender different political stances, which encompass both forms of empowerment and, in many ways, new modes of entrapment. Their convergence in what I call posthuman critical thought is producing a chain of theoretical, social and political effects that is more than the sum of its parts and points to a qualitative leap in new conceptual directions.[1]

The force of this convergence is enhanced contextually by the urgency of the Anthropocene condition, which, read in the light of Guattari's three ecologies,[2] becomes an environmental, socio-economical, as well as affective and psychical phenomenon of unprecedented proportions. The combination of fast technological advances on the one hand and the exacerbation of economic and social inequalities on the other, make for a multifaceted and conflict-ridden posthuman landscape.[3]

I understand the task of philosophy as both critical and creative. The critical side is operationalized through cartographies of the power relations at work in the production of discourses and social practices, with special emphasis on their effects upon subject-formation.[4] Cartographies are theoretically infused navigational tools across the complexities of the material and discursive complexities of the present. The posthuman is at present my preferred navigational tool and *conceptual persona*, following from the previous sequence that included the feminist philosopher and the nomadic subject.

I combine the cartographic approach with the feminist politics of locations, based on the notions of embodiment and lived experience, which I take as the original historical and theoretical manifestation of embodied and embedded immanence and of corporeal or sensible empiricism. Politics of locations emphasize the situated and accountable nature of knowledge.[5] Feminist epistemology includes, next to a sharp critical dimension, creative efforts aimed at the expression of new alternatives.[6] The encounter of feminist epistemology and Deleuze, in the framework of vital neo-materialism,[7] results in renewed emphasis on immanence and, therefore, the rejection not only of dualism but also of transcendental universalism.

My nomadic philosophy of immanence is rooted in feminist theory, but it flows nomadically in many other directions. Two main implications follow from this, and they are symbiotically intertwined: one about the function of cartographies and the other about the importance of subjectivity. Cartographies as embodied and embedded relational practices become both methods and political strategies. They produce theoretical and political accounts of one's multiple – and potentially contradictory – locations in terms of space (geophysical or eco-sophical dimension) and time (both Chronos and Aion, that is to say: historical memory and genealogical dimension). As relational objects produced and circulated in multiple networks of connection, cartographies become dialogical objects of exchange. The speed of their itineraries and the intensity of their discursive production compose the different planes of an 'assemblage',[8] that is to say a transindividual form of subjectivity. This assemblage – which includes non-human factors as well as technological mediation – composes a plane of immanence, that is to say, a space of relational encounter[9] or the composition of a community that was virtual until it gets materialized, embodied and embedded, as a 'people'. This nomadic transversal entity is bonded by what Genevieve Lloyd calls a 'collaborative morality',[10] which is to say, an ethics of affirmation (more on this later).

Subjectivity, therefore, is not linked to bound individuals – Deleuze and Guattari rejected liberal individualism. Nor is it 'collectivized' within a dialectical scheme that posits one entity, like class, or a multitude,[11] as the transcendent category that drives the progress of world history. Nomadic subjectivity rather gets actualized transversally, in between nature/technology; male/female; black/white; local/global; present/past – in assemblages that flow across and displace the binaries. These in between states are processes of becoming that defy the logic of the excluded middle. Although they allow an analytic function to the negative, they reject negativity and aim at the production of joyful or affirmative values and projects.[12] A new alliance of critique with creation is put to the task of actualizing alternatives to the dominant vision of the subject, resisting the hegemony of reason and the pull of transcendentalism.

A neo-materialist posthuman philosophy, which assumes that all matter is one; that it is intelligent and self-organizing (auto-poietic); that takes 'living matter' as *zoe*-centred process,[13] which is geophysical but also psychic and interacts with the technosphere; that resists over-coding by the profit principle, which is the axiomatic of advanced capitalism – results in proposing an affirmative composition of transversal subjectivities (i.e. assemblages). Subjectivity can then be redefined as a praxis, not a concept – it produces an expanded self, whose relational capacities are multifold and open to non-anthropomorphic elements. *Zoe*-centred egalitarianism, the non-human, the vital force of Life is the transversal entity that allows us to think across previously segregated species, categories and domains. Neo-materialist immanence requires ethical accountability for the sustainability of these assemblages or transversal compositions.[14]

The question of the posthuman in Deleuze

A consensus has emerged in recent Deleuze scholarship that Deleuze's philosophy is firmly inscribed in the Continental tradition of anti-humanism, going back to Nietzsche and beyond.[15] Deleuze's theoretical and personal relationship to Foucault is, in this respect, a crucial knot and one that I cannot untie here. But I do wish to foreground the critical distance that Deleuze takes both from the claims of European humanism and the (often rhetorical) celebrations of the human that ensue from it.

This distance is both conceptual and affective, as things often are in Deleuze's philosophical universe. European humanism is taken to task in view of the philosophical institutions it has created and supported. They are true mechanisms of capture of the singular and collective intelligence, instruments of intimidation and conformism that enforce the replication of the obvious, albeit in shrinking institutional spaces. At the affective level, far from displaying any anthropocentric arrogance or boastful self-satisfaction, Deleuze – the most ascetic of twentieth-century French philosophers – openly professes a kind of shame about being human. The sense of shame encompasses macro historical events, such as the Holocaust – think of the pages Deleuze dedicates to Primo Levi – colonialism and despotic power. It also extends, however, to daily micro-instances:

> we can feel shame at being human in utterly trivial situations, too: in the face of too great a vulgarization of thinking, in the face of TV entertainment, of a ministerial speech, of 'jolly people' gossiping. This is one of the most powerful incentives towards philosophy, and it's what makes all philosophy political.[16]

This deep-seated sense of shame about being human is not a form of self-hatred and nihilism, but exactly the contrary. As critical self-reflection, it lays the conditions of a possibility for overcoming negative passions and compose a life where generosity, ontological relationality and openness to human and non-human others, provide the ethical compass. The crucial point is the transcendence of negativity, which in this case means the transformation of shame as a negative state, from contempt and resentment (or Lack, ontological insecurity, original sin, structural guilt and perennial debt, as stipulated in the Hegelian-Lacanian model), into a becoming-minoritarian of the subject, aimed at the affirmation of other ways of being human. The ethical moment consists in the production of affirmative affects and generative relations, composing assemblages that can actualize virtual relations and projects. Shame about some of the facets of being human triggers the whole process, in the sense of instilling critical distance from the identities we are socially encouraged to take for granted. Feeling ashamed of how we are constructed and how we behave as humans, in other words, is a form of critical distance, of dis-identification from established conventions and values about the human itself. The co-author of *Anti-Oedipus* is asking us to experiment with de-familiarization from the norm, to experiment with nomadic becoming that actualizes virtual possibilities. In this particular case, the virtual encompasses other ways of becoming human.

What I especially value in Deleuze's thought is the radically non-nostalgic approach he develops to anti-humanism and the extent to which his transformational approach turns shame into de-familiarization and then works to construct affirmative becoming as the ethical solution to the impasse of negative passions. Thus, Deleuze explores the 'death of Man', the end of humanism and the crisis of the humanities, notably philosophy, without shedding a tear for these massive mechanisms of capture. He keeps instead clearly in focus that the purpose of contemporary thought is to deterritorialize philosophy from the despotic machine that has coded it over time, using transcendental reason as an instrument of power. Learning to think differently about what we are in the process of becoming is the aim of the game, which means that we need to unlearn many habits of thought and re-position thinking as a life-process, not a reductively cerebral or cognitive one. In my work, unlearning old habits and relinquishing the privileges that go with the reiteration of tradition is another productive point of contact between Spinozist neo-materialism and feminist theory.[17]

Not only is the anti-humanism palpable in Deleuze's vital materialism, but so is his relation to the inhuman and non-human facets of the philosophical enterprise, including animals, plants, weeds, the whole planet, but also machinery, technology, coal, oil, zombies and vampires. Deleuze's materialism is an immanent philosophy of life as becoming, in keeping with the illustrious French philosophical tradition of vital philosophies which encompass the non-human without reducing it. Notable figures in this tradition are Diderot, Sade, Canguilhem, Bachelard and Simondon, and I regret I cannot pursue the analysis of this connection here.

The force of Deleuze's work is that it traces a counter-genealogical line in the history of philosophy, to defend an alternative vision of both humanism and the human. Thus, Deleuze and Guattari's analysis of capitalism as schizophrenia[18] produces a materialist account of the codification of the human through successive de/reterritorializations

– with reference to the empiricists, Nietzsche,[19] Spinoza,[20] Hume,[21] Leibniz[22] and Foucault.[23] In other words, they operationalize anti-humanism as a critical-creative tool to compose a different understanding of how humans come into being as a philosophical event. They argue that capitalism installs a political economy – both material and discursive – that captures and subsumes the organic – matter, mind, *techne* included – through stratification processes and encapsulates them into the despotic state machine. Their critical vitalism stresses the extent to which all living matter – not only human but the Earth as a whole – is captured and reduced to the functional requirements of market economies. They aim to resist these mechanisms of entrapment and the opportunistic trans-species commodification of 'Life as surplus'.[24] In response to this self-serving reductionism, they uphold the vital unity of all living matter – human and non-human – thereby displacing human anthropocentric exceptionalism and opening up to post-anthropocentric relational ethics.

Further, they emphasize the generative force of life as a non-human phenomenon – which I defined as *zoe*[25] – and celebrate the diversity of life forms in a non-hierarchical manner, which recognizes the respective degrees of intelligence and creativity of all organisms. If thinking is *not* the prerogative of humans alone, and if vital-materialism generates a form of relational eco-sophical ethics, it then follows that posthuman materialism invites us to envisage the ecological co-creation of possible worlds; the genetic mode of mutual specification and the politics of radical immanence, while recognizing the specific abilities and capacities of humans. Let us follow closely the steps of this crucial argument.

If it is indeed the case, as Deleuze argues,[26] that thinking – in philosophy, art and the sciences – is the counterpart of the embodied and embrained subject's ability to enter into multiple modes of relation, then it is fair to say that thinking is the expression of ontological relationality, that is to say, of the power (*potentia*) to affect and be affected.[27] And if it is further the case that thinking is about the creation of new concepts in that it pursues the actualization of intensive or virtual relations, it then follows that posthuman thought is a vitalist and multidirectional philosophy of immanence and relational ethics, based on a time continuum that works in terms of transpositions and nomadic interconnections,[28] that is to say, generative cross-pollination.[29] Thinking is indeed the stuff of the world.[30]

The challenge for posthuman critical theory, therefore, is threefold. First to acknowledge that subjectivity is not the exclusive prerogative of *anthropos*; that it is not linked to transcendental reason and that it is unhinged from the dialectics of recognition, being based on the immanence of relations. Second, the challenge is also to develop a dynamic and sustainable notion of vitalist, self-organizing materialism which encompasses non-human agents, notably technological artefacts. Third, there is a need to enlarge the frame and scope of ethically accountable subjectivity along the transversal lines of post-anthropocentric relations or assemblages.

To sum up this section: the key features of Deleuze and Guattari's approach to the posthuman are: first, the unity of matter as a process ontology based on becoming, which entails vital materialism as a creative praxis of actualization of the virtual; second, a healthy detachment from both humanism and anthropocentrism, which gives to the non-human/inhuman elements a ubiquitous presence in Deleuze and

Guattari's materialist thought; third, the composition of transversal subjectivities in the mode of eco-sophical assemblages that include non-human actors; and, last but not least, the relational ethics of affirmation and the politics of radical immanence, which aim at composing a missing people and actualizing virtual capacities. Let me look at these in more details.

About vital materialism

Materialist ontologies have had a hard time in critical thought. A 'neo materialist universe', with its rejection of binary oppositions and dialectical negativity, as often been misunderstood or dismissed, despite its obvious positive implications for ecological ethics and environmental politics.[31] Critical Spinozism foregrounds the fact that matter, the world and humans themselves are not dualistic entities structured according to the dialectical principle of internal or external opposition, but rather materially embedded subjects-in-process circulating nomadically within webs of relation with forces, entities and encounters. Contemporary materialism does not eliminate or deny differences, but it dismantles the hierarchical structures within which they have been codified.

This shift results also in overcoming the classical opposition between materialism and idealism, moving instead towards a dynamic brand of 'materialist vitalism', or relational vision of subjectivity. A materially embedded and embodied, material, affective and relational approach offers the advantage of redefining old binary oppositions, such as nature/culture and human/non-human, therefore paving the way for a non-hierarchical and more egalitarian relationship to and between the species.

By embracing the turn to Spinozist politics, Deleuze and Foucault[32] target for explicit criticism the universalistic utopian elements of Marxism, which identified the dialectics of power as the motor of world history. They stress instead the need for a change of scale, to unveil power relations where they are most effective and invisible: in the specific locations of one's own intellectual and social practice. One has to start from micro-instances of embodied and embedded self and the complex web of social relations that compose the self. This self is not an atomized entity but a non-unitary relational subject, nomadic and outward-bound, which is then read within a Spinozist vital-materialist frame.

The rejection of dialectical oppositions, with their violent logic and the central role attributed to negativity, has historically caused intense criticism of Spinoza on the part of Hegel and later by the Marxist-Hegelians who see Spinoza's and Deleuze's world view as politically ineffective and even mystical at heart. I shall return to this point. But contemporary Spinozism was shaped by the critical intervention made by the French philosophers in the 1970s, when they elected to revisit Spinozist materialism precisely as an antidote to some of the contradictions of Marxism and as a way of clarifying Hegel's relationship to Marx.[33] The 'Spinozist legacy' therefore consists in a very active concept, which defines matter as vital and self-organizing, thereby producing the staggering combination of 'vitalist materialism', or 'radical immanence'. All vital matter or substance being one and immanent to itself, it is intelligent and self-organizing in both human and non-human organisms,[34] it is driven by the ontological desire for the expression of its innermost freedom (*conatus*). Materialism results in relocating difference outside the dialectical scheme, as a complex process of differing which is framed by both internal and external forces and is based on the centrality of the relation to multiple others. An updated version of Spinozism[35] as a democratic move towards radically immanent forms of immanence promotes a kind of ontological pacifism.[36]

This radical relocation of difference outside dialectics is especially relevant to feminist and anti-racist perspectives that take 'difference' not as a neutral category but as a term that indexes exclusion from the entitlements to subjectivity. The equation of difference with pejoration is built into the tradition, which defines the subject as coinciding with/being the same as consciousness, rationality and self-regulating ethical behaviour. This results in making entire section of living beings into marginal and disposable bodies: these are the sexualized, racialized and naturalized others who carry difference as a negative mark on their backs. Vital materialism encourages delinking these 'others' from these oppositional dialectics, resulting in different forms of political resistance. This is the nomadic politics of 'becoming-minoritarian' that produces a politics of affirmation based on a renewed concern for human vulnerability, which is, however, coupled with an analysis of and resistance to power, defined not dialectically, but in a multilayered and multidirectional relational manner.

The single most significant advantage of posthumanist materialism is that it introduces an inclusive post-anthropocentric vision of subjectivity, including also non-human agents. Vital neo-materialist theories lead to a productive 'eco-sophical' approach, that extends the ethical implications of one-matter ontology to a better understanding of the complex interaction of social, psychic, natural and technological factors in the construction of multiple ecologies of belonging: they all hang eco-sophically together.

To argue that posthuman materialism by stressing the unity of all living matter, introduces a methodological kind of naturalism which includes the displacement of anthropocentrism, however, is only the starting point, and it works to the extent that we are prepared to do some extra work ourselves. Deleuze is very keen to stress the proactive nature of critical thought by redefining thinking as the invention of new concepts, methods and *conceptual personae*. This challenge enlists the resources of the imagination, as well as the tools of critical intelligence, but it throws multiple challenges our way: from the de-familiarization of cognitive habits I mentioned above to the necessity to nurture more conceptual creativity. The collapse of the nature-culture divide, for instance, requires that we need to devise a new vocabulary, with new figurations to refer to the kind of subjects we are in the process of becoming.

This implies, for instance, that we cannot assume a theory of subjectivity that takes for granted naturalistic foundationalism, nor can we rely on a purely social constructivist and hence dualistic theory of the subject which disavows the ecological dimension. Thus, in order to activate neo-materialist approaches to a general understanding of subjectivity, we need to be prepared to leave behind familiar territories and accepted notions, so as to embrace new navigational tools and alternative figurations.[37] Posthuman critical theory needs to fulfil the multiple – and potentially contradictory – requirements of a neo-materialist ontology. It is crucial, for instance, to see the multiple interconnections among the greenhouse effect, the status of women and LBGTQ+, racism and xenophobia and frantic consumerism. We must not stop at any fragmented portions of these realities but rather trace transversal interconnections among them.

The subject of posthuman critical theory is therefore ontologically polyvocal. It rests on a plane of consistency including both the real that is already actualized, 'territorialized existential territories', and the real that is still virtual, 'deterritorialized incorporeal universes'.[38] Guattari calls for a collective reappropriation of the production of subjectivity through nomadic de-segregation of the different categories. For Deleuze and Guattari, the virtual is the universe of reference for ethical-political processes of becoming in the sense of the unfolding of transformative values. A qualitative step forward is necessary if we want subjectivity to escape the regime of sedentarization/commodification that is the dominant political economy of advanced capitalism and experiment with virtual possibilities.[39] A materialist ontology, in other words, sustains the process of constitution of the sorts of subjects who actively desire to reinvent their interaction as a set of transformations within a commonly shared matter and to draw our pleasure from that mode of affirmative relation, not from the perpetuation of familiar regimes and dominant values.

Species equality in a post-anthropocentric world does urge us to question the violence and the hierarchical thinking that result from human arrogance and the assumption of transcendental human exceptionalism. In my view, materialist relationality stresses instead the more compassionate aspect of subjectivity.

Nature-culture-media ecologies

Deleuze's vital materialism did *not* maintain a categorical separation between natural entities and manufactured artefacts. Spinozism challenges this separation by proposing the unity of all matter, based on a classification of all entities – things, objects and human organisms included – in terms of their forces and impact upon other entities in the world. An ethology of forces, in other words, produces a displacement of anthropocentric value systems and allows for a continuum nature-culture that includes media and digital networks, that is, 'media ecologies'.[40]

In other words, the vital-materialist understanding of 'Life' as a symbiotic system of co-dependence alters the terms of the nature-culture debate and of human interaction with what used to be called 'matter', which now can be approached as the continuum of self-organizing vital systems, of the environmental, technological, psychic, social and other kinds. Starting from such premises, neo-materialist theory moves away from the social constructivist methods and the deconstructive strategies of post-structuralism, to embrace differential becoming and the actualization of transversal alliances.

The core idea for the vital-materialist approach remains the nature-culture continuum, which is best expressed by the materialist insight that, as Lloyd put it, we are all 'part of nature'.[41] This statement, which in itself is as sobering as it is inspiring, is further complicated, for us citizens of the third millennium, by the fact that we actually inhabit a nature-culture continuum – 'naturacultures'[42] – which is both technologically mediated and globally interlinked. This deceptively simple step expresses a complex and fundamental insight, namely that all living matter today is mediated along multiple axes: we have become 'biomediated' bodies[43] and immersed in 'medianatures'.[44]

Félix Guattari broadened the principle of autopoiesis (originally coined by Varela to refer to biological organisms only) to cover also the machines or allopoietic systems of technological others. Another name for subjectivity, according to Guattari, is auto-poietic subjectivation, or self-styling, and it accounts for both living organisms, humans as self-organizing systems, and also for inorganic matter, the machines. Ever since Guattari, the notion of 'machinic autopoiesis' has been offered as an alternative to oppositional models of political subjectivity, thus establishing the qualitative link between organic matter and technological or machinic artefacts. The process of auto-poietic self-styling aims at self-organization and meta-stability by embedding the subject in transversal technologically mediated relations, while avoiding all kinds of reductive thinking. It engenders different notions of bio-social processes of subjectivation (Parisi, 2004) and non-anthropocentric posthuman ethics.[45]

Transversality actualizes an ethics based on the primacy of the relation, of interdependence, which values non-human or a-personal life. The focus is on the force and autonomy of affect and the logistics of its actualization.[46] Some Deleuzian thinkers push this position to call for the very abolition of the category of the human, supporting an 'a-human turn'.[47] Nomadic transversality actualizes *zoe*-centred egalitarianism as an ethics and also as a method to account for forms of alternative, posthuman subjectivity. An ethics based on the primacy of the relation, of interdependence, values *zoe* in itself. I also refer to these practices of becoming-machine as 'radical neo-materialism',[48] others call it 'neo-realism',[49] 'matter-realism',[50] and 'vibrant matter'.[51] These ideas are supported by and intersect with changing understandings of the conceptual structure of matter itself, under the impact of contemporary bio-genetics and information technologies, which constitute our new or 'second' nature. If Guattari's effort to expand auto-poietic vitality to the machines has shown that there is no such thing as 'originary humanicity',[52] then it follows that there is only 'originary technicity'.[53] We need to reconceptualize the technological apparatus as our new 'milieu'. This intimacy is far more complex and generative than the prosthetic, mechanical extension that modernity had made of it.[54] Our neo-materialist universe is 'smart', that is, 'medianaturecultural'.

Affirmative politics

This takes me to the last important corollary, which, as I mentioned before, has been at the heart of the many controversies that have surrounded the issue of neo-materialism, namely the question of the political. In the perspective of a materialist ontology, which assumes all subjects to be part of a common matter, a fundamental trust in what we could call, for lack of a better term, 'the world' is a crucial part of the deal. Conceptually, this means that political subjectivity need not be postulated along dialectical axes of negativity, nor must it be critical in the oppositional sense of the term in order to ensure the production of counter-subjectivities.

The most frequently raised objections to the case for affirmation date back to Spinoza's own times and comes down to the danger of acquiescence with the conditions of the present: if all matter is one and self-organizing, is there not a risk of mystical acceptance that all that lives is holy? Does radical immanence result in passivity rather than activity?

Politically, does it not open the danger of complicity with current forms of capitalist innovation? How does the posthuman critical subject differ from the neoliberal entrepreneurial self? As Benjamin Noys puts it,[55] the saturation of space through the concept of the virtual leaves little space for political freedom in the accepted sense of the term, to pursue new actualizations or realities: does it not just lead to rearrangements of existing conditions? What exactly is the politics of radical immanence? Is the appeal to ontological positivity not just a form of indifference to real-world relations and experiences? Does the Univocity of Being not entail a risk of dogmatic determinism, that is to say, a refusal of the 'messiness' of things in the world?

A second related objection, which was already raised to Spinoza himself, is the problem of evil: supposing that ontological relationality is the heart of the matter, what are we to make of the persistence of destructive, negative relations? Are we to assume that all relations are *a priori* positive? But that would be deterministic, of course. So when do the politics of transversal assemblages turn into geometries of dispossession? How can we tell the difference between these two distinctly opposed ethical modes?

The answers are clearly spelt out by Deleuze in his revisitation of Spinoza's work and of the standard Hegelian-Marxist objections against it. Deleuze is aware of the danger of pacification and, for instance, in *Difference and Repetition*, he warns us against the pious discourse of 'beautiful souls', that is to say, mystical harmonization of all conflicts. Both Deleuze and Guattari stress that we need a structure of *differentiation*, but they also insist that such a structure need not be antagonistic, in a dialectical mode, and hence violent. This is the same point made before about the negative structure of differences: this habit of thought need not become universalized, let alone be naturalized as 'the way things are'. Non-dialectical difference – aka the positivity of difference – is perfectly thinkable within a materialist world view. By extension, a non-antagonistic play of differences and disagreements is perfectly feasible and, to this purpose, Deleuze and Guattari devise a praxis based on the actualization of the virtual. This praxis is primarily ethical, but its ethics are supposed to guide our politics – and this is the ethics of affirmation. Let me explain.

I said earlier that I operationalize posthuman vital neo-materialism in the method of cartographies of the present. This assumes – following Foucault read with Deleuze – that the critical thinker can access and account for the present conditions – in order to analyse multiple formations of power as a complex strategic situation that is at work in the most intimate, as well as in the macro-formations of our subjectivity. Accounting for a set of conditions, however, does not mean endorsing them; producing an adequate cartography of the present conditions aims at identifying points of resistance, which compose a collective assemblage – transversal subjects – who labour to actualize virtual alternatives. Far from being a form of complicity with the system, this project aims at overturning it. Both nomadic subjects and posthuman critical subjects stand in ethical opposition to neoliberal schemes of possessive individualism and entrepreneurial selfhood. The ethics of affirmation proposes a critique of the basic tenets of neoliberal individual formation, and proposes to replace them with a relational, multilayered, non-profit-oriented vision of transversal subjectivity. What my posthuman neo-materialist approach does however assume is that all subject formation is immanent to the very political economy it is trying to overturn, and that capitalism is a process ontology that continues to reterritorialize and recode even the margins and relations of resistance, in constant lows of restratification.

This is why the question of subjectivity is so important – *pace* the object-oriented ontologists' hasty dismissal of this crucial political factor. Recasting subjectivity in the nomadic mode of a praxis that activates the capacity of transversal subjects – as compounds of human and non-human factors, including technological mediation – to detach themselves from the historically sedimented determinations of power, aims at releasing transversal lines of resistance and not integral lines of power. This is why I defend also the idea of *amor fati* as a way of accepting vital processes and the expressive intensity of a Life we share with multiple others, here and now. This is the possibility of 'subjectivation' as the becoming-nomadic of the subject. The aim is not to unfold affirmative differences in happy coexistence, but to bring about together productive subversions of the status quo by actualizing virtual possibilities.

Whereas Marxism would argue for ideological rupture, Deleuze and Guattari emphasize that, to actualize this rupture requires subjects who actively desire otherwise and are other-worldly and thus break with the *doxa*, the regime of commonsense. The function of the virtual is to actualize the real issues, which means precisely the effort to interrupt the acquiescent application of established norms and values, to deterritorialize them by introducing alternative ethical flows. The virtual is the laboratory of the new.

To accomplish this ethics, we need to engender together a qualitative leap that engages with but also breaks productively with the present, by understanding how it engenders the conditions of our bondage. The affirmative politics of becoming mobilizes a subject's ontological desire – the vital *potentia* of the subject – and collectively reframes it in disruptive directions capable of resisting codes and powers. This ethical transformation of negative critique into creative affirmation is the key to Deleuze's idea of revolutionary subjectivity, as being activated by the shared desire to create new conditions that break with the replication of the same and the reiteration of the obvious which are supported and marketed by the current system. This virtual or affirmative force is the motor of political change, not oppositional dialectics. There is also the input of a Bergsonian philosophy of time at work here,[56] in the form of a time continuum that makes the past not into a frozen block of half-accomplished deeds, but a heterogeneous mass of future pasts awaiting historical actualization.

The double challenge of delinking political subjectivity from oppositional consciousness and from critique defined as negativity is one of the main issues raised by a neo-materialist approach to a politics of radical immanence. Not only is human subjectivity redefined as an expanded relational self, which includes non-human others, but it also allows us to open up to the virtual forces of Life. Life as *zoe*[57] is what Deleuze refers to as the great animal, the cosmic 'machine'. This is not to be taken in any mechanistic or utilitarian way, but in order to avoid any reference to biological determinism on the one hand and overinflated, psychologized individualism on the other. Deleuze and Guattari also use the term 'Chaos',[58] or the neologism 'Chaosmosis',[59] to refer to the endless supply of cosmic energy. They are also careful to point out, however, that Chaos is not chaotic, but it rather contains the infinity of all virtual forces. These potentialities are real in so far as they call for actualization through pragmatic and sustainable practices, which require collective assemblages and praxis. Posthuman materialist politics places differential mechanisms of distribution of power effects at the core of all stratifications. Multiple mechanisms of capture also engender multiple forms of resistance. Power-formations are time-bound and consequently temporary and contingent upon social action and interaction. But time is a continuum and therefore it entails movement and speed, lines of sedimentation and lines of flight, which are the main factors that affect the formation of non-unitary, posthuman subjects.

Politically, neo-materialism produces a different scheme of activism and a non-dialectical politics of human and posthuman liberation. It assumes that political agency need not be critical in the negative sense of dialectical oppositions but rely instead on affirmation and the pursuit of counter-actualizations of the virtual. An activist embrace of *zoe* introduces a planetary dimension that involves not only continuous negotiations with dominant norms and values but also the politics of co-production of affirmative and sustainable alternatives. A materialist politics of posthuman differences works through potential becomings that call for actualization. The becoming-minor or nomadic is a counter-actualization in that it strives to sustain processes of subject-formation that do not comply with the dominant norms. These counter-subjectivities are enacted through a collectively shared praxis and support the process of recomposition of what is not yet there – a missing people.

'We' are a missing people: our subjectivity needs to be composed as a collective assemblage activated around the shared desire to actualize new potentials. 'We' are becoming posthuman ethical subjects in our multiple capacities for relations of all sorts and modes of communications by codes that transcend the linguistic sign by exceeding it in many directions.[60] At this particular point in our collective history, we simply do not know what our enfleshed selves, minds and bodies as one, can actually do. We need to find out by embracing an ethics of experiment with intensities. A sustainable ethics for non-unitary subjects rests on an enlarged sense of interconnection between self and others, including the non-human or 'earth' others, by removing the obstacle of self-centred individualism on the one hand and the barriers of negativity on the other.

In other words, to become posthuman does not mean to be undifferentiated from or indifferent to the humans or to be dehumanized. On the contrary, it rather implies a new way of combining ethical values with the well-being of an enlarged sense of community, which includes one's territorial or environmental interconnections. This is an ethical bond of an altogether different sort from that shaped by the self-interests of an individual subject, as defined along the canonical lines of classical humanism, or from the moral universalism of the Kantians and their reliance on extending Human Rights to all species, virtual entities and organisms.[61]

Becoming-posthuman consequently redefines one's sense of attachment and connection to a shared world, a territorial space: urban, social, psychic, ecological, technological, planetary as it may be. It expresses multiple ecologies of belonging, while it enacts the transformation of one's sensorial and perceptual coordinates, in order to acknowledge the collective nature and outward-bound direction of what we still call the self. This is in fact a moveable assemblage within a common life-space which the subject never masters nor possesses, but merely inhabits, crosses, always in a community, a pack, a group or a cluster. For posthuman theory, the subject is a transversal entity, fully immersed in and immanent to a network of non-human (animal, vegetable, viral) relations. The *zoe*-centred embodied subject is shot through with relational linkages of the contaminating/viral kind which interconnect it to a variety of others, starting from the environmental or eco-others, and include the 'medianaturecultural' technological apparatus.

This process-oriented vision of the subject is capable of a universalistic reach, though it rejects moral and cognitive universalism. It expresses a grounded, partial form of accountability, based on a strong sense of collectivity and relationality, which results in a renewed claim to community and belonging by singular subjects, bonded in collaborative ethics.[62] The stated criteria for this new ethics include nonprofit, emphasis on the collective, acceptance of relationality and of viral contaminations, concerted efforts at experimenting with and actualizing potential or virtual options, and a new link between theory and practice, including a central role for creativity. These are not moral injunctions, but dynamic frames for an ongoing experiment with intensities. These need to be enacted collectively, by composing the 'missing we', that is to say actualizing a 'missing people'. This 'we' is a collective assemblage, that is to say, an immanent complex singularity, not to be confused with a messianic entity to-come. It is rather the result of a collective praxis: the task of critical theory is to labor towards the emergence of this transversal subject, or 'missing we', by producing effective cartographies of and experiments with how much these embodied subjects can take. I index these experiments with intensity on an ethical scale that aims at creating collective bonds, a new affective community or polity. The limits of what these embodied transversal entities can take constitute the thresholds of ethical sustainability.[63]

The key notion in posthuman nomadic ethics is the transcendence of negativity. What this means concretely is that the conditions for renewed political and ethical agency cannot be drawn from the immediate context or the current state of the terrain. They have to be generated affirmatively and creatively by efforts geared to creating possible futures, by mobilizing resources and visions that have been left untapped and by actualizing them in daily practices of interconnection with others. This project requires more visionary power or prophetic energy, qualities which are neither especially in fashion in academic circles, nor highly valued scientifically in these times of coercive pursuit of globalized 'excellence'. Yet, the call for more vision is emerging from many quarters in critical theory. As I stated earlier, feminists have a long and rich genealogy in terms of pleading for increased visionary insight, and this constitutes the affirmative and innovative core of the radical epistemologies of feminism, gender, race and postcolonial studies.

A posthuman theory of the subject emerges, therefore, as an empirical project that aims at experimenting with what contemporary, bio-technologically mediated bodies are capable of doing. These non-profit experiments with contemporary subjectivity actualize the virtual possibilities of an expanded, relational self that functions in a nature-culture continuum and is technologically mediated. Not surprisingly, this non-profit, experimental approach to different practices of subjectivity runs against the spirit of contemporary capitalism. The perversity of this system, and its undeniable success, consists in reattaching the potential for experimentation with new subject formations, back to an overinflated notion of possessive individualism,[64] fuelled by a quantitative range of consumers' choices. This is precisely the opposite direction from the non-profit experimentations with intensity, which I defend in my theory of posthuman subjectivity.

Composing a community around the shared affects and concepts of becoming-minoritarian is the key to nomadic transformative politics. It expresses the affirmative, ethical dimension of becoming-posthuman as a gesture of collective self-styling, or mutual specification. It actualizes a community that is not bound negatively by shared vulnerability, the guilt of ancestral communal violence, or the melancholia of unpayable ontological debts, but rather by the compassionate acknowledgement of their interdependence with multiple others, most of which, in the age of the Anthropocene, are quite simply not anthropomorphic.

Notes

1. Rosi Braidotti, *The Posthuman*.
2. Félix Guattari, *The Three Ecologies*.
3. Rosi Braidotti, 'The Contested Posthumanities'.
4. Michel Foucault, *The Order of Things*.
5. See, for example, Sandra Harding, *The Science Question in Feminism*; Adrienne Rich, *Blood, Bread, and Poetry*; Donna Haraway, 'Situated Knowledges'; Patricia Hill Collins, *Black Feminist Thought*.
6. See Joan Kelly, 'The Double-edged Vision of Feminist Theory', and Donna Haraway, 'A Manifesto for Cyborgs'.
7. See Gilles Deleuze, *Bergsonism* and *Expressionism in Philosophy*; Rosi Braidotti, *Patterns of Dissonance* and *Nomadic Subjects*.
8. Gilles Deleuze and Félix Guattari, *A Thousand Plateaus*.
9. Gilles Deleuze, *Francis Bacon*.
10. Genevieve Lloyd, *Spinoza and the Ethics*, 74.
11. Michael Hardt and Antonio Negri, *Empire*.
12. Rosi Braidotti, *Nomadic Theory*.
13. Rosi Braidotti, *Transpositions*.
14. Rosi Braidotti, *Metamorphoses* and *Transpositions*.
15. See Rosi Braidotti, *Metamorphoses* and *The Posthuman*; Elizabeth Grosz, *Becoming Undone*; Claire Colebrook, *Death of the Posthuman*; John Protevi, *Life, War, Earth*.
16. Gilles Deleuze, *Negotiations*, 172.
17. Rosi Braidotti, 'The Posthuman in Feminist Theory'.
18. See Gilles Deleuze and Félix Guattari, *Anti-Oedipus* and *A Thousand Plateaus*.
19. Gilles Deleuze, *Nietzsche and Philosophy*.

20 Gilles Deleuze, *Expressionism in Philosophy*.
21 Gilles Deleuze, *Empiricism and Subjectivity*.
22 Gilles Deleuze, *The Fold*.
23 Gilles Deleuze, *Foucault*.
24 Melinda Cooper, *Life as Surplus*.
25 Rosi Braidotti, *Transpositions*.
26 Gilles Deleuze, *Bergsonism* and *Expressionism in Philosophy*.
27 Gilles Deleuze and Félix Guattari, *What Is Philosophy?*
28 Rosi Braidotti, *Transpositions*.
29 Keith Ansell-Pearson, *Germinal Life*.
30 Stacy Alaimo, 'Thinking as the Stuff of the World'.
31 Rosi Braidotti, *Transpositions*.
32 Michel Foucault, *Discipline and Punish*.
33 The group around Althusser started the debate in the mid-1960s; Deleuze's path-breaking study of Spinoza dates from 1968 (English in 1990); Macherey's Hegel-Spinoza analysis came out in 1979 (English in 2011); Negri's work on the imagination in Spinoza in 1981 (English in 1991).
34 See Genevieve Lloyd, *Spinoza and the Ethics*; John Protevi, *Life, War, Earth*.
35 Yves Citton and Frédéric Lordon, *Spinoza et les sciences sociales*.
36 Rosi Braidotti, 'Postface'.
37 Rosi Braidotti, *Nomadic Theory*.
38 Félix Guattari, *Chaosmosis*, 26.
39 Gilles Deleuze and Félix Guattari, *What Is Philosophy?*
40 Matthew Fuller, *Media Ecologies*.
41 Genevieve Lloyd, *Part of Nature*.
42 Donna Haraway, 'A Manifesto for Cyborgs', and *Modest_Witness@Second_Millennium*, *The Companion Species Manifesto*.
43 Patricia Clough, *The Affective Turn*, 3.
44 Jussi Parikka, *A Geology of Media*.
45 Patricia MacCormack, *Posthuman Ethics*.
46 Brian Massumi, *Parables for the Virtual*.
47 Patricia MacCormack. *The Animal Catalyst*.
48 Rosi Braidotti, *Patterns of Dissonance*.
49 Manuel DeLanda, *Intensive Science and Virtual Philosophy*.
50 Mariam Fraser, Saraha Kember and Celia Lury, eds., *Inventive Life*.
51 Jane Bennett, *Vibrant Matter*.
52 Vicki Kirby, *Quantum Anthropologies*.
53 Adrian MacKenzie, *Transductions*.
54 Rosi Braidotti, *Metamorphoses*.
55 Benjamin Noys, *The Persistence of the Negative*.
56 Gilles Deleuze, *Bergsonism*.
57 Rosi Braidotti, *Transpositions*.
58 Gilles Deleuze and Félix Guattari, *A Thousand Plateaus*.
59 Félix Guattari, *Chaosmosis*.
60 Gilles Deleuze and Félix Guattari, *A Thousand Plateaus*.
61 Martha Nussbaum, *Frontiers of Justice*.
62 Genevieve Lloyd, *Spinoza and the Ethics*.
63 Rosi Braidotti, *Transpositions*.
64 Crawford B. MacPherson, *The Theory of Possessive Individualism*.

Bibliography

Alaimo, Stacy. *Bodily Natures: Science, Environment and the Material Self*. Bloomington, IN: Indiana University Press, 2010.
Alaimo, Stacy. 'Thinking as the Stuff of the World'. *O-Zone: A Journal of Object-Oriented Studies* 1 (2014): 13–21.
Bennett, Jane. *Vibrant Matter: A Political Ecology of Things*. Durham, NC: Duke University Press, 2010.
Braidotti, Rosi. 'The Contested Posthumanities'. In *Contesting Humanities*, edited by Rosi Braidotti and Gilroy, Paul, 9–45. London and New York: Bloomsbury Academic, 2016.
Braidotti, Rosi. *Metamorphoses. Towards a Materialist Theory of Becoming*. Cambridge and Malden: Polity Press/Blackwell Publishers Ltd., 2002.
Braidotti, Rosi. *Nomadic Subjects*. New York: Columbia University Press, 1994 and 2011.
Braidotti, Rosi. *Nomadic Theory*. New York: Columbia University Press, 2011.
Braidotti, Rosi. *Patterns of Dissonance*. Cambridge: Polity Press, 1991.
Braidotti, Rosi. 'Postface: The Residual Spirituality in Critical Theory. A Case for Affirmative Postsecular Politics'. In *Transformations of Religion and the Public Sphere: Postsecular Publics*, edited by Rosi Braidotti, Bolette Blaagaard, Tobijn de Graauw and Eva Midden, 249–72. Hampshire: Palgrave Macmillan, 2014.
Braidotti, Rosi. *The Posthuman*. Cambridge: Polity Press, 2013.
Braidotti, Rosi. 'The Posthuman in Feminist Theory'. In *Oxford Handbook of Feminist Theory*, edited by Lisa Disch and Mary Hawkesworth, 673–98. Oxford: Oxford University Press, 2015.
Braidotti, Rosi. *Transpositions: On Nomadic Ethics*. Cambridge: Polity Press, 2006.
Citton, Yves and Frédéric Lordon. *Spinoza et les Sciences Sociales*. Paris: Editions Amsterdam, 2008.
Colebrook, Claire. *Death of the Posthuman*. Ann Arbor: Open Humanities Press/ University of Michigan Press, 2014.
Cooper, Melinda. *Life as Surplus. Biotechnology & Capitalism in the Neoliberal Era*. Seattle: University of Washington Press, 2008.
Clough, Patricia. 'The Affective Turn: Political Economy, Biomedia and Bodies'. *Theory, Culture & Society* 25, no.1 (2008): 1–22.
DeLanda, Manuel. *Intensive Science and Virtual Philosophy*. London: Bloomsbury, 2002.
Deleuze, Gilles. *Bergonism*. Translated by Hugh Tomlinson and Barbara Habber. New York; Zone Books, 1988.
Deleuze, Gilles. *Difference and Repetition*. Translated by Paul Patton. London: The Athlone Press, 1994.
Deleuze, Gilles. *Empiricism and Subjectivity*. Translated by Constantin V. Boundas. New York: Columbia University Press, 1991.
Deleuze, Gilles. *Expressionism in Philosophy: Spinoza*. Translated by Martin Joughin. New York: Zone Books, 1990.
Deleuze, Gilles. *The Fold: Leibniz and the Baroque*. Translated by Tom Conley. Minneapolis, MN: University of Minnesota Press, 1992.
Deleuze, Gilles. *Foucault*. Translated by Sean Hand. Minneapolis, MN: University of Minnesota Press, 1988.
Deleuze, Gilles. *Francis Bacon: The Logic of Sensation*. Translated by Daniel W. Smith. London and New York: Continuum, [1981] 2003.

Deleuze, Gilles. *Negotiations*. Translated by Martin Joughin. New York: Columbia University Press, 1995.
Deleuze, Gilles. *Nietzsche and Philosophy*. Translated by Hugh Tomlinson. New York: Columbia University Press, 1983.
Deleuze, Gilles and Félix Guattari. *A Thousand Plateaus: Capitalism and Schizophrenia*. Translated by Brian Massumi. Minneapolis, MN: University of Minnesota Press, 1987.
Deleuze, Gilles and Félix Guattari. *Anti-Oedipus. Capitalism and Schizophrenia*. Translated by Robert Hurley. New York: Viking Press/ Richard Seaver, 1977.
Deleuze, Gilles and Félix Guattari. *What is Philosophy?* Translated by Hugh Tomlinson. New York: Columbia University Press, 1994.
Foucault, Michel. *Discipline and Punish*. Translated by Alan Sheridan. New York: Pantheon Books, 1977.
Foucault, Michel. *The Order of Things*. Translated by D. W. Harding. New York: Vintage Books, 1970.
Fraser, Mariam, Saraha Kember and Celia Lury, eds. *Inventive Life. Approaches to the New Vitalism*. London: Sage, 2006.
Fuller, Matthew. *Media Ecologies: Materialist Energies in Art and Technoculture*. Cambridge, MA and London: MIT Press, 2005.
Grosz, Elizabeth. *Becoming Undone*. Durham, NC: Duke University Press, 2011.
Guattari, Félix. *Chaosmosis. An Ethico-aesthetic Paradigm*. Translated by Julian Pefanis. Sydney: Power Publications, 1995.
Guattari, Félix. *The Three Ecologies*. Translated by Ian Pindar. London: The Athlone Press, 2000.
Haraway, Donna. 'A Manifesto for Cyborgs: Science, Technology, and Socialist Feminism in the 1980s'. *Socialist Review* 5, no. 2 (1985): 65–107.
Haraway, Donna. *The Companion Species Manifesto. Dogs, People and Significant Otherness*. Chicago: Prickly Paradigm Press, 2003.
Haraway, Donna. *Modest_Witness@Second_Millennium. FemaleMan©_Meets_ Oncomouse™*. London and New York: Routledge, 1997.
Haraway, Donna. 'Situated Knowledges. The Science Question in Feminism as a Site of Discourse on the Privilege of Partial Perspective'. *Feminist Studies* 14, no. 3 (1988): 575–99.
Harding, Sandra. *The Science Question in Feminism*. Ithaca: Cornell University Press, 1986.
Hardt, Michael and Antonio Negri. *Empire*. Cambridge, MA: Harvard University Press, 2000.
Hill Collins, Patricia. *Black Feminist Thought. Knowledge, Consciousness and the Politics of Empowerment*. New York and London: Routledge, 1991.
Kelly, Joan. 'The Double-Edged Vision of Feminist Theory'. *Feminist Studies* 5, no.1 (1979): 216–27.
Kirby, Vicki. *Quantum Anthropologies: Life at Large*. Durham, NC: Duke University Press, 2011.
Lloyd, Genevieve. *Part of Nature: Self-knowledge in Spinoza's Ethic*. Ithaca and London: Cornell University Press, 1994.
Lloyd, Genevieve. *Spinoza and the Ethics*. London and New York: Routledge, 1996.
MacCormack, Patricia. *The Animal Catalyst*. London: Bloomsbury, 2014.
MacCormack, Patricia. *Posthuman Ethics*. London: Ashgate, 2012.
Macherey, Pierre. *Hegel or Spinoza*. Translated by Susan M. Ruddick. Minneapolis, MN: University of Minnesota Press, 2011.

MacKenzie, Adrian. *Transductions: Bodies and Machines at Speed.* New York: Continuum, 2002.
MacPherson, Crawford B. *The Theory of Possessive Individualism.* Oxford: Oxford University Press, 1962.
Massumi, Brian. *Parables for the Virtual: Movement, Affect, Sensation.* Durham, NC: Duke University Press, 2002.
Negri, Antonio. *The Savage Anomaly.* Minneapolis, MN: University of Minnesota Press, 1991.
Noys, Benjamin. *The Persistence of the Negative: A Critique of Contemporary Continental Theory.* Edinburgh: Edinburgh University Press, 2010.
Nussbaum, Marta. *Frontiers of Justice. Disability, Nationality, Species Membership.* Cambridge: Harvard University Press, 2006.
Parikka, Jussi. *A Geology of Media.* Minneapolis, MN: University of Minnesota Press, 2015.
Protevi, John. *Life War Earth.* Minneapolis, MN: University of Minnesota Press, 2013.
Rich, Adrienne. *Blood, Bread and Poetry.* London: Virago Press, 1987.

2

Deleuzian traces

The self of the polyp

Christine Daigle

The posthumanist philosophies I am interested in, including material feminism and new materialism, challenge the anthropocentric world view by rejecting human exceptionalism and emphasizing the material embeddedness and interconnectivity of all beings. It is not uncommon among posthumanist thinkers to posit a flat ontological plane in which no being takes precedence over others.[1] As Rosi Braidotti suggests, embracing such a position entails a far-reaching reconceptualization of that ontological plane and the beings it encompasses.[2] However, there is a risk involved with some posthumanist claims – some of which are inspired by Deleuze and Guattari – that deny that there is any core to the human subject and posit the human being as a fundamentally selfless fluctuating being. One worry is that such a fleeting being would not qualify as an agent to whom one can ascribe responsibility because it is incapable of constituting a self. In response to that concern, some have argued that we ought to establish at least a minimal self that can bear this responsibility. Braidotti, for example, says that we need to 'devise new social, ethical and discursive schemes of subject formation to match the profound transformations we are undergoing. This means that we need to learn to think differently about ourselves.'[3] My claim is that understanding our being as rooted in materiality, in discourse, in the experience of being a subject, and in intersubjective relations is key to reconceptualizing ourselves. The concept of transjectivity that I put forward captures this manifold constitution of the being we are and contributes to establishing the posthuman minimal agent we need to deal with the most urgent crises facing us such as climate change, global wars and violence, and the continued oppression and exploitation of groups of humans and non-humans to satisfy the exponentially growing demands of select few.

The posthumanism in which I ground my concept of transjectivity – what I also refer to as our polyp-being – is that which emerges from the lines of thinking connecting Spinoza, Nietzsche, Deleuze and material feminism. I see the latter as bringing an important angle of approach which successfully maintains a minimal agent in the midst of the radical challenge to subjectivity and notions of selfhood offered by Deleuze and Guattari and, arguably, their predecessors identified in the lineage above. With transjectivity, I am not offering a strictly Deleuzian concept – nor a

Spinozist or Nietzschean one for that matter. Rather, I aim to offer a concept that takes seriously Deleuze and Guattari's radical challenge while retaining some trace of the self that is grounded in the matter that constitutes it. This is why I begin my chapter by exploring that challenge and identifying what the 'trace of the self' can be for Deleuze and Guattari, if it can be anything. Building upon that notion of trace and appealing to material feminist views, I will explain how we can still emphasize materiality and interconnectivity without doing away with the self completely. I will propose that the transjective being is the foundation upon which a trace of the self can emerge, thereby satisfying our ethical and political need for an agent. In what may appear as a surprising move to some, I will appeal to Paul Ricœur's hermeneutics of the self, according to which the self can relate to itself and constitute the unity of itself and its life through a narrative reappropriation of the lived experience.[4] Indeed, even though his phenomenological understanding of the self is at odds with Deleuze and Guattari and potentially with what we find in posthumanist philosophies that are inspired by them – indeed, they would never subscribe to the notion of a conscious unity of the self, the self they offer being a perpetually fluctuating coalescing of tensions and forces, affects and percepts, upon which some flickering of consciousness may occur – the way in which Ricœur understands self-constitution as relating to one's embodied being is a useful theoretical strategy to explain how a posthumanist material feminist self may emerge. Ricœur's view, as expressed specifically in *Oneself as Another*, encompasses relating to one's own materiality in the way required by posthumanist and feminist materialist thinkers. My chapter will show how the transjective being and its self offer a reconceptualized view of the human that responds to Braidotti's call.

Deleuze and Guattari on subjectivity and the body

Deleuze and Guattari's proposals for a deterritorialization/reterritorialization of the concept of Man point to reconfigurings of the experience of subjectivity and being a body that moves away from traditional theorizations about the experience of being a conscious being and about subjectivity. They question and reject notions such as that of an autonomous transcendent subjectivity neatly separated from the body and the world. They thereby do away with the self of humanist philosophies that is a unified being meeting the world in a reflective manner. Their discussion of the body without organs (BwO) intriguingly points to the necessary trace the self must have indicating that this self is not done away with completely but, rather, reconfigured. They write, 'for it is not "my" body without organs, instead the "me" (*moi*) is on it, or what remains of me, unalterable and changing in form, crossing thresholds.'[5] I take this as an indication that as much as one needs to think beyond the narrow confines of subjectivity and consciousness, that is, as much as we must try to think beyond dualistic categories, there still remains a 'self', or at least a trace of one that I see as grounded in the material being that we also are. However, Deleuze and Guattari claim, 'The BwO is what remains when you take everything away. What you take away is precisely the phantasy, and significances and subjectivations as a whole.'[6] Processes of subjectivation are precisely that: processes. The human being, just like any other being, is dynamic becoming and, as such, constantly fluctuating as it enters in relations with other beings. As they put it in *What Is Philosophy?*, 'man [sic], as he is caught in stone, on the canvas, or by words, is himself a compound of percepts and affects'.[7] These are, as they put it, the non-human becoming and landscapes in which the human becomes; 'We are not in the world, we become with the world'.[8]

What, then, is the 'me' or 'we' they refer to? The entanglement of the human in this web of relations and the constant becoming that ensues undermines the erection of a stable and fixed identity. As they put it, '*I* is a habit',[9] one that emerges from the brain's thinking activity. 'It is the brain that says *I*, but *I* is an other'.[10] Deleuze and Guattari are clear: 'we are sick, so sick, of our *selves!*'[11] In *Anti-Oedipus*, they explain that the subject is a residuum; it is 'not at the center, which is occupied by the machine, but on the periphery, with no fixed identity, forever decentered, defined by the states through which it passes'.[12] This decentred subject, or self, represents a radical shift from philosophies that focus on consciousness as central to the human experience. For Deleuze and Guattari, the subject emerges from a process of stratification, it is part of a molar plane[13] and while it is important for them to destratify, there is no need to do so 'wildly': 'you have to keep small rations of subjectivity in sufficient quantity to enable you to respond to the dominant reality'.[14] But these small rations of subjectivity ought not to take the form of a humanist subject since we are dynamic becoming beings, and our selves are constantly done and undone by the affects and percepts that traverse us. And yet, they ask, 'Is it not necessary to retain a minimum of strata, a minimum of forms and functions, a minimal subject from which to extract materials, affects, and assemblages?'[15] Perhaps, but that self, however, is merely a threshold, 'a becoming between two multiplicities'.[16] The minimal subject is radically different from the subject of humanist philosophies. They explain:

> Thus each individual is an infinite multiplicity, and the whole of Nature is a multiplicity of perfectly individuated multiplicities. The plane of consistency of Nature is like an immense Abstract Machine, abstract yet real and individual; its pieces are the various assemblages and individuals, each of which groups together an infinity of particles entering into an infinity of more or less interconnected relations.[17]

Rather than talk of subjects or individuals, Deleuze and Guattari refer to haecceities. Haecceity is a mode of individuation that is not to be confused with that of a thing or a subject,[18] what del Río refers to as 'singularity stripped of subjectivity'.[19] In fact, 'There are only haecceities, affects, subjectless individuations that constitute collective assemblages. . . . Nothing subjectifies, but haecceities form according to compositions of nonsubjectified powers or affects'.[20] This makes us fleeting beings – never fixed or stable – that exist at the point of encounter of affects and tensions, beings that emerge and disappear as quickly through an encounter of relations because 'pure affects imply an enterprise of desubjectification'.[21] As del Río puts it, even the body, which is often conceived as the grounds for establishing individual subjectivity, 'is never a fixed or unified entity, but, instead, an open and unstable whole'.[22] There is, after all, no possibility for a self to have any kind of permanence and, therefore, no room for us to talk about subjectivity as anything but an illusory concept fabricated out of habit and fictive use of relations. The trace of the self alluded to in relation to the BwO is so tenuous that it is on the verge of vanishing.

Examining materiality

The move away from the centrality of subjectivity – initiated by Spinoza, pursued by Nietzsche, and intensified by Deleuze and Guattari – points to the many other elements of life that have been traditionally disregarded and devalued. Materiality and its action need to be examined anew leaving behind the notion of materiality as brute and devoid of agency, a view often held by philosophies that privilege the human. Deleuze and Guattari's focus on materiality, however, is not on matter itself, as it is, so much as on the relations between material beings. Their emphasis is not on materiality as it presents itself in the various beings populating the plane of immanence, or on its inner operations, but rather on materiality as engaged in dynamic becoming and relations. Joe Hughes notes, for example, and in relation to one specific type of material being, that there is very little in the whole Deleuzian corpus about the body itself and that 'even in those texts in which the body plays a prominent role, it is very quickly transcended'.[23] Deleuzian-inspired material feminists see this as a problem and want to refocus our attention on the very materiality of the being that we are as well as the materiality of the relations between beings. Matter matters to the relations.[24] Focusing on the body, on the biochemical processes animating bodies,[25] or on the agitation taking place in the quantum field[26] is the strategy chosen to establish the minimal self we need.

Braidotti's views on nomadic subjects, which inspire my own concept of transjectivity, also point to the necessity of thinking through materiality. She posits a subject that is fluid and hybrid and thereby challenges the traditional view of the subject as a self-contained unity. For her, selves are in the process of shaping themselves and being shaped by their manifold interactions and entanglements. Taking from Deleuze and Guattari, she claims that the self may be understood as a field of tensions. She says:

> The body refers to a layer of corporeal materiality, a substratum of living matter endowed with memory. Following Deleuze, I understand this as pure flows of energy, capable of multiple variations. The 'self', meaning an entity endowed with identity, is anchored in this living matter, whose materiality is coded and rendered in language. . . . *the body cannot be fully apprehended or represented: it exceeds representation.*[27]

The excess Braidotti refers to is the very materiality of the body as well as its dynamic material entanglement with other beings, animate and not, organic and not.[28] Even if it resists representation, if we cannot capture it with language and thinking and fully conceptualize it, we need to get as close to it as we can. This is what material feminists attempt. In that field, I find the set of ideas presented by Stacy Alaimo, Karen Barad, Jane Bennett, Claire Colebrook and Nancy Tuana particularly generative.[29]

Stacy Alaimo's view of the material self, for example, emphasizes the materiality of the body. For Alaimo we are transcorporeal beings, which means that our human corporeality is materially interconnected with the more-than-human world.[30] She uses 'trans' to indicate that we are dealing with a 'mobile space that acknowledges the often unpredictable and unwanted actions of human bodies, nonhuman creatures, ecological systems, chemical agents, and other actors'.[31] In short, we are 'always the very stuff of the messy, contingent, emergent mix of the material world'.[32] In her most recent work, she further emphasizes that human beings are always exposed: 'penetrated by substances and forces that can never be properly accounted for'.[33] She forms this view by incorporating Nancy Tuana's notions of viscous porosity and interactionism as well as Karen Barad's intra-activity which amount to a rethinking and rejection of the mind-body and human-non-human dualisms. As Alaimo puts it, viscous porosity 'with its emphasis on mediating membranes, which may be biological, social, and political, is a powerful model for understanding material interactions'.[34] As we will see shortly, we can put this model to work in explaining the transjective being we are.

Viscosity can be seen to serve as a response to views that choose to emphasize fluidity in order to move away from dualistic thinking.[35] Recently, for example, Astrida Neimanis has argued for the need to think of ourselves as bodies of water. She says, 'Attention to water's material capacities informs a new way of thinking about subjectivity in collective rather than individualist terms'.[36] However, as useful as such thinking may be, it conveys a false sense of a smooth process. Fluidity implies an easy flowing of liquids, a continuous movement that accelerates or decelerates but is not interrupted. This ease associated with fluidity seems to ignore the resistance to be found in materiality. The embrace of fluidity has been of service to a certain extent in opening up notions of fixed identity and bodily autonomy. However, as Mary K. Bloodsworth-Lugo claimed, conceiving of the human body as fluid runs the risk of losing sight of its materiality and the inherent resistance that matter can exercise.[37] Tuana's concept of viscous porosity therefore seems more appropriate. She explains:

> *Viscosity* is neither fluid nor solid, but intermediate between them. Attention to the porosity of interactions helps to undermine the notion that distinctions, as important as they might be in particular contexts, signify a natural or unchanging boundary, a natural kind. At the same time, 'viscosity' retains an emphasis on resistance to changing form, thereby a more helpful image than 'fluidity', which is too likely to promote a notion of open possibilities and to overlook sites of resistance and opposition or attention to the complex ways in which material agency is often involved in interactions, including, but not limited to, human agency.[38]

Viscous porosity is a metaphor Tuana uses to capture how 'subjects are constituted out of relationality',[39] but not merely intersubjective relationality. Rather, she is proposing to think of a 'complex network of relations' that involves various kinds of beings. An interactionist metaphysic, such as the one she embraces, understands the world and its beings in those terms and moves us beyond the dualistic split between nature and culture, eliminates the debates between realism and social constructivism[40] and puts us in a position to understand agency in a more complex manner as an assemblage that emerges out of the continuum that flows between terms previously erroneously conceived as in a binary relation that kept them separate. Karen Barad's intra-activity is a means to articulate that network of relations. She explains, 'the world is intra-activity in its differential mattering.'[41] For her, the world is a dynamic state of becoming in which agency is the after-effect of the field of forces and tensions that intra-act. This, however, has the potential to eliminate human agency, an elimination that is not desirable. I agree that we need a 'robust account of the materialization of all bodies'[42] but not at the cost of moving away completely from any processes of subjectivation necessary for the establishment of human agency. My claim is that we constitute a minimal self as the bodies that are materialized through the relations we are in. There is room for minimal agency in the swarm of relations that make us.[43] For Barad, 'matter is substance in its intra-active becoming – not a thing, but a doing, a congealing of agency. Matter is a stabilizing and destabilizing process of iterative intra-activity.'[44] However, this seems to exclude important processes of self-constitution that, even if they are grounded in the material intra-active becoming, are not themselves material. This is what the transsubjective brings to the transobjective in constituting transjectivity.

What is interesting to note is that even staunch materialists who want to make matter matter again are still caught up in discussions that focus on relations rather than matter itself.[45] It may be the case after all that matter eludes us to a certain degree. With that said, it may be sufficient to agree with Jane Bennett's project. She approaches her concept of 'vibrant matter' with a specific ethical and political goal in mind. In her preface, she indicates that her plan is to 'emphasize, even overemphasize, the agentic contributions of nonhuman forces (operating in nature, in the human body, and in human artifacts) in an attempt to counter the narcissistic reflex of human language and thought'.[46] She is forthcoming about her interest in human well-being and sees materialism as potent in addressing human issues:

> Such a newfound attentiveness to matter and its power will not solve the problem of human exploitation or oppression, but it can inspire a greater sense of the extent to which all bodies are kin in the sense of inextricably enmeshed in a dense network of relations. And in a knotted world of vibrant matter, to harm one section of the web may very well be to harm oneself. Such an enlightened or expanded notion of self-interest *is good for humans*.[47]

Bennett's concept of vibrant matter is part of a vitalist view according to which things are quasi agents[48] that act upon their vital impetus and that impact the being and agency of other beings, including the human. Those agents never act alone as they are always caught in a web of relations. Spinoza's notion of affective bodies and Deleuze and Guattari's concept of assemblage feed into her concept of agency by emphasizing the entanglement of all beings. Exploring this theoretical path leads her to reject completely the notion of passive matter which, as she puts it, weakens our understanding of the force things may exert.[49] She concludes:

I believe it is wrong to deny vitality to nonhuman bodies, forces, and forms, and that a careful course of anthropomorphization can help reveal that vitality, even though it resists full translation and exceeds my comprehensive grasp. I believe that encounters with lively matter can chasten my fantasies of human mastery, highlight the common materiality of all that is, expose a wider distribution of agency, and reshape the self and its interests.[50]

What the views I have explored point to is the power and force of materiality, its agential strength in interacting with all other agents, what has been referred to as the agentic capacity of all matter, including ours.[51] We are dealing with a world and life that is vibrant with activity, an affective material that is also a subjective fabric in which all beings are interconnected. Claire Colebrook sums this up very nicely: 'We are at once thrown into a situation of urgent interconnectedness, aware that the smallest events contribute to global mutations, at the same time as we come up against a complex multiplicity of diverging forces and timelines that exceed any manageable point of view.'[52] Such a view aligns with my view of transjectivity whereby we are always caught up in a field of tensions and forces, being done and undone, both by ourselves and by other beings we are entangled with, doing and undoing them as well.

Transjectivity – Thinking our polyp-being

My own posthumanist view of transjectivity emerges at the intersection of the views discussed thus far and builds upon them. Transjectivity is my ontological concept to refer to our polyp-being, a being that is concomitantly transsubjective and transobjective, always caught up in relations and fields of tensions, both contributing to and at the receiving end of agency and intra-action, an expression of agentic capacity in the midst of a manifold of capacities. This goes further than intersubjectivity and interobjectivity taken individually or together. Following Michèle Le Doeuff, who was dissatisfied with the limits she perceived as inherent to 'intersubjectivity', I wish to use *transsubjectivity* to capture an experience that is more encompassing.[53] I extend the use of 'trans' to the objective, material realm as well and propose that we are transjective beings. Interobjectivity, or intercorporeality for that matter, maintains separate entities or the idea that there are different and separate objects or bodies interacting and thereby engaging in the realm of interobjectivity or intercorporeality.[54] However, I propose that there are no such autonomous separate bodies and objects: they are always intermingled. My concept of transjectivity captures the concomitant experience of being a transsubjective and a transobjective being, and it acknowledges the mobility and permanent state of flux inherent in our being and in our very (self-)constitution. We are transsubjective beings that have experiences of being selves and are constituted and permeated by our relations with other selves, be it through personal encounters, the use of language, social construction,[55] and/or material entanglement. To repeat Tuana's claim, we are constituted through a complex web of relations, material and subjective. We are transobjective beings in that we are entangled and permeated by materiality: our own, that of other beings and of the world as a whole.[56]

I borrow from the powerful metaphor of the polyp that Nietzsche uses in *Daybreak* where he says: 'With every moment of our lives some of the polyp-arms of our being grow and others dry up, depending on the nourishment that the moment does or does not supply . . . all our experiences are, in this sense, types of nourishment.'[57] What does it mean to think of ourselves as polyps? Interestingly, Deleuze and Guattari quote William S. Burroughs's *Naked Lunch* in which he says, 'The human body is scandalously inefficient. Instead of a mouth and an anus to get out of order why not have one all-purpose hole to eat *and* eliminate?'[58] This corresponds to the polyp:[59] a soft-bodied organism that has a mouth that also serves as its anus, with tentacles to grab its nourishment. Marine polyps build for themselves a limestone skeleton, named calicle, to protect their translucent bodies. While some polyps live as solitary organisms, most live in colonies in which they are all interconnected via their calicles. The colony thereby constitutes one living organism composed of a multiplicity of 'individuals'. The coral reefs thus formed are multiplicities in another sense as they also host billions of colourful algae that inhabit them. This is what gives the coral reefs their spectacular colouration. However, polyps are highly sensitive and responsive to their environment and fluctuations caused by environmental stress may lead to bleaching of the reefs, when polyps evict their inhabitants in response to pollution or temperature change in the water.

One may be so bold as to say that polyps are transjective beings. They are materially interconnected with one another in the colony, making up one living organism firmly anchored to the seabed after the initial polyp 'decided' to attach itself to a rock and then proliferated. One may object, however, that it would be difficult to ascribe any kind of subjectivity, let alone transsubjectivity, to polyps since they are brainless creatures.[60] However, they are acting creatures that relate to other beings they are attached to or host as well as to their overall environment. They act by attaching themselves to a rock and creating a colony. They act by evicting hosts in reaction to environmental change. They act in welcoming them back. Now, this agency may not be of the same kind as that of other animals, if only because of its limited scope, and its ensuing subjective existence may thereby be extremely limited. But I don't think there is any reason to deny that a polyp may have an experience of itself and that some thinking may be occurring at that marine level. It may even be argued that the limited agency of the polyp – one that is limited individually but expanded via the collective action of the colony – is no more limited than that of any other being, including that of our human selves. In fact, using the metaphor of the polyp to give an account of human existence makes precisely that point and yet, that does not entail denying a subjective and transsubjective experience and being to the human. That said, I am not attempting to prove or disprove the transsubjective life of a coral polyp – that may very well be impossible and therefore foolish to attempt – but want to use the polyp as an analogy for our human transjective being that gives us a potent image of how we exist transsubjectively and transobjectively. Like polyps, we exist as interconnected with others. We host organisms that may be said to give us our 'colour', namely our microbiological constitution as a multiplicity. Polyps are attached to a material foundation in a literal way while we are mobile creatures, but our mobility is always and ever grounded in materiality. And like polyps, that grounding constrains and shapes our agency. We are indeed polyps. It may be argued that the materiality to which the marine polyp is attached does not fluctuate and is not changing dynamically the way materiality does for a transjective human being. However, I think that this claim does not hold if one considers the different types of dynamic becoming in which a rock exists. There are geological and temporal scales that differ for every being, impacting the speed at which change may occur thereby making it sometimes invisible in its slowness or speed for other beings.[61] This does not mean that the material object is not becoming. Furthermore, the polyp is not merely anchored in materiality via its attachment to the rock. It is also transobjective in its interactions with water, the food particles and other beings in it, nearby interconnected polyps and their bodies, the algae it hosts, fishes that pass by or make the reef their home, etc. The relations between these beings and their materiality constitute the transobjective being of the polyp, just as our transjective being is impacted by the set of relations and fields of tensions in which we live.

The polyp is a transsubjective and transobjective being, entangled with other subjectivities and with objects and materiality. What is notable with the quote from *Daybreak*, cited above, and other passages where Nietzsche discusses the self, is that the polyp engages in self-constitution but is also the object of processes of self-constitution that lay outside the scope of its consciousness and are not the outcome of a wilful decision or action on its own part. Nietzsche proposes that 'the way is open for new versions and refinements of the soul-hypothesis; and such conceptions as "mortal soul", and "soul as subjective multiplicity", and "soul as social structure of drives and affects", want henceforth to have citizen's rights in science'.[62] As we have seen, Deleuze and Guattari's notion of individual multiplicity is at risk of being completely desubjectified, thereby exacerbating Nietzsche's notion of subjective multiplicity. Transjectivity avoids that risk, anchored in the reef of our polyp-being, a vibrant transobjective and transsubjective multiplicity with undefined porous – and viscous – boundaries.

The transjective being incorporates in its being the fields of tension in which it exists but also acts upon it. Incorporating these fields of tension in the constitution of the transjective beings that we are leads us to a position where we are fundamentally vulnerable because we are always in that dynamic flux of making ourselves and being made by and through our radical entanglement with other subjectivities and materiality, a materiality which is also in dynamic flux, albeit on different scales.[63] This poses a great challenge to self-constitution that stands to be undone at any point in time through the changes and various actions of the intra-active realm, or the flux of affects that traverse the immanent realm in which the transjective being finds itself. The experience of being a transjective self that emerges out of this field of tensions makes the transjective being similar to Deleuze and Guattari's haecceity, namely the point at which latitude and longitude intersect (materiality and affects). In the plane of immanence, multiple interactions occur and the body emerges as that 'sum total of the material elements belonging to it under given relations of movement and rest, speed and slowness (longitude); the sum total of the intensive affects it is capable of at a given power or degree of potential (latitude)'.[64] This view takes its point of departure in Spinoza and his take on the body and its potential to affect and be affected. Being caught in this plane of immanence where forces interact and are in tension, the body is a fluctuating thing and the 'self' that may emerge even more tenuous. From this, Brian Massumi observes that:

> The charge of indeterminacy carried by a body is inseparable from it. It strictly coincides with it, to the extent that the body is in passage or in process (to the extent that it is dynamic and alive). . . . to think the body in movement thus means accepting the paradox that there is an incorporeal dimension *of the body*.[65]

While I do think that this view of affect and how it operates reflects what happens in the realm of the transsubjective and transobjective and their criss-crossing, there is definite risk there too to lose the self as affects continually alter and shape it. Narrative theories of self-constitution can help us deal with this conundrum in providing a strategy for a self-reprise. Recall, as per the material feminists, that there are many different modes of self-constitution that occur in a complex network of relations.

For each 'individual', for each self, experiences are had as an ambiguous multiplicity, as a field of tensions, as a transjective being. Various elements of our experiences as bodies that are also conscious are incorporated and become part of our being. As Massumi puts it:

> The intensity is experience. The emptiness or in-betweenness filled by experience is the incorporeal dimension of the body . . . The conversion of surface distance into intensity is also the conversion of the materiality of the body into an *event*. . . . It is a relay between its corporeal and incorporeal dimensions. This is not yet a subject. But it may well be the conditions of emergence of a subject: an incipient subjectivity. Call it a 'self-'. The hyphen is retained as a reminder that 'self' is not a substantive but rather a relation.[66]

All we can say about the self is that it is a relation, that is, if we stick to an ontological description of these relations. However, phenomenologically, a narrative theory of self-constitution, such as Paul Ricœur elaborates, can still emerge on the grounds of this moving field of tension. It offers an explanation for how a self can erect itself narratively on the fluctuating material basis that it also is as transjective being through a reflective self-reprise.[67]

Narratively constructing the polyp

According to Ricœur, the self can relate to itself and constitute the unity of itself and its life through a narrative reappropriation of the lived experience.[68] This encompasses relating to one's own materiality. Ricœur speaks of an internal dialectic whereby the *ipse* is fundamentally shaped by the *idem* which is also appropriated reflectively through a narrative constitution of the self by the *ipse*-identity. The distinction between *idem* and *ipse* in Ricœur pertains to personal identity as it relates to materiality and continuity in time (*idem*) and the relation a self has to its own history along with its capacity to relate to it reflectively via a narrative reconstruction (*ipse*). While materiality plays a role in that it affects the *idem*, the self is really established and consolidated by consciousness. In that, Ricœur remains faithful to phenomenology's emphasis on and prioritization of consciousness. All narrative theories of selfhood share in this in that they ground selfhood in the act of telling oneself one's story. For Ricœur, personal identity is the dialectic between *idem* and *ipse* as they are inscribed in corporeity. They are equiprimordial and the dialectic between them is constitutive of our self *as we relate to our selves*. More precisely, narrativity is the mediation that allows us to relate to our whatness – a portion of the transobjective, in my terms – and constitute our whoness – portion of the transsubjective, in my terms – on that basis. There may be some immutable elements of the what, for example, one's physiology, one's geographical location, etc., but through the constitution of one's self, one may relate to this immutability in a variety of ways. As we construct our narrative, we relate and value such in different ways. However, life narratives are intertwined with those of others. No life narrative is ever put in place in complete isolation from that of others. As Butler explains in *Giving an Account of Oneself*, 'When the "I" seeks to give an account of itself, it can start with itself, but it will find that this self is already implicated in a social temporality that exceeds its own capacities for narration.'[69] And, quite simply for Butler, 'my narrative begins *in media res*, when many things have already taken place to make me and my story possible in language.'[70] While Butler has a Foucauldian view of discourse in mind when she says this, I see how it relates to Ricœur's phenomenological commitments. It points to a vulnerability inherent to the self as well as its fragmented aspect. Indeed, a great portion of our self's constitution depends on other narratives and on language as a social phenomenon, the fabric of the transsubjective realm. Alterity is constitutive of us also via language and narrative construction.[71]

Susan J. Brison and Adriana Cavarero have picked up on the Ricœurian notion of narrative self and expanded it to emphasize the relationality of the self. In her book *Aftermath. Violence and the Remaking of a Self*, Brison offers that 'the self is both autonomous and socially dependent, vulnerable enough to be undone by violence and yet resilient enough to be reconstructed with the help of empathic others'.[72] This requires that one reconstructs oneself narratively and that this narrative be heard and acknowledged by others. The implication is that we always constitute our selves in this fashion. Violence to the self undoes and impacts this process, and we need to reactivate it. Cavarero agrees with this and posits that 'lives are disjointed and fragmentary' but that one may attain a 'fleeting and unstable unity' by giving a narrative structure to one's life through one's life story.[73] This implies a relation to another to whom the story is told. Cavarero speaks of a 'spontaneous narrating structure of memory'.[74] This spontaneity is constantly active and productive of the self. But it is a pre-reflective type of narrative and it is a process that remains internal to consciousness, making the self narratable. She says, 'the life-story that memory recounts is not enough for the narratable self.'[75] For the self to truly consolidate, there needs to be a relation between two where one gives their life story and the other receives it. For her then, 'the ontological status of the *who* – as exposed, relational, altruistic – is totally external.'[76] There is, therefore, an inherent vulnerability to the relational self as described by Cavarero and Brison. For Brison, however,

> If we are socially constructed, as I believe we are, in large part through our group-based narratives, the self is not a single, unified, coherent entity. Its structure is more chaotic, with harmonious and contradictory aspects, like the particles of an atom, attracting and repelling each other, hanging together in a whirling, ever-changing dance that any attempt at observation – or narration – alters.[77]

This points to the transsubjective realm. But what her account of her own rape also indicates is that there is a material inscription of trauma in the body and that the transobjective realm is also operative in the disruption and in the reconstruction of the self via narrative. As she indicates, it is impossible to recover in the sense of going back to the pre-traumatic self. The best one can do is reconstruct oneself by relating to the trauma, narrating it for oneself and for others. To a great extent, though, a large part of the trauma remains ineffable. This points to the necessary excess of narrative.

Ricœur's view is interesting for me as it allows me to discuss the transjective being's self and its relation to oneself and self-constitution. However, I agree with Annemie Halsema's assessment that Ricœur's proposal misses the excess of bodily, corporeal, material being that is also constitutive of the self and may escape one's own narrativization and self-constitution. She criticizes Ricœur because his emphasis on coherence amounts to a dismissal of the fact that 'the self is never completely narratable'.[78] She explains: 'Life exceeds narrative identity and self: we are merely *co-authors* of the meaning of our lives. Life exceeds narrative but is also not recognizable and cannot be constructed without the narrative.'[79] Some events which may fall on the wayside of narrative may still exist and operate within one's life. They are inscribed in our beings and constitutive of our selves without finding their way in narrative. There is an excess of meaning, of determination to the self that does not reduce to the narrative self. What Halsema is pointing to here is what I refer to as transobjectivity. As transjective beings, we are always also constituted by our transobjectivity. One may even question whether such excess is ever narrativizable. Perhaps it is the case that this excess constitutes the narrative. It certainly impacts the narrative; it is the material fabric of the narrative. In that sense, it is interesting to ask the question of whether it is 'the' narrator or a co-narrator along with the transsubjective.

In his *Sources of the Self*, Charles Taylor suggests that 'our identity is deeper and more many-sided than any of our possible articulations of it'.[80] Indeed, if we are the transjective beings I propose we are, narrative identity that is constructed subjectively is but a small part of who and what we are and one that is constantly being disrupted. Discussing Cavarero's views, Judith Butler speaks of the limits of the narrative self, 'The singular body to which a narrative refers cannot be captured by a full narration, not only because the body has a formative history that remains irrecoverable by reflection, but because primary relations are formative in ways that produce a necessary opacity in our understanding of ourselves.'[81] To her, the narrative self is always and necessarily a fiction, one we construct within a mode of subjectivation in a Foucauldian sense.[82] It is debatable whether identity matches the actual content of the narrative. One's identity might also be constituted by the various omissions or plain erasures that accompany narrative construction. As she puts it, 'To be a body is, in some sense, to be deprived of having a full recollection of one's life. There is a history to my body of which I can have no recollection.'[83] Claire Colebrook has a very interesting take on this. While discussing Butler's *Bodies That Matter*, she explains:

> The self may be performative – having no being that grounds its life other than its own doing – but those performances are materially constrained. Bodies matter, not because they cause our being, but because the living of them *as material* – as the very nature that is our own – is made possible only through regarding ourselves as subjects, as beings who have some recognizable, repeatable, and accountable identity. And to have identity, or to be *someone*, is to possess some minimal degree of self-definition.[84]

One could replace 'performative' in this quote with 'narrative' and it would work really well to explain the excess of narrative and how narrative is indeed grounded in the body, in materiality as interconnected, in the transobjective which is always also transsubjective. Colebrook is a Deleuzian who posits that bodies and materiality are in relation. As mentioned, we exist in a field of forces and tensions. Matter, of which we are, is a process of relations out of which fleeting moments of self-constitution and consolidation may occur. They occur thanks to narrative. But they can as easily be undone thanks to those relations and multitude of affects stemming from the various encounters among dynamic beings. In this sense, affects are generative of the narratives we may end up constructing on the basis of how we relate to them. As Declan Sheerin puts it in his analysis of Ricœur's relation to Deleuze, 'the self does not tell a story – it is told in the telling of the story . . . the question that [Ricœur] initially establishes: Who says I? Who is the author, the agent of action? . . . is a badly posed question, because it carries with it the presupposition that there is an extant narrator in the first place.'[85] This leads him to suggest that we ought to adopt the verb 'to selve' in order to capture this process through which a self emerges out of the poetic creation of its narrative by itself and by the swarm of dynamic tensions and interrelations out of which it emerges. This process is aptly described by him as a poetics of the potential, of the not-yet.[86]

What this all illuminates for me is that the self is constituted subjectively, through its own narrative, constructing a fiction about itself as it is relating to itself and shaping itself, experiencing itself, 'selving' as Sheerin would have it, while relating to others and to interconnected materiality in the transsubjective and transobjective realms. Both realms are deeply interwoven and cannot be separated. This is the field of forces and tensions that life is, generating affects and events and allowing for a self – as per Massumi above – to emerge. Narrative allows that self- to consolidate itself amid the fluctuating, dynamic, ever-changing being that it is. The 'self-' (relation) becomes a self (identity) as a means to resist change and its own dissolution, but it does so in a tenuous and constantly vulnerable manner. This process, however, is subjective and, as such, represents a minimal part of what/who we are as humans. It is grounded in the doings of a multiplicity of narrators that narrate each in their own way. That multiplicity is the bundle of experiences and forces that our embodied material beings affect or are affected by. The multiplicity itself is a narrator – a doer, a creator – that constructs our selves and finds a narrow expression in the notion of a self constructing itself narratively. The excess of narrative is, therefore, only an excess in that narrative theory of self-constitution merely contemplates the operations of subjective narrative self-constitution. In fact, it is not an excess, but it is the narrator and creator of the self- that we are. Through narrative then, the self is always processing affects and reconstituting its interconnectedness with the world as well as the porous boundaries that allow it to reflect back on itself as an identity or a self. This is a necessary, if tenuous, process if we are ever to have an ethics for it allows for the creation of agents.

Posthuman ethical pathways

In her discussion of narrative construction of selves, Butler suggests that 'a theory of subject formation that acknowledges the limits of self-knowledge can serve a conception of ethics and, indeed, responsibility. If the subject is opaque to itself, not fully translucent and knowable to itself, it is not thereby licensed to do what it wants or ignore its obligations to others.'[87] As we have seen, the opacity in question is one that we have also contributed to render opaque through our disregard for materiality. The 'newfound attentiveness to matter'[88] that posthumanist thinking, and material feminism, in particular, introduces opens up pathways for ethical thinking in which the human and the non-human may thrive in their entangled web of relations. It allows us to recognize that the polyp-being that we are as transjective being is embedded in such networks and constitutes its self while entangled in this web. The interconnectivity is constitutive and potentially disruptive of the self.

Understanding these mechanisms and processes is helpful in terms of formulating an ethics of the polyp-being for the polyp-being. What I mean by that is that while a posthuman ethics ought to encompass all beings and all elements of the web of relations and rest on an ontology that conceives of the human in terms of transjectivity, an ontology that also conceives of all being as agential and affective, it remains an ethics for the human itself. Recognizing agency in non-human beings and materiality itself does not entail devising ethical rules and principles that apply to them as agents who ought to perform certain duties, for example. Whatever ethics we elaborate will be for the human and will be grounded on the understanding of the human as radically entangled with all other beings. In fact, what matters most here is not to come up with an ethical theory with its full set of moral prescriptions and imperatives. What is more important is the development of an ethos. Embracing our beings as transjective, acknowledging our radical entanglement and shared agency, experiencing ourselves as vulnerable, understanding our transsubjective and transobjective constitution, our affective, subjective, material fabric, will necessarily change how we exist in the world and with others. The ethos of a being who conceives of themselves in this way would govern actions and decisions in ways that would be attentive to the radical entanglement of all beings including their own. Any decision or action would be based at all times on the particular set of circumstances and relations all the while recognizing the fluctuating nature of said set and beings involved in it.

An awareness of one's transjectivity will bring about a new posthuman ethos that represents a profound shift in our thinking. This is made possible by a posthumanism that has emerged via a radical undoing of subjectivity as proposed by Deleuze and Guattari, one that inspires a new attention to processes of subjectivation that exceed traditional notions of subjectivity and agency, but one that also rejects the complete elimination of agency. The path is now opened for views of the agent as that self that continually constructs itself and is constructed by its transjective being. This self's agency may be minimal when compared to the free autonomous self posited by humanist types of philosophies. After all, its foundation is much less stable and fixed than that of the good old humanist autonomous and free agent. It is, however, a more accurate view that, if embraced, may lead us to more potent ethical flourishing than a view that distorts and disregards fundamental aspects of our beings.

Notes

1 This is taken to its extreme in the works of object-oriented ontologists, such as Graham Harman and Ian Bogost, for example. However, I will not discuss these views here.
2 See Rosi Braidotti, *The Posthuman*, 2.
3 Ibid., 12.
4 It may be more appropriate to say 'surprising to most' since Deleuze is often taken at his word with regards to his rejection of phenomenology. Yet, a work like Declan Sheerin's *Deleuze and Ricœur* challenges that. Despite acknowledging that surface differences between the two thinkers are stark (5), Sheerin works to unearth the convergence 'in the depths, in the movements therein, in that which struggles in each philosophy to find expression' (7). Sheerin refers to this as the 'unthought' and 'unsaid'. My own approach certainly has affinities with Sheerin's even if my goal is not to do a comparative study of Deleuze and Ricœur. I only use them and portions of their thinking as it allows me to think what a transjective agent could be and how it may come to be. With that said, like Sheerin, I acknowledge that Ricœur's embrace of the notion of identity goes against Deleuzian difference (62) but there is, at the heart of Ricœur's ontology of the narrative self, an 'unacknowledged philosophy of difference' (107). Sheerin sees it as grounded in their respective readings and appropriations (or lack thereof) of Spinoza and Bergson. I come back to some of Sheerin's points in a later section.
5 Gilles Deleuze and Félix Guattari, *A Thousand Plateaus*, 179. The plateau is titled 'Comment se faire un Corps sans Organes?' The question itself contains the traces of a self in the verb 'se faire'. The title is translated as 'How Do You Make Yourself a Body without Organs?' But it could also be rendered as 'How to make for oneself a BwO?' Whichever way you translate it or read it in French, the self is minimally present as that which constitutes itself or is constituted, as that which makes for itself that BwO. I take this as the BwO pointing to the materiality and other elements of constitution of the self, one that has eluded investigation but is the foundation for the self. But the self is not eradicated by the BwO. The deterritorialization of the self is always also a

reterritorialization. This may be why Deleuze and Guattari say that we never quite get to the BwO. Granted, however, the BwO is not a concept that pertains strictly to the human body: it is much more than that but also that as deterritorialized.
6   Ibid., 151.
7   Gilles Deleuze and Félix Guattari, *What Is Philosophy?*, 164.
8   Ibid., 169.
9   Ibid., 105. This is said in reference to David Hume's view on personal identity. In his essay on Hume, in *Pure Immanence. Essays on A Life*, Deleuze praises Hume's emphasis on a logic of relations and points out that he showed that the 'positing of an identity of the self requires the intervention of all sorts of fictive uses of relations' (43).
10 Gilles Deleuze and Félix Guattari, *What Is Philosophy?*, 211. This is a reprise of Arthur Rimbaud's punny claim in a letter to Georges Izambard from 13 May 1871. He says: 'C'est faux de dire: Je pense: On devrait dire: On me pense. – Pardon du jeu de mots. – Je est un autre' (Arthur Rimbaud, *Complete Works*, 370). The last sentence is translated as 'I is someone else' (Ibid., 371) but it would be more precise to translate as 'I is an other'. Deleuze and Guattari explain that 'It is the brain that thinks and not man – the latter being only a cerebral crystallization. . . . Philosophy, art, and science are not the mental objects of an objectified brain but the three aspects under which the brain becomes subject, Thought-brain. They are the three planes, the rafts on which the brain plunges into and confronts the chaos' (Gilles Deleuze and Félix Guattari, *What Is Philosophy?*, 210). This idea of crystallization relates to the notion of haecceity to which I turn shortly.
11 Gilles Deleuze and Félix Guattari, *Anti-Oedipus*, xxi.
12 Ibid., 20.
13 Elena del Río sums this up really well: 'while the molar plane refers to traditional, humanist notions of identity and subjectivity, the molecular plane is understood as a perpetual becoming freed from the constraints of a stable territory, position, or goal' (*Deleuze and the Cinemas of Performance*, 153).
14 Gilles Deleuze and Félix Guattari, *A Thousand Plateaus*, 160.
15 Ibid., 270.
16 Ibid., 249.
17 Ibid., 254. As we will see below, such a description would aptly fit the polyp-being.
18 See Ibid., 261.
19 Elena del Río, *Deleuze and the Cinemas of Performance*, 50.
20 Gilles Deleuze and Félix Guattari, *A Thousand Plateaus*, 266.
21 Ibid., 270.
22 Elena del Río, *Deleuze and the Cinema of Performance*, 27. This is the object of investigation for material feminists as we will see below.
23 Joe Hughes, 'Introduction', 2.
24 Talking about the linguistic, semiotic, interpretative and cultural turns, Karen Barad quips that 'there is an important sense in which the only thing that does not seem to matter anymore is matter' ('Posthumanist Performativity', 801). Her proposals and those of other material feminists seek to remedy that.
25 This is Samantha Frost's approach in *Biocultural Creatures*.
26 Karen Barad famously takes the quantum leap in her work.
27 Rosi Braidotti, *Nomadic Subjects*, 165–6, emphasis added.
28 In her attempt at queering phenomenology, Sarah Ahmed thinks through the impact our surroundings have on self-constitution. For example, she says, 'The "here" of bodily dwelling is thus what takes the body outside of itself, as it is affected and

shaped by its surroundings: the skin that seems to contain the body is also where the atmosphere creates an impression; just think of goose bumps, textures on the skin surface, as body traces of the coldness of the air. Bodies may become oriented in this responsiveness to the world around them, given this capacity to be affected. In turn, given the history of such responses, which accumulate as impressions on the skin, bodies do not dwell in spaces that are exterior but rather are shaped by their dwellings and take shape by dwelling' (*Queer Phenomenology*, 9). Ahmed's famous notion of orientation rests on this responsiveness to surroundings. Such a phenomenological approach, queer as it may be, is not sufficient for my purposes, however, since it maintains a dualistic split between the self and its surroundings, the body and its surroundings. To be fair, Ahmed's project is more properly to think orientation, specifically sexual orientation. She thus says, 'the orientations we have toward others shape the contours of space by affecting relations of proximity and distance between bodies. Importantly, even what is kept at a distance must still be proximate enough if it is to make or leave an impression' (Ibid., 3). In explaining things in this way, Ahmed retains the distinctions posited by classical phenomenology. Regardless of these limitations, I think it is useful to think about the impact surroundings have on self-constitution. With the current project, I wish to go beyond the limitations of phenomenology in that regard.

29 Elsewhere I explain how Simone de Beauvoir's existential phenomenology and its emphasis on embodiment launched a much-needed focus on the body and its material conditions which led to the current thinking in material feminism. See my 'Trans-Subjectivity/Trans-Objectivity'. That essay also presents my view of transjectivity in its first iteration, a view I revisit and expand here.
30 See Stacy Alaimo, *Bodily Natures*, 2.
31 Ibid. Alaimo's use of 'trans' is what leads me to adopt the term 'transjectivity' in order to convey the criss-crossing movement in-between beings, one that undermines boundaries and limits and goes beyond intersubjective and interobjective relations. More on this below.
32 Ibid., 11. She also says, 'a recognition of trans-corporeality entails a rather disconcerting sense of being immersed within incalculable, interconnected material agencies that erode even our most sophisticated modes of understanding' (Ibid., 17).
33 Stacy Alaimo, *Exposed*, 5. Thinking the human being as material, as 'subject to the agencies of the compromised, entangled world'; means that we need to embrace 'an environmental posthumanism, insisting that what we are as bodies and minds is inextricably interlinked with the circulating substances, materialities, and forces'. This requires a radical change in how we conceive of ourselves, our world and our relations to and within it.
34 Ibid., 15.
35 Such as Elizabeth Grosz in *Volatile Bodies* where she also talks, in a Deleuzian vein, about the body as a borderline concept and a hinge. Luce Irigaray's 'Mechanics of Fluids' also uses the concept of fluidity but, in her case, this does not help her move away from gender binaries.
36 Astrida Neimanis, 'Feminist Subjectivity, Watered', 34.
37 See Mary K. Bloodsworth-Lugo, *In-Between Bodies*, 60.
38 Nancy Tuana, 'Viscous Porosity', 194.
39 Ibid., 188. She insists that 'The boundaries between our flesh and the flesh of the world we are of and in is porous' (Ibid., 198).
40 See Ibid. 191.

41 Karen Barad, 'Posthumanist Performativity', 817.
42 Ibid., 810.
43 In fact, not only is there room for it, but it does happen as can be attested by our mundane, everyday experience of existing as such selves. See note 67 below.
44 Ibid., 822. Barad's views are established upon her examination of quantum field theory in physics. There is, however, a great degree of uncertainty and unpredictability in the quantum field. While this serves to dismantle any strong notion of self or agency, it is problematic in many ways. Samantha Frost proposes to focus on the predictable and known biochemical processes instead. These require permeability and transit of matter through matter while providing for a less unpredictable foundation for a material feminist minimal self. Frost still wonders what it means for her to position herself as a materialist when her inquiries into atoms and their particles and biochemical processes show that matter is not matter at all but energy (*Biocultural Creatures*, 32). I examine Frost's views in some details in an essay co-authored with Olga Cielemęcka, 'Posthuman Sustainability'.
45 A similar critique may be levelled at object-oriented ontology that wishes to focus entirely on objects and matter and yet always do so from a human perspective and through a human's relation to objects. I merely want to point to the difficulty of extracting ourselves entirely from the anthropocentric perspective here and do not aim to discuss this extensively or even attempt to solve the issue. It may very well be irresolvable.
46 Jane Bennett, *Vibrant Matter*, xvi.
47 Ibid., 13. So, while some thinkers like Braidotti wish to embrace a strategic essentialism to fight some political battles, with regards to gender equity for example, Bennett offers that we need to embrace something like a strategic materialism to arrive at some political goals. Perhaps it is the case that whichever philosophical position one chooses need be strategic. Indeed, one does not ontologize for ontology's sake but most often than not to achieve other goals.
48 Ibid., viii.
49 See Ibid., 65. She indicates that only a small step may be needed from that view to the view of materiality as creative agent.
50 Ibid., 122.
51 By scholars such as Diana Coole and Samantha Frost, for example, in an attempt to depersonalize agency and break down the tendency to conceive of human agency as isolated, self-sufficient and exceptional. See the introduction to their *New Materialisms* and Frost's *Biocultural Creatures*.
52 Claire Colebrook, *Death of the Posthuman*, 11.
53 See Le Dœuff, 1989, p. 39. While the prefix 'inter' conveys a static sense of 'between' and 'among', '*Trans* indicates movement across different sites' (Stacy Alaimo, *Bodily Natures*, 2). Given that the polyp-being is in constant flux, *transjectivity* is a more appropriate name to give this concept.
54 I thank Margrit Shildrick for that point about intercorporeality and how it retains the sense of distinct independent bodies.
55 However, as Brian Massumi puts it, 'Ideas about cultural or social construction have dead-ended because they have insisted on bracketing the *nature* of the process' (*Parables for the Virtual*, 12). Richard Grusin also underscores this problem, saying, 'Practitioners of the nonhuman turn find problematic the emphasis of constructivism on the social or cultural constructions of the human subject because, taken to its logical extreme, it strips the world of any ontological or agential status' (Joe Hughes,

'Introduction', xi). Posthumanist thinking that focuses on materiality, its role, and effects remedies that.
56 This differs from the concept of interobjectivity that emerges from a phenomenological context like Vivian Sobchack's inquiries in her *Carnal Thoughts*. She explains that phenomenology's question of the limit between the body and the world necessarily brings up that of the objectivity of the embodied subject and how much it shares with other objects (see *Carnal Thoughts*, 286). The process of objectification that one suffers when encountering an other consciousness is one wherein the body-subject "'suffers" a *diminution of subjectivity* and, in this diminution, comes to experience – within subjectivity – an increased awareness of *what it is to be a material object*' (Ibid., 288). This, however, rings of dualism and Sobchack offers instead that 'the body-subject experiences not a diminution of subjectivity but its *sensual* and *sensible* expansion – and an enhanced awareness of what it is *to be material*' (Ibid., 290). She uses interobjectivity to refer to the 'complementary experience we have of ourselves and others as material objects' (Ibid., 296). However, as she puts it, we can never experience our objectivity *qua* objectivity. She thereby poses the problem of the limits of phenomenology in a similar way than speculative realism does. Nevertheless, her notion of interobjectivity remains steeped in phenomenological intentionality and thereby fails to capture the way in which materiality constitutes our selves.
57 Friedrich Nietzsche, *Daybreak*, 74.
58 Quoted in Gilles Deleuze and Félix Guattari, *A Thousand Plateaus*, 150.
59 It should be noted that it is one specific type of polyp I have in mind: the coral polyp, a marine invertebrate that, more often than not, lives in colonies. See http://coral.org/coral-reefs-101/coral-reef-ecology/coral-polyps/. See also http://animals.nationalgeographic.com/animals/invertebrates/coral/.
60 I thank Dorothea Olkowski for her forceful objection to my use of the metaphor which has pushed my thinking on the matter. Although they do not have brains, they may be said to have structures similar to nerve cells and, perhaps in that sense, may be considered to be pure affectivity. I thank Antonio Calcagno for that suggestion. That said, it may very well be that if it is the material body that thinks, polyps are also capable of thought despite their lacking a brain.
61 Thanks to Terrance McDonald for raising that point.
62 Friedrich Nietzsche, *Beyond Good and Evil*, 20–1. Further, in aphorism 19, he analyses the will and how it relates to sensations and argues that 'the will is not only a complex of sensation and thinking, but it is above all an affect, and specifically the affect of the command' (Ibid., 25). There is no will in-itself but rather the will is the expression of a commanding affect or sensation: 'In all willing it is absolutely a question of commanding and obeying, on the basis, as already said, of a social structure composed of many "souls"' (Ibid., 27).
63 While I do not explore this question in this chapter – I merely allude to it in relation to Brison and Cavarero's views on relationality – vulnerability is an essential characteristic of the polyp. Rather than seeing it as entirely negative, one must see its potential to contribute to our growth and flourishing as a being that nourishes itself from its experiences, whichever they are qualitatively. As Simone Drichel puts it, 'In seeking to defend ourselves, we – perversely – come to violate ourselves, or, to put this differently, what we preserve in "self-preservation" is what makes the self "inhuman" rather than human' ('Reframing Vulnerability', 22). So in an effort to protect ourselves and make ourselves invulnerable, we in fact do violence to ourselves and dehumanize

ourselves. It is better to accept and multiply experiences as well as acknowledge that many of those are fortuitous, outside the reach of our consciousness, and yet constitutive of our selves. Colebrook also thinks that to ignore the vulnerable being that we are is problematic. She identifies this approach with humanist thinking: 'The fact that we forget our *impotentiality* – that we treat humans as factual beings with a normality that dictates action – has reached crisis point in modernity, especially as we increasingly suspend the thought of our fragility for the sake of ongoing efficiency' (*Death of the Posthuman*, 13).

64 Gilles Deleuze and Félix Guattari, *A Thousand Plateaus*, 387.
65 Brian Massumi, *Parables for the Virtual*, 5. He explains that this incorporeal dimension is real and material and is to the body just like energy is to matter. They are two concrete aspects of the same reality.
66 Ibid., 14.
67 It, thereby, offers an explanation for how the self we experience in a mundane, daily setting can even exist. That self experiences itself as having a certain continuity, being connected to its past self via experiences and memories. It also experiences connections with its future self, making plans for oneself and preparing oneself for future experiences to be had. Phenomenology and its emphasis on conscious experience takes these seriously, perhaps even too much as it ends up overemphasizing consciousness and its self. See note 43 above.
68 See Paul Ricœur, *Oneself as Another*. For my purposes, I choose to focus on this work because it provides me with the tools I need to articulate my views. As Declan Sheerin puts it, this work best explicates Ricœur's hermeneutic view of the narrative self. Sheerin distinguishes this concept as it is explained in *Oneself as Another* 'both from its own genetic origins (in the three-volume *Time and Narrative* where it is first posited) and from its progeny (specifically the late work of Ricœur, *Memory, History, Forgetting*)' (*Deleuze and Ricœur*, 1). Given that I seek to provide myself with tools to articulate a self on the fluctuating swarm of interconnectedness, rather than seek to adopt a Ricœurian view of the self, my chosen focus will be sufficient for the task at hand as will its necessary shortcomings and inadequacies in giving an accurate account of Ricœur's full view of the self.
69 Judith Butler, *Giving an Account of Oneself*, 7–8.
70 Ibid., 39.
71 This view continues to be steeped in dualistic thinking. This is why I wish to move beyond a phenomenological view and only consider Ricœur's approach for the value of his strategies to help explain how a self can still endure, albeit tenuously, in the midst of the dynamic becoming of materiality constituting it.
72 Susan J. Brison, *Aftermath*, 38.
73 See Paul A. Kottman, *Translator's Introduction to Relating Narratives*, xxii.
74 Adriana Cavarero, *Relating Narratives*, 34.
75 Ibid., 40.
76 Ibid., 89.
77 Susan J. Brison, *Aftermath*, 95.
78 Annemie Halsema, 'The Time of the Self', 116.
79 Ibid., 117; emphasis added.
80 Charles Taylor, *Sources of the Self*, 29.
81 Judith Butler, *Giving an Account of Oneself*, 20–1.
82 As a Foucauldian, she posits that 'There is no making of oneself (*poiesis*) outside of a mode of subjectivation (*assujettissement*) and, hence, no self-making outside of the

norms that orchestrate the possible forms that a subject may take' (Ibid., 17). The language we use to build our narratives is also pre-given and social and therefore always somewhat inadequate.
83 Ibid., 38.
84 Claire Colebrook, 'On Not Becoming-Man', 68.
85 Declan Sheerin, *Deleuze and Ricœur*, 152. He adds 'nobody is the author or producer of his own life story' (Ibid.).
86 Ibid., 173. Sheerin establishes that connection between Deleuze and Ricœur by way of a complex analysis of both thinkers' relation to Aristotle's notion of the potential and the actual. Sheerin's comparative work is detailed and a full account of it lays outside the scope of the present chapter.
87 Judith Butler, *Giving an Account of Oneself*, 19–20.
88 Jane, Bennett, *Vibrant Matter*, 13. While it does not illuminate everything and eliminate opacity entirely – there will always be some material resistance and processes that will resist our understanding and thereby remain opaque – it does change our approach to beings in a generative manner.

Bibliography

Ahmed, Sara. *Queer Phenomenology. Orientations, Objects, Others*. Durham, NC and London: Duke University Press, 2006.

Alaimo, Stacy. *Bodily Natures: Science, Environment, and the Material Self*. Bloomington, IN: Indiana University Press, 2010.

Alaimo, Stacy. *Exposed. Environmental Politics and Pleasures in Posthuman Times*. Minneapolis, MN and London: University of Minnesota Press, 2016.

Barad, Karen. 'Posthumanist Performativity: Toward an Understanding of How Matter Comes to Matter'. *Signs* 28, no. 3 (2003): 801–31.

Bloodsworth-Lugo, Mary K. *In-Between Bodies. Sexual Difference, Race, and Sexuality*. Albany: SUNY Press, 2007.

Braidotti, Rosi. *Nomadic Subjects. Embodiment and Sexual Difference in Contemporary Feminist Theory*. New York: Columbia University Press. 1994.

Braidotti, Rosi. *The Posthuman*. Cambridge: Polity Press, 2013.

Brison, Susan J. *Aftermath. Violence and the Remaking of a Self*. Princeton, NJ: Princeton University Press, 2003.

Butler, Judith. *Giving an Account of Oneself*. New York: Fordham University Press, 2005.

Cavarero, Adriana. *Relating Narratives. Storytelling and Selfhood*. Translated by Paul A. Kottman. London and New York: Routledge, 2000.

Colebrook, Claire. *Death of the Posthuman. Essays on Extinction I*. Ann Arbor, MI: Open Humanities Press, 2014.

Colebrook, Claire. 'On Not Becoming-Man: The Materialist Politics of Unactualized Potential'. In *Material Feminisms*, edited by Stacey Alaimo and Susan Hekman, 52–84. Indianapolis: Indiana University Press, 2008.

Daigle, Christine. 'Trans-Subjectivity/Trans-Objectivity'. In *Future Directions in Feminist Phenomenology*, edited by Helen Fielding and Dorothea Olkowski, 183–99. Bloomington, IN: Indiana University Press, 2017.

Daigle, Christine and Olga Cielemęcka. 'Posthuman Sustainability: An Ethos for our Anthropocenic Future'. *Theory, Culture & Society* 36, 7–8 (2019): 67–87.

Deleuze, Gilles. *Pure Immanence. Essays on a Life*. Translated by Anne Boyman. New York: Zone Books, 2001.
Deleuze, Gilles and Félix Guattari. *Anti-Oedipus. Capitalism and Schizophrenia*. Translated by Robert Hurley, Mark Seem and Helen R. Lane. Minneapolis, MN: University of Minnesota Press, 1983.
Deleuze, Gilles and Félix Guattari. *A Thousand Plateaus. Capitalism and Schizophrenia*. Translated by Brian Massumi. Minneapolis, MN and London: University of Minnesota Press, 1987.
Deleuze, Gilles and Félix Guattari. *What Is Philosophy?* Translated by Hugh Tomlinson and Graham Burchell. New York: Columbia University Press, 1994.
del Río, Elena. *Deleuze and the Cinemas of Performance. Powers of Affection*. Edinburgh: Edinburgh University Press, 2012.
Drichel, Simone. 'Reframing Vulnerability: "so Obviously the Problem . . ."?' *SubStance* 42, no. 3 (2013): 3–27.
Frost, Samantha. *Biocultural Creatures. Toward a New Theory of the Human*. Durham, NC and London: Duke University Press, 2016.
Grosz, Elizabeth. *Volatile Bodies: Toward a Corporeal Feminism*. Bloomington, IN and Indianapolis: Indiana University Press, 1994.
Halsema, Annemie. 'The Time of the Self: A Feminist Reflection on Ricœur's Notion of Narrative Identity'. In *Time in Feminist Phenomenology*, edited by Christina Schües, Helen Fielding and Dorothea Olkowski, 111–31. Bloomington, IN and Indianapolis: Indiana University Press, 2011.
Hughes, Joe. 'Introduction: Pity the Meat?: Deleuze and the Body'. In *Deleuze and the Body*, edited by Laura Guillaume and Joe Hughes, 1–6. Edinburgh: Edinburgh University Press, 2011.
Kottman, Paul A. *Translator's Introduction to Relating Narratives. Storytelling and Selfhood*. Edited by Adriana Cavarero. Translated by Paul A. Kottman, vii–xxxi. London and New York: Routledge, 2000.
Massumi, Brian. *Parables for the Virtual. Movement, Affect, Sensation*. Durham, NC and London: Duke University Press, 2002.
Neimanis, Astrida. 'Feminist Subjectivity, Watered'. *Feminist Review* 103 (2013), 23–41.
Nietzsche, Friedrich. *Beyond Good and Evil. Prelude to a Philosophy of the Future*. Translated by Walter Kaufmann. New York: Vintage, 1966.
Nietzsche, Friedrich. *Daybreak. Thoughts on the Prejudices of Morality*. Translated by R. J. Hollingdale. Cambridge: Cambridge University Press, 1997.
Ricœur, Paul. *Oneself as Another*. Translated by Kathleen Blamey. Chicago: Chicago University Press, 1992.
Rimbaud, Arthur. *Complete Works, Selected Letters. A Bilingual Edition*. Translated by Wallace Fowlie. Chicago and London: The University of Chicago Press, 2005.
Sheerin, Declan. *Deleuze and Ricœur: Disavowed Affinities and the Narrative Self*. London: Continuum, 2009.
Sobchack, Vivian. *Carnal Thoughts. Embodiment and Moving Image Culture*. Berkeley, CA: University of California Press, 2004.
Taylor, Charles. *Sources of the Self. The Making of the Modern Identity*. Cambridge: Cambridge University Press, 1989.
Tuana, Nancy. 'Viscous Porosity: Witnessing Katrina'. In *Material Feminisms*, edited by Stacy Alaimo and Susan Hekman, 188–213. Bloomington, IN and Indianapolis: Indiana University Press, 2008.

3

The art of good encounters

Spinoza, Deleuze and Macherey on moving from passive to active joy

Bruce Baugh

The problem

Is it the case, as Descartes and his rationalist successors have argued, that the body and its affects impede thinking? Or is it rather the case that the body and its affects are indispensable to thinking? A number of contemporary philosophers and psychologists argue for the latter position, including Martha Nussbaum, Ronald de Sousa, Richard Lazarus, Robert Zajonc, Antonio Damasio and Nico Frijda. In different ways, these scholars argue that the relevance and significance of facts and situations relative to our goals and concerns are revealed and even guided by affects and emotions; without affects and emotions, rational thought would lack the lines of salience and relevance necessary to arrive at an organized, coherent and rational response to the situation at the level of judgement, decision and action. Frijda, taking his inspiration from Spinoza, argues that positive affects, such as joy, provide an aid to rational thought. Joy is the feeling of the mind passing to a greater degree of perfection; it signals accomplishment (attaining or coming closer to a goal) and, because of its pleasurable nature, reinforces successful behaviours, thereby providing guidance for behaviours in a way that facilitates goal accomplishment. Rather than being contrary to reason, the affect of joy actually promotes rational thinking and acting.[1] Joy signals that the individual has enjoyed what Gilles Deleuze calls a 'good encounter' with its environment or with other human beings. In that way, joy helps guide us towards further good encounters, as well as increasing our self-confidence and energy, enabling us to think and act better.[2]

Frijda's arguments are similar to Deleuze's in his works on Spinoza that passive joys (or joyful passions) can be a means to active joys.[3] Pierre Macherey, however, argues that Deleuze is mistaken.[4] Passive joys result from a good encounter between two bodies having the same relation among their parts, such that the bodies can be harmoniously joined together or 'composed'. The joy resulting from this harmonious 'composition', says Deleuze, motivates the mind to investigate what the two bodies have in common that would result in this harmony, promoting the search for a 'common notion' concerning what two particular bodies specifically have in common. Since common notions are 'adequate ideas' in Spinoza's view, and the mind is active when it makes use of adequate ideas, common notions lead to the active joy that results from the mind's enjoyment of its increased power of thinking. Macherey, however, argues that the passivity inherent in all passions – including joyful ones – alienates the mind from its own powers and renders it more passive. For Macherey, all passive joys are marked by the sadness characteristic of passivity, as all passivity involves a decrease in the mind's active power of thinking. Spinoza's teaching, argues Macherey, is that the liberation of the mind comes from reason, liberated from the passions, and so operating free of all the passive influences that come to the mind from the body and its reactions to its environment.

Behind the disagreement over whether good encounters help or hinder the mind in forming common notions and thinking rationally lie Deleuze's and Macherey's fundamentally different conceptions of the role of the body. Deleuze takes Spinoza's statement, 'Nobody knows what a body can do', as 'a war cry' and as the guiding thread of his Spinozism.[5] Macherey considers the body's influence on the mind as an impediment to reason. Even though, as a Spinozist, he cannot accept the notion of a disembodied reason, Macherey argues that reason requires surmounting the point of view of any particular body and grasping interactions from the point of view of the entire universe.

The disagreement also stems from the hybrid nature of joyful passions. Like all passions, joyful passions are *passive* insofar as they result from my encounter with something external to myself; these passions are experienced in the mind as a kind of feeling or affect that results from the external object acting upon me, rather than being explicable through my mind's active powers of understanding. The feeling only registers the effect of the interaction between my body and an external thing without presenting the cause. For that reason, it is what Spinoza calls an 'inadequate idea', that is, a confused idea of the changes occurring in my body.[6] To the extent that an idea is caused by something other than the activity of our rational understanding, we are passive in relation to it, and so we are always passive in relation to inadequate ideas. On the other hand, joy is the emotion felt by the mind when the body's power of activity is increased, which is concomitant with an increase in the mind's power of activity;[7] it is a 'transition from a state of less perfection to a state of greater perfection'.[8] In that respect, even though joyful passions are *passive* insofar as they are passions at all, they also involve both mind and body becoming more *active*, and in that way lead us towards coming into possession of our active powers. For Spinoza, 'the more we are affected by joy, the more we pass to a state of greater perfection, and consequently the more we participate in the divine nature' (E IV Appendix Item 31).

As Macherey comments, joyful passions 'seem to occupy an intermediate place between the two extremes of freedom and slavery',[9] freedom being when our lives are governed by a rational understanding of the causes of things and events, slavery being subjection to mental states we don't understand, and at its worst, subjection to sad passions, the feelings that result from a decrease in our power of acting.[10] Yet, from the hybrid nature of joyful passions, Deleuze infers that 'Before becoming active we must select and link together passions that increase our power of action'.[11] We can use joyful passions to leverage the mind from passivity and feeling to activity and understanding. Since joy is what results when we encounter something which agrees with our nature or is good for us,[12] the art of living well would then be the art of arranging as many 'good encounters' as possible and the avoidance of bad encounters: we should seek encounters with things which bring us joy and avoid encounters with things which make us sad and diminish our power of acting. Of course, encounters will always involve an element of passivity insofar as they result from a deterministic chain of cause and effect over which we do not have complete control. We can, nevertheless, use our agency to increase the probability of having more encounters that increase our powers of acting and thinking; much of Book IV of the *Ethics* deals with how forming associations with other rational agents can help to diminish the share of external circumstances in our affective life.

Spinoza does not say that emotions in themselves are bad; only sad passions, emotions contrary to our nature, diminish our power of acting and the mind's power of understanding.[13] The right way of living, then, would be to seek out what is good so that we may always be determined to act from joyful passions.[14] This would not eliminate emotions altogether but would help us to replace passive emotions with active ones. For passive emotions based on inadequate ideas, we could substitute emotions based upon adequate ideas, emotions which reflect the passage to a higher level of perfection or the greater level of activity intrinsic in rationally understanding something.[15] Deleuze summarizes: 'The ethical question in Spinoza is thus two-fold: *How can we come to produce active affections?* But first of all: *How can we come to experience [éprouver] a maximum of joyful passions?*'[16]

I want to note an obvious danger in Deleuze's approach. The pursuit of 'good encounters' *may* lead to active joy, increased understanding and the self-contentment that arises from this,[17] and in the final instance, the intellectual love of God, 'the highest good we can aim at according to the dictates of reason'.[18] But it may not. It could lead instead to a restless search for new stimuli and new joys, leading to boredom and finally despair. That is, Macherey is right that the passivity of joyful passions might increase heteronomy rather than autonomy and lead to a dissolution and loss of self. I am thinking of what Fichte and Kierkegaard have to say about such matters, namely, that the person who pursues a life of sensuousness or feeling (what Kierkegaard calls 'the aesthetic') and chooses to have her mind be determined by external forces can lose her very self,[19] but I am also thinking of Spinoza's remark that 'The ignorant man, besides being driven hither and thither by external causes, never possessing true contentment of spirit, lives as if he were unconscious of himself, God, and things, and as soon as he ceases to be passive, he at once ceases to be at all'.[20]

The danger, then, is twofold: the seeker of good encounters is, to the extent that external circumstances do not lie entirely within our control, a hostage to fortune, and worse, in identifying the good life with arranging good encounters, is apt to dissipate the self in a series of transient pleasures and the external circumstances that produce them. Might one become, if I can put it this way, a good encounter junkie, always in need of a stronger fix, and so becoming less and less self-reliant the more one seeks external stimuli as a means of increasing one's activity? Are joyful passions, as Macherey maintains, necessarily alienating insofar as every passion alienates us from our power of understanding things rationally? Or is there a way of using good encounters prudently, so that they always remain a means, and do not become ends in themselves?

A second difficulty presents itself: why should good encounters and passive joys be more apt than passive sorrows to lead to an active understanding of the necessity with which every event takes place, since the necessity involved in sorrow is the same as that involved in joy, and so can also be understood and in that way surmounted? I will argue, however, that although the active mind, which has adequate ideas that follow from its power of understanding,[21] can equally understand both passive joy and sorrow, sorrow nevertheless impedes or inhibits the mind's power of understanding. Consequently, the best way for the mind to enhance the mind's active power of understanding is through arranging one's life in order to have a maximum of good encounters.[22]

Spinoza does not share the Stoicism of Milton's Satan, according to whom 'the mind is its own place, and in itself can make a heaven of hell, a hell of heaven',[23] for he recognizes that as long as the mind is united with the body, it will be subject to all the body's vicissitudes and 'necessarily always subject to passive emotions',[24] whether sad or joyful. Human existence is not 'an empire within an empire',[25] but a part of nature. Rather than vainly seeking to overcome or avoid passive emotions altogether, as Macherey proposes, the more prudent course of action is to seek out a maximum of joyful passions: 'The more we are affected with pleasure, the more we pass to a state of greater perfection; that is, the more we participate in the divine nature. Therefore it is the part of a wise man to make use of things and to take pleasure in them as far as he can . . . without harm to another.'[26]

Deleuze's proposal

Deleuze outlines a 'program' with four stages for becoming-active:

(1) passive joy, which increases our power of action, and from which flow desires and passions based on a still inadequate idea; (2) the formation by way of these joyful passions of a common notion (adequate idea); (3) active joy, which follows from this common notion and is explained by our power of action; (4) this active joy is added to passive joy, but *replaces* the passion-desires born of passive joy with desires belonging to reason, which are genuine actions.[27]

The passivity involved in joyful passions resulting from our not understanding the cause of our emotion not only leaves us subject to chance, or the fortuitous run of circumstance, but makes us liable to form desires based on ignorance, thinking that something is good for us because at one point it gave us joy, and neglecting to take into account the changes that may have occurred in us, in the object, or in the relation between us and the object that would render the object no longer good. Since we cannot ensure good encounters by bending circumstances to our will, the solution is to replace our inadequate idea with an adequate one; this is the second and crucial phase of Deleuze's programme. Joys based on an adequate idea follow from our own power of thinking and are thus active rather than passive. The 'adequate idea' in question would explain why the external object caused my power of acting to increase. Such an explanation would have to take into account the nature of the external object, my nature, and what the object and I have in common that allows for our interaction. This is what Spinoza calls a 'common notion': 'Those things that are common to all things and equally in the part as in the whole, can be conceived only adequately.'[28] An idea of 'that which is common and proper to the human body and to some external bodies by which the human body is customarily affected'[29] will be an adequate one and form the basis for a rational explanation of the interaction of the human body with external bodies.[30]

Deleuze's argument is that passive joys, or joyful passions, aid us in the formation of common notions, and thus aid us in achieving active joys based on adequate ideas. Active joys flow from our rational understanding *of* our passive joy, as such increased understanding amounts to an increase in our mind's powers of acting.[31] This is why 'active joy is added to passive joy, but replaces the passion-desires born of passive joy with desires belonging to reason',[32] that is, with the rational desires for those things that really do help us persist in our essence and aid our power of action, and which are thus truly good[33] because they are *necessarily* good in virtue of agreeing with our nature,[34] rather than merely fortuitous sources of transient joys that can, under changing circumstances, become sources of sadness. Rational understanding and adequate ideas eliminate the passivity in desires arising from passive joys without eliminating either joy or desire itself; rather, the feeling of joy is retained, and irrational desires are replaced by rational, active ones.[35]

Active joys are more stable and more secure than passive ones insofar as their source is our active power of thinking, which always lies to hand, rather than variable external circumstances, which lie beyond our direct control. Moreover, since active joys are based on common notions, they are related to the universal and always present aspect of things rather than those qualities that are transient and changing.[36] An active joy, then, is the feeling of an increase in our power of acting caused by our own power of thinking being directed towards the universal and unchanging aspects that external things share with us and united with the rational desire for things whose nature agrees with our own. Although 'a passive emotion ceases to be a *passive* emotion as soon as we form a clear and distinct idea of it',[37] that means that the emotion ceases to be passive, not that it either ceases to be a feeling or that it no longer gives rise to a desire. The pleasurable *feeling* of passing to a higher degree of activity functions both as a reward and as an incentive to behaviours that will produce similar results.

Good encounters producing passive joys, then, are only a first step towards forming adequate ideas. But even this step requires some explanation. Taking 'body' to mean any more or less coherent organization of parts, such that the body can be said to continue to exist for as long as its parts remain within their characteristic relationship, we can distinguish broadly between two kinds of encounters: those where the parts of two bodies enter into contact and mingle in such a way that the power of acting of one or both is enhanced (a good encounter) and those where the power of acting of one or both is diminished or destroyed. The first sort of encounter, where bodies combine together harmoniously, Deleuze calls 'composition'; the bad sort, he calls 'decomposition'. When someone ingests a poison, for example, the parts of the external body combine with her body in such a way as to 'decompose' the vital relationship among the parts of her body: the parts of her body enter into a relationship incompatible with her continued existence.[38] Deleuze extends the concept of poison and toxicity to include any sort of encounter that is bad for me because the external object – whether a thing, an event, another person, a relationship – has a constitutive relation among its parts that cannot be combined with my own, leading to a reduction of my power of acting and the concomitant feeling of sadness.[39] A good encounter, on the other hand, is when the external body 'agrees with my nature' and enhances my power of acting because the relation among its parts is harmonious with the relation among my parts constitutive of my vitality. Although in both cases, I am passive in relation to an external cause, I can turn that passivity to my advantage by trying to organize my encounters so that more often than not I encounter things that agree with my nature.[40]

Since nothing can increase my power of acting more than another human being, I must endeavour to combine with other individuals, who not only increase my power of acting and bring me joy, but with whom I can pursue the common advantage of all.[41] This is what removes us from the state of nature and gives rise to society. 'In the state of nature, I live at the mercy of encounters';[42] in society, I have the chance to remove some of the haphazardness of the fortuitous run of circumstances. I cannot eliminate chance or master the forces of nature, but together with others, I can try to minimize the deleterious effects of chance encounters. As Deleuze says, 'The effort to organize encounters is thus first of all the effort to form an association of men under relations that can be composed together [*qui se composent*].'[43] I can thus hope to maximize my joyful passions through 'this art of organizing encounters, or of forming a *totality* under relations that can be composed together'.[44]

Still, why should passive joys be more useful than sorrow in leading us to the active joys of the understanding when it is equally possible to use reason to understand both? Sorrow also involves an interaction between bodies that can only be adequately explained through common notions inasmuch as bodies can interact only if they share some properties in common, and common notions are applicable to all bodies, of whatever nature.

Here it is necessary to make some distinctions. In the first place, we must distinguish between, on the one hand, what the mind is capable of understanding once it has become active, and grasps things through adequate ideas of which it is the full cause, and, on the other hand, the *process* by which the mind becomes active. An active mind is capable of understanding any affection of the body,[45] including those bad encounters or setbacks that would normally lead to sorrow but which the active mind, seeing the necessity in all things, forms an adequate idea of, such that the emotion ceases to be passive.[46] The sadness or sorrow involved in the emotion, being entirely due to passivity and weakness, is thereby destroyed,[47] and replaced with an active emotion that is necessarily joyful inasmuch as it expresses the mind's power of understanding. But such 'strength of mind'[48] is the result of a long process during which the mind undergoes a kind of apprenticeship, passing from passivity to activity through the midpoint of passive joys that increase the activity and vital powers of both mind and body.[49] Although bad encounters leading to sorrow result from whatever common factors allow two bodies to interact at all, the resulting sadness decreases vital and mental activity and impedes the mind's ability to understand rationally how the external body affected its own body in such a manner. A mind gripped by sorrow, depression, or other painful passions, does not think well or clearly. The way for the mind to reach the goal of being able to comprehend sad passions, then, is through joyful ones that express the mind's becoming more active and reinforce that activity, which is why 'in arranging our thoughts and images we should always concentrate on that which is good in every single thing'[50] so that in so doing 'we may determine ourselves to act always from the emotion of pleasure' or joy.[51]

There are other reasons why good encounters are more apt than bad ones to provide us with common notions. This question hinges on the differing levels of generality of common notions, a point to which I will return in Part IV of this chapter. Bodies agree with one another, and so constitute a good encounter, when the *relations* among their constituent parts, a relation constitutive of the bodies' essences, agree. In a bad encounter, where these relations disagree and decompose each other, the interaction between bodies can be accounted for only at the most universal level of particles in motion and rest interacting with one another. In short, the *interaction* is understood at the level of the constituent *parts*, which must share something in common in order to interact at all, through the broadest and most universal common notions, and the interaction between relations, 'decomposition', is understood only insofar as the negative affect registers the specific incompatibility of the *relations*. But in that case, it is the *incompatibility* of relations which is felt and inadequately grasped through the sad affect, and not that which the two bodies have in common. Something can 'diminish or check our power of activity' only to the extent that it is contrary to us, not in virtue of what it has in common with us.[52]

'Composition' and 'decomposition' thus have to do with relations between *essences*, not just between parts; 'that which is common to all things and is equally in the part as in the whole does not constitute the essence of any particular thing.'[53] In a good encounter, a more specific commonality, that of the constitutive *relations* of the two bodies, is grasped, however implicitly, in the feeling of joy. The understanding of a good encounter between bodies is thus more apt to be more complete and adequate insofar as the compatibility of essences reflects bodies having more 'in common' than does incompatibility. By means of more specific common notions having to do with the agreement of an external body's constitutive relation with its own, the mind rises to more universal common notions capable of explaining bad encounters as well as good ones. Here, once again, it is important to distinguish the endpoint from the process leading up to it. Good encounters are the basis of the first common notions found in experience, and to begin with, these notions are the most specific and least universal.

It is important to keep in mind that 'common notions' are not commonly accepted ideas or the ideas that result from what Spinoza calls 'the common run of experience'. Received, 'common sense' ideas are always inadequate; they are based on how a particular body and mind are affected by particular encounters with other things but comprehend only the effects of those encounters, not the causes. Ideas based on the common run of experience give us only the subjective impression of 'how it felt' when a certain encounter occurred but have no explanatory value. Common notions, on the other hand, are principles that explain the interactions between different bodies based on the features those bodies share in common. They help explain not only interhuman interactions but the interactions between humans and non-human things (animal, vegetable or mineral) by looking for the common factors that make it possible for those things to affect each other. Chemistry, for example, explains the effects on two or more material substances involved in a chemical interaction with respect to the properties those substances share in common (electrons, protons, etc.) and the laws governing such interactions. Common notions are products of reason, not sensibility; they involve finding relations of agreement or disagreement between the essences of things at the level of universal principles, much in the manner that logical reasoning determines relations of contradiction or agreement among ideas. As such, common notions often overturn or contradict the commonly held ideas based on what usually or normally occurs in human experience. They are indispensable to the liberation of the mind from inadequate ideas and the passions based on them.

By taking into account the capacities for affecting and for being affected of both bodies involved in an encounter, common notions help us to transcend a narrowly anthropocentric viewpoint; common notions explain non-human bodies' capacities for affecting and being affected based on what those bodies share in common with the bodies that they encounter, and whether the capacities for acting and being affected of those non-human bodies are increased or diminished in virtue of the encounter. Animals, plants and even minerals have their joys and sorrows, as every body has a corresponding mind capable of registering that body's increase or decrease in its power of existing.[54] But given that how a mind thinks depends on the capacities of the body to affect and be affected by other bodies,[55] the more dissimilar a body of an animal, plant or mineral is from the human body, the less its mental states will resemble ours, and the less comprehensible those mental states will be to us. No one knows what a body can do, but a human body can only do so much, and the limits of what the body can do are the limits of what the mind can grasp.

Vacillation and ambivalence

Even supposing that good encounters are more likely to lead to greater mental activity through common notions, the art of organizing good encounters is far from easy. Part of the difficulty here is that one and the same external object can enter into many different relations with me, both through the intermediary of other relations – *per accidens* rather than in itself – and also because of the complexity of the relations constitutive of my being. The result is that I can love and hate the same object, a state of ambivalence or vacillation (*fluctuatio animi*).[56]

This can happen in two ways. The first, as Spinoza explains, is that different parts of the body can be affected in different ways, such that an external object that produces joy in one part at the same time produces sadness in another, in which case my power of acting is simultaneously both increased and diminished.[57] What Spinoza calls 'titillation', for example, 'consists in one or more of the body's parts being affected more than the rest'[58] to the extent that it impairs the body's ability to be affected in other ways, and thus one part of the body's power of acting is enhanced at the expense of another part, often to the detriment of the whole. The joy involved in one part of the body being affected more than the others can easily become excessive and turn into an obsession: with honour, with material gain, with another person. As Spinoza says, this amounts to mania, madness.[59] Obsessive desires override or suppress the desires that arise from other joyful passions and stunt the development or fulfilment of other parts of the person, leading to more sadness than joy. At the very least, they enter into conflict with those other desires, so that a person can become internally divided and contrary to herself, which is in itself an unhappy state.[60] But because 'partial joys' can be so intense or so powerful, they can cause us to lose sight of how other aspects of our being are being stunted or repressed, and can do so for quite a long time. A poison might first be experienced as stimulating or calming, revealing its true nature only much later.

A genuinely good encounter would be one that, by increasing one's power of activity, made one increasingly more able to combine other parts of oneself with other bodies in the world; it would make one more open to more good encounters or dispose one's body so that it can be affected by and can affect external bodies in many ways.[61] Obsession and the dependency on a particular person, activity or substance for one's happiness, on the contrary, make it seem that one cannot live without that on which one is dependent and prevent the mind from even thinking of anything else.[62] Obsession leads to the sad passions of jealousy and longing that will outweigh the joy.[63] Such encounters leave one's powers more diminished than enhanced, enervated both by sadness and the conflict between joy and sadness inherent in obsessive desires.

The second source of ambivalence is the association in the mind of one thing with another, often because of some resemblance between the two things, or because two things were experienced at the same time, or because of some other relation between the things that cause us to think of the one whenever we think of the other.[64] If a thing apt to cause us sadness calls to mind another thing apt to cause us joy, then the 'sad' thing will call to mind the 'joy' linked with the idea of the associated object, so that the same thing will affect us with both joy and sadness, and we will then both love and hate it. Imagine, if you will, a person whom you hate – a rival, a political opponent – and yet who calls to mind the idea of a person you love because of some similarity between the two, such as physical resemblance, or because of some relation between the two, such as the enemy being the parent of a child you love. In one respect, you hate that person, and in another respect, you love that person; or, much the same thing, part of you hates that person and another part loves that person. Now imagine further that the person you hate suffers some setback or injury: part of you will rejoice in this because things we hate are things that cause us sadness and diminish our power of acting, so that their destruction amounts to the removal of an obstacle and increases our power of action; but another part will be saddened because of the love based on the association of this person with someone else, and when we love someone, whatever harms or causes that person sadness will make us sad as well. This extends to the love connected with the idea of ourselves, an idea to which the other person is related simply in virtue of being another living being capable of affects. Sometimes this is all the resemblance needed to create ambivalence; we rejoice in a rival's misfortune insofar as that person is a rival, but we are saddened to the extent that the rival is a human being like us.[65] The inhibition of my power of acting manifested in sad passions comes to contaminate the malicious joys of hatred.[66]

This is where 'the concrete factors of existence' make things rather messy.[67] Not only is it the case that many external objects – things, events, persons, relationships – can be both good for me and bad for me, and can increase my power of acting in some ways but diminish it in others, but the ambivalence this arouses in me sets against myself. Even worse, the very strength of 'partial' joys – based on an increase in the power of acting of one part of me – prevents other joys from being realized, and this blockage or inhibition of an increase in my power of acting is, in and of itself, sadness. As Deleuze puts it, 'We now seem farther than ever from coming into possession of our power of action; our capacity to be affected is exercised not only by passive affections, but, above all, by sad passions, involving an ever lower degree of the power of action.'[68]

The problems of ambivalence take us to the heart of Pierre Macherey's critique of Deleuze. Macherey says that Deleuze gives short shrift to 'the theme of ambivalence and the associated dialectical inversions that he sees as depending on negativity',[69] as Deleuze is practically allergic to the Hegelian dialectic of negativity and 'the negation of the negation',[70] to which Deleuze contrasts Spinoza as a philosopher of affirmation 'in the great lineage that goes from Epicurus to Nietzsche'. But Macherey argues that far from being a rare occurrence or an extreme case, the mental confusion of ambivalence 'corresponds to a situation in which the soul regularly finds itself while under the sway of the passions and their "forces", *vires*'.[71] Insofar as all passions are under the sway of an external object, they all 'alienate the soul by subjecting it to a law foreign to its own nature',[72] and in that respect, all our passive joys are tainted with ambivalence merely as a result of their passivity. Any time the soul or mind feels itself to be determined by something other than its own powers, it becomes aware of its impotence, and this feeling of 'not being able' is a feeling of being cut off from one's own power, that is, a sad passion.[73] Such a feeling can actually prevent us from acting, says Spinoza: 'Whenever a man thinks something is beyond his capacity ... he is so conditioned by this belief that he *really* cannot do what he *thinks* he cannot do.'[74] The passivity of the passions, even joyful ones, says Macherey, contains 'nothing positive to provide a foothold for the liberation of desire', but rather deepens our subjection to the force of circumstance.[75]

All passions thus lead to *fluctuatio animi* and leave us, in Spinoza's words, 'at the mercy of external causes' by which we 'are tossed about like the waves of the sea when driven by contrary winds, unsure of the outcome and of our fate'.[76] Worse, says Macherey, 'all passions, without exception, are sad – even those that appear to be joys',[77] insofar as all passions involve both a feeling of passivity and impotence and 'an imaginary fixation' on external things beyond our control.[78] We have already seen how fixation on a single object as the source of our happiness is an impediment to realizing good encounters with other things and events, and monopolizes our passive capacity for being affected as well as stultifying our active powers.[79]

Only an active joy that follows from our power of thinking *alone*, rather than any external cause, would be pure joy, unalloyed with sadness; only it could lead to an increase in our power of acting that is not off-set by a concomitant decrease.[80] The way to achieve such positive joys, says Macherey, is not by multiplying passive joys, but by changing our way of thinking, and, in particular, by bringing the imagination under the control of reason, which he takes to be the main point of the first twenty propositions of Part Five of the *Ethics*. Spinoza's *ars vivendi* involves basing our affective life on adequate ideas and a rational understanding of what occurs in the body, rather than on our bodily reactions taken at face value. The only way in which the mind can be active is through adequate ideas; the only reason it is passive is because its ideas are inadequate.[81]

All of our affects reflect variable increases or decreases of our *vis existendi*, the ideas of which are necessarily inadequate insofar as they do not grasp the real causes of these transitions.[82] In passive joys, 'the mind is entirely under the mechanisms of the imagination', forming inadequate ideas of its own powers insofar as 'it undergoes impulses communicated to it through the intermediary of the body's affections' and so of the body's encounters with other bodies 'following the common order of nature', or temporal succession.[83] The intermediate status of passive joys, combining both an increase in the *vis existendi* and the passivity of the imagination, rather than being an advantage, renders the ideas of them even more confused – 'hallucinatory' – and the mind even more passive.[84] Passive joys only destabilize the mind's power of thinking by communicating to it the variability of the body's chance encounters with other bodies,[85] deepening the mind's alienation from 'an authentically active life'.[86]

Macherey rather strangely seems to want to confine reason to a citadel in which it is immune from the slings and arrows of outrageous fortune. Given that the order of ideas in the mind is the same as the order of changes in the body,[87] the *independence* of reason from the vicissitudes of the body is not something a Spinozist could seriously maintain. The question is then not whether the variability of the body's chance encounters with other bodies can be avoided (it cannot), but whether the mind can arrange those encounters in such a way as to promote more rational and active thought – that is, whether one can arrange one's life such that one can increase the probability of good encounters and joyful passions. The desideratum that the mind should be as free as possible from affect and emotion also seems misguided. Without affects originating in the body, the mind has no indication of where the embodied individual stands in relation to goal achievement.[88] One sometimes has the impression reading Macherey that the ultimate goal of reason would be 'thought thinking itself', an Aristotelian *autonoeia*. But the function of reason is to promote the strategies for goal achievement with the highest probability of success, and although thinking clearly about how to achieve those goals is a goal of reason itself, most of those goals will arise from the individual's bodily and organic existence. To be free of passive affects, in that sense, would amount to being without any goals other than the goal of thinking rationally – a goal which, taken by itself, is purely formal and devoid of the concrete content that could guide an individual through life. Freedom from ambivalence would amount to freedom from the contingencies of life itself.

The necessity of emotions

Macherey's critique of emotions and affects takes for granted that they are 'irrational' phenomena: not just 'not rational', but impediments to rational thinking and action.

Yet many contemporary philosophers and psychologists argue the contrary: that not only are emotions not necessarily impediments to thinking and acting rationally, but that emotions can actually promote rationality and even possess a 'rationality' of their own. The philosopher Ronald de Sousa, for example, has long argued for 'the rationality of emotions'.[89] Emotions can be assessed for both cognitive and strategic rationality. An emotion is cognitively rational if the belief on which it is based is rational – that is, arrived at through a procedure with a high probability of arriving at the truth. An emotion is strategically rational if it constitutes a rational way of achieving our goals – that is, if it is expressed through or promotes behaviour with a good to high probability of achieving our goals.

But more than that, emotions can reveal when our goals are out of alignment: when they are in conflict with each other, when lower order goals have taken precedence over more important ones, or when our behaviour is self-defeating. In that respect, as Patricia Greenspan has argued, the internal emotional conflict of ambivalence can be salutary.[90] Certain negative emotions (regret, anger) can also reveal when our goals and beliefs – and the emotions connected with them – are products of an ideology that is harmful to our interests or the interests of those whom we care about, such as when women become angry and frustrated when told that prioritizing the pursuit of a career over rearing children is unnatural and bound to be unfulfilling. Negative and ambivalent emotions can signal a dissonance among our various goals, or between emergent goals and traditional ones, and thus reveal the necessity for reflecting on our goals and attempting to give them some sort of coherent and ordered ranking. In short, negative emotions signal that something has gone wrong in relation to our concerns and motivate us to undertake corrective actions. Even at their most negative and passive, then – even at their 'saddest' – emotions can promote the rational pursuit of our goals. In that respect, even bad encounters contain an element of good.

More broadly, says De Sousa, emotions can determine lines of salience and relevance for evaluating and assessing a situation in relation to our goals: which facts need to be attended to, which facts matter to us, and in what way they matter. Without emotions as a way of sorting and filtering the vast amount of cognitive information at hand, we would be unable to arrive at decisions or to act. Like Buridan's ass, we would have no reason to prefer one line of conduct or strategy over another, such as whether it would be better to minimize loss or maximize gain. Worse, without grief or sadness, and without joy or pleasure, we would have only a pale, cognitive apprehension of loss and gain (to paraphrase William James), much as if we were appraising someone else's behaviour, rather than experiencing the life that we ourselves are living.

Affect and emotion reflect our involvement in the world: how we are faring is a matter of our relations with others, with our environment, and the relation between our thoughts and actions and our goals and concerns, and all of these relations are revealed through how things *affect* us: through affect and emotion, which do not merely reflect our bodily states, but relate those states to our goals and desires through positive or negative feeling (pleasure and pain) and the judgements and behaviour sets implicit in emotions. Although De Sousa would not put it this way, we can see how affect and emotion express our *being-in-the-world*: our necessarily embodied involvement with the world and the goals and concerns related to our embodied and worldly existence.[91]

As indicating how states of affairs and events stand in relation to our concerns, or how they matter to us, emotion and affect express the way in which we relate our concerns to our world, and they thereby constitute a fundamental orientation to ourselves and the world that is the basis of the meaning and significance of events and things relative to our own personal existence and projects. Emotions and affect provide us with the felt meaning or *sense* of things, without which we would have no reason to pursue one course of action or line of inquiry rather than another. In that way, affect and emotion are indispensable to acting in and thinking about the world.

As already mentioned, a similar line of argument is pursued by Nico Frijda, who argues that emotions reveal the relevance of aspects of the situation to our concerns and goals, and act as motivators promoting goal achievement. This line of argument extends at least as far back as the work of Richard Lazarus and Magda B. Arnold, who had also argued that emotions involve appraisals of a substantive relation between a person's goals and environment, together with a response (somatic and behavioural) that addresses the person's concerns and promotes goal achievement.[92] Negative emotions indicate that a concern has been harmed or that there is apprehension that a concern is at risk, whereas positive affect (such as enjoyment) shows that either a desire has been satisfied or that one has come closer to achieving satisfaction. These affects serve to motivate coping behaviour: acting to prevent loss or to deal with a loss in the case of negative affect, positively reinforcing 'the successful exercise of one's capabilities' in the case of positive affect.[93] Affect signals 'the optimal or non-optimal functioning' of our capabilities,[94] either (in Damasio's words) 'optimal physiological coordination and the smooth running of the operations of life' together with 'a greater ease in the capacity to act' (joy) or 'physiological discord' and a diminished power and freedom to act (sorrow).[95] Such signals are indispensable to the rational pursuit of our well-being. We can dispense then with Macherey's concern that affects, even joyful ones, necessarily alienate us from our powers of thinking and acting.

From joyful passions to common notions

Macherey states that in Deleuze's interpretation of Spinoza, 'Everything turns on whether ... our transition to a greater perfection as a result of the chance composition of our being with that of something else which agrees with it in nature allows one to speak ... of "joyful passions" *whose very passivity* ... prepares the way for the transition to greater activity'.[96] But this is not what Deleuze says. He acknowledges that 'every passion is in itself bad insofar as it involves sadness' or passivity.[97] Although he does say that 'joy is the only passive affection that increases our power of action', and so in general, a good life involves a maximum of joys, passive and active,[98] he emphasizes that even passive joys do not occur often in the normal course of events. We have very few opportunities for good encounters, and to the degree to which we are determined by our passions, we are more likely to have bad encounters than good ones. Even if 'in principle' one human being *should* 'agree' in nature with another, different people are affected in different ways by external objects, and so come to have contrary loves and hates that cause them to be opposed to each other.[99] Moreover, 'This is hardly surprising, as Nature is not constructed for our convenience, but through a "common order" to which man, as a part of Nature, is subject.'[100] Good encounters, then, rarely occur *naturally* or spontaneously, but must be made the object of an *art*. We cannot simply passively await good encounters and 'hope for the best'; we must so arrange our life that good encounters become more probable.

No amount of joyful passions will give us possession of our power of action. For us to become active, we must move from passive joys to active ones based on adequate ideas.[101] This move is made possible through the formation of common notions, that is, an idea of what my body has in common with other bodies and which would explain our interactions. Everything turns, then, not on the *passivity* of joyful passions, but on the way in which joyful passions aid us in forming common notions: how the positive affect of joy, which expresses an increase in the functioning of our capabilities, helps us to understand our interactions and relations with our world and with others.

As earlier noted, what Spinoza calls 'common notions' have varying levels of generality. At the most general level, all bodies 'agree' in virtue of the attribute of extension and the infinite mode of motion and rest.[102] Yet, it is also in virtue of motion and rest, quickness and slowness that bodies *differ* from one another.[103] In that respect, the most universal common notions represent 'what is common to all things', 'that is, the universal similarity of relations as combined *ad infinitum* from the viewpoint of Nature as a whole'.[104] These similarities account for *both* the *general* agreement among two bodies (all bodies have constituent parts in a constitutive relation or ratio of motion and rest) and their *specific* disagreements, as a disagreement of natures is explicable by reference to an incompatibility between the ratios of motion and rest among parts that constitute the natures or essences of the two bodies in question.[105]

This most general sort of 'common notion' does not account for the direct and specific agreement in nature of two bodies whose constitutive ratios of motion and rest can be combined in a greater whole of which those bodies would be the parts.[106] When bodies having systems of relations among their parts are thus composed in a harmonious relation that encompasses them both, they agree from their own viewpoint, rather than from the viewpoint of the universe as a whole:[107]

> The first common notions we form are thus the least universal, those, that is, that apply to our body and to another that agrees directly with our own and affects it with joy.... When we experience a joyful passive affection, we are induced to form the idea of what is common to that body and our own.[108]

Because common notions have to do with the genuinely universal properties of things that fall under scientific laws of cause and effect, they offer us a *rational explanation* for the agreements in natures first revealed in joy: the similarity of composition or structure of the two bodies is grasped as the *necessary and internal reason* for their agreement,[109] and it is the nature of reason to regard things as necessary rather than contingent.[110] At the same time, it is joy that provides the motivation to inquire into what common notions would account for it: joy, as Frijda says, wants more joy, and in order for a repetition of joy to be more than just an accident, we must inquire into its causes at the level of universal laws of cause and effect. When the mind by its own power forms the idea of what is common to our own body and that of another body that agrees with ours, it becomes more active, resulting in an active joy caused by the mind's active power of understanding.[111]

There is thus in Spinoza an *apprenticeship* of becoming-active, starting from the least universal common notions, those having to do with the agreement in nature between our body and an external body as revealed in passive joy, and from there working our way up to more universal common notions, including even those which explain interactions with bodies whose nature disagrees with our own and cause negative affects and a decrease in our powers of thinking and feeling.[112] When the mind grasps an affect through an adequate idea, and so understands it 'as governed by necessity', that affect becomes an emotion arising from reason, one necessarily related to the common properties of things. As these common properties of things are regarded as always present, an active emotion thus has a stability lacking in the passions.[113] Active joys are thus not subject to vacillation or ambivalence; they are not accompanied by any sad passions and so do not hinder any of the mind's operations. Rather, active joys, caused by adequate ideas, give rise to the *active* desire for more adequate ideas,[114] and so give rise to an increase in our power of understanding. This in turn leads to more active joys, culminating in the mind's enjoyment of its own powers, *acquiescientia in se ipso*,[115] the highest form of which consists in the mind being affected by joy when it has adequate knowledge of the essence of things.[116]

Despite his disagreements with Deleuze, Macherey also makes common notions key to the transition from passivity to activity. 'All the affections of the body, of whatever sort . . . must obey the common laws' of motion and rest and 'thus fall under the jurisdiction of common notions through which they admit of a rational explanation'.[117] Common notions thus move the mind from passive perception to active conception by stabilizing the imagination and subjecting it to the order of rational rules or laws.[118] Moreover, 'the fact that through the intermediary of common notions there are adequate ideas in the human mind makes possible the development of active affects, rational affects that are not passions' and that lead 'the power of being and acting that is within each person to function at its maximum'.[119] In that case, 'the path to liberation consists in desiring only those things that *really* agree with our nature' so that we unite with things that really unite with and reinforce our power,[120] especially with other human beings, both because human beings, sharing mostly the same nature, can be combined into communities,[121] but more importantly because what is most useful to a reasonable human being is another reasonable human being.[122] By forming common notions, which are necessarily adequate, people can achieve genuine agreement and be really united in a free community,[123] seeking a common good based on a common nature, such that, governed by reason, each seeks for himself only what he also desires for others.[124]

In that case, is there a real difference between Macherey and Deleuze? Both agree that common notions are the hinge leading from inadequate to adequate ideas and so from passive to active joys.[125] The difference would seem to be whether there can be 'good encounters' *prior* to there being common notions. For Deleuze, the encounter between two beings which can combine or 'compose' with each other not only can but must precede the formation of those common notions based on what two beings have in common at the most general or universal level. For Macherey, by contrast, it is only common notions that allow human beings to be truly united by common rational interests,[126] and these common notions pertain to 'the uniform and unvarying relations that unite them,'[127] that is, to the universal laws governing motion and rest, not to the confused and fleeting encounters of two bodies being passively affected by each other.[128] In short, for Macherey, we must work from the most universal common notions concerning what all bodies have in common (ratios of motion and rest) in order to explain particular interactions between bodies, whereas for Deleuze, we must start from particular good encounters between particular bodies that have in common certain specific ratios of motion and rest that allow them to be 'composed' together harmoniously.

In plain terms, Deleuze argues that it is on the basis of harmony or compatibility between their basic modes of acting and feeling that two individuals can arrive at a specific common notion regarding the relationship between them, paving the way to mutual understanding and a union of goals and interests based on that mutual understanding. The starting point for grasping a specific common notion is the passive joy that results from a 'good encounter' between two individuals. In essence, the question comes down to whether fortuitous good encounters and passive joys can pave the way for a genuine union based on adequate ideas and common notions. Deleuze argues that they can: that even if the reason for our joy is inadequately understood, we are more apt to think well when our power of activity is increased, and we feel joy, than when our powers are diminished and we feel sad. Macherey, though, argues that when the mind uses common notions to grasp universal relations among bodies, and uses universal relations to understand how it is affected through the body by other bodies, then the mind attains a 'completely disincarnated point of view',[129] an assertion that sounds more Cartesian than Spinozist. If we are to take seriously Spinoza's idea that the mind and body are one thing considered under different attributes, then joy, even in its passive form, is a transition from passivity to a greater degree of activity in both body *and* mind: a real transition, not just an imagined one, as Macherey alleges.[130] But the greater objection to Macherey is that what bodies have in common on the most general level is also what can differentiate them and even put them in opposition to each other. We cannot then move from the most universal agreement in relations between bodies to the most specific, but rather must move from specific good encounters between bodies to common notions of greater and greater scope and generality.

Conclusion

We have seen then how it is that joyful passions supposedly lead to common notions, and how these in turn serve as the basis for active joys. In transforming passionate joys into active ones, we can then gain 'the power to arrange and associate affections of the body according to the order of the intellect', as Spinoza says, so that 'we are not easily affected by bad emotions'[131] and act always from the emotion of joy.[132] Only one question remains: will this actually work?

To be as brief as possible: yes, but only provided that we do not simply try to maximize the number of good encounters and passive joys in our lives, but that we use passive joys as a means of arriving at common notions. No amount of joyful passions will, in and of itself, give us the understanding of the necessity involved in the agreement of the natures of two bodies.[133] There is a 'genuine leap' from passive joys to common notions,[134] but passive joys, by revealing a commonality or agreement between my body and another body, can be the *occasion* for arriving at a common notion: that is, both the opportunity and the *motive* for understanding what two bodies have in common. It is in the reflective moment, when we are not immersed in experience but rather turn around and examine it 'at arm's length', that we move from joyful passions to common notions, and from there to active joys. In Spinoza's terms, we must move beyond perceiving things through images determined externally by the fortuitous run of circumstance to an internal determination of mind that follows from the mind regarding 'several things at the same time, to understand their agreement, their differences and their oppositions'.[135] It is only in that way that arranging good encounters can be an art leading to common notions and active joys, and not just an addiction in which we lose ourselves in a multitude of passive pleasures.

The starting point must be affect itself, the mind's awareness of an increase or decrease in the functioning of the body. It is joy which first reveals to us, affectively, an agreement between our own nature and the nature of something else. The fact that this joy is 'passive' does not impede us from arriving at a rational understanding of ourselves and our emotional life. On the contrary, it is this first affective experience of the agreement of two natures that leads to the formation of ideas pertaining to the agreement or disagreement between things, ideas that form the very essence of rational thought. Reason *depends* on affects, and affects express the agreements and disagreements between the constitutive relations among parts of bodies of all sorts: human, non-human, organic and inorganic. It is through joyful affects that we discover what in the world can compose with the relations among parts and vital forces that both constitute our being and link us to nature as whole.

Notes

1 Some psychologists and philosophers argue that all emotions in principle aid rational thought and action. See Antonio Damasio, *Looking for Spinoza*, 147–8: 'Covertly or overtly, [an emotion] focuses attention on certain aspects of the problem and thus enhances the quality of reasoning over it . . . the [emotional] signal *marks* options and outcomes with a positive or negative signal that narrows the decision-making space and increases the probability that the action will conform to past experience . . . increasing the efficiency of the reasoning process and making it speedier.'
2 Nico Frijda, 'Emotions Are Functional', 131–41. Parenthetical references are to the Solomon volume.
3 Gilles Deleuze, *Spinoza et le problème de l'expression*, hereafter *SPE*; translated as *Expressionism in Philosophy*, hereafter *EPS*; *Spinoza: Practical Philosophy*, hereafter *SPP*.

4 Pierre Macherey, 'The Encounter with Spinoza', 139–61. Macherey's interpretation of Spinoza's theory of affects is presented more fully in Macherey's *Introduction à l'Éthique de Spinoza*; vol. 1, *La première partie. La nature des choses*; vol. 2, *La seconde partie. La réalité mentale*; vol. 3, *La troisième partie. La vie affective*; vol. 4, *La quatrième partie. La condition humaine*; vol. 5, *La cinquième partie. Les voies de la libération*. Hereafter these are indicated by the abbreviations M1 for volume one and so forth.
5 See Gilles Deleuze, *Nietzsche and Philosophy*, 39: 'Spinoza . . . said that we do not even know what a body *can do*, we talk about consciousness and mind [*esprit*] and chatter on about it all, but we do not know what a body is capable of, what forces belong to it or what they are preparing for.' See also Ibid., 62 and 262 on affects as capacities for being affected and hence as degrees of power (*puissance*).
6 EPS 147/SPE 132. Spinoza, *Ethics*, hereafter E, followed by Part, Proposition number, D for demonstration, S for Scholium, C for Corollary. See E I Ax4, 'The knowledge of an effect depends on, and involves, the knowledge of the cause' and E II Def. 4, 'By an adequate idea I mean an idea which, in so far as it is considered in itself without relation to its object, has all the . . . intrinsic characteristics of a true idea.' See E II P24-28 and their Demonstrations, III Def. 2, III P1 and Demonstration, and III General Definition of Emotions.
7 E III P11.
8 E III Def. 3, III P 2 S and Definitions of the Emotions, Def. 2.
9 Pierre Macherey, 'The Encounter with Spinoza', 152.
10 E III Def. 3 and Definitions of Emotions, Def. 3.
11 EPS 294.
12 E IV P31.
13 E V P10.
14 see E V P10 S.
15 E IV Appendix items 2 and 3.
16 EPS 246/SPE 225.
17 E IV P 52.
18 E V P15, P20.
19 See J. G. Fichte, *The Vocation of Man* and Søren Kierkegaard, *Either/Or*.
20 E V P42 S.
21 E III Def 1 and 2, P1.
22 See E V P10 S.
23 See E V Preface.
24 E IV P4 C; see V P34.
25 An *imperium in imperio*; E III Preface.
26 E IV P45 S.
27 EPS 285/SPE 264.
28 E II P 38.
29 E II P39.
30 See E II P40 S2; EPS 283.
31 EPS 274.
32 EPS 285.
33 See E IV P8, P15, P24, P26.
34 E IV P31.
35 E III P58-59, IV P15D, IV P59 S, IV Appendix items 2, 3 and 30.
36 E V P7.

37 E V P3.
38 E IV P39.
39 SPP 33–4; EPS 241; E IV P39 and IV Appendix item 30.
40 SPP 103.
41 E IV 18 S.
42 EPS 260.
43 EPS 261/SPE 240.
44 EPS 262/SPE 241.
45 E V P4.
46 E V P3.
47 E V P4S, V P18 S.
48 E III P59 S; see V P20 S.
49 See E III P11, III General Definition of Emotions, Explication, IV Appendix item 30.
50 E IV P63 C, III P59.
51 E V P10 S.
52 E IV P30 D.
53 E II P37.
54 E II P7.
55 E IV P38.
56 E III P17.
57 E III P17 S.
58 E IV P43.
59 E IV P44 S.
60 EPS 244–5.
61 E IV P38.
62 E IV P44 S.
63 E III P35 S and E III P36 S.
64 E II P18.
65 E III P47.
66 E III P44 and P47.
67 EPS 243.
68 EPS 245.
69 Pierre Macherey, 'The Encounter with Spinoza', 156.
70 For Deleuze's critique of Hegelian negativity, see in particular Gilles Deleuze, *Nietzsche and Philosophy* and *Difference and Repetition*. Macherey himself, however, is equally insistent that for Spinoza, the negation of a negation can never result in something positive. See Pierre Macherey, *Introduction à l'Éthique de Spinoza*, passim, and *Hegel or Spinoza*, chapter 4, '*Omnis determinatio est negatio*'. It would be pointless to cite specific instances; Macherey repeats the point time and time again.
71 Pierre Macherey, 'The Encounter with Spinoza', 155.
72 Ibid.
73 E III P55.
74 E III Definitions of Emotions, item 28, Explication.
75 Pierre Macherey, 'The Encounter with Spinoza', 156.
76 E III P59 S.
77 Pierre Macherey, 'The Encounter with Spinoza', 153.
78 Ibid., 155.

79 This point is developed by Pascal Sévérac in 'Passivité et désir d'activité chez Spinoza', and at greater length in *Le devenir actif chez Spinoza*. Sévérac's interpretation supports Macherey's.
80 M 3 375–90.
81 M 3 352.
82 M 3 355–6.
83 M 3 345–6.
84 M 3 357–9.
85 M 3 358–9.
86 M 3 377.
87 E II P 7.
88 See Nico Frijda, 'Emotions are Functional, Most of the Time'; see also Richard Lazarus, 'Appraisal', 125–30. An emotion involves an appraisal of the relationship of one's situation to one's goals without one necessarily being cognitively aware of that relationship; see Antonio Damasio, *Looking for Spinoza*, 54–5.
89 Ronald de Sousa, 'Self-Deceptive Emotions'; 'The Rationality of Emotions'; *The Rationality of Emotions*. My summary of De Sousa's theory draws freely from all these sources.
90 See also Patricia Greenspan, 'A Case of Mixed Emotions'. Greenspan argues that emotions grasp the relations between things, events and persons, on the one hand, and our desires and goals, on the other hand, in a pre-cognitive and pre-reflective way. Ambivalence signals a conflict in our goals and concerns prior to any rational and reflective assessment of them. That is one way in which 'emotions play an important role in motivating rational behaviour' (243).
91 I realize that my Heideggerian gloss is one that de Sousa would not necessarily accept. Nevertheless, I think that de Sousa's position regarding emotions are determinants of lines of relevance and salience has a great deal in common with Heidegger's analysis of human affect. See my 'Heidegger on *Befindlichkeit*'.
92 Both Lazarus and Arnold have written a good deal about emotions. For Lazarus, see also *Psychological Stress* and R. Lazarus, J. R. Averill and E. Opton, 'Towards a Cognitive Theory of Emotion'.
93 Antonio Damasio, *Looking for Spinoza*, 133–5.
94 Ibid. 138.
95 Ibid., 137–9.
96 Pierre Macherey, 'The Encounter with Spinoza', 153; my emphasis.
97 EPS 271.
98 EPS 272.
99 EPS 244, 265.
100 EPS 245/SPE 224.
101 EPS 274.
102 E II P13 Lemma 2.
103 E II P13 Lemma 1.
104 EPS 276.
105 SPP 55; E II P29 S.
106 EPS 275, 278.
107 EPS 276, 281.
108 EPS 282.
109 EPS 276/SPE 255.
110 E II P44.

111 EPS 284.
112 SPE 266-7, 278/EPS 287-8, 298.
113 E V P7.
114 see E III P58 D, IV P15 D.
115 E III P55 S and III Definitions of the Emotions, #25.
116 E V P 25-7. See Syliane Malinowski-Charles, *Affects et conscience chez Spinoza*. 151-77; 176: '*Acquiescientia* is quite simply the joy of being active itself.' See also Malinowski-Charles, 'Le salut par les Affects'. Malinowski-Charles' interpretation is more in line with Deleuze's than with Macherey's in that she also maintains that passive joys, despite their passivity, can lead to active joys and blessedness. She does, however, agree with Macherey concerning the connection between *acquiescientia* and blessedness; see M 5 89.
117 M 2 285 n. 3.
118 M 2 288-9.
119 M 2 291 n. 1.
120 M 4 120.
121 M 4 122-3.
122 M 4 416.
123 M 2 290-1.
124 M 4 124-5, 134-5, 137-8, 416, 421.
125 See M 3 375-90.
126 M 2 290.
127 M 2 294.
128 M 2 217-23.
129 M 2 282.
130 See M 3 332-5.
131 E V P10.
132 E V P10 S.
133 See EPS 295.
134 EPS 283.
135 E II P29 S.

Bibliography

Baugh, Bruce. 'Heidegger on *Befindlichkeit*'. *Journal of the British Society for Phenomenology* 20 (1989): 124-35.

Damasio, Antonio. *Looking for Spinoza: Joy, Sorrow, and the Feeling Brain*. New York: Harcourt, 2003.

Deleuze, Gilles. *Expressionism in Philosophy*. Translated by Martin Joughin. New York: Zone Books, 1990.

Deleuze, Gilles. *Nietzsche and Philosophy*. Translated by Hugh Tomlinson. New York: Columbia University Press, 1983.

Deleuze, Gilles. *Spinoza et le problème de l'expression*. Paris: Éditions de Minuit, 1968.

Deleuze, Gilles. *Spinoza. Practical Philosophy*. Translated by Robert Hurley. San Francisco: City Lights Books, 1988.

de Sousa, Ronald. 'The Rationality of Emotions'. *Dialogue: The Review of Canadian Philosophy* 18 (1979): 41-63.

de Sousa, Ronald. *Rationality of Emotions*. Cambridge, MA: MIT Press, 1987.
de Sousa, Ronald. 'Self-deceptive Emotions'. *Journal of Philosophy* 75 (1978): 684–97.
Fichte, Johann Gottlieb. *The Vocation of Man*. Translated by Peter Preuss. Indianapolis: Hackett, 1987.
Frijda, Nico. 'Emotions are Functional, Most of the Time'. In *What Is an Emotion?*, edited by Robert C. Solomon, 2nd ed., 131–41. Oxford and New York: Oxford University Press, 2003.
Greenspan, Patricia. 'A Case of Mixed Emotions: Ambivalence and the Logic of Emotions'. In *Explaining Emotions*, edited by Amélie Oksenberg Rorty, 223–50. Berkeley, CA: University of California Press, 1980.
Kierkegaard, Søren. *Either/Or*. Translated by Howard V. Hong and Edna H. Hong. Princeton, NJ: Princeton University Press, 1987.
Lazarus, Richard. 'Appraisal: The Minimal Cognitive Prerequisites of Emotion'. In *What Is an Emotion?*, edited by Robert C. Solomon, 2nd ed., 125–30. Oxford and New York: Oxford University Press, 2003.
Lazarus, Richard. *Psychological Stress and the Coping Process*. New York: McGraw-Hill, 1966.
Lazarus, Richard, James R. Averill and Edward Opton. 'Towards a Cognitive Theory of Emotion'. In *Feelings and Emotions*, edited by Magda B. Arnold, 207–32. New York: Academic Press, 1970.
Macherey, Pierre. 'The Encounter with Spinoza'. In *Deleuze: A Critical Reader*, edited by Paul Patton, 139–61. Oxford and Cambridge: Blackwell, 1996.
Macherey, Pierre. *Introduction à l'Éthique de Spinoza. La première partie. La nature des choses*, Vol. 1. Paris: Presses Universitaires de France, 1998.
Macherey, Pierre. *Introduction à l'Éthique de Spinoza. La seconde partie. La réalité mentale*, Vol. 2. Paris: Presses Universitaires de France, 1997.
Macherey, Pierre. *Introduction à l'Éthique de Spinoza. La troisième partie. La vie affective*, Vol. 3. Paris: Presses Universitaires de France, 1995.
Macherey, Pierre. *Introduction à l'Éthique de Spinoza. La quatrième partie. La condition humaine*, Vol. 4. Paris: Presses Universitaires de France, 1997.
Macherey, Pierre. *Introduction à l'Éthique de Spinoza. La cinquième partie. Les voies de la libération*, Vol. 5. Paris: Presses Universitaires de France, 1994.
Malinowski-Charles, Syliane. *Affects et conscience chez Spinoza. L'automatisme dans le progrès éthique*. Hildesheim Zurich-New York: Georg Olms Verlag, 2004.
Malinowski-Charles, Syliane. 'Le salut par les affects: la joie comme ressort du progrès éthique chez Spinoza'. *Philosophiques* 29, no. 1 (2002): 73–87.
Sévérac, Pascal. *Le devenir actif chez Spinoza*. Paris: Honoré Champion, 2005.
Sévérac, Pascal. 'Passivité et désir d'activité chez Spinoza'. In *Spinoza et les affects*, edited by Fabienne Brugère and Pierre-François Moreau, 39–54. Paris: Presses de l'Université Paris-Sorbonne, 1998.
Spinoza, Benedict de. *Ethics*. Translated by Samuel Shirley. Edited by Seymour Feldman. Indianapolis: Hackett, 1992.

4

Symmetry and asymmetry in conceptual and morphological formations

The difference plant body growth can make to human thought[1]

Karen L. F. Houle

Ontological orientation: Conceptual bodiliness

As a Spinozist philosopher, my working hypothesis is that the concepts with which we think are formed, or *have* form. The colloquial phrase – *a body of thought* – is rendered literal through a Spinozist lens: concepts *are* thought's body. The body that thought is, or that thought has, is not a thing. Rather, it is the always animated typology of active and reactive forces *in* or *as* a concept, when acting as an act of thought.[2] The concept has, or is, a singular body when it is a thinking-thing-thinking: when it is an idea as it *ideas*.

In *What Is Philosophy?* Deleuze and Guattari state, 'concepts are not made from nothing'.[3] What does this imply? It implies that concepts are ontogenetic: that they emerge, change, recede. As primordial bodily mental mutations, they emerge from, and vanish into a non-totalizable, heterotopic[4] 'zone of productivity . . . a ground of plural becoming'[5] from the 'primordial asymmetry'[6] of the infinity of attributes of a single substance. As determined, existent modes, concepts are animated via relational intensities among themselves: that is, they differ. They differ one from the other not in terms of their 'content' or the 'objects' in the world they denote, but rather in terms of their immanent relational intensities; their peculiar active and reactive dynamic typologies as these typologies are enmeshed with others.

Patterning and stabilization

As thought's bodiliness, then, concepts undergo morphogenesis. This takes place at two key sites: at, or in the individual thinking thing that thinks *with* them,[7] and at or in, the cultural norms of thought and thinking that lives its particular *life of the mind* in and through this living mesh of ideas. Through morphogenesis, concepts take on patterns. This is clearly evident in human social domains of meaning: the emergence and clumping of concepts into the semi-independent fields of ethics, history, law, geography, medicine, theology, education, botany, economics, art and sexuality, to name but a few. But what is completely overlooked is that this is also true about the shape or form of the concepts themselves. In their emergence, deployment and redeployment, concepts *themselves* 'are concrete assemblages',[8] come to take on distinct patternings of shape and form: vertical, curvy, linear, radial, dyadic, horizontal, concentric, scattershot, triangular, diagonalist, isometric, spiral, spherical. And, they come to express the concomitant action-operations (and combinations thereof) of these forms and shapes: binarizing, centripetal (exteriorizing), flattening, wobbling, abstracting, flip-flopping, speedy, centrifugal (interiorizing), clambering, hierarching, leaning to one side, accreting, withdrawing, dissipating, equipoised, inefficient, truncating, grounding out, oppositional, unbudgeable.[9] Moreover, their usage – *thinking* – begins to express upscale discernable patterns or forms: what we sometimes call *styles of thinking*[10] is simply the name for a certain stable typology of active and reactive forces of constellations of concepts in action. Now, because they are heritable, those living geometries of conceptual habits – our *thinking* – tend to give rise, in turn, to those same bodily forms. We are not, as we sometimes like to imagine, independent thinkers with our own unique and groovy style of cognition: we have in fact inherited a narrow repertoire of prefab concepts, and we find ourselves thinking as thinking-things on highly ramified architectonics of ideas, and along deeply grooved paths of thought-action. Finally, we should note that, just as we can say about the periodic table of the elements, certain concepts have come to form large families of practically inert (stable, non-reactive) thought-body forms. And, just like the salts or the inert gases, this family of concepts dominates the field of our thinking-action: the *ways that thought happens*, whether it is *about* ethics, history, law, geography, medicine, theology, education, botany, economics, art or sexuality.[11] More than any other, this family of concepts *shapes* our individual and collective thinking. We will return to this claim shortly, with respect to the way that thought and thinking shapes our thinking *about* ethics.

Evolution, deformation, growth

The dominant, legible or 'normal' things to think about; the dominant, legible or 'normal' ways to think-about-things was named by Deleuze and Guattari 'a regime of thought'. The translation of the French term *régime* into the English 'regime' implies that thought and thinking are quasi-military prison houses ruled by strong armed dictators. This does not get it right; it doesn't leave enough space for our basic working claim that 'concepts are ontogenetic. They emerge, change, recede.' Without this latitude, there could be no conversation about ethics; the ethics of thinking. An ethics of thinking involves the almost paradoxical undertaking of shifting the patterns that express one's self as a legible self. How? 'Comment ces régimes de pensées, l'architecture de notre imaginaire fondamentale, le plan de nos concepts de base, sont-ils capables d'être décolonisées, disassemblées, rassemblées selon un plan différent?'[12] And, yet, concepts and the character of conceptual terrains *do* change, grow, deform, evolve. How? Consider three possible ways. They can evolve due to random background mutations – the surprising 'pure becoming'[13] of concepts: events of thought itself which testify to the ground of plural becoming. Events of 'pure becoming' secure the fact that the appearance of a new form does not automatically entail the disappearance of an old one: one form or operational tendency does not simply take the place of an other, like Pez-mind; rather, a plurality of genuinely different modes of thinking always coexist on the plane of becoming: what varies is the degree of differenciation[14] happening at any given time. Second, concepts can mutate due to exposure events: potent factors conjured or found within the milieu of thinking bodies that are capable of destabilizing them. Third, they can evolve through strategically and continuously applied micro-selection pressures operating via the immanent mechanics of thought (thinking-things-thinking differently) to effect subtle but felt, or sensed shifts in the established patterns of intensities and forces of, or as, thinking. I suspect that this is what the phenomenon we name 'understanding' involves, and feels like, as a lived cognized phenomenon. Also, this latter evolution path is what Deleuze and Guattari have in mind when they say 'concepts must be created'.[15] New concepts can be made, and made by us when adequately and strategically pressured by 'our problems, our history'.[16] Unlike background spontaneous mutation which always maintains a degree of differenciation, within this third domain of concept-making, they identify a special situation: 'concepts can only be replaced by others if there are new problems relative to which it loses all meaning.'[17] In this chapter, I will argue that 'plant ethics' is exactly that: a genuinely new problem relative to which the old concepts, the concepts with which we thought about, and conducted, (human)animal ethics, lose all meaning. Hence, for the question of plant ethics, new ethical concepts need to be created which replace, rather than merely extend or work alongside norms of, and for, animality.

The key point in this section on conceptual morphogenesis is that although concepts and styles of thought *are* conditioned relations and practices – they *are* determinable – and these determinations tend to accrue quasi-stable mechanisms, patterns and tendencies; they are also, in principle, always mutable: 'a permanent condition of their existence . . . is an insubordination . . . a certain essential obstinacy . . . a means of escape.'[18] These two facts – the mutability of concepts – the permanent amenability of thinking to an event of thought – and our possible involvement in that mutation – serve as the central axis of this whole chapter.[19] In the next section, we will see how, in some cases – I will focus on the case of posthumanist ethics – concepts and styles of thinking *should* be altered. What we establish in this section is the ontological claim that, as thinking-things-thinking, and as thinking-things-thinking-about-thinking, we are immanent to those very mechanics and forces of thought by which evolution can happen. In short: we are sites of change, growth, mutation, deformation and evolution of thinking, both as individual thinking-things and as systems of thought-norms. We *are* thinking-things. Our concept bodies are affected by, and as thought, but can also affect thought. We can literally *be* thought differently. It is in the nature of ourselves as thinking bodies to enjoy the latent capacity to think-the-difference back into the bodies of those very concepts and the regimes of thought which have become inert, and in which we participate whether directly or indirectly, intentionally or unintentionally. We have, or perhaps *are*, a capacity to make 'something new . . . finally come about; to make thinking reach thought'.[20] This profound capacity, the capacity to bring about an event of thought, is not sufficiently targeted nor actualized when a given individual undertakes to think-*about*-something-differently (i.e. an intentional, rational shift in the content or target of one's cogitations or obsessions such as Epicurus or Freud or CBT [Cognitive Behavioural Therapy] might advise, a mere change in the objects of one's 'wishes'[21]) but rather, by system-wide base-level deformations in the very bodies of thought with which we think: by changing the *form* of the concepts used *to think*, to *imagine*, to *evaluate*, to *understand*, to *wish*. Sustained meditation practice, for instance, has been shown to alter the very speed of reactivity of one's thinking:[22] 'to reduce the *force* of anger';[23] that is, to mutate the very suppleness and morph-*ology* of mental-bodies we carry in, and as, wholly and deeply thinking *beings*.

The animal's body of thought

As I have argued elsewhere,[24] *thinking-the-animal* has saturated Western thought. It continues to dominate its images, its stories, its metaphors, its grammars, its logic and all its philosophies. By this, I do not mean that the modern West is obsessed by thinking *about* the animal (though that is also certainly true in the case of *the human animal*): what I mean is that *thinking-as-animal-thinking* has stabilized as the dominant *form* of ratiocination: *how* thought is; how thinking behaves.

The concepts which we – the human animal – have inherited, and with which we think, are strongly marked by an animal form; or, put otherwise, have, and give rise to a pronounced animal bodiliness of thought. The actual fleshed animal body, whether found in the human animal or the panther or the guinea pig, exhibits four stable morphological formal traits (though their admixture varies across species and among individuals): a front and a back, a right and a left side, a top and a bottom, a core and a periphery. Indeed, one way that the kingdom *Animalia* is divided up taxonomically is in terms of arrays of these bodily axes of symmetry. In a parallel fashion, the repertoire of concepts with which we think *about* anything has evolved within this immensely potent animalesque lineage. Put otherwise, all our concepts, no matter the subject domain in which they appear – ethics, history, law, medicine, geography, theology, education, botany, economics, art and sexuality – express a dominant animal bodiliness, both in terms of the forms of the concepts we deploy, and in terms of ideational functions (their concomitant form, or style, of thinking). Whereas in principle, there could be a plurality of forms of thinking-forms and styles, in fact, our concepts are a veritable monoculture of four formal characteristics: right-left bilaterality, a front-to-back split, stable up and downness, and radial concentricity (inside versus outside). We should note that each of these is a dualism. The concomitant thinking styles (of individuals, of entire domains of meaning, and whole cultures) which these dualistic architectures tend to operationalize are 'either-or' judgement (strict rules for classifying and organizing perceptions of objects), oppositionality, linearity, one-to-one object-subject pairing, problem-solvers, ranking, grasping, naming, technocratic forward progress, results-orientation, efficiency, atomistic individualism, grandiosity and feeling at home in one's world.

My claim about the animalesque nature of thought's body can be corroborated by scrutinizing any modern sociocultural domain. The logic body of late capitalist neoliberalism perhaps offers many examples: the single-mindedness of homogeneous commodity production (Jules: 'What do they call a Big Mac in France?' Vincent: 'A Big Mac's a Big Mac, but they call it Le Big Mac');[25] the immediacy of consumption and endless deferral of the 'problem of waste', a winner-takes-all global resource extraction game, the craving for innovation over the desire to, as Francis Alÿs says, 'do more with what we already have',[26] an obscene results-driven competitiveness; the categorization of followers as losers; a near-total disregard of the lessons and wisdoms of history; an inability to 'see' ecology (which is a mesh and not a thing that can be 'seen' with the same eyes), a pathological lack of empathy for Others; the valorization of efficiency; its 'march-of-progress-as-necessary' narratives at every turn. Each of these *difficulties* emanates from an either-or binary logic, and that is the morpho-logic of the animal body, at work, in and as late capitalism, producing the same problem over and over and over again, and merely appearing to offer different solutions to them.

It is interesting (and alarming) to notice just how deeply and consistently gouged our most critical domains are by these same either-or animalesque qualities. A rich example comes from current political theory. We simply lack an holonic[27] thought-body up to the task of responding to anthropogenic climate change.[28] For example, 'climate change is conceived of as a problem in need of a solution (as opposed to a condition).'[29] A 'condition' is simply not the kind of ontological situation in which one can situate oneself, automatically or unselfconsciously as a subject (the problem-solver), nor name the situation in which one finds oneself as an object (a problem) in need of a solution towards which one *can* innovate.[30] Adding another layer to this same issue of impoverished dualistically fixed imaginaries, Biro, drawing on Walter Benjamin, makes the apt observation that CC solution response campaigns – mitigation or adaptation – 'focus on "hardware" solutions [which] rely on a kind of "homogeneous, empty time", a reification of temporality, drawing on the metaphorical power of what is perhaps the paradigmatic technology of modernity: the ticking clock'.[31] He points out the inefficacy (and growing tragicomedy) of various urgency-ramping campaigns that have been anchored in a conception of linear time (now . . . and then . . . and then), with a regular tempo (moving towards it at a calculable, steady rate), and time itself marked by the character of a resource (running out from current amounts). Biro writes: 'The deadline, while conveying a certain political urgency, and clearly useful for the purposes of mobilization, also turns the politics into a situation of absolutes: either we make the deadline or we don't. . . . This way of *thinking about* and practically approaching the issue makes the prospect of what comes after the deadline, in practical terms, unimaginable.'[32]

Even in this tiny sliver of (sincere) theorizing about the future of the living planet, one spies the mobilization of a large, functional meshwork of very stable binary axes: problem-solution, subject-object, now-then, us-them.[33] Those are the political imaginaries we have inherited. We *do* have this thought-body and are mobilizing it over and over again by way of response to climate change, to practically no avail.

Undoubtedly, this same body plan dominated the thinking-activity that produced the situation we now call 'climate change'. Audre Lorde's oft-repeated warning that 'we will never dismantle the master's house with the master's tools' takes on a new sense through our analysis: the shape or form of the conceptual tools which built (in this case) the Anthropocene greenhouse cannot be the same mental tools with which we try to live in it or *even think about it*.

The animal body of ethics

Let us now focus on the domain of ethics. As I showed in my recent book,[34] 'contemporary ethics' is also dominated – in ethical pedagogy, in ethical scholarship and in practical ethical training – by a ubiquitous, deeply oppositional style: Which of the two positions, pro-life or pro-choice, should I take? Is euthanasia for the terminally ill right or wrong? Should I attempt to save the drowning child or not? Should I pull the trolley car lever or not? Are harms reduced or increased by making the survey participant anonymous? Take a stance. Attack the other position with knock-down arguments. *All* the concepts we use to do that thinking *about* ethical phenomena like abortion or the liveability of the planet for future generations of beings – concepts like integrity, dignity, compassion, responsibility, harm, justice, fairness, subjectivity, collectivity, utility – are marked by those same cut-in-half patterns: higher versus lower, in versus out, front versus back, right versus left. While this operation of thought is often effective, appropriate, even at times elegant, as a posthumanist ethical philosopher, my assessment is that this thought-body trait can also be an obstacle to ethicality. It is an obstacle in two closely linked senses.

First, it is an obstacle *when the site of ethicality* – the ethical situation *from* which a call for ethical response emerges for us – is simply not the *kind of object* or question or situation which *bears* the ontological feature of being split or bifurcatable. Timothy Morton has said as much about the nature of the claims climate change makes; Yves Besson argues the same is true about organic agriculture,[35] and I have made this argument about unwanted pregnancy. In complex ethical cases, responding to stock normative concepts with their dualistic form and cutting operations is intellectually inappropriate. It is like taking a hammer to water. As Biro rightly diagnosed, 'this *way of thinking about* and practically approaching these sorts of issues' blocks the ethical imagination from encountering the ethical at issue – that is, actually seeing *what* it is faced with – and hence in this sense is a form or style of conceptualization which is an obstacle for *doing right* by this sort of an object or condition.

Animal ethics

This is precisely what is happening in the sub-area of ethics concerned with the moral standing of 'the non-human': animals, plants, bacteria, species, ecosystems; even Gaia herself. Which other *animals* are matters of ethical concern? What, if anything, are they owed, and from whom? What does the good life consist in, or mean, for cows, chickens, fish, penguins, panthers, guinea pigs? What, morally speaking, are we permitted, obliged, forbidden to do *with* or *to them*? These are the sorts of questions asked *by ethically minded human individuals* about other animals. These are the starting block questions which one finds in every single area of animal concern today, theoretical or practical: comparative ethology, government policy in animal shelters, airports, city park by-laws, empirical animal welfare science and theoretical ethics. They might very well be the right questions. However, the concepts deployed, the clinical tests designed in light of these concepts, and the styles of reasoning through the evidence garnered which have *followed* from these questions have actually pushed *the deeply powerful question of the animal* out of reach. This is happening by way of a sort of undercurrent. It looks as if there is a sincere reaching for and caring about animals. For example, thousands of scientists spend umpteen years designing and carrying out experiments to prove that animals suffer *just as we do*. Or cognize *just as we do*. They are operating with a dual epistemic and moral certitude that the suffering or cogitation of any given sentient individual animal is, *just like* the suffering or cognition of individual innocent humans, *and thus* morally pertinent. The above-horizon attempt to reach for and include particular examples of *the non-human animals* within our moral community, to extend moral status to particular demonstrably worthy others like the Great Apes project, needs the presumption and demonstration of similitude, whether biochemical, emotional or sociocultural. However, that similitude *always* moves from an anchored, stable, human-modelled, centre outwards towards others in the moral periphery (*them*) and measures them against the standard we take ourselves to have set. And then, if there is deemed to be adequate resemblance, we must conceptually tow those Others back inside the perimeter of the moral community of equals, thus reifying that very same perimeter. Almost all current moral reasoning *about animals* operates by this gesture of conceptual extension, and yet the more potent undertow of this gesture is that it redeploys a strict boundary, an either-or, an us-them, a human and *non*. As I[36] and many others have argued, this gesture not only flattens to a single horizon the immense plurality – the difference – which all other forms of life in fact are, but continually excludes other others, thus requiring starting 'the ethics game' all over again. Another invisible mechanism is that each time it is deployed, this entire apparatus recertifies the moral standing *of the human animal* thus, maintaining a background moral hierarchy, despite appearing to be aiming for equality.

Moreover, some theorists have argued that this entire approach is a non-starter because what matters, morally, is not this or that isolated morally relevant feature *in* this or that individual animal, or *in* this or that keystone species, but complex nested holons of eco-relations: chunks of life big enough to continue to *be* alive, in all their complex vitality, a vitality in no way measurable according to some feature of any isolated human individual or a general property said to inhere in the human. Marc Bekoff's late onset apprehensions even of his prior involvement in the Great Ape Animal Project is telling:

> People often ask whether 'lower' nonhuman animals such as fish or dogs perform sophisticated patterns of behaviour that are usually associated with 'higher'

nonhuman primates. . . . In my view, these are misguided questions . . . because animals have to be able to do what they need to do in order to live in their own worlds. . . . I want to reemphasize that the use of the words 'higher' and 'lower' and activities such as line drawing to place different groups of animals 'above' and 'below' others are extremely misleading and fail to take into account the lives and worlds of the animals themselves.[37]

Even in the sub-domain of ethics known as animal ethics – sites of moral concern that are, after all, very much *like* us – we see a concern arising on the edges of ethical labour over the intellectual appropriateness of deploying the normative repertoire we have inherited: doing 'animal ethics' using animalesque concepts and styles of reasoning is like slicing at water with a hammer.

Plant ethics

Why would an ethicist persist in this vein and try to 'do plant ethics'? There are a number of good reasons. Plants are so crucially important to the health and vitality of all other living beings on this planet that working up some kind of theoretically sound protectorate and deriving a policy of conservation on their behalf by way of that protectorate is prudent. But, if the reason we care about plants (trees, for instance) is because they perform the vital service of making oxygen for us, then the protection need not specify anything more precise than safeguarding a certain minimum amount of CO-fixing biomass. From a less crass angle, we might want to defend the view that human-induced plant species loss – biodiversity loss – of orchids, sequoias and grasses is just as egregious as it is for polar bears, tuna and newts, and that if we have a duty to mitigate with respect to the latter, then we also have a duty to mitigate with respect to the former. Yet, another intelligible angle is the possibility that individual plants – trees, grassland communities, potted jade plants – have a kind of dignity and integrity, or can be harmed in some non-trivial way, or enjoy a kind of well-being when cared for, and as such, are as worthy of our moral care and considerability as any comparably complex individual animal creature. This is a view that is expressed in the skill of the avid gardener and also enshrined in several national constitutions (Switzerland, Ecuador). However, one attempts to angle one's justificatory motivation, it should come as no surprise to hear that even the relatively few ethical theorists who have been 'working on plants' admit that 'granting moral standing to plants remains a difficult endeavor at this stage'.[38] Any humanist (animal) ethics is really not going to work for plants because plants *really* are not animals.

I said a bit earlier that thinking-with-animal-thinking is an obstacle to ethicality in two senses. The first sense is that it has a mechanism which actually prevents us, as Levinas might say, from being confronted by the ostensible object of ethical concern: the 'irreducible difference between the worldhood of other existences and that of human beings'.[39] We saw how that was increasingly true with other-than-human-animals as they looked or acted less and less like us, and if one takes a good hard look at the plant kingdom, one sees it would be even more true there. Perhaps impossible. 'By considering morphogenic forces embodied in biophysical forms and organic performances of plants, it can be shown that plants exhibit completely original features that make them incommensurable with animals'.[40] We can never arrive even in the vicinity of the worldhood of plants if we set out equipped with the sorts of ideas that can only orient themselves, and behave, like an animal body does: 'the animal seems to stand more as a theoretical block than a useful reference for the moral consideration of plants'.[41]

My interest in 'plant ethics' has as its point of departure this very impasse. Although I care very much about plants (possibly more than anyone I know), I am drawn to the work of thinking-about-plants-ethically as a philosopher – that is, for what this work, done differently, might actually accomplish for thinking itself. How might 'plant ethics' cause a mutation in our dominant conceptual habits, given, as we have already established, that such a mutation is sometimes required: 'Because of their literally outstanding nature, plants require a completely new ethical approach'?[42] The second sense, therefore, in which 'animal ethics' is an obstacle to ethicality is that it is incapable of provoking such a mutation. When we automatically deploy *as* our ethical thoughts, that animal thought-body repertoire of concepts, we miss out on an occasion by which thought itself might *become*. A condition for the creation of concepts is the appearance of a genuinely new problem. The genuine heterogeneity of plant and animal modes of existence means that plant ethics *is* a new problem for ethics and ethical thinking. The inadequacy of animal-based or animal-quality ethics for discovering and grounding our obligation to vegetal life is a unique problem in need of its own concepts. And so, the conferring of moral standing for plants cannot pass with, or through the animal referent, for if it does, it not only misses the mark entirely (plants), but it bypasses the moment or site immanent to the active and reactive force relations that we are, or do, as thinking-things-thinking where there might arise from our (so to speak) *pluripotent ethical-conceptual stem cells* a mutation in ethical thought.

And insofar as the becoming of thought enables us *to respond* more subtly and vitally to the full array of *what is* that presents itself to us *as* questions of value and meaning, then this becoming of thought – *a completely new approach* – is an ethical event as well. And, if this becoming of thought takes place by way of fully exposing our morally considering selves to planthood as far as possible on its own terms (a sort of vegetal moral pedagogy), then the outcome just might be an ethical event of ethics: the *becoming* of our very 'moral' subjectivity as 'a free, anonymous and nomadic singularity which traverses men as well as plants and animals independently of the matter of their individuation and the forms of their personality'.[43] Pouteau spies the same radical potential:

> Finally, history seems to be making a feed-back loop: plant domestication was the foundational act of agriculture and moral consideration of plants is now making this foundational act a matter of conscious, cognitive comprehensiveness ... it is proposed that, as a mirror-image, the moral consideration of plants may involve a mental revolution potentially as paramount as the 'Neolithic revolution'.[44]

Active exposure: Becoming, becoming-plant

'Becoming' is the term Deleuze and Guattari use to name the process by which a primordially differentiating reality enters into compositions and decompositions, giving rise to 'another power'. What is this *other power*? The capacity to mutate; to be or do something other than what one is or does: to *differenciate*. In *A Thousand Plateaus*, Deleuze and Guattari list various becomings: becoming-woman, becoming-child, becoming-animal, becoming-molecular, becoming-imperceptible and becoming-plant. Either these list mere variants on a more fundamental category of becoming, or they are also meant to name *hétérotopiques* becomings: *genuinely other* other-powers given rise to when 'woman' or 'animal' or 'plant' enter into novel compositions. Given the central role that the concept of difference plays in Deleuze and Guattari's thought, it is likely that each of these becomings names a unique capacity.

What would an endeavour *to become* involve? We are instructed as to what it isn't: 'Do not look for a resemblance or analogy.'[45] *Becoming-dog* does not mean you imitate a dog but 'make your organism enter into composition with something else in such a way that the particles emitted from the aggregate thus composed will be canine as a function of the relation of movement and rest, or of molecular proximity, in which they can enter.' This *something else* 'can be quite varied, and be more or less directly related to the animal in question.'[46]

What, then of becoming-plant? Although Deleuze and Guattari did not elaborate on this mode of becoming, we know what it doesn't involve: we don't literally unite our bodies 'with' a plant or impersonate plants like some sort of photosynthetic circus. Put positively, and in light of the project at hand, we can infer that the *becoming-plant* of our animalesque forms and habits of thought would enter into composition with *something else* – something absolutely different, for instance, plant forms and habits – in such a way that the conceptual or thinking *particles we emit* from that composition would express another power: the singular qualities of *vegetality qua* forms and habits of thought.

The next question, then, is: What are these singular qualities of vegetality? What exactly makes 'plants radically and unconditionally different from animals'?[47] What is the distinct 'worldhood of plants'[48] to which we should expose ourselves in order to *become*? I am most interested in what current sciences (botanists, biophysicists, developmental biologists, ecologists) have to say about that based on their systematic, longitudinal assessments of those very questions. And then, bringing those discoveries into direct, productive proximity with philosophy: exposing our concepts (especially our normative concepts) and ways of thinking (especially our valuing) to that other version of being. This is a 'hermeneutic new realism' in the tradition of Goethe and Jakob von Uexküll. It embodies a commitment to 'finding' the significance of plants that does not go by way of an external referent like God or humans – that is, looking for empirical evidence of 'intelligence' or 'capacity for feeling' or 'higher order intentionality' – it passes immediately to the natural forms that are internal to plants; readily on display in plant life itself. This approach reveals the details of the many non-superficial ways that sessile vegetal existence differs from the kingdom *Animalia*.[49]

I wish to now focus the discussion on plant body form: the radically non-animal developmental plans of plants; their cellular and bodily symmetries and asymmetries. In the next section, I will report from scientific findings on plant morphogenesis, noting the uniqueness of this vegetal characteristic by comparison with the same in animal cells and bodies. The point of scavenging from natural science and inserting 'data' into philosophy is neither to reify an empirical approach, nor to 'depart from science but rather to raise science beyond its currently limited scope'.[50] The *departure* I am interested in is a becoming-plant: not simply by way of informatic description *of* plant cell growth and morphology that we read here and think *about*, but by way of direct exposure of our thinking *to* what plants are and do. As a Spinozist knows, this doesn't mean we have to stop theorizing and go hang out with the lawn and trees outside. Recall that the vegetal *something* with which we enter into composition does not 'even have to have a localizable relation' to any particular plant or plant kind:[51] it could simply involve an exposure event – mental or physical – to a powerfully strange quality strongly manifested in, or by, plantness: in this case, the peculiar symmetry and asymmetry of plant embodiment. That departure just might be a deterritorialization of our conceptual-thinking animal form as it *becomes vegetal*. A concept is, after all, an act. A new or deformed concept is a different act.

Finally, what is of real interest and value in this new naturalist Deleuzian hermeneutic is the actualization of a latent power *in* and *as* thought – thought itself changing its force patterns; thinking itself expressing *another power*. A becoming-plant of thought is, as I argued above, an ethical event. It is first an ethical event *appropriate to* vegetal life: 'an ethics oriented toward and arising from plants [which] would preclude human self-recognition in and projection onto the world of the flora, or, more positively, would entail an affirmation of the irreducible difference between this world and that of human beings.'[52] And it is also an ethical event insofar as it is a successful occasion for the emergence and free circulation of the meaningfulness of life itself. 'The power of life, a vital power that cannot be confined within the species, environment or path of a particular diagram. Is not the force that comes from outside a certain idea of life, a certain vitalism?'[53]

Plant bodies and living: Morphogenesis

Molecular biologists working with plants in a laboratory isolate mutant cell lines, introduce these into living organisms at germination, and track the results through developmental studies: embryogenesis and morphogenesis. The technique of tampering at the level of cells and genes has revealed the presence of extraordinarily complex, multi-level mechanisms in plant development that would not otherwise be apparent. This work has recently raised an entirely new set of questions about the precise relationship between genetic information (coding for protein synthesis and amino acids) and the concrete volumetric orientation living plants must eventually manifest. In the domain of molecular plant biology, the stories about how DNA and RNA determine *which* components will appear and *how much* matter a part or an entity will eventually be comprised of, have been fairly well worked out, but not the stories about '*how the spatial expression of these genes is controlled*:[54] What *are* the spatial ordering occasions, from germination and 'early embryogenesis, stomatal development, and ground tissue formation in the root'?[55] How *do* plant cells increasingly differentiate in terms of their symmetries? 'An important and exciting question is why are new axes formed only in lateral organs?'[56] How do leaves, all of which have a left-right axis, happen when leaves come out of stems and trunks which are always and only cylindrical, that is, have neither left nor right? How exactly is the 3-D, highly stabilized body plan such as 'Old Tijikko, a 9550-year-old Norway Spruce'[57] exhibits actually *accomplished*?

Spatial mechanics and significance

Plant architecture is currently the 'hottest area of plant developmental biology'.[58] Mechanistic explanations of organisms are the most common in current biological sciences. 'Mechanism is (in part) the view that to explain the properties of a complex system, one appeals to the causal capacities and relations of its parts.'[59] In other words, what happens happens due to the powers contained within atomistic self-regulating entities. Current thinking on plant architecture is that the formal elaboration of organisms – their shape – *is* under genetic control ('patterning genes' and 'transcription cascades'[60] controlling for the functional protein 'auxin' is where most of the current bets lie[61]) and it is just a matter of time before the molecular pathways are mapped. Yet, can we look at this incredible 'natural secret' with fresh eyes and make sense of it with any other thoughts?

All higher plant bodies have only three organs: stem, root and leaf. This body originally develops from a pollinated seed, though it may be propagated by graft or pinning. The human body also begins from a rounded object, the fertilized egg. The first symmetry-breaking development within the embryo, whether animal or vegetal, happens along what is called the apical-basal axis (up-down). This axis, which organizes 'shoot or root fate',[62] arises in embryogenesis and is the result of the establishment of polarities: a symmetry breaking. But, how these chemical-mechanical polarities even get established in the non-polarized zygote in the first place 'remains enigmatic';[63] the 'initiation event' is 'largely unknown'.[64] The possibility that symmetry breaking gets going inside an organism by virtue of an external cue, possibly an entirely random one, cannot be ruled out. There is evidence that initial polarity in all living beings is formed in response to *external* gradients like the direction of light hitting the earth, or lines of gravity, or metallic gradients associated with the earth's patterns of longitude and latitude, or the location of the ovule relative to the female body in which the ovule is fertilized, or even the angle of entry of sperm (or pollen) into the spherical egg (or ovule).

The most maximally symmetrical object is a sphere: any plane that passes through its midpoint would still preserve its symmetry. Fertilization thus must involve a morphing from a sphere-like object into an elliptically shaped object having an up versus a down.[65] In the mature plant embryo, there are already distinct zones comprised of a first order cell polarity labelled SAM (the 'shoot apical meristem') and RAM (the 'root apical meristem') which exhibit 'differential sensitivity to auxin transport',[66] in other words, levels or zones of 'shoot indeterminacy'[67] where differenciation (the phenomenon being explained) is already somehow established. Throughout the life of the plant, certain cells are devoted to being 'ranged' along this apical-basal axis – that is, to continuing to reach up while others only ever reach down. The up and downness of plants is maintained or regulated by the stiff plant *cell wall*. The cellular division operation along this first and sustained polarity is one of elongation, establishing in the plant a permanent vertical axis for upwardness and downwardness divided exactly at the horizon of the earth. How is this like or unlike the spatialization of the animal embryo and later body? If the plant protoplasts are isolated from that plant cell, the embryo it develops will again be 'a sphere of tissue' and sensitive to *environmental cues*.[68] One speculation is that the external cell wall of all plant cells is a descendant of the original external wall of the zygote (like an infinite Moscow doll scaffolding remembering the gesture of the hand that shaped the first one), 'and therefore all plant cells inherit a determinant of outside identity'.[69] The human, whether in the early embryonic stage or at age 48, also enjoys an up-down axis. Like plants, we elongate along an up-down axis, and maintain that verticality all our lives. However, that verticality comes from deep within us – our spinal cord – rather than from the way that the pliable organ cells on our very outside – the skin – preserve an original 'environmental cue' of directionality.

We also have something like a midpoint, though it is not a point of immobilization, as if up to our waists in concrete or snow. And unlike plants, we aren't constrained to stay in that upward position. Even in an embryo state, we can twist into an L-shape or hang upside-down position. We sleep, swim, bathe, star-gaze, bobsled, fix the car, have sex and die as horizontal beings. We are not sessile and rooted. We are free. Our free motility depends upon, takes advantage of, and habituates in us as our mode of living, the forward-pressing, backward-ignoring adaxial-abaxial plane, the fact that our basality meets and pushes up from the surface of the earth rather than being below it; and the side-to-side swing of our left and our right. This is true from the micro (cellular) to the organismic (body) level: cell migration does not occur in plant embryogenesis whereas it is a key mechanism in animal development. Petrika points out that this makes 'regulated asymmetrical cell division of particular importance to plants'.[70]

The second symmetry development within the embryo, whether animal or vegetal, is radial. Gradients build up between the centre and the periphery (c-p) establishing in the plant a pull of outwardness against a point of inwardness. The overall morphological result is a concentric thickening.[71] A horizontal elongation is not the same as the vertical, however. There must be a greater 'radial than tangential velocity of growth'[72] towards the outside and a spreading of this thickening along an emerging arc so that the periphery becomes continuously rounded. Indeed, this c-p pathway exhibits a 'cellular pattern which commences with the division of a triangular cell and continues until a complete set of ten different cells, including new triangular cells, is formed among the descendants'.[73] Furthermore, while neither of these two primordial axes is determined by the other, the horizontal and vertical must become integrated, coordinated. In other words, two entirely separate and distinct planes of dynamic growth must enter into composition so as to build a wholly integrated 3-D plant body out of cylindrical stems and tapering roots.

Yet – and this is a crucial point – in the upper part of the plant, unlike the animal body, this coordination of symmetries does not lead the plant to have the same inside-outsideness.[74] Plants face only outward.[75] Stem and roots have continual cell growth in upward, downward, and outward *directions* (think of the laying down of yearly tree rings). In addition to these cellular actions, though, animals undergo another major shape change early on in embryogenesis. This change called gastrulation[76] consists in an invagination of the embryo and the creation of an actual space inside: an empty tube. This inner space is in fact an internalization of what was initially facing outward. The inside of animal bodies – mouth cavity, throat, oesophagus, stomach, intestines, anus – is the outside world now hanging through the inside, *as* inside. This mechanism of gastrulation is significant 'because it gives rise to . . . an actual dualistic state of being',[77] whereas plants 'are un-split beings (having neither inside nor outside),[78] i.e., they live as "non-topos" in an undivided, unlimited, non-centered state of being'.[79]

The leaves always develop last. An adaxial-abaxial axis (also called dorsal-ventral [dv]) orients a leaf in space front to back such that you could cut a plane right through its thickness from top to bottom and you would get two roughly equal parts: a front and a back. The leaf has a bilateral left-right axis (lr) such that you could fold it in half lengthwise, from tip to stem and you would get two roughly equal pieces: a left side and a right side. And, like the rest of the plant, leaves have an up-down apical-basal axis ordered tip to base such that you could fold it in half widthwise and have a roughly similarly shaped and sized top and bottom. But the leaf organ also has two new axes of symmetry not found elsewhere on the plant. The peculiarly complex spatial development of the leaf challenges the assumption that genes *within the cells* alone encode for these features, in other words, that the development of plant bodies is strictly 'lineage dependent'. Having a left and a right is *dependent upon* having a front and a back: 'Proteins encoded by these genes probably function to respond to *positional information* along the adaxial-abaxial axis.'[80] What the fact of the leaf form tells us is that the way an entity takes up positionality and spatiality is dependent upon other positions and spaces: that the architectures of beings are elaborations of the architectures of other existents. It is hypothesized that this is also true of the incredible array of floral morphologies: that the initiating factor driving the diversification of the shape of flowers were its insect pollinators.[81] These interpretations challenge the basic mechanistic paradigm that 'to explain the properties of a complex system, one appeals to the causal capacities and relations of its parts'.[82] What these findings suggest, by contrast, is that to explain the properties of complex systems one has to appeal to the causal capacities and relations of more than what is 'found inside' a living being: genes and their mutations; proteins and their functions. Plants thrive only insofar as they are wide open, totally vulnerable to what happens to it. A permanent self-shaping relation to what is alien, other, outside – in this case, to a line of differenciating force – *is* a pronounced feature of vegetal ontology.[83]

Though the lower part of a plant is dominated by cylindricality, in the mature leaf you won't find a centre around which a radial pattern spirals. This high up in the vegetal body plan circles and spheres are found in fruiting bodies, seeds and flowers, and in an astonishing geometry of expression,[84] that is, parts having to do with making another embryo. Finally in some plants, there is a fifth plane: chirality or 'spiral phyllotaxy' (sp)[85] which is a complex of radial, lengthening upward and dorsality whereby branches or leaves or parts of flowers twist up and around. The total number of axes of symmetry any plant can exhibit is five.[86] Animal bodies can also exhibit all five of these axes. However, the ratio and distribution of these regions differ. While plants, especially angiosperms, are dominated by central-peripheral axis (or radial symmetry) and apicality, or elongation upward and downward, animals, especially mammals, are dominated by the adaxial-abaxial (front-back, anterior-posterior) and left-right planes. And, this leftness and rightness distributed *throughout* the animal body plan: two ears, two kidneys, two gluteus maxima, two big toes, whereas the leftness and rightness of plants are constrained to its extremities. However, perfect bilaterality is not preserved within our extremities: the hand or foot, those parts of us which also happen to be capable of an exceptionally high degree of activity (being affected in many ways and affecting in many others). An 'opposable thumb' makes our hands the furthest degree of symmetry breaking from the fertilized egg.

This is interestingly true, too, of leaves. In a mature plant leaf, there is actually asymmetry where once there was uniformity: the front and back and asymmetrical, the top and bottom are asymmetrical, and the midpoint outwards are also asymmetrical. So we can say it loses its uniformity and/or asymmetry itself must develop (different than a privation of symmetry). Axes of asymmetry (gradients which do not distribute equally on both sides) must build up.[87] As both animal and vegetal life develops, it deviates more and more from a simple spatial plan and is able to express a degree of singularity: to become an individual. This singularity (and correlate sensitivity; responsiveness) is a result of increased symmetry breaking – that is, a gradual privation of the initial state of maximum symmetry and stability. Or, to put it in more Deleuzian and positive terms, the individual plant testifies to the fact that vegetal and animal bodies are co-constituted by order and disorder out of, and likely towards, what Primo Levi named the 'primordial asymmetry of all things'.[88]

Conclusion: An open how

It is noteworthy that the oldest living individual things are plants. And that their longevity is of an order of magnitude greater than that found among the oldest living members of animality: tortoises, geoducks, koi, sea urchins, quahogs, ocean sponges and bowhead whales. The longest-living animals are aquatic. Their lives are stuck in water. Plant bodies are even more constrained: stuck in dirt and stuck in one position. But, despite this constraint, the peculiar spatial ontologies of the plant kingdom's development – that all of a plant faces outward, that it really does lack an 'inner life', that it is completely unfree in the earth, that plants' impressive capacity for geometrical morphological variation is wholly dependent on externals – seem to enable a profound vitality, interconnectedness and resilience.

Could we take up that model and express it: *becoming-plant*? Could we figure out a way to make our concepts, our ethical norms, even our bodily sensibilities face only outward, and yet in all directions at once? What productive deformations, for instance, could the concept of justice undergo if we insisted it, too, look in all directions at once?

Could we, tutored by the example of plant bodily being, experience intense positional vulnerability and yet come to know and value ourselves as singular through that very impingement? What would a concept like dignity do, or feel like, if it was absolutely rooted in incapacity, rather than capacity, especially as those capacities dwindle? Could we respond differently in ethically charged situations if our mental and physical propensity for binary action was pushed to the edges of what we do, what we say, and curled like a spiral? Could we live a good life with, and as an 'indeterminate ontology, [without] clear spatial and temporal boundaries and ... never be conceived of as complete'?[89] Could we sense the capacity for immense variation that waits at our extremities rather than in our core, our egos, and develop a new tonal range of virtues that know nothing of our 'innermost selves'? Could we welcome disorder with gratitude and grace, following the plant's model of axes destabilizations? To learn to be skillfully and positively affected by random externals, we would need concepts whose own bodily plan and range of action is activated not in a gesture of 'autonomous choosing' but in a gesture of exposure.

The giant ethical question that confronts us all, perhaps more now than ever, is, does life even matter? If we prefer to answer yes, then we have some sort of stakes and duty in light of that. This entails that we be ruthless in our assessment of whether our ways of being contribute to, or detract from, the capacity of life *to matter*. One corner of our being to aim that scrutiny is at our forms of thought-being. Does *how* our thinking happens actually contribute to a life of vitality, interconnectedness and resilience? If the answer is no, or even *maybe not*, then we really do need to change our minds.

Notes

1 A preliminary version of this essay appeared in French under the title 'Les Différentes Symétries des Plantes', in the journal *Chimères* (issue 82, 2014, 165–8) © Éditions érès.
2 'The concept is an *act* of thought.' Gilles Deleuze and Félix Guatarri, *What Is Philosophy?*, 21. My emphasis.
3 Ibid., 19.
4 *Hétérotopique* is the term for the non-same primordial character of reality I borrow from Foucault: 'there is a worse kind of disorder than that of the incongruous ... I mean the disorder in which a large number of possible orders glitter separately ... in such a state, things are "laid", "placed", "arranged" in sites so very different from one another that it is impossible to find a common place beneath them all' (Michel Foucault, *The Order of Things*, 48).
5 Jay Lampert, 'Limit, Ground, Judgment ... Syllogism', 187–9.
6 Primo Levi, *The Black Hole of Auschwitz*, 42.
7 'Every body, whether human, animal, vegetable or otherwise might have been considered inanimate, has an idea of everything that happens in and to it. This idea constitutes its mind. Every body imagines' (Spinoza, *Ethics*, Part II, P13 schol). 'The order of actions and passions of our body is, by nature, at one with the order of actions and passions of the mind' (Ibid. Part III, P2 schol).
8 Gilles Deleuze and Félix Guattari, *What Is Philosophy?*, 36.

9 This intra-conceptual spatio-temporal character of territories of intelligibility draws directly from Spinoza's understanding of bodies in *The Ethics* Part II, Proposition 13, Lemma 1 through 7 and is intended to connect with Foucault's analysis of 'the diagram', the name he gives to the operation or 'functioning' by which pre-linguistic forces ('statements') take up objects and carve out discursive fields ('spatio-temporal multiplicities' characterized by different forms and layers of modes of power (see Gilles Deleuze, *Foucault*, 34–44).
10 This is not dissimilar to what we hear Foucault claiming about the way that power relations take up particular forms and those forms are apparent at all scales of the sociocultural reality: he named these power-patterns 'dispositifs'.
11 What Deleuze calls 'hegemonic images of thought' must be similar to what I am assessing here. And Foucault, though he did not speak about regimes of power *in or as* concepts themselves would not have disagreed with this assessment as yet further micro-sites of the operation of 'sovereign regimes of thought'.
12 Serge Latouche, *Décoloniser L`imaginaire : La Pensée Créative Contre L'économie de L'absurde*, 23. Italics added. 'How can these regimes of thought, the architecture of our fundamental imaginary, the model of our basic concepts, be decolonized, disassembled, reassembled according to a different plan?' (my translation).
13 Gilles Deleuze, *Nietzsche and Philosophy*, 47.
14 Gilles Deleuze, *Difference and Repetition*, 209–21.
15 Gilles Deleuze and Félix Guattari, *What Is Philosophy?*, 27.
16 Ibid.
17 Ibid.
18 Michel Foucault, 'The Subject and Power', 225.
19 As I will argue in the next section, they can and should, in some cases, be altered; and this mutability of thought – the amenability of thinking to an event of thought – is an operation in which we can, and often should, intervene.
20 Deleuze, *Foucault*, 119.
21 His Holiness the XIV Dalai Lama, *Transforming the Mind*, 4.
22 Evan Thompson, 'Contemplative Neuroscience as an Approach to Volitional Consciousness', 187–97.
23 His Holiness the XIV Dalai Lama, *Transforming the Mind*, 5.
24 Karen Houle, 'Animal, Vegetable, Mineral'.
25 Pulp Fiction (1994, Miramax), written and directed by Quentin Tarantino.
26 A Story of Deception (Tate Modern, 2006), p. 12.
27 See Arthur Koestler, *Janus*.
28 See Timothy Morton, *Hyperobjects*.
29 Andrew Biro, 'The Good Life in the Greenhouse?', 36.
30 The Existential Analytic (Kierkegaard, Derrida, Heidegger, Levinas) makes similar remarks about grief and death. These are not problems we can solve: they are conditions we must face and endure. Entirely different qualities and kinds of relations are sketched here; different virtues are called out or called for.
31 Andrew Biro, 'The Good Life in the Greenhouse?', 36.
32 Ibid., my emphasis. Biro introduces from James Howard Kunstler a new concept: 'the long emergency'. This concept can anchor a genuine shift in thinking and thinking-about 'the environment' because it is a nearly, but not quite, unthinkable paradox: something that is urgent (now) *and* something that is slow (not quite now; in a while; coming along). The sense that accompanies this concept is similarly almost nonsensical, but it nevertheless can register as meaningful: the planet needs us to

do something radical and absolutely fully committed-to now *and* it needs us to be careful, to slow down, to look out onto the longest possible horizon of futurality. Its nearly paradoxical conjunctive form is a better term than 'deadline' with which to consider the question of appropriate political tempo since it does not give rise to the defeatist and self-serving disjunct: it's too late *and* it's not yet happening.
33 Ibid., 20. He notes that many counsel that, in order to make climate change feel like an issue that matters to more people, it has to appear on their 'emotional radar', to become 'ours' because 'it means something valuable in their own terms'.
34 See Karen Houle, *Complexity, Responsibility, Abortion*.
35 Yves Besson, 'Une histoire d'exigences'.
36 See Karen Houle, 'Infinite, Indifferent Kinship'.
37 Marc Bekoff, 'Animal Rights', 152.
38 Sylvie Pouteau, 'Providing Grounds', 154.
39 Michael Marder, 'The Life of Plants', 260–1.
40 Sylvie Pouteau, 'Providing Grounds', 154.
41 Ibid., 155.
42 Ibid., 154.
43 Gilles Deleuze, *The Logic of Sense*, 107.
44 Sylvie Pouteau, 'Providing Grounds', 158. In this article, Pouteau explores what the moral concept of 'integrity' might come to mean once it is actually exposed to the complex facticity of vegetal life. It cannot and does not retain a resemblance to the concept of integrity as we apply it to an animal body or animal life.
45 Gilles Deleuze and Félix Guatarri, *A Thousand Plateaus*, 275.
46 Ibid., 274.
47 Sylvie Pouteau, 'Providing Grounds', 155.
48 Michael Marder, 'The Life of Plants', 264.
49 I have used this approach with plant signalling. See Karen Houle, 'Devenir Plante'.
50 Sylvie Pouteau, 'Beyond "Second Animals"', 18–19.
51 Gilles Deleuze and Félix Guatarri, *A Thousand Plateaus*, 274.
52 Michael Marder, 'The Life of Plants', 260–1.
53 Gilles Deleuze, *Foucault*, 92–3.
54 Masao Tasaka, 'From Central-Peripheral to Adaxial-Abaxial', 549.
55 J. J. Petricka et al., 'Symmetry Breaking in Plants', 11.
56 Masao Tasaka, 'From Central-Peripheral to Adaxial-Abaxial', 548.
57 'Old Tijikko'.
58 Yonghong Wang and Jiayang Li, 'Molecular Basis of Plant Architecture', 253.
59 Denis M. Walsh, 'Mechanism, Emergence and Miscibility', 44.
60 See Moriyah Zik and Vivian F. Irish, 'Flower Development'.
61 See John L. Bowman and Sandra K. Floyd, 'Patterning and Polarity'; Cm. Liu, Zh. Xu and N. H. Chua, 'Auxin Polar Transport'.
62 Masao Tasaka, 'From Central-Peripheral to Adaxial-Abaxial', 548.
63 A. Hudson, 'Development of Symmetry in Plants', 351.
64 See Steffen Lau et al., 'Early Embryogenesis in Flowering Plants'.
65 Though I don't consider it in this chapter, it is also true of flowers. The ancestral form of all flowers was radial symmetry. Evolutionary diversification enabled first a bilateral (l-r) axis, then a dorsal-ventral axis to occur. One of the most 'striking aspects of flowering plants is the diversity of floral symmetry' (Lena Hileman, 'Trends in flower symmetry evolution', 1648).
66 John L. Bowman and Sandra K. Floyd, 'Patterning and Polarity in Seed Plant Shoots', 81.

67 Yonghong Wang and Jiayang Li, 'Molecular Basis of Plant Architecture', 253.
68 A. Hudson, 'Development of Symmetry in Plants', 356.
69 Ibid., 355.
70 J. J. Petricka et al., 'Symmetry Breaking in Plants', 2.
71 See T. Laux et al., 'Genetic Regulation'.
72 D'Arcy Wentworth Thompson, *On Growth and Form*, 279.
73 P. W. Barlow, H.B. Luck and J. Luck, 'The Natural Philosophy of Plant Form', 1141.
74 See A. Hudson, 'Development of Symmetry in Plants'.
75 Sylvie Pouteau, 'Providing Grounds', 156.
76 Sylvie Pouteau, 'Beyond "Second Animals"', 19.
77 Ibid.
78 G.W.F. Hegel, *Philosophy of Nature*, 307.
79 Sylvie Pouteau, 'Beyond "Second Animals"', 20.
80 Masao Tasaka, 'From Central-Peripheral to Adaxial-Abaxial', 549.
81 See Wenheng Zhang, Elena M. Kramer and Charles C. Davis, 'Floral Symmetry Genes'.
82 Denis M. Walsh, 'Mechanism, Emergence and Miscibility', 44.
83 Epigenetics is corroborating this explanatory shift. See Pilar Cubas, Coral Vincent and Enrico Coen, 'An Epigenetic Mutation'.
84 See Paul R. Neal, Amots Dafri and Martin Giurfa, 'Floral Symmetry'.
85 A. Hudson, 'Development of Symmetry in Plants', 349.
86 Masao Tasaka, 'From Central-Peripheral to Adaxial-Abaxial', 548–550.
87 A. Hudson, 'Development of Symmetry in Plants', 345–73.
88 Primo Levi, *The Black Hole of Auschwitz*, 45.
89 Sylvie Pouteau, 'Providing Grounds', 156.

Bibliography

Barlow, P. W., H.B. Luck and J. Luck. 'The Natural Philosophy of Plant Form: Cellular Autoreproduction as a Component of a Structural Explanation of Plant Form'. *Annals of Botany* 88 (2001): 1141–52.

Bekoff, Marc. 'Animal Rights and the Great Ape Animal Project'. In *The Animal Ethics Reader*, edited by Susan J. Armstrong and Richard G. Botzler, 2nd ed., 151–56. New York: Routledge, 2008.

Biro, Andrew. 'The Good Life in the Greenhouse? Autonomy, Democracy, and Citizenship in the Anthropocene'. *Telos* 172 (fall 2015): 15–37.

Bowman, John L. and Sandra K. Floyd. 'Patterning and Polarity in Seed Plant Shoots'. *Annual Review of Plant Biology* 59 (2008): 67–88. doi:10.1146/annurev.arplant.57.032905.105356.

Cubas, Pilar, Coral Vincent and Enrico Coen, 'An Epigenetic Mutation Responsible for Natural Variation in Floral Symmetry'. *Nature* 401 (1999): 157–61.

Deleuze, Gilles. *Difference and Repetition*. Translated by Paul Patton. New York: Columbia University Press.

Deleuze, Gilles. *Foucault*. Translated by Séan Hand. Minneapolis: University of Minnesota Press, 1986.

Deleuze, Gilles. *The Logic of Sense*. Translated by M. Lester with C. Stivale. New York: Columbian University Press, 1990, 107.

Deleuze, Gilles. *Nietzsche and Philosophy*. Translated by Hugh Tomlinson. New York: Columbia University Press, 2006.
Deleuze, Gilles and Félix Guattari. *A Thousand Plateaus: Capitalism and Schizophrenia*. Translated by B. Massumi. Minneapolis, MN: University of Minnesota Press, 1987.
Deleuze, Gilles and Félix Guattari. *What is Philosophy?* New York: Columbia University Press, 1994.
Foucault, Michel. *The Order of Things*. Translated by D.W. Harding. New York: Pantheon, 1970.
Foucault, Michel. 'The Subject and Power'. In *Michel Foucault: Beyond Structuralism and Hermeneutics*, edited by Hubert Dreyfus and Paul Rabinow, 2nd ed., 208–26. Chicago, IL: University of Chicago Press, 1983.
Hegel, G.W.F. *Philosophy of Nature: Encyclopedia of the Philosophical Sciences, Part II*. Translated by A.V. Miller. Oxford: Oxford University Press, 2004.
Hileman, Lena. 'Trends in Flower Symmetry Evolution Revealed Through Phylogenetic and Developmental Genetic Advances'. *Philosophical Transactions of the Royal Society B* 369: 1648, Published 23 June 2014. doi:10.1098/rstb.2013.0348, http://rstb.royalsoc ietypublishing.org/content/369/1648/20130348.full.
Houle, Karen. 'Animal, Vegetable, Mineral: Ethics as Extension or Becoming?' *Symposium* 19, no. 2 (2015): 37–56.
Houle, Karen. *Complexity, Responsibility, Abortion: Toward a New Image of Ethical Thinking*. Lanham, MD: Lexington, 2014.
Houle, Karen. 'Devenir Plante'. *Chimères* 76 (2012): 183–94.
Houle, Karen. 'Les Différentes Symétries des Plantes'. Translated by Anne Querrien. *Chimères* 82 (2014): 155–68.
Houle, Karen. 'Infinite, Indifferent Kinship'. *C Magazine (Toronto)* 107 (2010): 12–23.
Hudson, A. 'Development of Symmetry in Plants'. *Annual Review of Plant Physiology and Plant Molecular Biology* 51 (2000): 349–70.
Koestler, Arthur. *Janus: A Summing Up*. New York: Random House, 1978.
Lampert, Jay. 'Limit, Ground, Judgment . . . Syllogism'. In *Hegel and Deleuze: Together Again for the First Time*, edited by Karen Houle and Jim Vernon, 183–203. Evanston, IL: Northwestern, 2013.
Latouche, Serge. *Décoloniser L'imaginaire : La Pensée Créative contre L'économie de L'absurde*. Lyon: Parangon, 2003.
Lau, Steffen, Daniel Slane, Ole Herud, Jixiang Kong and Gerd Jürgens. 'Early Embryogenesis in Flowering Plants: Setting Up the Basic Body Pattern'. *Annual Review of Plant Biology* 63 (2012): 483–506. First published online as a Review in Advance on January 3, 2012. doi:10.1146/annurev-arplant-042811-105507.
Laux et al. 'Genetic Regulation of Embryonic Pattern Formation'. *The Plant Cell* 16 (Supplement 2004): 190–202.
Levi, Primo. *The Black Hole of Auschwitz*. Cambridge: Polity Press, 2005.
Liu, Cm, Zh. Xu and N. H. Chua. 'Auxin Polar Transport Is Essential for the Establishment of Bilateral Symmetry during Early Plant Embryogenesis'. *The Plant Cell* 5, no. 6 (June 1993): 621–30.
Marder, Michael. 'The Life of Plants and the Limits of Empathy'. *Dialogue* 51, no. 2 (2012): 259–73.
Morton, Timothy. *Hyperobjects: Philosophy and Ecology After the End of the World*. Minneapolis, MN: University of Minnesota Press, 2013.
Neal, Paul R., Amots Dafri and Martin Giurfa. 'Floral Symmetry and its Role in Plant-Pollinator Systems'. *Annual Review of Ecological Systems* 29 (1998): 345–73.

'Old Tijikko'. Last modified 12 April 2016 https://en.wikipedia.org/wiki/Old_Tjikko
Pouteau, Sylvie. 'Beyond 'Second Animals': Making Sense of Plant Ethics'. *Journal of Agricultural and Environmental Ethics* 27 (2014): 1–25.
Pouteau, Sylvie. 'Providing Grounds for Agricultural Ethics: The Wider Philosophical Significance of Plant Life Integrity'. In *Climate Change and Sustainable Development: Ethical Perspectives on Land Use and Food Production*, edited by Thomas Potthast and Simon Meisch, 154–9. Wageningen: EurSafe, 2012.
Spinoza, Benedict de. *Ethics*. Translated by G. H. R. Parkinson. Oxford: Oxford University Press, 2000.
Tasaka, Masao. 'From Central-Peripheral to Adaxial-Abaxial'. *Trends in Plant Science* 6, no. 12 (2001): 548–50.
Walsh, Denis M. 'Mechanism, Emergence and Miscibility: The Autonomy of Evo-Devo'. In *Functions: Selection and Mechanisms*, edited by Philippe Huneman, 43–65. Netherlands: Springer, 2013.
Wang, Yonghong and Jiayang Li. 'Molecular Basis of Plant Architecture'. *Annual Review of Plant Biology* 59 (2008): 253–79. doi:10.1146/annurev.arplant.59.032607.092902
Wentworth, Thompson D'Arcy. *On Growth and Form*. Cambridge: Cambridge University Press, 1961.
Zhang, Wenheng, Elena M. Kramer and Charles C. Davis. 'Floral Symmetry Genes and the Origin and Maintenance of Zygomorphy in a Plant-Pollinator Mutualism'. *PNAS* 107, no. 14 (2010): 6388–93.
Zik, Moriyah and Vivian F. Irish. 'Flower Development: Initiation, Differentiation, and Diversification'. *Annual Review of Cell and Developmental Biology* 19 (2003): 119–40. First published online as a Review in Advance on June 6, 2003 doi:10.1146/annurev.cellbio.19.111301.134635.

5

Back to earth!

A comparative study between Husserl's and Deleuze's cosmologies

Alain Beaulieu

Introduction

Edmund Husserl (1859-1938) and Gilles Deleuze (1925-95) are some of the few contemporary continental philosophers who incorporated cosmological questioning into their thought, thus renewing an old and partly lost way of seeing philosophy's task. The type of cosmological questioning they keep alive has a clear link with what has come to be known as posthumanism. Indeed, asking, as Husserl and Deleuze do, about our place in the universe, and more specifically about the cosmological status of planet earth, necessarily involves situating the earth in relation to other planets, other solar systems and potential non-terrestrial life forms. As such, it also involves relativizing our cosmic situation. These questions are timely as technological improvement and scientific discoveries will probably make our generation the first one ever to get the confirmation that inhabitants of the earth are not alone in the universe and that other living creatures exist elsewhere. This breakthrough takes place in a posthuman context where new questions are emerging: What is the earth? What is it to be an earthly creature? How do the non-terrestrial forces and entities affect the earth and its inhabitants?

The posthuman condition, therefore, finds a cosmological resonance,[1] and this chapter intends to study this condition by exploring Husserl's and Deleuze's[2] take on several cosmological issues. More precisely, this study explores Husserl's geostatic earth and Deleuze's geodynamic earth in order to elucidate the similarities and differences between both philosophers' reformations of the traditional speculative and transcendent cosmologies in favour of an immanent experience of the earth. The chapter begins with a discussion of Husserl's conception of the 'Ark-Earth' and segues to a presentation of Deleuze's 'cosmic earth'. This serves as the foundation for my analysis of Deleuze's and Guattari's critique of Husserl's earth, which the formers rather briefly formulated at the beginning of the chapter 'Geophilosophy' in *What Is Philosophy?*

Husserl

In his 1934 essay, 'The Originary Ark, the Earth, Does Not Move',[3] Husserl provides a geostatic view defending the immobility of the earth, which he considers more fundamental than its conditions of movement or rest. Doing so, Husserl bypasses modern science and its experimental method of observation in favour of an intuitive science, for example, phenomenology. It is important to provide some background to this short meditation by discussing Husserl's well-known book *The Crisis of European Sciences and Transcendental Phenomenology*, written between 1934 and 1937, and so overlapping with the Ark-Earth essay.

Crisis

In *Crisis*, Husserl suggests reconnecting with the Greek teleological and purely spiritual experience of *teoria* with the aim of neutralizing modern science and its empirical method. It is Galileo Galilei (1564–1642) whom Husserl recognizes as the chief proponent of modern science, and it is not surprising if we consider that Galileo was the scientist who, with the help of his telescope, paved the way for observational astronomy. His contribution to modern science and, more specifically, astronomy implies major discoveries such as the phases of Venus, Jupiter's moons and the sunspots. A few decades earlier, Nicolaus Copernicus (1473–1543) certainly made a determining astronomical discovery, namely, the heliocentric system, but this revolutionary discovery was made purely on mathematical grounds. It is Galileo who first used instruments of observation and applied the experimental method with the more or less explicit intention to become 'like masters and possessors of nature',[4] to use Descartes's famous assertion. This path taken by modern science, according to Husserl, initiated a deep crisis, which is symptomatic of current European sciences and their 'delirious' attempt to objectivize the *cosmos*, including the planets, which are now considered celestial objects whose motion is ready to be scientifically determined. The roots of the crisis are to be found in the misleading rationalism that objectifies nature and the world. The cure for Husserl, who for a moment becomes a 'doctor of civilization', lies in reconnecting phenomenology with the Greek teleological experience of science as *teoria*. The task of phenomenology as a rigorous science is not finite, for it does not look for definitive answers, exactitude or certainties. Rather, its task is infinite since constitution is a process destined to be ever unaccomplished.

The phenomenological problems of constitution cannot be solved by modern science. Conversely, Husserl posits that modern science goes against and indeed destroys the originary teleological spirit of science, which shall animate Western civilization. Reconnecting with the Greek sense of scientific teleology should reveal that modern science has been historically constituted, and for that reason it could not claim to have the last say on the 'truth'. In other words, modern science's regional take on truth jeopardizes the survival of a more universal truth, which is linked to wisdom and which pushes back the destructive aims of modernity.

Husserl's rhetoric of crisis can certainly be criticized, along with his sense of urgency, the idea of an increasing danger, and even a cultural devastation linked with the collapse of reason in the alleged time of crisis. After all, modern science is not utterly evil; it contributes to the advancement of humanity. Moreover, modern science dismantled many mythical conceptions, thereby contributing to mankind's maturity (in Kant's categories). Husserl is not particularly keen on the rationality of the Enlightenment, which he does not hesitate to consider a 'mistake'.[5] However, we must supplement it by saying that Husserl's critique of rationality does not lead to mere irrationality. Rather, it is an attempt to reconnect with what he considers to be a more fundamental experience of rationality, a reawakening to the Greek teleological *logos*, which Galileo and others disregarded and pushed back into the realm of useless abstractions.

In chapter 9, the lengthiest of the book, Husserl minutely explains his critique of Galileo who incarnates the modern project of objectivation of nature through empirical observation and life-world (*Lebenswelt*). From Galileo to Einstein, modern scientists missed the *telos* of science, which enables a connection with the life-world, a world that cannot be 'known' by the intellect or experienced by the senses: it can only be intuited. For as long as scientists fail to recognize the pre-predicative level of experience, says Husserl, they will remain prisoners of a false conception of evidence. For as long as the natural attitude prevails, European sciences will remain in the state of crisis.

Husserl distinguishes between three kinds of perceptions: subjective perceptions (such as personal feelings or desires), objective perceptions (such as natural laws), and perceptions that belong to the life-world. First, this distinction allows us to consider that knowledge is, for Husserl, nothing but a series of perceptions. And second, that the fundamental task of science is not only to relativize the false pretences of modern science but also to grant an epistemological right to the 'originary intuitions'[6] that pertain to the life-world.

This critique of modern science provides the necessary context for reading 'The Originary Ark, the Earth, Does Not Move'. Incidentally, Husserl's critique of modern science reveals his cosmological affectivity. Indeed, he does not target medicine, biology or chemistry, even if Claude Bernard, Dmitri Mendeleev or Charles Darwin did contribute to implementing the empirical method with their science. Rather, Husserl targets astronomy through Galileo in *Krisis* and Copernicus in 'The Originary Ark', perhaps to emphasize the opposition between the modern world view and a new cosmic view. After all, phenomenology makes the 'world' (and its constitution) one of its core concepts. It is as though Husserl saw himself as a philosopher-saviour while depicting phenomenology as the incarnation of a new world view, free from the natural attitude.

The earth as an Originary Ark (*Ur-Archè*)

In his essay 'The Originary Ark, the Earth, Does Not Move', Husserl asserts that all past cosmologists, whether geocentrist or heliocentrist (or Tycho Brahe's hybrid geo-heliocentric system), share something in common: they conceive the earth as a celestial body while missing a more fundamental aspect of the earth as 'originary Ark'. How are we to understand this notion? There is certainly a polysemy involved here as the Ark might refer to Noah's Ark as a metaphor for our cosmic ship; it might equally refer to the Greek *archè*, or 'basic principle'; or it might be linked with the adjective 'archaic' as synonymous with 'primordial' and 'ancestral'. In fact, Husserl's Ark-Earth implies all of the above. The Ark stands for a spaceship that carries the fundamental Greek and teleological principles of the European sciences. Husserl sums up these meanings in his 1934 essay when he considers the phenomenological earth not a celestial body but our originary living 'ground' (*Boden*).[7] The living bodies coexist with and are the extension of this centred ground.

Husserl's claim that the earth does not move is, of course, a provocation. Since Copernicus and Galileo, it has been established that the earth, being a celestial body, moves. *Eppur si muove* ('And yet it moves!'), Galileo secretly wrote after his trial where he was forced to disavow the heliocentric model. Indeed, the earth as a celestial body moves, and it moves quite fast: 465 millisecond for the rotation around its axis, and over 107,000 kilometres per hour for its revolution around the sun, without mentioning the 850,000 kilometres per hour rotation speed of our solar system around the centre of the Milky Way, which in turns travels across the universe at the speed of 2.3 million kilometres per hour. These movements are not perceptible by humans. It is as though the earth was not moving. Our daily experience demonstrates that the earth might not be at rest either. The sunrise and the sunset give us the impression that something is moving. However, if we ask our perceptions: 'What exactly is moving?' The answer: 'the sun revolves around the earth' is no less absurd, or no more meaningful, than the answer 'the earth revolves around the sun'. Based solely on our perceptions, then, the earth does not move since the absence of acceleration or deceleration gives the impression of an absence of movement. And it is not meaningless to consider that the earth is not at rest since we experience the passing of the sun in the sky. Thus, fundamentally, the earth for Husserl is neither moving nor at rest, it is rather an immobile ground. All of the movements and non-movements are relative to this immobile ground that renders them possible.

Husserl transposes to the Ark-Earth the undecidedness of movement for the perceptions. As a celestial body, the earth moves. But this natural view is methodologically bracketed (*épochè*) by the phenomenological reduction, and as a result the earth turns into an unmoving originary Ark. And it is in this sense that the earth does not move. This primordial phenomenological experience of the Ark-Earth corresponds to the fixed and stable Greco-European cultural ground we carry wherever we go, whether on the physical earth or beyond. Each and every experience of movement and rest is relative to this originary ground, which is also our immobile 'primitive home', considered by Husserl as more fundamental than any scientific view. In other words, both the Ptolemean and the Copernican systems are relative to the unmoving Ark-Earth, which is their universal common ground.

In his 1934 essay, Husserl suggests a series of eidetic variations: a flying bird, a pilot, an astronaut and a human living on another planet. All of them share the same intuitive reference system: the Ark-Earth from which all of the possible perceptions of the intuitive world originate. How are we to understand Husserl's originary Ark-

Earth, then? Husserl's original conception of the earth becomes clear when compared to previous ways of experiencing the earth:[8] a stable earth at the centre of the universe (Ptolemy), the earth that moves around the sun (Copernicus), and the moving bodies that depend on the frame of reference of the observer (Einstein).[9] For Husserl, the earth as Ark-Earth does not belong to any of these, for it is not a celestial body but rather a pre-scientific ground for the lived experiences and perceptions. Phenomenologically speaking, the earth is not a celestial body, *Körper*, but rather a lived experience, *Leib*, which is part of the ground of the life-world.

Even if a group of astronauts left the earth to land on another celestial body (in the 1934 essay, Husserl gives the examples of Venus and the Moon), their Ark-Earth would continue to be their immobile source of prejudices and perceptions. Modern astrophysicists tend to value solely the latest dominant perception while forgetting that the history of astronomy displays a series of conflicts of perceptions. Once put in their historical contexts, each of these perceptions is relatively valid, and there is no reason for Husserl to give priority to one perception (Copernicus's or Einstein's perception considered 'objective') over others (Ptolemy's, Plato's or Aristotle's considered *passé*). Rather, Husserl's pheno-cosmological view implies that all of these perceptions are relative to the static Ark-Earth. All of them did (and new ones will) contribute to the phenomenological constitution of the earth, that is, like any phenomenological task, to an infinite constitution oriented by a *telos*, forever remaining ahead of us. This constitution is also guided by the universal *logos* inherited from the Greeks, for which the quest for certainties represents only one possibility among others, perhaps the lowest on the pheno-epistemological scale.

Carrying this fundamental ground across the universe means that the Ark-Earth has no boundaries. From a modern scientific point of view, the earth is a celestial body located in a certain space and time,[10] but for Husserl the originary Ark is spatio-temporally inescapable. Humans will carry it everywhere they go with no possibility for them to engage with a different *telos* or with a new *logos*, distinct from the one determined once and for all by the Greeks. For Husserl, then, it is as though the history of cosmology went from geocentrism, where the earth as a celestial body is at the centre, to heliocentrism, where the sun as a celestial body is at the centre, to an intentionalist egocentrism, where a shared geostatic earth now becomes intersubjectively and historically constituted.

Weightlessness

There is an experience, cosmological for that matter, which might support Husserl's views regarding the existence of an immobile Ark-Earth: the experience of the living body in weightlessness. Over the last decades, a series of weightlessness experiences has been performed and studied.[11] These experiments in zero-gravity environment show that the classical conception of space is misleading in the sense that there is no natural or *a priori* sensation of 'left', 'right', 'up', and 'down'. This research proves that while experiencing weightlessness, the body creates a new sense of orientation. Husserl might qualify it as pre-scientific, pre-subjective, intuitive and kinesthetic. That is to say, as a living experience.

On earth, the force of gravity provides a sense of space significant for locomotion, posture and orientation. The gravitational force on earth provides spatial references, but these spatial references do not exist in weightlessness. The vast majority of space travellers, or those who experience weightlessness in controlled environments on earth, have difficulty to adapt. A study showed that in 98 per cent of cases, subjects experience 'impairment of spatial perception' (ISP), such as feeling upside down, dizziness and illusory orientation of self, accompanied by physiological reactions such as nausea and gastrointestinal symptoms.[12] In most cases, subjects will adapt to weightlessness and the ISP will pass, but only after a certain period of time, which varies from one subject to another. A similar situation occurs in other extreme environments such as high mountain climbing or scuba diving where most of the subjects suffer from high altitude or pressure. While most take more time to adapt, few do not suffer significantly from altitude or pressure.

Of particular interest with regard to weightlessness are the remaining 2 per cent who defy the norm, do not suffer from the ISP, and quickly adapt to weightlessness, reacting as though they never left the physical ground. More research in weightlessness needs to be conducted to understand the treatment of sensory information, brain functions, and, more specifically, the role of the inner ear, which is responsible for balance and orientation in the three-dimensional gravitational space. However, one can still ask: Do these 2 per cent of people who do not suffer from the ISP carry something similar to Husserl's Ark-Earth with them? Is there a phenomenological explanation for these 2 per cent of people who experience weightlessness without the ISP? If these 2 per cent are endowed with physico-biological 'super inner ears', then the phenomenological explanation, due to its methodological reduction of the natural world, cannot be taken into account. Until the existence of these super inner ears as the sole cause of the absence of the ISP has been proven, the possibility of these 2 per cent of people carrying Husserl's Ark-Earth with them remains valid. Perhaps the possibility of a combination between special inner ears and the Ark-Earth can also be considered. Of course, in the context of weightlessness experiments, the Ark-Earth phenomenon remains quite rudimentary. It would only provide a sense of ground (*Boden*) without the cultural aspects that come with Husserl's authentic Ark-Earth. Still, we cannot exclude that there is indeed something like a phenomenological pre-scientific experience of our living body attached to the Ark-Earth, distinct from the physical human body attached to the earth as a celestial object.

Deleuze

Deleuzian literature has paid little attention to cosmology, even though Deleuze remains one of the few important figures in contemporary philosophy to integrate an original cosmological questioning. More precisely, the secondary literature on Deleuze has either proposed a fragmentary reading of his take on cosmology[13] or suggested ways in which it can be applied to specific fields such as music,[14] theology[15] and politics.[16] A systematic analysis of Deleuze and cosmology is still undeveloped,[17] and the debate between Deleuze and Husserl regarding the question of the earth has not been carefully considered. As we will see, Deleuze's perspective on these matters is more posthuman than Husserl's own take as it involves non-human c(ha)osmic forces affecting humans. Conversely, Husserl systematically positions humans living outside the earth when he considers living entities in space, on the moon or Venus through his series of eidetic variations.

In *A Thousand Plateaus* and *What Is Philosophy?*, Deleuze and Guattari demonstrate their attachment to the earth affected by chaosmic forces, composed of a series of territories more or less juxtaposed to one another, where lines of flight create unknown spaces and where the edges of territories become uncertain. The deterritorializing lines of flight do not only take place at the surface of the earth, but they also find an extension in the whole universe as the earth itself is in a constant process of losing its identity and creating a new one: 'the Earth [. . .] is a body without organs.'[18] In this context, Husserl's model of an originary Ark-Earth as the ground (*Boden*) becomes obsolete. Before exploring this divergence in detail, a few words ought to be said on the status of cosmology in Deleuze and Guattari's thinking.

Cosmology

Deleuzian readers are not unfamiliar with such topics as black holes, space-time, equivalence between matter and energy, supernovae, Big Bang, speed of light, Einstein's theory and the Hubble constant, which are sporadic in his writing. Deleuze also enthusiastically refers to the work of such astrophysicists as Roland Omnès[19] and Jean-Pierre Luminet.[20] There are numerous other signs of Deleuze's cosmological sensibility. They are evocative, for instance, in his appreciation of Whitehead's *Process and Reality. An Essay in Cosmology*,[21] considered 'one of the greatest books of modern philosophy',[22] or in his borrowing of James Joyce's neologism 'chaosmology', which implies that the cosmos is never fully conquered, as opposed to classical views such as Hesiod's *Theogony* where the cosmos takes shape once and for all after being separated from chaos. One could also think of Deleuze's use of the notion 'Outside', borrowed from Artaud and Blanchot and conceived as being '*farther away* than any external world and even any form of exteriority, which henceforth becomes infinitely closer'.[23] Another example of Deleuze's cosmological sensibility can be found in his book on Bergson where he analyses Bergson's critique of Einstein's theory of relativity by discussing the 'cosmic Memory' and the 'mystic soul [that] actively plays the whole of the universe'.[24] In *Bergsonism*, Deleuze does not enter a debate about the possibility of telepathy, but it is nonetheless implied by the experience of duration, which belongs to the 'Whole of the Universe' and which allows simultaneity (against Einstein's theory) for the famous twin brothers, one of whom remains on earth while the other is travelling in a high-speed rocket and might be able to use telepathic means of communication.[25]

Despite these cosmological considerations, which are well integrated in Deleuze's work, one of the main *philosophical* challenges for Deleuze has less to do with knowing what is 'out of the world we live in' and more with 'how to live in this one'. Valéry's famous assertion that 'the deepest is the skin'[26] overlaps with Deleuze's take on cosmology: the deep mysteries of the universe are down here, in the immanent world.

Deleuze's earth, then, belongs to Samuel Butler's category of the 'Erewon': it is a 'now here' deprived of transcendences, but also a 'nowhere', for it exceeds representation. Philosophy's primary task, it follows, is to create concepts while experiencing the paradoxical unfamiliarity of this earth. In order to do so, philosophy must become a geophilosophy.

Geophilosophy versus cosmo-philosophy

Deleuze and Guattari's geophilosophy offers a critical answer to historicism, to the philosophies of history, and to the reduction of philosophy to its own history. They are fierce opponents of the hermeneutic turn of philosophy, which they consider, in a very Nietzschean way, anti-creative. To the 'interpretosis' as a philosophical disease,[27] they oppose experiencing with intensities, creativity, untimeliness, all irreducible to historical contexts. Deleuze also grants privilege to geography over history by stating that true becomings are not historical but geographical.

It is certainly true to consider that geophilosophy is critically defined in opposition to historicism, but it is equally true to acknowledge that geophilosophy takes a critical distance, perhaps more implicitly, from another way of practising philosophy, namely, 'cosmo-philosophy'. For the ancient Greeks, Plato and Aristotle in particular, cosmology was closely linked with philosophy. For them, one could not claim to have reached the highest degree of wisdom without seeing the close connection between the harmony in us and the harmony of the universe. The speculative aspect of Plato's cosmological questioning serves a higher ethical goal since it ideally leads to, as Plato puts it in a very poetic way, experiencing the harmony of the celestial bodies' motion and the orbits in our soul.[28] The movement of the human soul must align with the harmony of the celestial orbits. Simply put, as Pierre Hadot argued,[29] observing the sky for the ancient cosmologies was a spiritual exercise that aimed at improving the self. One of the philosopher's main tasks, then, consisted in integrating this cosmological aspect in his journey to wisdom. In that sense, philosophy was indeed a cosmo-philosophy.

Deleuze's geophilosophy is suspicious about these cosmo-philosophies. We could say that the passage from geo- to cosmo-philosophy is blocked in Deleuze in order to avoid restoring a supraearthly transcendence.[30] The task of geophilosophy is not to contemplate harmonious links between the micro- and macro-cosmos, but rather to experience with the earth's deterritorializing forces, which makes of this immanent environment a surprising, creative and non-familiar place to live. Deleuze's geophilosophy implies a 'de-Œdipalisation' of the former cosmo-philosophies. In other words, geophilosophy breaks with the intimacy and transcendences of the old cosmo-philosophies in favour of the conquest of an immanent earth.

Territorialization, deterritorialization and reterritorialization become paradigmatic for this quest, a quest that promotes a very specific conceptuality (including striated and smooth spaces, extensive and intensive spaces, and cartography). Incidentally, it is worth noting that something is lost in translation here. In French, there is an obvious etymological and conceptual connection between *terre* (our planet) and *territoire* that is lost in the English translation where these notions are rendered by 'earth' and 'territory' respectively. What the English reader might miss is the celestial and cosmic aspect of the territory. Thus, processes of 'deterritorialization' and 'reterritorialization' not only have a geographical aspect but also a cosmological connotation, without the cosmo-philosophical aspect outlined above.

From a geophilosophical standpoint, philosophy is not concerned with the relationship between the human mind and the 'soul of the world', to follow Plato in *Timaeus*, as 'thinking takes place in the relationship of territory and the earth'.[31] This complex thinking/earth relationship involves movements of de- and reterritorialization, with the lines of flights being their transformative vectors and each territory providing a temporary state of equilibrium, an ephemeral 'order to protect from chaos',[32] which, moreover, is sent back to the realm of mere opinion. Territorial movements are not defined in opposition to more perfect extra-terrestrial territories such as Plato's sky of Ideas or Augustine's City of God, which are mere illusions from a geophilosophical perspective.

Past cosmo-philosophies leave the earth behind and in doing so oversee the thinking/earth relationship. In other words, geophilosophy is an immanent philosophy and it is terrestrial by nature. This is one way to understand Deleuze and Guattari's provocative affirmation: 'We are no longer Greeks'.[33] Geophilosophy strongly denies cosmo-philosophy as the former is not interested in the supraearthly but the very earth.

Moreover, the dynamic earth, which is the playground for deterritorializing processes, is not a perfectly organized hylemorphic organism that would harmoniously connect all parts. Deleuze and Guattari take a position against these ideal and abstract conceptions of the earth formulated by Conan Doyle and Gustav Fechner.[34] The earth is not in a stable state, a ground or a *Boden*, but it is rather affected by chaosmic forces that mystically originate from an outside farther away than any external world. Deprived of any fixed identity, the earth is in the middle of deterritorializing processes or, as Deleuze and Guattari put it, 'the Earth [. . .] is a body without organs. This body without organs is permeated by unformed, unstable matters, by flows in all directions, by free intensities or nomadic singularities, by mad or transitory particles'.[35]

Philosophy as a geophilosophical endeavour is not cosmological in the traditional sense in that it is not a cosmo-philosophy. This might explain why Deleuze, despite his obvious cosmological sensitivity, does not venture into developing a new philosophical cosmology. Yet, cosmology remains part of the metaphysical quest as Deleuze shows a clear sympathy for the 'cosmic' in art. More precisely, he believes that one of the main undertakings of modern artists (Klee, Stockhausen and others) is to cultivate a healthy detachment, which allows levitating above the earth. Philosophers must remain earthly in order to avoid losing themselves in the illusions of the supraearthly, whereas the task of modern art has to do with creating a 'new people' and a 'new earth' while grasping and rendering the cosmic forces sensible.

Cosmic art

Deleuze and Guattari are unequivocal in their statement: modern art's main concern is the cosmos.[36] Modern art does not express terrestrial forces in the way classicism (organized territory) and romanticism (Natal and individualistic territory) did, but rather renders the cosmic forces sensible. Modern art deals primarily with a 'universe-cosmos'[37] and with a 'planetary Cosmos'.[38] One of the objectives of *What Is Philosophy?* consists in defining the logic at play behind the three forms of thought (philosophy, science, art). While philosophy has to remain faithful to the earth by creating concepts and laying out its immanent plane of consistency, art is basically concerned with the cosmos as it creates blocks of sensation to lay out its immanent plane of composition.

Every self-respecting modern art's de- and reterritorializing processes, according to Deleuze and Guattari, do not take place on the earth's surface. Modern art's nomadism takes a step beyond the terrestrial borders. Without expressing an ideal and abstract world, the plane of composition it lays out remains immanent to this world. Modern art evokes unearthly or semi-earthly sounds, shapes or images, but it shall also remain sober in order to avoid plunging the work into pure chaos. Art, therefore, plays a key role in deterritorializing the earth as it paves the way for a new earth while suggesting a new system of signs, new perspectives, new ways of living, new possibilities for thinking and a new people. It becomes clear that there is not one universal earth common to all but a multiplicity of virtual earths, or, as Deleuze and Guattari posit: the earth is 'not only a point in a galaxy, but one galaxy among others'.[39]

A wrong way of explaining the peculiar relationship of art and the cosmos, according to Deleuze, would be to evoke, for instance, the Pythagorian idea of a *Musica universalis*, which implies a harmonious ratio and connection among celestial movements. One could also think, mistakenly for that matter, that Gustav Holst's piece *The Planets*, which proposes a musical rendition of the planets' mythological characters, is adequate for Deleuze's conception of cosmic art. But because Pythagoras and Holst use an essentialist language of representation their enterprises remain non-Deleuzian forms of cosmological expression. Grasping and expressing cosmic forces by rendering them sensible challenges representation, exceeds figuration and gives a sense of unfamiliarity. One example Deleuze and Guattari offer is Paul Klee, who once wrote: one 'tries convulsively to fly from the earth, but at the following level one actually rises above it . . . powered by centrifugal forces that triumph over gravity',[40] as well as the work of the composer Karlheinz Stockhausen,[41] whose pieces, such as *Comet* (1999) or *Cosmic Pulse* (2007), give a sense of Deleuze and Guattari's conception of modern art.[42]

Philosophy's and art's main concerns are the earth and the cosmos respectively. However, it becomes more complex if one considers these forms of thought as not completely isolated from each other. There is a possible 'junction' of the planes[43] and possible 'interferences' between the planes.[44] In that sense, the capacity to grasp cosmic forces and to express a 'new people' and a 'new earth' is not the exclusive privilege of the artist, since philosophical concepts could potentially 'resonate' with cosmic blocks of sensation. This happens, one could say, when the philosopher becomes a 'philosopher-artist'. Philosophy and art then combine their efforts and possibly succeed in bringing geophilosophy and the cosmic together in order to produce a conceptual-artistic 'cosmic earth'.[45]

Deleuze and Guattari's critique of Husserl's earth

Past philosophical cosmologies, from Plato's *Timaeus*[46] to Kant's *Theory of the Heavens*,[47] are dominated by a speculative attempt at knowing everything about heaven in terms of its organization, finality and perfection. Husserl and Deleuze take a different stance, as they implore the philosophers to come 'Back to Earth' after getting lost in speculation over transcendent cosmological issues. Thus, both thinkers take a critical distance from traditional ways of integrating cosmological questioning within the philosophical endeavour. Husserl and Deleuze agree to abandon the old quest for the supraearthly in favour of an experimentation of the earth.

That said, as we can imagine, a series of divergences quickly arise between Husserl's earth as originary Ark and Deleuze's earth as chaosmic celestial body. At the beginning of 'Geophilosophy' in *What Is Philosophy?*, Deleuze and Guattari articulate what seems to be their only explicit critique of Husserl's Ark-Earth when they oppose geodynamism to Husserl's geostatism: 'Husserl demands a ground for thought as original intuition, which is like the earth inasmuch as it neither moves nor is at rest. Yet we have seen that the earth constantly carries out a movement of deterritorialization on the spot, by which it goes beyond any territory; it is deterritorializing and deterritorialized.'[48]

First, the bones of contention between Husserl and Deleuze/Guattari should be elucidated in order to give consistency to their critique of Husserl's geostatism. Husserl's methodological *épochè* is a major sign of the incompatibility between the Ark-Earth and Deleuze's earth. Husserl brackets the natural world and proposes a radical critique of the natural attitude, which leads him to question the validity of the heliocentric system that is reduced to a mere perception. This leaves place to a purely symbolic earth that stands for the spiritual, universal and immortal root of the Euro-Western tradition. The price of reaching this ideal is high, for Husserl has to position phenomenology against scientific advancements, including astronomical and astrophysical discoveries. In that sense, Didier Franck might be right when he considers the 1934 essay the most audacious reduction ever attempted by Husserl.[49] Deleuze's earth, on the other hand, is both physical and animated, or effected by immaterial forces. Deleuze does not discard scientific discoveries. On the contrary, as I have mentioned, he often refers to the works of astrophysicists to illustrate some aspects of his philosophy. Science is for Deleuze a form of thought no more and no less valuable than the two others, philosophy and art.

Husserl also exposes a pre-modern and romantic view of the earth depicted as a new mythical figure as he presents a phenomenological version of Mother Earth who brings food, protection and comfort, whom we do not want to leave behind. It is as though there existed a phenomenological umbilical cord that tied us (us who belong to the spiritual Europe) to the Ark-Earth. It sounds quite Œdipal for Deleuze who does not hesitate to consider the posthuman possibility of deterritorializing the earth and to create a new, non-romantic 'cosmic earth',[50] if not an infinite number of new earths. Moreover, Deleuze does not endorse the image of the earth as a tiny 'pale blue dot'[51] lost in the immensity of the intergalactic space but rather as offering richness and diversity in terms of encounters, deterritorializing processes, assemblages, networks of virtualities; as a galaxy in itself among other galaxies.

Another difference concerns cosmology itself. Husserl's cosmology is in fact a 'pseudo-cosmology'. His conception of the earth certainly brings a cosmological dimension to phenomenology, but his attachment to an 'originary earth' leaves no room for real encounters with worlds fundamentally different than ours as these potential other worlds are condemned by him to be forever experienced through the inescapable Greco-teleological lense. According to Husserl, it remains strictly impossible for humans to create new ways of perceiving things philosophically without grounding the perceptions in the spiritual *logos* inherited from the Greeks. In other words, potential life on exoplanets will never modify the human perspectives and will never suggest fundamental new ways of perception. For true Euro-Westerners, the system of perceptions extends to what they perceive and there is no way to reverse it, even partially. Husserl believes that humans can never abandon the ground of *this* earth. Ultimately, he asserts that the deterritorialization of human perceptions is a mere illusion.[52] Contrary to Husserl, Deleuze presents a much broader posthumanist cosmological view, one that is not concerned with the earth only, one that suggests the possibility of a deterritorialization of perceptions, and one that implies the possibility of human metamorphoses via contact with outer (real or artistically expressed) forms of life. Modern art imagines such posthuman transformations. Husserl's pseudo-cosmology and anthropocentric conservatism is immersed in a typical German nostalgia for Greece,[53] whereas Deleuze and Guattari consider the possibility of an impure beginning of Euro-Western thought. This is precisely what Deleuze and Guattari's geophilosophy recalls: philosophy was contingently brought to Greece by foreigners and it reshaped earth with the rational form of thought that we know, and that Husserl considers inescapable. For Deleuze and Guattari, Greece is not an absolute origin[54] but a contingent milieu where an encounter between foreigners and indigenous peoples took place. Today, modern artists are such foreigners who grasp cosmic forces and give shape to a new earth, to a new people or even to a posthumanity. True modern cosmology must shake the ideal purity of the 'Greek miracle' in its very foundation. Only then will the trap of an anthropo/Euro-centric pseudo-cosmology be avoided, only then will a revolutionary role be granted to the supralunar, only then will the extra-terrestrial environment be the source of encounters, only then will the incapacity to think be overcome, and only then will the awareness to the 'forces of the outside'[55] affecting the geodynamic earth rise.

Although from a phenomenological point of view, weightlessness questions the objectivity of the 'left', 'right', 'up', and 'down' in favour of an intuitive sense of space, it does not fundamentally question the existence of gravity. A phenomenogical force of gravity always brings us back to the Ark-Earth. Deleuze and Guattari's exploration of the body without organs leads them to believe not only in the contingent aspect of the sense of space but also in the body's capacity to defy gravity. In *A Thousand Plateaus*, Deleuze and Guattari often refer to the opposition between gravity associated with the state and the striated space and celerity associated with war machines, smooth space, and nomadism.[56] Further, in *Cinema 2*, Deleuze is clearly fascinated by the aberration of movement that defies the vertical line of gravity: 'masses have lost the centres of gravity around which they were ordered, forces have lost the dynamic centres around which they organize space.'[57] Deleuze challenges gravity at a qualitative level. However, this should not obscure the scientific hypothesis of the graviton, a massless elementary particle predicted by the string theory and able to travel from one braneworld to another.[58]

While phenomenology remains within the limits of liveable experiences by the human lived body, Deleuze and Guattari go a step further so as to suggest that the unfamiliar and non-human cosmic forces are properly unliveable as they escape the commonly anthropomorphic capacities of representation. They, therefore, call for a body without organs (BwO) intensified by impersonal forces as a critical alternative to the phenomenological lived body (*Leib*). In this context, Deleuze and Guattari's critique of phenomenology or art and of the phenomenological flesh gains a cosmological value as it promotes non-human cosmic becomings that open up to the 'universe-cosmos' beyond the safe and protective house[59] understood as Husserl's *Boden* (ground) or Heidegger's *Wohnen* (dwelling).

Finally, Husserl's and Deleuze's respective concept of earth have different political implications. From a political standpoint, the phenomenological conversion from the natural to the phenomenological attitude shall ideally lead to the formation of a community of phenomenologists who will stand as 'functionaries of humanity',[60] that is, not the employees of the state affiliated with a political party but the Euro-Western bearers of teleological truth in charge of guiding people by providing the teleological idea of science, including the fundamental meaning of the earth as originary Ark. This assembly of phenomenological functionaries shall then give birth to a spiritual 'community of love' (*Liebesgemeinschaft*).[61] Deleuze might agree with some phenomenological standpoints, including the distrust in societal politics or the inappropriateness of the earth that could provide arguments for today's environmental debates. Deleuze also shares Husserl's doubt about the universe being merely defined by a series of natural and mechanical laws. However, this doubt remains partial for Deleuze, considering his acknowledgement of science as a form of thought and the way he promotes the 'machines' and the 'mecanosphere' at the rank of philosophical concepts. For the most part, however, Deleuze remains light years away from Husserl's political views as he considers phenomenology to be a 'modern scholasticism'.[62] Indeed, Husserl admits that the *épochè* is akin to a religious conversion and even compares the living body (*Leib*) to a 'phenomenologized Christic incarnation'.[63] For both Husserl and Deleuze, the true inhabitants of the earth are missing. Husserl integrates this idea in a political rhetoric of crisis, which aims at asserting that phenomenology serves as a saviour for humanity. This situation is rather different for Deleuze as the depopulation of the earth has already been prophetically announced by an untimely community. Deleuze gathers artists and writers who explicitly referred to the idea of a 'missing people', including the poet Mallarmé,[64] the painter Klee,[65] the dramatist Carmelo Bene,[66] the writer Kafka,[67] and several post-war filmmakers.[68] Deleuze becomes more original than these artists and writers and gives a cosmological twist to the 'new people' by associating them with a 'new earth': 'The creation of concepts in itself calls for a future form, for a new earth and people that do not yet exist.'[69] In other words, leaving a territorial assemblage and the existing people behind ultimately means for Deleuze finding another 'logic of the earth' (following Deleuze's new 'logic of sense' and a new 'logic of sensation'). This new 'logic of the earth' would imply not only new, posthuman ways of perceiving but also posthuman ways of living, thinking and inhabiting the earth unheard of. The integration of cosmology and politics is not a choice made by modern artists but an obligation imposed by modern sociopolitical conditions: 'The established powers have occupied the earth, [...] [they] have placed us in a situation of a combat at once atomic and cosmic, galactic.'[70] If the new people win the combat, then the cosmos will become art, the earth will not suffer from a depopulation and it will overcome the romantic perspective, new collective assemblages of enunciation will be created, a new people and a new earth will arise. However, if the new people do not triumph over the existing and dominant ones, this earth will continue to depopulate, collapse and disappear. Husserl would not adhere to this 'hope in the new' as he prefers to rely on tradition, but for Deleuze, to fall back on tradition is nihilistic as it destroys life's creative forces. Relying on tradition is part of the earth's problem. Both Husserl and Deleuze ultimately make of the earth a political affair, but Husserl's normative and universal conception of the Ark-Earth constituted by the phenomenological functionaries obeys a different political agenda than Deleuze's politics of the deterritorializing earth. This cosmological debate boils down to the opposition between Husserl, the conservative thinker of identity, and Deleuze, the progressive thinker of difference.

Conclusion

Traditionally, the earth has been taken for granted, either as the centre of the universe for Greek philosophers, an unquestionable creation by religious believers, or as a celestial object by scientists. Dissatisfied with these explicitly obvious ways to conceive the earth, Husserl and Deleuze open up a new philosophical question, namely, 'What is the earth?' The *quid* of the earth is, for them, not as obvious as it used to be thought. They abandon the quest regarding the organization of the whole universe and focus instead, philosophically and with a relative degree of modesty, on *this* earth.

Nietzsche is potentially thought to be the initiator of this quest. In *Zarathustra*, he explicitly leaves aside the supraearthly concerns of the origin and destiny of the universe. He invites us to 'remain earthly':

> I beseech you, my brothers, *stay true to the earth* and do not believe those who talk of over-earthly hopes! They are poisoners, whether they know it or not. . . . Once sacrilege against God was the greatest sacrilege . . . Sacrilege against the earth is now the most terrible thing. . . . I love those who do not first seek behind the stars for a reason to go under and be sacrifices, but who sacrifice themselves to the earth, that the earth may one day belong to the Overman.[71]

From the Nietzschean perspective, we can assert that Husserl and Deleuze understood Nietzsche's call to remain earthly differently. While Husserl could be seen as a logocentric thinker who tries to conquer the spiritual unity of the earth, for Deleuze this unity leaves place to a deterritorializing earth, that is, an earth that has the capacity to deterritorialize itself. Husserl searches for a definitive representation of the earth as originary Ark. The way humans perceive, wherever they are in the whole universe and whatever experiences they go through, is limited for Husserl to the Greco-European abilities of earth's inhabitants to perceive logically and teleologically. He may well consider the possibility of many 'earths'[72] but ultimately only 'our' earth is grounded. The other earths, for example, exoplanets where complex forms of life could be found, remain solely celestial bodies deprived of any spiritual aim. If one were to be born on a spaceship, as Husserl imagines, the spaceship would not be another ground but the same earth-ground which expands, for there cannot be two fundamental earths but only two fragments of the same earth.[73]

Conversely, the human perspective is not inescapable for Deleuze. He aptly sums up this divergence when he says: 'The world is neither finite nor infinite as representation would have it: it is completed and unlimited.'[74] For Deleuze, the cosmological challenge does not consist in developing a more fundamental, intimate and familiar relationship with the earth, but it concerns the creative potential of the earth, which has a non-limited capacity to generate posthuman, unheard of and unseen environments where a new people can live and think. Moreover, there is not *one* earth for Deleuze but a multiplicity of virtual earths as complex as galaxies. Ultimately, heaven and earth lie in the same pragmasphere. The whole cosmos is not a hyper-earth or a giant organism but a vast plane of immanence where intensive movements of deterritorialization are taking place. In that sense, perhaps, Nietzsche's quest for earthliness opens up to a 'Cosmos philosophy'.[75]

Husserl's conviction about the universal *telos* of European science imposes a certain number of restrictions on the earth and its inhabitants. In Crisis, he explicitly limits the theoretical attitude and the spiritual life to Greco-Westerners.[76] But what if a non-Greco-Westerner travels through space? Will that person remain spiritually attached to any earth? Furthermore, references to the 'primordial home' (*Urheimat*) of a 'primordial people' (*Urfolk*) with their 'primordial territory' (*Urgebiet*) and 'primordial history' (*Urgeschichte*)[77] point to the originary Ark-Earth (*Ur-Archè*) that annihilates all terrestrial and extra-terrestrial differences. What if a cosmonaut was to experience extra-terrestrial becomings while travelling through a black hole or a wormhole? Would the Ark-Earth emerge unscathed from these becomings? And what if an inter-planeraty creature was to be born, either as a result of copulation or scientific experiment? How can this posthuman creature still carry the Ark-Earth? Husserl's cosmology, as opposed to Deleuze's cosmological questioning, does not provide conceptual tools to address these thought experiments.[78]

Notes

1 Rosi Braidotti, *The Posthuman*, 55, 81, 131, 137 and 159.
2 Along with Félix Guattari, even if the two names will not always be mentioned.
3 Edmund Husserl, 'The Originary Ark, the Earth, Does Not Move', translated by Fred Kersten. Another English translation: 'Foundational Investigations of the Phenomenological Origin of the Spatiality of Nature' (*Husserl. Shorter Works*, 222–33). Original text in German (Manuscript D17): 'Umsturz der Kopernikanischen Lehre in der gewöhnlichen weltanschaulichen Interpretation. Die Ur-Arche Erde bewegt sich nicht. Grundlegende Untersuchungen zum phänomenologischen Ursprung der

Körperlichkeit der Räumlichkeit der Natur im ersten naturwissenschaftlichen Sinne. Alles notwendiges Anfanguntersuchungen', (*Philosophical Essays*, 307–25).
4 René Descartes, *A Discourse on the Method*, Part Six.
5 Edmund Husserl, *The Crisis of European Sciences*, 290.
6 Edmund Husserl, *Ideas I*, §24.
7 Heidegger uses the notion *Bodenstandigkeit*, sometimes translated as 'autochthony'. See, for instance: Martin Heidegger, 'Memorial Address'. Similarly to Husserl, Heidegger does not understand *Boden* geographically but rather as a spiritual ground able to travel through time. However, as opposed to Husserl, Heidegger does not seem to consider the possibility of travelling through the cosmic space of this spiritual ground. Heidegger's essay 'On the Origin of the Work of Art', which was published one year after Husserl's Ark-Earth essay, suggests a reconnection between thinking and the earth without locating the earth in a cosmic environment. Nonetheless, Janae Sholtz points out possible links between Heidegger's and Deleuze's calls for the creation of a new earthly people. See Janae Sholtz, *The Invention of a People*. The ramifications between the phenomenological movement and Deleuze's cosmological views are numerous. This chapter explores only one facet of these connections, namely, Husserl's and Deleuze's conceptions of the earth.
8 Raluca Mocan, 'La terre ne se meut pas', 1–7.
9 Pierre Kerszberg thinks of Husserl's 1934 essay as the most detailed critique of Einstein by Husserl. See Pierre Kerszberg, 'The Phenomenological Analysis of Earth's Motion'. For another philosophical critique of Einstein's theory of relativity, see Henri Bergson, *Duration and Simultaneity*.
10 I leave aside the mathematical hypothesis of the multiverse.
11 See L. N. Korlinova, Ch. Muller and L. M. Chernobyl'skii, 'Phenomenology of Spatial Illusory Reactions'; James R. Lackner, 'Spatial Orientation in Weightless Environments'; James R. Lackner and Ashton Graybiel, 'Parabolic Flight'; David Morris, *The Sense of Space*.
12 L. N. Korlinova et al., 'Phenomenology of Spatial Illusory Reactions', 345.
13 John Sellars, 'The Point of View of the Cosmos'; Alain Beaulieu, 'La réforme du concept phénoménologique de 'monde' par Gilles Deleuze'.
14 Ronald Bogue, 'Rhizomusicosmology'; Mikos Solomos, 'De la ritournelle-Cosmos à la puissance du son'.
15 Paul A. Harris, 'Deleuze's Cinematic Universe of Light'.
16 Janae Sholtz, *The Invention of a People*.
17 Alain Beaulieu, 'Introduction to Gilles Deleuze's Cosmological Sensibility'; Daniel Falb, 'The Circumference of the Earth'.
18 Gilles Deleuze and Félix Guattari, *A Thousand Plateaus*, 40.
19 Deleuze and Guattari, *A Thousand Plateaus*, 521n1.
20 Gilles Deleuze and Félix Guattari, *What Is Philosophy?*, 220n2.
21 Alfred N. Whitehead, *Process & Reality*.
22 Gilles Deleuze, *Difference and Repetition*, 284–5.
23 Gilles Deleuze, *Foucault*, 86. Deleuze credits Foucault for the distinction between 'exteriority' and 'outside' (*Foucault*, 143, n. 24). He refers to Foucault's essay 'This Is Not a Pipe', where Foucault supposedly opposes the outside of forces ('another space') to external forms. Indeed, Foucault presents this 'other space' as being undetermined by the 'form', but it does not primarily have the 'cosmological' meaning attributed by Deleuze to the forces.
24 Gilles Deleuze, *Bergsonism*, 111–2.
25 Ibid., chap. IV.

26 Paul Valéry, *L'Idée fixe*, 216.
27 Deleuze and Guattari, *A Thousand Plateaus*, 114.
28 Plato, *Timaeus*, 47d.
29 Pierre Hadot, 'La terre vue d'en haut', 31–9.
30 Daniel Falb, 'The Circumference of the Earth'.
31 Deleuze and Guattari, *What Is Philosophy?*, 85.
32 Ibid., 201.
33 Ibid., 107.
34 Ibid., 213. We could also think of James Lovelock's Gaïa hypothesis: James E. Lovelock and Lynn Margulis, 'Atmospheric Homeostasis', 2–10.
35 Deleuze and Guattari, *A Thousand Plateaus*, 40.
36 Ibid., 310–50. That said, there is nothing like a universal history for Deleuze, but rather singular histories produced by philosophers and artists. See Alain Beaulieu, 'La pratique deleuzienne de l'histoire'.
37 Deleuze and Guattari, *What Is Philosophy?*, 180.
38 Ibid., 189.
39 Deleuze and Guattari, *A Thousand Plateaus*, 345.
40 Quoted in Deleuze and Guattari, *A Thousand Plateaus*, 312.
41 Ibid., 342. See also Karlheinz Stockhausen, *Towards a Cosmic Music*.
42 Ronald Bogue offers an inspiring analysis of Deleuze and Guattari's musi-cosmology. Deleuze and Guattari are said to take their distance from the paradigm of the 'harmony of the spheres'. For them, 'the essence of music is to be found not in the macroscopic order of celestial cycles but in the molecular domain of transverse becoming', thus music is 'in relation to the world' (becoming, territory, birds, etc.). Ronald Bogue, 'Rhizomusicosmology', 87–8 and 98.
43 Deleuze and Guattari, *What Is Philosophy?*, 208.
44 Ibid., 216–8.
45 Deleuze and Guattari, *A Thousand Plateaus*, 346.
46 Plato, *Timaeus*.
47 Emmanuel Kant, *Universal Natural History and Theory of the Heavens*.
48 Deleuze and Guattari, *What Is Philosophy?*, 85. In the chapter 'Geophilosophy', Husserl's two texts discussed in this chapter, namely, the 1934 essay and *Crisis*, are the object of harsh critique.
49 Didier Franck, 'Introduction', in Edmund Husserl, *La Terre ne se meut pas*, 9.
50 Deleuze and Guattari, *A Thousand Plateaus*, 346.
51 The romantic aspect of this metaphor, borrowed from Carl Sagan, might be compatible with Husserl's conception of the earth as unique, fragile and isolated. See Carl Sagan, *Pale Blue Dot*.
52 Paul Ducros, 'La Terre', 51: "Il n'y a *jamais*, pour la vie réelle, un abandon de la Terre-sol-fonds-immobile. Le propre de l'homme moderne n'est en rien sa déterritorialisation, mais l'illusion de l'avoir effectuée."
53 Jacques Taminiaux, *La Nostalgie de la Grèce à l'aube de l'idéalisme allemand*.
54 Deleuze and Guattari, *What Is Philosophy?*, 96–7.
55 Gilles Deleuze, *Foucault*, 87.
56 See, for instance, Deleuze and Guattari, *A Thousand Plateaus*, 372: 'when one escapes the force of gravity to enter a field of celerity'.
57 Gilles Deleuze, *Cinema 2*, 142.
58 Brian Greene, *The Hidden Reality*. For a critical account of this hypothesis, see Lee Smolin, *The Trouble with Physics*.

59 Deleuze and Guattari, *What Is Philosophy?*, 163–99.
60 Edmund Husserl, *The Crisis of European Sciences*, §7.
61 Philip Buckley, 'Husserl's Rational *Liebesgemeinschaft*', 116–29.
62 Gilles Deleuze, *Nietzsche and Philosophy*, 195.
63 Natalie Depraz, 'L'incarnation phénoménologique'; Alain Beaulieu, 'L'incarnation phénoménologique à l'épreuve du 'corps sans organes'.
64 Deleuze and Guattari, *A Thousand Plateaus*, 346.
65 Ibid.; Gilles Deleuze, *Cinema 2*, 320n41.
66 Gilles Deleuze, 'Le théâtre et sa politique'.
67 Gilles Deleuze and Félix Guattari, *Kafka*, 17–18.
68 Gilles Deleuze, 'Cinema and Politics', in *Cinema 2.*, 215–24. One could also add the filmmakers Jean-Marie Straub and Danièle Huillet who share a similar idea: Jean-Louis Raymond, ed., *Rencontres avec Jean-Marie Straub et Danièle Huillet*, 46.
69 Deleuze and Guattari, *What Is Philosophy?*, 108.
70 Deleuze and Guattari, *A Thousand Plateaus*, 345.
71 Friedrich Nietzsche, *Thus Spoke Zarathustra*, 12–14.
72 Edmund Husserl, 'The Originary Ark, the Earth, does not Move', 122.
73 Ibid., 126.
74 Gilles Deleuze, *Difference and Repetition*, 57.
75 Deleuze and Guattari, *A Thousand Plateaus*, 342.
76 Edmund Husserl, *The Crisis of European Sciences*, 273.
77 Edmund Husserl, 'The Originary Ark, the Earth, does not Move', 126–7.
78 First versions of this chapter were presented at the conferences *Thinking Through Deleuze: Nomadic Subjects, Global Citizenship and Posthumanism* (Brock University, Canada, 6–8 February 2015) and *Gilles Deleuze and Félix Guattari. Refrain of Freedom* (Panteion University, Athens, Greece, 24–26 April 2015). I would like to thank the organizers of the events, in particular Terrance McDonald, Christine Daigle and Constantin Boundas, as well as Laurentian University for the financial support and Izabela Zdun for the translation of this chapter.

Bibliography

Aristotle. *On the Heavens*. Translated by W. K. C. Guthrie. Cambridge: Harvard University Press, 1937.

Beaulieu, Alain. 'Introduction to Gilles Deleuze's Cosmological Sensibility'. *Philosophy and Cosmology. The Journal of the International Society of Philosophy and Cosmology* 16 (2016): 199–211.

Beaulieu, Alain. 'L'incarnation phénoménologique à l'épreuve du "corps sans organes"'. *Laval théologique et philosophique* 60, no. 2 (2004): 301–16.

Beaulieu, Alain. 'La pratique deleuzienne de l'histoire'. In *Contr'hommage pour Gilles Deleuze*, edited by Dalie Giroux, René Lemieux and Pierre-Luc Chénier, 3–21. Sainte-Foy: Presses de l'Université Laval, 2009.

Beaulieu, Alain. 'La réforme du concept phénoménologique de 'monde' par Gilles Deleuze'. *Studia Phaenomenologica. Romanian Journal for Phenomenology* 3, no. 3/4 (2003): 257–87.

Bergson, Henri. *Duration and Simultaneity*. Translated by Leon Jacobson. Manchester: Clinamen Press, 1999.

Bogue, Ronald. 'Rhizomusicosmology'. *Substance* 20, no. 3 (1991): 85–101.
Braidotti, Rosi. *The Posthuman*. Cambridge: Polity Press, 2013.
Buckley, Philip. 'Husserl's Rational *Liebesgemeinschaft*'. *Research in Phenomenology* 26 (1996): 116–29.
Deleuze, Gilles. *Bergsonism*. Translated by Hugh Tomlinson and Barbara Habberjam. New York: Zone Books, 1988.
Deleuze, Gilles. *Cinema 2. The Time-Image*. Translated by Hugh Tomlinson and Robert Galeta. Minneapolis, MN: Minnesota University Press, 1989.
Deleuze, Gilles. *Difference and Repetition*. Translated by Paul Patton. New York: Columbia University Press, 1994.
Deleuze, Gilles. *Foucault*. Translated by Sean Hand. Minneapolis, MN: Minnesota University Press, 1988.
Deleuze, Gilles and Carmelo Bene. *Superpositions*. Paris: Minuit, 1979.
Deleuze, Gilles and Félix Guattari. *A Thousand Plateaus*. Translated by Brian Massumi. Minneapolis, MN: Minnesota University Press, 1987.
Deleuze, Gilles and Félix Guattari. *Kafka. Toward a Minor Literature*. Translated by Dana Polan. Minneapolis, MN: Minnesota University Press, 1986.
Deleuze, Gilles and Félix Guattari. *What is Philosophy?* Translated by Hugh Tomlinson and Graham Burchell. New York: Columbia University Press, 1996.
Depraz, Natalie. 'L'incarnation phénoménologique. Un problème théologique?'. *Tijdschrift voor filosofie* 55, no. 3 (1993): 496–517.
Descartes, René. *A Discourse on the Method of Correctly Conducting one's Reason and Seeking Truth in the Sciences*. Translated by Ian Maclean. Oxford: Oxford University Press, 2006.
Ducros, Paul. 'La Terre: La théorie du géostatisme d'Edmund Husserl'. *Bulletin d'analyse phénoménologique* 3, no. 5 (2007): 1–88.
Falb, Daniel. 'The Circumference of the Earth. Deleuze and Cosmology'. Available at www.academia.edu/10683650/The_Circumference_of_the_Earth._Deleuze_and_Cosmology.
Greene, Brian. *The Hidden Reality. Parallel Universes and the Deep Laws of the Cosmos*. New York: Vintage Books, 2011.
Hadot, Pierre. 'La terre vue d'en haut et le voyage cosmique: le point de vue du poète, du philosophe et de l'historien'. In *Frontières et conquête spatiale. La philosophie à l'épreuve*, edited by Jean Schneider, and Monique Léger-Orine, 31–9. Dordrecht, Boston and London: Kluwer Academic Publishers, 1987.
Harris, Paul A. 'Deleuze's Cinematic Universe of Light: A Cosmic Plane of Immanence'. *Substance* 39, no. 1 (2010): 115–24.
Heidegger, Martin. *Basic Writings*. Translated by David Farell Krell. New York: Harper Collins, 2008.
Heidegger, Martin. *Discourse on Thinking*. Translated by John M. Anderson and Hans E. Freund. New York: Harper Collins, 1955.
Husserl, Edmund. 'Foundational Investigations of the Phenomenological Origin of the Spatiality of Nature: The Originary Ark, the Earth, Does Not Move'. Translated by Fred Kersten. In *Husserl at the Limits of Phenomenology. Including Texts by Edmund Husserl and Maurice Merleau-Ponty*, edited by Leonard Lawlor and Bettina Bergo, 117–31. Evanston, IL: Northwestern University Press, 2002. Another English translation: 'Foundational Investigations of the Phenomenological Origin of the Spatiality of Nature'. Translated by Fred Kersten. In *Husserl. Shorter Works*, edited by Peter McCormick and Frederick A. Elliston, 222–33. Notre-Dame: Notre-Dame

University Press, 1981. Original text in German (Manuscript D17): 'Umsturz der Kopernikanischen Lehre in der gewöhnlichen weltanschaulichen Interpretation. Die Ur-Arche Erde bewegt sich nicht. Grundlegende Untersuchungen zum phänomenologischen Ursprung der Körperlichkeit der Räumlichkeit der Natur im ersten naturwissenschaftlichen Sinne. Alles notwendiges Anfanguntersuchungen'. In *Philosophical Essays in Memory of Edmund Husserl*, edited by Marvin Farber, 307–25. New York: Greenwood Press, 1968.

Husserl, Edmund. *La Terre ne se meut pas*. Translated by Didier Franck. Paris: Minuit, 1989.

Husserl, Edmund. *The Crisis of European Sciences and Transcendental Phenomenology*. Translated by David Carr. Evanston, IL: Northwestern University Press, 1970.

Kant, Emmanuel. *Universal Natural History and Theory of the Heavens*. Translated by Ian Johnston. Arlington: Richer Resources Publications, 2009.

Kerszberg, Pierre. 'The Phenomenological Analysis of Earth's Motion'. *Philosophy and Phenomenological Research* 48, no. 2 (1987): 177–208.

Korlinova, Ludmila N., Christopher Muller and Lyudmila M. Chernobyl'skii. 'Phenomenology of Spatial Illusory Reactions Under Conditions of Weightlessness'. *Human Physiology* 21, no. 4 (1995): 344–51.

Lackner, James R. 'Spatial Orientation in Weightless Environments'. *Perception* 21 (1992): 803–12.

Lackner, James R. and Ashton Graybiel. 'Parabolic Flight: Loss of Sense of Orientation'. *Science* 206, no. 4422 (1979): 1105–08.

Lovelock, James E. and Lynn Margulis. 'Atmospheric Homeostasis by and for the Biosphere: The Gaia Hypothesis'. *Tellus. Series A. Dynamic Meteorology and Oceanography* 26, no. 1–2 (1974): 2–10.

Mocan, Raluca. 'La terre ne se meut pas. Husserl contre Copernic'. *Alliage* 65 (2009): 1–7.

Morris, David. *The Sense of Space*. New York: SUNY Press, 2012.

Nietzsche, Friedrich. *Thus Spoke Zarathustra*. Translated by Graham Parkes. Oxford: Oxford University Press, 2009.

Plato. *Timaeus*. Translated by Desmond Lee. New York: Penguin Classics, 2008.

Raymond, Jean-Louis, ed. *Rencontres avec Jean-Marie Straub et Danièle Huillet*. Le Mans: École régionale des beaux-arts, 1995.

Sagan, Carl. *Pale Blue Dot. A Vision of Human Future in Space*. New York: Ballantine Books, 1994.

Sellars, John. 'The Point of View of the Cosmos: Deleuze, Romanticism, Stoicism'. *Pli* 8 (1999): 1–24.

Sholtz, Janae. *The Invention of a People. Heidegger and Deleuze on Art and the Political*. Edinburgh: Edinburgh University Press, 2015.

Smolin, Lee. *The Trouble with Physics*. Boston: Houghton Mifflin Company, 2007.

Solomos, Mikos. 'De la ritournelle-Cosmos à la puissance du son. Cinq essais pour écouter *Mille plateaux*'. In *Gilles Deleuze. La Pensée-musique*, edited by Pascale Criton and Jean-Marc Chouvel, 153–62. Paris: Publication Cdmc, 2015.

Stockhausen, Karlheinz. *Towards a Cosmic Music*. Shaftesbury: Element, 1989.

Taminiaux, Jacques. *La Nostalgie de la Grèce à l'aube de l'idéalisme allemand. Kant et les Grecs dans l'itinéraire de Schiller, de Hölderlin et de Hegel*. La Haye: Martinus Nijhoff, 1967.

Valéry, Paul. *L'Idée fixe*. Paris: Gallimard, 1931.

Whitehead, Alfred N. *Process & Reality. An Essay in Cosmology*. New York: Macmillan, 1960.

Part Two

From Deleuze and Guattari to posthuman aesthetics

6

Posthuman cinema

Terrence Malick and a Cinema of Life

Terrance H. McDonald[1]

Introduction

From many perspectives, cinema is always already human. Whether filming the fictional embraces of imaginary characters, the tangled aspects of real issues, or the abstract constructions of human minds, the moving images of cinema, both analogue and digital, constantly appear human-centric. Nevertheless, this generalization may seem unsatisfactory. We could point to the mechanical processes of a camera or the binary operations of a computer in order to fracture the human-centric claim to cinema. 'Today the making of images', argues André Bazin, 'no longer shares an anthropocentric, utilitarian purpose.'[2] Bazin is one of the first to champion the anti-anthropocentric potentialities of the cinema. However, even with this fracture, it is difficult to support the claim that fiction and documentary films are not primarily human-centric because films are created primarily by the efforts of humans, and these films focus on the interests of humans. 'The conventions of mainstream film', states Laura Mulvey, 'focus attention on the human form. Scale, space, stories are all anthropomorphic.'[3] In terms of representation, most fiction and documentary films offer anthropocentric narratives, which encapsulate scales, spaces, and stories that can be read as replicating and translating a belief in human privilege into the image. Initially, we may expect that a posthuman cinema will challenge these representations by seeking different scales, spaces, and stories that could rupture and displace this prominent focus on human form, and by extension focus on non-human forms. This is certainly a worthwhile endeavour, but I also think that cinema has the capacity to unfold intensities by juxtaposing human and non-human forms, which can be mobilized to generate new perspectives, new images and new conceptualizations of life. Therefore, rather than focusing on a film as projecting posthuman or non-human representations, this chapter aims to explore the cinematic forms of Terrence Malick's *The Tree of Life* through the lens of Deleuze's transcendental empiricism to read how the film takes shape as a form of life.

The aim of this chapter is not to trace what is already posthuman about our sociocultural milieu, but rather to collapse the boundaries between cinema and life to generate new posthuman images – both cinematic and worldly – yet to come. In other words, it imagines where cinema is an experience with the capacity to shake the perspectives that we have chosen to see the world through, even if we only ever have the ability to choose those perspectives. The goal being: recognize the limits of our perspective as opposed to trying to force ourselves into the perspectives of non-humans. That being said, thinking a cinema of life does not entail the embrace of a new theoretical artifice to be placed and written overtop of images as a means of demonstrating the novelty of a new philosophical approach. Furthermore, this chapter does not embrace posthumanism as the latest theoretical trend that promises to break all ties with the past in an attempt to start anew. On the contrary, I see posthumanism as an alteration of theoretical approaches as such that develops as we move from humanist towards posthumanist methodologies. Rosi Braidotti outlines this position in her important work *The Posthuman*, which maps the forces and projects being generated by the posthuman condition. 'Far from being the nth variation in a sequence of prefixes that may appear both endless and somehow arbitrary', states Braidotti, 'the posthuman condition introduces a qualitative shift in our thinking about what exactly is the basic unit of common reference for our species, our polity and our relationship to the other inhabitants of this planet.'[4] The notion of posthumanism as a qualitative shift immediately leads me to recall Gilles Deleuze's transcendental empiricism, which maps all species, all polities, all relationships and all everything as generated by experience.

From a theoretical perspective, I take this to be profoundly posthuman and one pathway for thinking posthumanisms through Deleuze. Transcendental empiricism launches this pathway because it reveals a field of experience as the basic common reference for everything. Furthermore, Deleuze's transcendental empiricism maps how experiencing this field generates all things. It is important to note that this is not the recognition and processing of an experience by a mind or an agency that then comes to be a thing, a being, a subject or a something, but rather it is the experiencing itself that is a thing, a being, a subject or a something. This is complex and I will develop this position shortly, but for the moment it is also important to acknowledge how difficult it is to grasp the field of experience as a basic common reference because, as humans, we access the world through our subjective images of that field of experience. Therefore, we can map all the complex theoretical positions imaginable, but this will not ensure that we recognize the limits of our own views. Here is where I see *The Tree of Life* taking shape as a form of experience and gesturing to the field of experience that structures life.[5] In this sense, a cinema of life generates the capacity to challenge the linear assumptions of humanism through cinematic forms that continuously vacate the human subject in gestures towards the whole. This position progresses through Deleuze's transcendental empiricism to read *The Tree of Life* as a series of images of any-instant-whatever.[6] However, I am not seeking to fit the film within Deleuze's cinematic taxonomy because this risks forcing a recent film into a period gone by or, and perhaps more troubling, attempting to declare the emergence of a third image. These are, at times, generative endeavours, but, for my purposes, the key theoretical claim runs through Deleuze's transcendental empiricism to posthumanist thought which takes shape within Malick's film. The cinema books do explicitly and implicitly come to bear on this conversation, but more potential exists than simply relying on the cinema books when Deleuze and moving images come together. No matter how conspicuous, I will risk forging the new.

The Tree of Life: A form of life

How do we make sense of the space, or cosmos, sequence in the film? Scholars approach this question in a multiplicity of ways,[7] but my focus seeks to consider what potentialities for speculation do these sequences launch. Malick's film leaves open, in a glaring way, the potentiality of interpretation. There is no set of answers given and no frame of reference established by the opening shot of space that transitions to a discussion of the way of grace and the way of nature. From the first moment, the film takes shape through images of any-instant-whatever as in the formation of a universe or a shot of sunflowers or the view of a girl in a field. However, if the images themselves and the arrangement of these images are unique, the general cinematic approach could be understood as belonging to Deleuze's time-image. 'We run in fact into a principle of indeterminability', states Deleuze of the time-image, 'of indiscernibility: we no longer know what is imaginary or real, physical or mental, in the situation, not because they are confused, but because we do not have to know and there is no longer even a place from which to ask.'[8] *The Tree of Life* embraces this principle, and I read the film as taking shape through a continuous deterritorialization that emphasizes the fact that a place from which to ask these questions does not exist.[9] In this sense, *The Tree of Life* can be read at the intersections of cinema and life, or posthuman cinema, because it fractures the subject from the centre of the film by stressing that any voice-over, any point-of-view shot, or any image of a human can only ever be an any-instant-whatever amid a multiplicity of images without humans, such as a cosmos sequence or a dinosaur sequence, that are linked by a field of experience, or life, and not by linear narrative. In other words, the dinosaurs in the film do not interact with humans, such as in Steven Spielberg's *Jurassic Park* (1993), and instead, this sequence of dinosaur images becomes an abrupt gesture towards the whole by having no discernible link to the human sequences other than sharing the same film and happening, presumably, on the same planet.

While a pathway from a closed set to the whole always remains present, *The Tree of Life* makes this pathway explicit. 'Every closed system also communicates. There is always a thread', argues Deleuze, 'to link the glass of sugared water to the solar system, and any set whatever to a larger set.'[10] Malick's film offers more than a thread when it transitions to images of the solar system. However, this film does not follow the linear life of a boy or a family that becomes interrupted by a cosmos sequence and flashbacks to a time of dinosaurs. Within the images of this boy (and his experiences as a man) as well as the images of the family in general, there is always a thread to link an event to another without taking a linear pathway and by reaffirming a principle of indeterminability. 'And love is smiling through all things,'[11] states Jessica Chastain's voice-over narration during the childhood play sequence that follows from the two ways through life sequence, which comes just after the opening cosmos sequence. Although some might wish to link this statement to the way of grace that Mrs O'Brien

(Chastain) can be said to model in the film, the cinematic form of Malick's film can be read to emphasize that this love shares with immanence the structure that smiles through all images of the film. Therefore, following this childhood play sequence, which offers little if any principle of determinability to situate these characters and actions as the sequence jumps from one moment of play to the next, there is a cut to an overhead shot of a waterfall to a cut that places the camera at the base of a tree moving up towards a glowing sun. Then there is a cut to a black screen and finally a cut to another sequence when Mrs O'Brien is older, and she receives the infamous Western Union telegram in the yellow envelope that one often associates with the horrible news that a family member has died in the Vietnam War. This moment brings a rush of emotions to characters in this actual moment and to the many moments that will follow when the images of the film flow. However, this narrative event becomes dislodged from narrative.

In the film, the images of this moment are glimpsed as any-instant-whatever, but not because they lack important or affective performance. Rather, this sequence becomes any-instant-whatever because it does not follow from a causal chain of events and instead springs forth amid a set of sequences that juxtapose human and non-human images. In short, *The Tree of Life* takes shape through a field of experience where human perspectives are only one possibility through which life materializes. The film can be read in terms of posthuman cinema because the form of the film continuously reminds us that our view of the world and the way in which we process it remains one possible condition as opposed to the real condition of experience. To map this form, it becomes necessary to unfold Deleuze's transcendental empiricism as a vibrant pathway to posthumanism.

Deleuze's transcendental empiricism

There is, perhaps, no simple definition of transcendental empiricism. Moreover, to adequately map this mode would require much more space than there exists within this chapter.[12] In place of a complex definition of transcendental empiricism, this section explores the interconnections between Deleuze's transcendental empiricism and posthumanism to mobilize a philosophical position in relation to the forms unfolded by *The Tree of Life*. Thinking through Deleuze towards posthumanism reveals how Deleuze's philosophies – both his independent work as well as his work with Félix Guattari – can be read as always already posthuman, especially in terms of a de-hierarchization of life. This de-hierarchization entails a rethinking and a dismantling of human privilege and the transcendental subject in order to understand those views as illusions, which develop when the conditions of possible experience are taken to be the conditions of real experience. Therefore, rather than seeking what gives rise to images that are then perceived as privileges and subjects, human privilege and the transcendental subject (among other perceptions) are taken to be foundational and primary structures of experience. Composing this position is a detailed and complex set of claims and outcomes, which I will need to set aside for the sake of the task at hand and the space given. However, it is important to state that Deleuze observes errors in both transcendental positions as well as empirical ones. Hence, transcendental empiricism is not simply an empiricism.

What transcendental empiricism unfolds is a philosophy of immanence. Although I previously stated that there is, perhaps, no simple definition of transcendental empiricism, Levi R. Bryant's work claims that there is 'Deleuze's definition of transcendental empiricism is very simple: transcendental empiricism is that philosophical position which determines the conditions of real rather than possible experience'.[13] Whether or not we agree with Bryant's claim that this is a very simple definition, we can distinguish between the conditions of real and possible experience as inspired by Deleuze's position. In the most simple terms, real experience is generated by sensations as they unfold and express, while possible experience is composed of representations established from unacknowledged sensations and then reproduced as if they are the exact essence of sensation themselves and able to encapsulate all possibilities and all givens. Therefore, where real experience is an open field of sensations that is continuous difference, possible experience is a sealed compilation that could never be anything more than a different arrangement of what it already is. 'Deleuze argues that far from being prior to experience, the possible expressed in the concept', Bruce Baugh explains, 'is only the reflected image of the real, "a retrograde movement of the true", intelligible structures abstracted from real experience and then projected backward in time, creating the illusion of being prior to, and of conditioning, the experience.'[14] The issue here is not so much that this occurs, but it is the assumptions we make about these reflected images of the real that are structures disconnected from, all the while mistaken to be, real experience.

After all, humans and, in all likelihood, most non-humans engage with a field of experience in a related manner. That is to say, we take an image or a perception out of continuous unfolding sensations in various attempts to understand what we view as our past, present and future locations in what we deem to be a world. A subject or subjectivity is then an intelligible structure, but one that is abstracted from real experience. This is an important aspect to grasp because Deleuze is not seeking to completely eradicate representation, identity and recognition – as some readers of Deleuze assume – rather his transcendental empiricism seeks to uncover what makes these images and perceptions occur and, moreover, what is generating this potentiality. Bryant's reading of Deleuze informs this claim:

> Contrary to what some of the more romantic Deleuzians might think, Deleuze is quite happy to say that representation, identity, and recognition are real phenomena of our experience. We recognize things. We identify things. We represent things. If we did not do these things, then there would be no problem of representation and identity. The problem, rather, is what emerges when representation and identity are taken as metaphysically or epistemically primitive terms upon which the questions of philosophy are posed. According to Deleuze, when representation and identity are taken as metaphysically primitive, philosophy falls into insoluble problems. Transcendental empiricism attempts to navigate a way through or beyond these insoluble problems.[15]

Here we arrive at the issue, which occurs when representation and identity are assumed to be the conditions of real experience when they are, in Baugh's terms, actually reflected images of the real.

While Deleuze engages the history of philosophy as a means of navigating insoluble problems stemming from taking representation and identity as metaphysically primitive, I read this position as invigorating posthumanism because it provides a pathway to the de-hierarchization of life that exposes human privilege as an illusion, or as a condition of possible experience. This position exposes the fallacy that humans and transcendental subjects produce, manipulate and exist prior to experience through their own agency and power. By embracing transcendental empiricism, posthumanism has the capacity to rethink relations between all matter, living and nonliving, as interconnections in a continuous field of experience. Such a move displaces thought from the clutches of the subject and disperses it back within the chaos of being. 'The thought involved in the production of intuition is not the thought of a subject', as Bryant states, 'but is thought that unfolds on the part of being itself.'[16] Therefore, whether or not we claim to think something or to know something or to produce something, the field of experience and the force of living matter, as auto-poietic, continuously unfolds. Because this field of experience gives what is given – in terms of all things that come to materialize and then be perceived as this or that – the possibility for human privilege disintegrates. Consequently, in *The Tree of Life*, the movement between images of human life – and family life – continuously gives way to images of the universe, which take shape through the experiences of a sunflower or a cosmic glow or a rush of flowing lava. I read such sequences to illuminate the fact that human perspectives and stories are within a field of experience as opposed to determining it. In short, the sunflowers appear for no one and are images of experience on the same plane as any of the images of Jack.

Again, this can be difficult to grasp from our world view or perspective, because the field of experience and the sensations that are processed as a world and as objects appear to occur for us and even within us. The use of voice-over narration in *The Tree of Life* that emerges at the beginning of the film exposes this fact, especially the two ways through life that Chastain's character introduces. While the way of nature and the way of grace is voiced over images of the young girl as well as images of non-human animals and plants, the film lacks a link between these two perspectives or methodologies and the images of the world. Instead, this sequence gives shape to the processes through which humans work to place their subjective positions at the centre of experience and take them as the primary condition that structures an image of the world. Deleuze's transcendental empiricism, on the contrary, reveals that whenever the subject is assumed to be the primary condition to bring about this world view or perspective or image – or whatever conceptualization – this subject should be understood as actually removed and constructed outside of the conditions of real experience. In this sense, the way of grace and the way of nature are read to be possible conditions of experience.

Transcendental empiricism is then precisely a posthumanist position because it does not privilege any living matter as exceptional. Braidotti articulates such a position when discussing advances in molecular biology and monistic philosophy. 'These insights combine in defining intelligent vitality or self-organizing capacity as force', argues Braidotti, 'that is not confined within feedback loops internal to the individual human self, but is present in all living matter.'[17] Here intelligent vitality is dispersed to all living matter[18] where sensations and difference continuously unfold the new as matter is continuously becoming. Therefore, we arrive at the claim: 'Insofar as time is whole, open, and not dependent upon subjects, any thought founding itself on the form of identity or the same with respect to subjects or essences shows itself to be dogmatic.'[19] Consequently, if we embrace this position, we put not only all living matter on the same plane, but we also conceive of that plane as a field of experience transcendent to any and all formations. Taking this position further, we view the conditions of real experience as this field of experience where sensations and difference continuously unfold new relations, concepts and formations.

This may appear to suggest that we can then as a subject, identity, object or thing come to grasp the field of experience in its entirety. It could be expected that if we were able to rethink identity or the self in some less stringent manner and point our focus towards intersubjective and interobjective relations then we would somehow be better equipped to trace the field of experience in its entirety. However, such a tracing would only ever encapsulate some of the images or glimpses within our fold, and despite the most valiant of efforts this tracing would always already be a reflected image of the real, a retrograde moment projected back on a non-existent foundation. For even if we were to somehow project simultaneously every image or every glimpse of experience encapsulated by our fold, this would be an inadequate understanding because images and glimpses of the field of experience are always exceeded by a multiplicity of alterations – what we experience as more images. Beyond this inadequate understanding, it would also always be missing a swarm of other images of the field of experience because any one fold can never occupy the multiplicity of folds in any given moment. 'While all experience may be produced', argues Bryant, 'by differentials – may be the integration of differentials – not all experience can be deduced or constructed in mathematical thought by subjects such as ourselves.'[20] Therefore, beyond our human images or glimpse of the field of experience there is a manifold of images and glimpses, some of which we can deduce or construct while others forever escape our being and our thoughts. Moreover, because not all experience can be thought by humans, this realization links with posthuman conceptualizations of life through a de-hierarchization and eradication of human exceptionalism. *The Tree of Life* becomes, through this perspective, posthuman cinema and not a cinema-posthumans because the many sequences of the film that have no direct connection to humans and the human experiences of the characters are by no means an exhaustive set that encapsulates life. I read these sequences instead as giving shape to the fact that the field of experience structures many conditions of possible experience and the human-centric images are only one of many.

When there ceases to be an image, we cease being, but the field of experience persists. It gives rise to conditions of possible experience before us, such as the dinosaur sequence, as well as to conditions of possible experience that have yet to come, such as the sequences on the beach where in death or in dream – there is a principle of indeterminability here – humans may walk with their past selves and with family members who have passed. Rather than assuming that our subjectivities or identities passively receive images or glimpses, it is the potentiality for subjectivity or identity that is generated actively by the field of experience. Furthermore, we should not take an image to be simply a visual, or a perception. An image is anything that arises from a percept or an affect – moreover, a sensation – which is generated by forces or intensities unfolding new relations. Existence is then always something new. 'Essences, whether expressed through Kantian concepts or Hegelian Ideas, do not determine existence; coming into existence is not a transition from the possible (the concept) to the real (its instantiation)', Baugh explains, 'but the production of something new by already existing forces entering into new relations through chance encounters, where these encounters are nevertheless the extrinsically determined effects of previous encounters.'[21] It is important here to stress the positivity of the field of experience so it does not become conceived in terms of a negative or a void waiting to be formed by a concept or an Idea. Consequently, concepts and Ideas do not determine what it is. In place of a void in search of form, there is positive substance continuously entering into new relations and new forms as a myriad of forces and intensities remake, reimagine and rethink it. What we perceive as subjectivity or identity is a fold within this field of experience that gives a glimpse as it is generated by the ongoing multiplicity of chance encounters. In other words, it is the field of experience and our image of it that forms us in the becoming of each image over and over again. *The Tree of Life* takes shape through such a fold because narrative events do not follow a linear and causal chain of events, and instead they flow as encounters thrust upon various characters and as situations opening threads towards remaking, reimagining and rethinking images of life.

Our perceptions or our glimpses of the field of experience may be conceived as stable or even as *a priori* in structure to this field because we are often oblivious of the imperceptible forces and intensities continuously generated by and generating new relations. 'Deleuze's transcendental empiricism', states Bryant, 'attempts to overcome the opposition between concepts and intuitions, *noesis* and *aisthesis*, that has characterized most of the history of philosophy and which arises from the assumption of a finite subject whose receptivity is conceived of as passive.'[22] We think, feel, understand, or even experience images of the field of experience as if they are passively received by our being conceived to exist outside this field and perceiving it as something we engage with. However, it is being itself that is the image as a fold generated by forces and intensities continuously stirring. If there really was some sort of stability, or even some trace of ourselves, as a structure that passively received images or glimpses of the field of experience, then why can we not recall every image, every glimpse of experience, that we have ever lived? In some ways, *The Tree of Life* could be interpreted as a series of Jack's memories or images of childhood. However, we do not start with Jack, and it would be difficult to reconcile the moments attached solely to Mr or Mrs O'Brien, let alone the cosmos sequence. Through Deleuze's transcendental empiricism, we might read these images of Jack's childhood alongside the cosmos sequence, the dinosaur sequence, the cuts to black, the shots of sunflowers and trees that are not connected to any character within the film, and any of the other random images precisely as images of any-instant-whatever. Whether or not Jack or Mrs O'Brien is remembering, or if the childhood sequence is a flashback or understood as the present, these were all sensations unfolded by the field of experience. Consciousness, in this sense, becomes understood to be a delicate image fluctuating from moment to moment as it is always remaking and reimagining our conception of subjectivities and identities through each chance encounter as forces continuously bring about the new. Even if there are some moments we could deem to be major events within the childhood sequence – such as the drowning death of another boy – there are just as many moments that pass without a dramatic event. 'If these are privileged instants', states Deleuze in a discussion of Muybridge's equidistant snapshots of a horse's gallop, 'it is as remarkable or singular points which belong to movement, and not as the moments of actualisation of a transcendent form.'[23] The same can be said of the childhood sequence, the cosmos sequence, and *The Tree of Life* as a whole: they belong to movement and time and, moreover, to life. A chance encounter, a force or intensity, brings forth these images within the materiality of the world and our brains. These images themselves become bodies – understood as things or forms – capable of entering into new relations so that the materiality of a life belongs to no one but itself, or the field of experience.

The cinema is perhaps the most vibrant demonstration of this reality, where it is evident that two images put side by side or one after the other generate more than just two images.[24] Whether we claim that our minds produce a third image, which develops from the combination of the two given images, or that the moving images themselves create the third image, there can be no doubt that there is always something new when one image encounters another. Deleuze's transcendental empiricism, however, reveals that we do not receive these two images passively to create a third image – the effect of the two images – but that a multiplicity of indiscernible forces and intensities generate a third image, which we can only know in terms of their effect. 'In other words', Bryant states, 'in most cases we are unconscious of the productive rules governing our intuitions and must thereby have recourse to receptive affectivity – which consists only of the effects of these rules – in order to arrive at a knowledge of being.'[25] By focusing only on the effects of the rules or the forces generating images of experience, we are led to assume all kinds of systems and procedures that not only take possible experience to be real experience, but we also limit the maximization of our potentiality. Transcendental empiricism forms a methodology to overcome this limiting.

Transcendental empiricism and life

Transcendental empiricism offers a pathway towards posthumanism because 'Deleuze argues for the openness, and the endlessness of experience in such a way that we can no longer define the limits of experience a priori.'[26] Therefore, the openness and the endlessness of experience would not define what in life we should preserve nor would it fold life or the earth around human survival,[27] but in its place pursue an exploration of what life had yet to become. This entails a fracturing of any individualistic notions of existence, which transcendental empiricism launches by exposing the concept of the individual as motivated by the conditions of possible, not real, experience. *The Tree of Life* materializes a form of life in this way through the fleeting identities of Jack, Mrs O'Brien, and Mr. O'Brien that, at times, seem to seize the flow of the film through their voice-overs and even their visual perspectives, but, at other times, are ceaselessly undone by the intrusion of other characters and their perspectives, dreams, and images as well as the sequences that wander into the cosmos or offer extended takes of sunflowers moving in the wind unconnected to any character's perspective through a shot-reverse-shot. The individual becomes a central concern of the voice-overs as well as in the moments when the characters struggle with their existential condition, yet the images continuously push towards conditions of real experience and the open.

Furthermore, Deleuze's transcendental empiricism provides a basis for dismantling barriers to a de-hierarchization of life by exposing the tenets of human exceptionalism to be abstracted from real experience. The subject, identity, and individuality are such barriers that posthumanism works to undo in order to conceptualize a more holistic image of life. 'Individualism is not an intrinsic part of "human nature"', argues Braidotti, 'as liberal thinkers are prone to believe, but rather a historically and culturally specific discursive formation, one which, moreover, is becoming increasingly problematic.'[28] The individual then is an image projected back as removed from experience and assumed as a site of passive receptivity as opposed to being one more element within a field of experience. Here, within a field of experience, not only are elements or forms different from one another, but they exist as pure difference, which occludes any stability or linearity as an assumption that is necessary to assert what we perceive to be our self. However, it is important to stress that such an occlusion does not eradicate our ability to conceive of experience as containing the stability or linearity necessary to establish a self. Rather, it reveals that such processes exclude the conditions of real experience and the forces that compose actuality in order to frame a system of sameness that in turn justifies a hierarchization of life.

We may think we are one and we may think we are whole. We may even consider ourselves to be an individual, a subject, or to have an identity. But, where do we assert the boundaries of this container? How can we assign a central master of this so-called self when a multiplicity of forces form what we perceive to be a body and in turn allow it to persevere? Not only are there forces within what we perceive to be a contained body – such as churning bacteria, pumping organs and sparking chemicals, among others – but also so many intensities affecting this 'body' from the outside – such as air containing oxygen generated by the complex processes of plants and trees or toxins produced by mechanical sources, sunlight beaming from a massive star at the centre of the solar system, and gravity pushing minerals and materials into a formation recognizable as a body, among others. Furthermore, there are the chance encounters from what we deem to be our past, or the past of our ancestors – this should be read as human and non-human – which contributed to the forces and intensities that generated the experience we perceive as our own potential. Likewise, perhaps beyond any capacities we have to conceptualize time or duration, we may wish to acknowledge or imagine the forces that could have sparked life on earth and earth itself. 'To open ourselves up to superior and inferior durations', Bryant states, 'is to open ourselves up to greater and lesser rhythms of time or difference which go beyond our own subject-centered experience.'[29] Therefore, while we have an image of experience, transcendental empiricism has the capacity to open up a perception of the conditions of real experience as well as to reveal that what we deem to be us is only ever an image of experience itself.

Terrence Malick and a cinema of life

A radical capacity for overwhelming openness takes shape in Malick's film as demonstrated by the multiplicity of ways in which it has already been interpreted.[30] More than the sum of an interpretation or interpretations, Malick's *The Tree of Life* also expresses the capacity to launch a multiplicity of speculations – as do his other films – which can pose a challenge for viewers. Challenges are not always welcome, but they often force thinking and speculation that in turn generates new relations. An aversion to challenges is most likely why some people were critical of Malick's *The Tree of Life*. Referencing several reviews of the film, Lee Carruthers notes that some reviewers 'did not discern much connective tissue in Malick's film, binding its form to content' which leads to viewing *The Tree of Life* 'as a kind of broken signal whose intermittent "flashes" are too scant, or widely spaced, to plausibly produce meaning'.[31] However, the claim that there is a missing connective tissue, or that the film is a broken signal, reflects a desire, on the part of the reviewers, to engage with a film that is more capable of being explicitly understood in a linear way – Y and Z occur in the film, which represents X. *The Tree of Life* does not readily make form available to link or connect with content for direct and clear observations. 'Admittedly', concedes even Carruthers in terms of her own interpretation, 'this broad segmentation is somewhat provisional: one could easily propose alternative ways of construing the film's material to read it differently.'[32] This concession points not to a lack of validity within Carruthers's speculation, but rather to the openness of the film itself and to the fact that it unfolds a form in need of reading.

The form of the film, in my reading, takes shape as life. Which materializes life not in terms of a subjectivity or a boy's life, because the film works through much more than the life of Jack and offers far less than a complete and discernable overview of his identity – or anyone else's. Transcendental empiricism frames the life that takes shape in my reading: the film forms through images of any-instant-whatever to structure a multiplicity of possible conditions beyond that of Jack's or any other human. 'The story of *The Tree of Life*', states Steven Rybin, 'defies encapsulation. Its complexity is due not only to the subject matter – which takes on nothing less than the meaning and origins of life itself – but also to the further sundering of Malick's imagery and his narrative structure.'[33] I want to put pressure on Rybin's claim that the film's subject matter is the meaning and origins of life to gesture towards the claim that *The Tree of Life* forms life through the inability and the indiscernibility that fractures any clear subjective totality to know, or need to know, who Jack or even Mrs O'Brien is. In its place, the images map a becoming that never remains stable and always asks questions – such as the voice-overs that continue throughout the film – and this always cracks in a given moment to exceed the concerns or conditions of any given person to move back into other conditions of possible experience. Therefore, the form of Malick's cinema takes on an openness that makes what would be a major narrative event in many other films – such as Mr. O'Brien leaving after a fight with Mrs O'Brien – and marks this event as something that becomes only as singular and remarkable as any other moment – such as a roaring waterfall or the O'Brien brothers playing in a field.

The end of the film materializes through such singular and remarkable images on an even plane when, cutting from the beach sequence, the camera pans down to a field of sunflowers and lingers with them moving in the wind. Then there is a cut to inside a glass elevator going down – this is presumably a point-of-view shot for adult Jack, but again there is a principle of indiscernibility. A cut then goes to an image with the camera tracking back and tilted up following a tree to a glass ceiling with the sun shining before cutting back to the same position within the elevator going down. The next cut takes us to adult Jack turning in the space outside the glass buildings with a cut that goes to a close-up of his face. Finally, three more cuts go to a low angle shot of a glass building, a long shot that lingers on a bridge, and then the same shot that begins the film with a light formation. The end. 'What *The Tree of Life* finally offers', argues Carruthers, 'is not simply a form that mimics its content, but rather an effect that is visceral and generative.'[34] However, with this ending, I am less interested in the affective experience the film offers: the visceral and generative offering that Carruthers identifies. Rather, inspired by Brinkema's reading of the forms of the affects,[35] I take the structure of this ending to elucidate the fact that Jack's subjectivity only ever holds a condition of possible experience, which is exceeded by the many other possible conditions materializing in any given moment. Therefore, the film is a form of life not because it traces the linear events of Jack's life from start to finish – such as occurs more visibly in a film such as Richard Linklater's *Boyhood* (2014) – but because it refuses to contextualize Jack's life in a linear and discernable manner. Avoiding a mimicking of a boy's life or a person's life, *The Tree of Life* can be read through Deleuze's transcendental empiricism as rupturing the tenets that what privilege Jack's or Mrs O'Brien's or even a sunflower's view of the world. Many images do walk and feel and live with Jack's and Mrs O'Brien's experiences in a manner that structures our own human modes for making sense of the world, but these modes continually become undermined by and tangled with other modes to remind us that the real conditions of experience bring any given image to bear in fleeting glimpses.

For some, *The Tree of Life* can be seen as a film that takes a grand perspective through an exploration of the cosmos. As Marc Furstenau points out, this focus on the cosmos 'plays a curiously central role' in the film, 'which is otherwise a quite modest tale, the story of a childhood in small-town Texas in the 1950s'.[36] Despite this supposed curiosity surrounding Malick's inclusion of the cosmos sequence, Furstenau identifies[37] this portion of the film as aligning with Malick's tendency to reflexively navigate film genres within this work – such as his exploration of the western in *Days of Heaven* (1978) or the war film in *The Thin Red Line* (1998) – even if initial readings suggest that *The Tree of Life* 'may appear to be less obviously concerned with genre than Malick's other films'.[38] Despite the appearance that the film has a lack of generic conventions, Furstenau's careful and logical analysis outlines how 'the structure and logic' of the science fiction film 'informs *The Tree of Life*'.[39] What fascinates me within *The Tree of Life*, in relation to the science fiction genre, becomes realized through Furstenau's work. The science fiction film focuses on outer space as space-for-humans. From Georges Méliès's *A Trip to the Moon* (1902) to Fred Wilcox's *Forbidden Planet* (1956) to Stanley Kubrick's *2001: A Space Odyssey* (1968) to George Lucas's *Star Wars* (1977) to Christopher Nolan's *Interstellar* (2014), and before and beyond, images of outer space in science fiction films – as well as other films set within space, such as Ron Howard's *Apollo 13* (1995) or Alfonso Cuarón's *Gravity* (2013) – become framed as a space looked at by humans, a space explored by humans, a space impacting the lives of humans, a potential new home for humans, and, moreover as space-for-humans. In short, a subjective place always exists from which to ask: who is this space for and what does it do? Malick's cosmos sequence fractures this place and eradicates it from the science fiction film in order to render it, through the lens of transcendental empiricism, to be another image of the field of experience and without a character's perspective to bend it to the interest of a human.

The cinematic forms of Malick appear at odds with the core narrative concentrations of the science fiction film. While films such as *Days of Heaven* (1978) and *The Thin Red Line* (1998) dedicate close-ups to non-humans that can be said to appear monstrous, alien bodies and the looming danger they impose to humans seem unfathomable within a Malick film. Of course, he does include the occasional dinosaur, but, again, these are far from the dinosaurs of *Jurassic Park* and they too are no longer dinosaurs-for-humans because they remain a distinct image without a direct connection to a human narrative. Consequently, *The Tree of Life* pushes visuals of the science fiction film towards new pathways. This is no doubt motivated by 'Malick's aesthetic', which Carruthers states, 'has tended toward spare images, as though deliberately emptied out, lengthy descriptions of the natural environment, and compositions in which the human figure appears diminished in scale against an expansive context'.[40] These aspects of Malick's aesthetic, as identified by Carruthers, already situate his cinema within the posthuman realm by offering scales and spaces that represent non-human forms. However, juxtaposed or against these non-human forms – primarily the cosmos sequence and the images of outer space – is a film intently bound up and tangled with the life of a boy and his family. Much like the voice-overs that inform us of the way of nature and a way of grace, the cosmos and the boy could be considered as two competing aspects of the film.

To put it bluntly, the film would be simpler without the cosmos sequence. Even with a disconnect remaining between imagery and narrative structure, a sole focus on the boy and his family would be more readily interpreted as a poetic reflection on growing up and the difficulties one encounters as an adult searching for meaning in life. Again, Furstenau's reading is picking up on these tensions between cosmos and childhood sequences. '*The Tree of Life* is concerned with, among many other things, this delicate balance between the human and the cosmological', he continues, 'which has been most thoroughly dramatized in science fiction, and the film stages, in exceptionally stark terms, the potential for specifically human concerns to be lost in the vast space within which we may now so easily roam in our imaginations.'[41] There is a challenge within this delicate balance that Furstenau notes and this challenge tests the ability of viewers to 'maintain an interest in more earthly matters' against the journey into the depths of the cosmos.[42] While Furstenau's interpretation of the film recognizes important features of the cosmos-earthly divide, I argue there is also the capacity to collapse the two as expressions of a singular process in much the same way that Vernon W. Cisney takes the two approaches to life offered by the film – the way of nature and the way of grace – and collapses them as one.[43]

This collapsing occurs, through Deleuze's transcendental empiricism, when we speculate about the potential links between the cosmos sections and the rest of the film about small-town life. In most other films with images of outer space, there would be obvious links that frame images as space-for-humans, but *The Tree of Life* does not frame outer space in that way and, as a result, the images of outer space are, what I deem, space-as-immanence – in terms of outer space for space itself and open to potentialities as there is no direct or explicit cause for the images. Space-as-immanence becomes more images of any-instant-whatever, or images that frames additional conditions of possible experience beyond human subjectivity. 'The universe', Furstenau argues, 'is revealed in this long sequence to be a space of simple unfolding, of process without change, barren when compared to the ostensibly simpler but in fact far more mysterious stories of life and death on earth.'[44] This interpretation of the contrasting sequences is reasonable, especially from a humanist perspective grounded in human exceptionalism. There does, at first glance, appear to be much more happening and changing within the sequences focused on the boy and his life than there does within the cosmos sequence. Conversely, I could imagine an anti-humanist argument that would posit the cosmos sequence as much more complex – it is the creation of a universe, a planet and a multiplicity of lives – when compared to a few humans undergoing periods of thriving and struggling that are insignificant when compared to cosmos-time. That being said, I do feel both positions are equally compelling. While there is something to be said for the mystery of how the universe could have been created, there is also a possibility that there is little interest in a film with digital sequences of this endlessly ongoing creation.

In contrast, I can see the validity in Furstenau's reading: the film 'seems interested in contrasting our world with an apparently empty universe, devoid of other intelligent life'.[45] However, I cannot help but identify the privileging of human intelligence here over other forms of intelligence that are unfolding a universe in the cosmos sequence. The type of thought that unfolds on the part of being itself, which is generated by the forces and intensities within a field of experience far beyond any perceived boundaries of earth. 'The vital order', argues Colebrook, 'exceeds life as it is, which is a way of saying that life, or the vital, beyond the lived, possesses a reality beyond organisms, experience, subjects, and – most importantly – thought.'[46] In the cosmos sequence, the film expresses superior durations in comparison to that of humans as the creation of a universe occupies a time and a rhythm in many ways greater as well as lesser than the life of a boy. Yet, the film expresses all of these durations that can only be grasped as a multiplicity of durations, rhythms and times. In other words, all images become images on the same plane of any-instant-whatever. The film is not only about human life, a human life in context or the narrative of life from beginning to near present. *The Tree of Life* is also about what exceeds life as it is, especially for humans. In many ways, it could be argued that this exceeding of a life of a boy is merely represented by the cosmos sequence, which could be said to serve as a reminder that there are always greater forces beyond any human subjectivity. While this is an important observation, this reading only begins to grasp the speculative capacity to think these sequences as one and a form of life.

It is one thing to offer a reading that traces the life of a boy against the background of the cosmos that unfolds seemingly in a ceaseless flow. It is another thing to open up potentiality beyond a subject-centred experience to explore the capacities of the boy within the cosmos and the cosmos within the boy. I come to this reading by grasping the images of outer space to be space-as-immanence as opposed to space-for-humans. The images of outer space are only ever outer space as continuous forces and intensities. The durations, rhythms and times of this space are not bound within a human's travel, a human's search for a new home, a human's intergalactic battle with aliens, or simply a human's gaze.[47] Yet, given the images and narrative of childhood in small-town Texas in the 1950s, the life of a boy is open to these durations, rhythms and times. While the images of outer space remain space-as-immanence, their relations cascade throughout the rest of the film expressing the superior and inferior durations as well as the greater and lesser rhythms of human and, moreover, earthly life. Beyond a human, subject-centred experience, there is a multiplicity of images and vibrations as the camera flows and grasps the intensities of the sun's beams, the forces of water, the intensities of a poisonous smoke, the forces of a field of sunflowers, the intensities of a father's disposition, and the forces of a mother's embrace. Life forms the interrelations of all of these aspects as well as so much more. In this way, Malick's film forms a cinema of life, but not as a film that contains the story of the universe or the story of a boy's life. *The Tree of Life* forms a cinema of life precisely because it does not claim to show the totality of life, and instead, it is a multiplicity of images of any-instant-whatever that are strung together as distinct conditions of possible experience as each shot, and each sequence has the potential for becoming something new. What I read forming in *The Tree of Life*, through Deleuze's transcendental empiricism, becomes a de-centred, de-hierarchized glimpse of life. In this glimpse, the human remains an integral vehicle in which the world can be experienced, but the fleeting nature of these glimpses – through Jack or Mrs O'Brien or whoever else – reduces them to the same plane as all other images – such as images of the cosmos sequence or shots of sunflowers. Therefore, despite the possibility of reading Jack's subjective position as primary, the images and *The Tree of Life* as a form of life pushes us to reconcile them with the conditions of real experience, or a posthuman cinema moving us beyond the centre of ourselves.

Notes

1 I would like to acknowledge that *This research was supported by the Social Sciences and Humanities Research Council of Canada*.
2 André Bazin, 'The Ontology of the Photographic Image', 10.
3 Laura Mulvey, 'Visual Pleasure and Narrative Cinema', 17.
4 Rosi Braidotti, *The Posthuman*, 1–2.
5 This film philosophy methodology I am using is inspired by Eugenie Brinkema, *The Forms of the Affects*.
6 This is a reference to Giles Deleuze's cinema books, *Cinema 1* and *Cinema 2*.
7 I discuss these readings in a later section.
8 Gilles Deleuze, *Cinema 2*, 7.
9 There are other films that do this: Andrei Tarkovsky's films are also analysed in a large and related project. However, what strikes me as unique about Malick, as I go on to discuss, resides in the extent to which he gestures towards the whole through images.

10 Gilles Deleuze, *Cinema 1*, 17.
11 Terrence Malick, dir., *Tree of Life*.
12 For an extensive and generative account of Deleuze's transcendental empiricism, see Levi R. Bryant's, *Difference and Givenness*.
13 Levi R. Bryant, *Difference and Givenness*, 8.
14 Bruce Baugh, 'Transcendental Empiricism: Deleuze's Response to Hegel', 138.
15 Levi R. Bryant, *Difference and Givenness*, 5.
16 Ibid., 12.
17 Rosi Braidotti, *The Posthuman*, 60.
18 We may wish to further extend this to all matter (such as in Jane Bennett's concept of vibrant matter) or to think through Braidotti's conceptualization of living matter as being far more encompassing than merely human and non-human animals as well as plants, but this discussion runs outside the task at hand.
19 Levi R. Bryant, *Difference and Givenness*, 219.
20 Ibid., 47.
21 Bruce Baugh, 'Transcendental Empiricism', 139.
22 Levi R. Bryant, *Difference and Givenness*, ix.
23 Gilles Deleuze, *Cinema 1*, 6.
24 There is a complex history of film theory related to this claim – especially the work of Soviet filmmakers such as Kuleshov, Vertov and Eisenstein – which I am gesturing towards but I have no intention of summarizing here, as I see no need for another summary of these theories.
25 Levi R. Bryant, *Difference and Givenness*, 12.
26 Ibid., 41.
27 I take this notion of folding the earth around human survival from Claire Colebrook. In *Death of the Posthuman*, she asks: 'can we imagine a mode of reading the world, and its anthropogenic scars, that frees itself from folding the earth's surface around human survival?' (23). In a related paper on the cinema of life, I explore this question in relation to the films of Andrei Tarkovsky.
28 Rosi Braidotti, *The Posthuman*, 24.
29 Levi R. Bryant, *Difference and Givenness*, 77.
30 This includes Russell J. A. Kilbourn's examination of the film as an adaptation/remediation of the book of Job in '(No) Voice Out of the Whirlwind', Selmin Kara's analysis of the analogue and digital aspects of the film in order to gesture towards a speculative realist aesthetics in 'Beasts of the Digital World', Sarah French and Zoë Shacklock's exploration of the sublime aesthetics of the film and their affective potential in 'The Affective Sublime', and Jonathan Beever and Vernon Cisney's entire edited volume dedicated to philosophical footholds in the film, among others discussed here.
31 Lee Carruthers, 'Deep Time', 118.
32 Ibid., 131.
33 Steven Rybin, 'On *The Tree of Life*', 171.
34 Lee Carruthers, 'Deep Time', 138.
35 Eugenie Brinkema, *The Forms of the Affects*.
36 Marc Furstenau, 'Technologies of Observation', 59.
37 I want to point out that I am focusing on one aspect of Furstenau's argument. His reading of the film analyses the use of visual effects in relation to the science fiction, the meaning of life and other aspects, which are outside the scope of my interests within this chapter. However, his framing of the film within the science fiction genre is important here.

38 Ibid., 76-7.
39 Ibid., 60.
40 Lee Carruthers, 'Doing Time', 126-7.
41 Marc Furstenau, 'Technologies of Observation', 71.
42 Ibid.
43 Vernon Cisney, 'All the World Is Shining', 224-9.
44 Marc Furstenau, 'Technologies of Observation', 62.
45 Ibid., 63.
46 Claire Colebrook, *Deleuze and the Meaning of Life*, 34.
47 Of course, one could raise the counterpoint that the film has a spectator that is 'gazing' at the images of outer space, but I am concerned here with the convention that outer space within science fiction films is always something for humans in some way.

Bibliography

Baugh, Bruce. 'Transcendental Empiricism: Deleuze's Response to Hegel'. *Man and World* 25 (April 1992): 133-48.
Bazin, André. 'The Ontology of the Photographic Image'. In *What is Cinema? Volume 1*, translated by Hugh Gray, 9-16. Berkeley, CA: University of California Press, 2005.
Beever, Jonathan and Vernon W. Cisney. *The Way of Nature and the Way of Grace: Philosophical Footholds on Terrence Malick's The Tree of Life*. Evanston, IL: Northwestern University Press, 2016.
Bennett, Jane. *Vibrant Matter: A Political Ecology of Things*. Durham, NC: Duke University Press, 2010.
Braidotti, Rosi. *The Posthuman*. Cambridge: Polity Press, 2013.
Brinkema, Eugenie. *The Forms of the Affects*. Durham, NC: Duke University Press, 2014.
Bryant, Levi R. *Difference and Givenness: Deleuze's Transcendental Empiricism and the Ontology of Immanence*. Evanston, IL: Northwestern University Press, 2008.
Carruthers, Lee. 'Deep Time: Methods of Montage in Terrence Malick's *The Tree of Life*'. In *Doing Time: Temporality, Hermeneutics, and Contemporary Cinema*, 115-38. Albany, NY: State University of New York Press, 2016.
Cisney, Vernon W. 'All the World Is Shining, and Love Is Smiling through All Things: The Collapse of the 'Two Ways' in *The Tree of Life*'. In *The Way of Nature and the Way of Grace: Philosophical Footholds on Terrence Malick's The Tree of Life*, edited by Jonathan Beever and Vernon W. Cisney, 213-32. Evanston, IL: Northwestern University Press, 2016.
Colebrook, Claire. *Death of the Posthuman: Essays on Extinction, Vol. 1*. Ann Arbor, MI: Open Humanities Press, 2014.
Colebrook, Claire. *Deleuze and the Meaning of Life*. London: Continuum, 2010.
Deleuze, Gilles. *Cinema 1*. Translated by Hugh Tomlinson and Barbara Habberjam. London: Continuum, 2005.
Deleuze, Gilles. *Cinema 2*. Translated by Hugh Tomlinson and Robert Galeta. London: Continuum, 2005.
French, Sarah and Zoë Shacklock. 'The Affective Sublime in Lars von Trier's *Melancholia* and Terrence Malick's *The Tree of Life*'. *New Review of Film and Television Studies* 12, no. 4 (2014): 339-56.

Furstenau, Marc. 'Technologies of Observation: Terrence Malick's *The Tree of Life* and the Philosophy of Science Fiction'. In *The Way of Nature and the Way of Grace: Philosophical Footholds on Terrence Malick's The Tree of Life*, edited by Jonathan Beever and Vernon W. Cisney, 59–87. Evanston, IL: Northwestern University Press, 2016.

Kara, Selmin. 'Beasts of the Digital World: Primordigital Cinema and the Question of Origins'. *Sequence* 1, no. 4 (2014): 1–15.

Kilbourn, Russell J. A. ' (No) Voice Out of the Whirlwind: The Book of Job and the End of the World in *A Serious Man*, *Take Shelter*, and *The Tree of Life*'. *Adaptation* 7, no. 1: 25–46.

Malick, Terrence, dir. *Tree of Life*. Written by Terrence Malick. United States of America: Fox Searchlight Pictures, 2011.

Mulvey, Laura. 'Visual Pleasure and Narrative Cinema'. In *Visual and Other Pleasures*, 13–27. New York: Palgrave Macmillan, 2009.

Rybin, Steven. 'On *The Tree of Life*'. In *Terrence Malick and the Thought of Film*, 171–81. Lanham, MD: Lexington Books, 2012.

7

Affect/face/close-up

Beyond the affection-image in postsecular cinema

Russell J. A. Kilbourn

How is one to conceive of the subject in a posthuman, post-cinematic era – an era more awash in images than any prior period in human history, the great majority of which, moreover, are of people: a plenitude of faces. To what extent can we still find guidance in the writings of Gilles Deleuze, a thinker who has done more than most to destroy the psychoanalytic foundations of modern subjectivity inherited from the post-Enlightenment humanist tradition? How might his theories be productively inflected in relation to a certain twentieth-century counter-tradition of ethical thought grounded in the primacy of the other over the self? The latter will be exemplified here by Martin Buber's theory of dialogue set over against the Levinasian ethical model, in part at least because the former's formulation of otherness (in the self-other relation) is more amenable to application within a cinematic context.[1]

In *Cinema 2*, Deleuze elaborates the 'time image' characteristic of the post-war art cinema, ushering in a highly influential philosophical approach to the cinematic representation of time – simultaneously a diagnosis of European subjectivity in the aftermath of the Second World War – and to the idea of film itself as philosophy. In order to negotiate the gap between the modern cinematic subject, constituted in and through the post-war crisis of the action-image and resulting emergence of the time-image, and the radical epistemological transformations in subjectivity since the mid-1980s and into the twenty-first century, I focus here on the close-up as a uniquely cinematic technique; my discussion, therefore, concludes with a close analysis of a scene from Xavier Beauvois's *Of Gods and Men* (2010), a particularly striking example of postsecular film. At the same time, I seek to investigate the relation, such as it is, between the human face as subject of the paradigmatic close-up, what Deleuze calls the affection-image, and the 'face' as elaborated in the thought of Martin Buber, who had few words to spare for visual images.[2] The invocation of Buber shifts my consideration of the close-up into not so much a theological context as an explicitly ethical-philosophical context. My other contemporary film-theoretical reference points in this endeavour are Mary Ann Doane's 2003 essay 'The Close-up: Scale and Detail in the Cinema', and especially Paul Coates's 2012 book *Screening the Face*. Unlike Doane, however, whose primary focus is the close-up in classical Hollywood cinema,[3] mine is on the close-up more generally, as it signifies in relation to the transformations in the cinematic image Deleuze describes. And, unlike Coates, whose focus is primarily upon the face, the human visage as content of a given shot, mine is on the relation between the close-up as cinematic technique and the face as philosophical concept. As the following discussion will show, I would always insist on the radical distinction among the filmic close-up, the photographic still image of a face, and the face in itself.

Published in the mid-1980s, Deleuze's contribution to film theory, *Cinema 1 and 2*, appeared at the end of the celluloid and the dawning of the digital era in film. Historically speaking, Deleuze does not consider any films produced after the 1970s Hollywood Renaissance and is mainly concerned with the legacy of the postwar art cinema. It seems legitimate, therefore, to question the ongoing relevance of Deleuze's film theory, in light of his famous contention, in the seventh chapter of *Cinema 2*, that 'the link between man [sic] and the world has been broken. Henceforth this link must become an object of belief: it is the impossible which can only be restored within a faith' (62). According to Deleuze, the task or capacity of 'modern cinema' is to restore 'our belief in the world' (ibid.). What he meant by 'modern cinema' seems clear; what he meant by 'faith' or 'belief' somewhat less so. This passage has become a point of contention for research on film in the context of a world characterized with respect to economic, pop-cultural and above all technological globalization and media convergence, but which, in religious terms, is fractious and de-centralized. By announcing the 'death of God' at the end of the nineteenth century, Nietzsche opened a Pandora's box whose effects remain undiluted in the twenty-first century. What happens to a notion like the 'sacred' in the wake of this attempt to deconstruct Western culture's dominant ethical model? How do filmmakers confront this challenge? And what are we to make of the contradictions inherent in the contemporary love affair with the image, in the face of long-standing iconoclastic resistance to representations of the human, the transhuman or the radically Other? In other words, in the postsecular view, the question of belief is now only meaningful in an ethical context, defining a relationship not with God – or the transcendent or the sacred – but, in a much more urgent sense, with another human being whose very 'humanity' is localized in the face.

Deleuze has been and continues to be everyone's theorist and is often invoked to shore up manifestly contradictory positions. This is testament, among other things, to the fact that his philosophy as a whole is not systematic. When I invoke his work with Félix Guattari, for instance, I do so with the understanding that it is quite distinct from his mid-1980s film theory, which is *in itself* highly systematic.[4] As my approach does extend beyond the purely film-theoretical, I will also refer to Deleuze and Guattari's idiosyncratic critique, in *A Thousand Plateaus*, of the Christological underpinnings of the European colonialist subject. In the end, though, the focus here is Deleuze's contribution to contemporary theories of affect, and all that these pages in his first *Cinema* volume contribute to our understanding of what, cinematically speaking, comes after the subject as conceived in dualist Cartesian terms.[5] For, paradoxically, if the affection-image and the close-up teach us one thing, it is that we cannot do without some notion of the subject.

Deleuze and Derrida, for all their differences, were two of the key theorists in the post-structuralist project of displacing the Enlightenment subject from its position of conceptual-ideological centrality, and the deconstruction of its metaphysical foundations – a project that resonates to this day in Cultural Studies programmes and their disciplinary offshoots. Derrida's late 1980s forays into negative theology and his long-standing relation with Emmanuel Levinas extended his initial, late 1960s work of dismantling the metaphysics of presence, laying the ground for the subsequent emergence in the early twenty-first century of posthumanist thought.[6] And yet, it is Deleuze, even more than Derrida, who continues to be the key post-structuralist theorist for the current posthuman moment, particularly in its turn towards affect.

Affect and the affection-image

Contemporary popular culture is characterized by its melodramatic appeal to the emotions, behind which lurks the affectivity that has supplanted the subject in much contemporary critical-theoretical discourse. The attention to affect and its transcendence of representation is widespread, thanks largely to the influence since the 1990s of the work of Eve Kosovsky Sedgwick, Sarah Ahmed, Brian Massumi, Steven Shaviro and others. As will be explored next, one of the major theories of affect is that developed by Massumi, whose understanding of affect is deeply indebted to Deleuze's film theory, in particular what the latter calls the 'final avatar of the movement image': the affection-image.[7] It is, therefore, necessary to try to look back, past Massumian affect theory, in order to perceive the value in Deleuze's contribution to a discussion that most affect theorists would likely disavow. Key to my argument here is the affinity between the affection-image and the cinematic close-up, and the link between this shot/image and the human face. In Deleuze's formulation, 'the affection image is the close-up, and the close-up is the face'.[8]

This focus on the face/close-up as affection-image troubles the reading of affect we get from Massumi onwards, since the affectivity of the face comes down to a question of the emotions that can be read therein; in other words, we are firmly in the realm of representation, of readable signs, of affect as emotional trace of something deeper that escapes representation.[9] Confusion persists in the various theories of affect between affect and emotion. According to Eric Shouse, '[f]eelings are personal and biographical, emotions are social, and affects are prepersonal.'[10] Following Deleuze, Massumi equates affect with intensity: 'Affect is more often used loosely as a synonym for emotion. But one of the clearest lessons [here] is that emotion and affect – if affect is intensity – follow different logics and pertain to different orders.'[11] By 'The Autonomy of Affect', Massumi refers to 'autonomic' processes, as in the involuntary or 'unconscious' operations of the central nervous system. As Shaviro explains:

> For Massumi, affect is primary, non-conscious, asubjective or presubjective, asignified, unqualifying and intensive; while emotion is derivative, conscious, qualified, and meaningful, a 'content' that can be attributed to an already-constituted subject. Emotion is affect captured by a subject, or tamed and reduced to the extent that it becomes commensurate with that subject. Subjects

are overwhelmed and traversed by affect, but they have or possess their own emotions.[12]

Emotion, in this view, is a quality a subject takes on or puts off, while affect is the necessary condition for such attribution or divestment. This is one of the principal reasons why Deleuze concerns himself not with feelings or emotions per se but with affect, whose home is precisely the visual medium of film and whose locus is the face in the close-up. The non-rational, perceptual or 'pre-conscious' value the close-up represents resides in its affective dimension, and not in the emotion pictured there. Emotion falls under the regime of representation, while affect precedes and therefore escapes representation (Shaviro 4). In Deleuze's affection-image, however, this distinction is less clear, and the terminological issues around affect and emotion raise pertinent questions around representation and representability. Complications arise in particular when one traces back from Massumian affect per se to its source in Deleuze's affection-*image*. Indeed, for reasons to be explored next, these complications are similar to those arising from any attempt to 'apply', for example, Levinasian concepts in the analysis of a given film. Using Beauvois's film as example, I therefore invoke Buber's concept of 'dialogue' in an attempt to mitigate these problems with respect to actual filmic analysis. It is first necessary, however, to briefly address the significance of the cinematic close-up in relation to philosophical notions of the human face as ground of ethical thought.

The close-up and the face

The close-up as shot type and as uniquely cinematic technique is virtually as old as narrative cinema. According to Doane, '[t]he close-up, together with an editing that penetrates space and is at least partially rationalized by that close-up, seems to mark the moment of the very emergence of film as a discourse, as an art.'[13] It should not be overlooked that, unlike the conventional portrait photograph[14] or, in the twenty-first century, the 'selfie',[15] the classical close-up occurs within a flow of other shots, preceded and followed by a cut or other transition. As with other basic techniques, the close-up is a fundamental component of a narrative film grammar that manifests in a variety of different vernaculars. As the photo portrait analogy suggests, the shift from analogue/celluloid to digital has not altered this basic dimension of film language. One can then differentiate between the function and meaning of the classical close-up, as opposed to the uses to which the shot type has been put in alternative cinematic traditions. This becomes a crucial question when one addresses the distinction between Deleuze's movement- and time-images.

As Coates reminds us, the close-up comes into its own as cinematic signifier with the advent of the Hollywood star system, in which the face in close-up becomes icon/iconic, even as it remains – paradoxically – the ultimate reminder of predigital film's indexical connection to death.[16] These dimensions merge in an example from one of the earliest narrative films: the final frame of Edwin S. Porter's *The Great Train Robbery* (1903), in which a cowboy train robber, in close-up, fires his revolver point-blank towards the camera/viewer.[17] With certain significant exceptions, for example, Bergman and Kieslowski,[18] the close-up is statistically less common in the post-war modernist art cinema; however, 'one reason for political modernism's general lack of interest in close-ups is obvious: their capacity to mobilize compassion recalls a tabooed "identification"'.[19] But Porter's face-forward cowboy exemplifies a specific issue that remains rare even now, over one hundred years later.

If not affective identification, the close-up as distinct shot type has always addressed the viewer in a peculiarly intimate fashion. In one of the very first works of film theory in 1916, Hugo Münsterberg focuses on the mental experience of the viewer, anticipating contemporary theories of film spectatorship in a pre-Freudian discourse. Münsterberg introduces the new terminology of the 'photoplay', including the 'close-up': 'Here begins the art of the photoplay. [. . .] *The close-up has objectified in our world of perception our mental act of attention and by it has furnished art with a means which far transcends the power of any theater stage.*'[20] Echoing Henri Bergson's theory of affect, to which his is most directly indebted, Deleuze remarks that, in the movement-image, 'the moving body has lost its movement of extension, and movement has become movement of expression. It is this combination of a reflecting, immobile unity and of intensive, expressive movements which constitutes the affect. But is this not the same as a Face itself?'[21] When is a close-up of a non-human or partial object a 'face', and when not? Deleuze paraphrases Bela Bálàsz: 'As for the face itself, we will not say that the close-up deals with it or subjects it to some kind of treatment: there is no close-up *of* the face, the face is in itself close-up, the close-up is by itself face and both are affect, affection-image.'[22] According to Deleuze, this also works for close-ups of things other than human faces, through the process of 'faceification' (*visagéification*), which produces 'faceicity' (*visagéité*).[23] Coates therefore asks: 'Does this mean that . . . all close-ups disclose a face: that anything seen in close-up is not merely significant or powerful, but a "face," "affective," permitting something to be "faceified" . . . even if it does not resemble a face?' (24).[24] Bearing the attributes of focused attention and affective impact, Deleuze's affection-image is epitomized by the face, or by an object bearing the attribute of *faceicity* – a kind of baseline quality of 'humanness' – by virtue of its isolation as close-up (Deleuze, *Cinema 1*, 88). In the latter case, the close-up becomes an entity in its own right, in an echo of other early theorists such as Eisenstein and Bálàsz.[25] According to Deleuze, '[t]he close-up does not tear away its object from a set of which it would form part, of which it would be a part, but on the contrary it *abstracts it from all spatio-temporal co-ordinates*, that is to say it raises it to the state of Entity.[26] [. . .] What expresses [affect] is a face, or a facial equivalent (a faceified object)' (*Cinema 1*, 95–97). The question of objectification is at stake: when the close-up is *of* an object or when the close-up itself as image *becomes* an object. Recall Coates's observation about political modernism's lack of interest in close-ups:[27] Soviet cinema, and Eisenstein in particular, represents an attempt to deny the face in close-up its subjective specificity and, through 'typage', assign it an objective value as personification of a specific social class.[28] The distinction emerges, therefore, between the various cinemas that have arisen historically that treat the face in close-up generically or allegorically, as a metonym for the mass group (i.e. social class)[29] and those – classical Hollywood foremost among them – that evolved to treat the human face in close-up as the locus of individuality, the seat and source of emotional, if not affective, content. In the most extreme cases, such close-ups function independently of the preceding or subsequent flow of shots, as pointed out in 1970s feminist critiques of classical Hollywood's typical fragmentation of the female form. That is, in the classical Hollywood model, the close-up is at once a unit in a larger structure and a stand-alone image, producing meaning both in context and in a fashion intrinsic to itself. A distinction emerges, in other words, between cinematic permutations of the human countenance Coates identifies as the anti-realist 'mask' or *persona* versus the realism of the 'face'.[30]

This tension between inauthentic 'mask' and authentic 'face' beneath it reminds us of the subject's lingering value for our thinking of the ethical relation between self and other, in the movement from human to post- or non-human. Massumi, once again, insists on the affect-emotion distinction presumably because affect as he formulates it affords a new basis for subjectivity, a quasi-universalist – albeit radically negativized – foundation for human or posthuman identity, which seems to fly in the face of philosophies of immanence that embrace, perhaps too confidently, the positive and affirmative.[31] Richard Grusin goes further, extending Massumi's theory to the non-human realm. Apart from operating 'autonomously and automatically, independent of – and, according to Massumi, prior to – cognition, emotion, will, desire, purpose, intention or belief – all conventional attributes of the traditional liberal humanist subject', affectivity also 'belongs to nonhuman animals as well as to nonhuman plants or inanimate objects, technical or natural'.[32] Grusin rightly points out that Deleuze does claim affect for 'things as well as people'. The close-up of a thing other than a human face may become 'faceified'.[33] But such a reading of Deleuze's notion of the face in light of Massumi's privileging of the non-human distorts the former in the name of a posthumanist ethics. The example Grusin cites is from Deleuze's discussion of G. W. Pabst's *Pandora's Box* (1929),[34] one of whose characters is Jack the Ripper: 'And why is expression not available to things? There are affects of things. The "edge," the "blade," or rather the "point" of Jack the Ripper's knife is no less an affect than the fear which overcomes his features and the resignation which finally seizes hold of the whole of his whole face'.[35] What Grusin fails to note, however, is that Deleuze cites Pabst's film to show how the close-up of the object indicates for the viewer what the *character* is thinking/feeling – in the sequence of shots this is *Jack the Ripper* looking at a knife, after all, and, while the knife's point may very well be the locus of the affect, it is an altogether 'human' affect.[36] Grusin's error here is that he wants to keep the 'non-human' *within* the realm of representation – whether cinematic or otherwise. It seems to me, however, that a much better example of the non- or, for that matter, posthuman[37] – one that neither Grusin nor, for different reasons, Deleuze discusses – is God (in the parlance of negative theology) as 'absolute Other'.[38]

Towards a beyond of the affection-image

In *Cinema 1*, Deleuze breaks down the movement-image into three types according to conventional shot scale: the long shot corresponds to the perception-image, the medium shot to the action-image, the close-up to the affection-image. '[A]t the same time', he writes, 'each of these movement-images is a point of view on the whole of the film, a way of grasping this whole, which becomes affective in the close up, active in the medium shot, perceptive in the long shot.'[39] Deleuze elaborates the grammatical analogy of parts of speech to shot-types: the perception-image = noun; action-image = verb; affection-image = adjective[40] – although a better analogy for the latter might be the adverb, insofar as it modifies an action. What counts here is not simply the link between close-up shot and what Deleuze calls the 'final avatar of the movement image' – the affection-image[41] – but also the fact that this image occupies a specific position in a sequence of shots, the interval between 'an incoming perception and an outgoing action'.[42] The affection-image, as locus of affectivity, is what we might call the adjectival or adverbial interval, neither noun nor verb but modifier of each, the signifying space between inside and outside, in which the subject – what Deleuze calls a 'centre of indetermination' – 'perceives itself, or rather experiences itself or "feels itself" from the inside'.[43] Through the affection-image, the subject 'experiences its own interiority'.[44] 'This is the origin', for Deleuze, 'of Bergson's wonderful definition of affection as "a kind of motor tendency on a sensible nerve, that is, a motor effort on an immobilized, receptive plate"'.[45] This 'plate' is a photographic plate, the analogy directing attention to affect's visual, photographic, even analog, origins, and radically inflecting the status of this 'interiority'. This 'plate' or affection-image has its locus, moreover, in the *face*, the human visage, with its 'primary concentration of immobile receptors',[46] in other words, the eyes. To repeat: 'the affection image is the close-up, and the close-up is the face',[47] for Deleuze an eminently visual, visible structure. The face is a receptive surface, a photosensitive plate, which registers the emotional traces of affective stimuli. This is undoubtedly why Deleuze makes the further connection between the face/affection-image/photographic plate analogy and C. S. Peirce's iconic sign.[48] Deleuze thus privileges the positive dimension of the indexical sign even as he also privileges the iconic sign as site of stillness in the close-up, as perceptions are registered in the eyes and other 'organs' of the face, generating an affective response that precipitates an action or reaction.[49]

As noted, the close-up only signifies as affection-image within the basic sequence: perception/long shot > affection/close-up > action/medium shot. In other words, a conventional shot sequence that will as likely as not in any concrete example break down into a more or less complex series of shots and reverse-shots, where each close-up of a face is preceded and/or followed by the answering close-up of the interlocutor's face, until the action, whether a conversation or an exchange of looks, is completed and the specific constellation of shots delineating that action is superseded by the next, and so on. In terms of the function of the affection-image as a specific shot type, in the classical context each close-up tends to be of a face in three quarters or at times in profile. As Coates explains, 'the dominant face of mainstream cinema is the three-quarter one . . . because it lubricates the shot-counter shot movements that are the small change of dialogue.'[50] The straight on full-frontal close-up of a face (as in Porter's *The Great Train Robbery*) remains rare in narrative film until the emergence of the post-war art film in Europe. In 1959, Truffaut's *400 Blows* ended with the famous freeze-frame close-up of Jean-Pierre Léaud's face. The same strategy is replicated in the final shot of Fellini's *La Dolce Vita* (1960), with the difference that Valeria Ciangottini, the actress playing Paola, the young woman who reminds the protagonist of an 'Umbrian angel', turns to look straight into the camera, anticipating such mid-1960s self-reflexive works as *Persona* (1966), whose full-face and composite close-ups of Bibi Anderson and Liv Ullmann still read as radically anti-realist.[51]

Films as diverse as Godard's *Alphaville* (1965) and Bertolucci's *The Conformist* (1970) also exploit this highly formalized use of the full-face close-up. As Coates suggests, the difference between three-quarter and full-face close-ups in each case bespeaks a distinctly different meaning and a different relationship to realism: the 'partial averting of the face' suggests motion, action in process, if only because, as Coates points out, something is left 'unseen': both the other half of the face but also whatever it is that lies offscreen, in the direction of the eyeline indicated by the three-quarter angle of the face.[52] The full-frontal angle potentially militates against the onward flow of the narrative, bringing the viewer up short as if in a challenge to meet the character's gaze, to look her/him directly in the eyes – an action that in our daily lives can be very discomfiting when facing another person. Confronted by such a gaze in a film, the viewer's first response may be something like what Brecht meant by *Verfremdung*; thus, the full-face close-up can also function self-reflexively, as the *Persona* example shows. In Coates's words, the direct gaze potentially generates 'uncomfortable intensities of fear and love';[53] therefore, '"classical" filmmaking shields us from damage by the violence at play in the fictional world by employing a face that is habitually averted rather than directed towards us.'[54] It is to avoid such discomfort, while indirectly encouraging spectatorial identification, that the indirect gaze is employed: the performance of a face-to-face encounter. But whereas identification results from a perception leading to an affective response, with a more self-aware cinema (including Eisenstein's), the sequence is from perception to concept,[55] and affectivity is complicated or 'tainted' by intellectual engagement.

Alterity and the face

The affection-image corresponds to the close-up shot in classical style, and therefore the locus of affect or emotion in this kind of cinema is the face. For Deleuze, for instance, Carl Theodor Dreyer's 1928 *The Passion of Joan of Arc*, a film made up almost entirely of close-ups, is 'an almost exclusively affective film'.[56] Paul Schrader, in his theory of 'transcendental' film style, echoes 1 Cor. 13.12 in claiming that the cinematic representation or mediation of one's relationship to the sacred is only of value as long as that relationship is *not* 'face to face', for the face to face signals the end of images. In the New Revised Standard English translation, this passage reads: 'For now we see in a mirror dimly, but then face to face. Now I know in part; then I shall understand fully.'[57] The King James mistranslates the first line as 'through a glass darkly', which remains one of the most frequently misquoted lines in the Bible, for the point here is that if one could meet God face to face, there would be no need of images to mediate such an encounter. 'Like transcendental religion, transcendental art merges with mysticism: "Absolute religion is mysticism: it is without shape and without sound. Absolute art can neither be seen nor heard"' (Schrader 7). Paul's 'face to face' of course has nothing to do with the face to face instantiated by the close-up, any more than it has to do with a real-world face-to-face encounter between two people. And neither of these corresponds precisely with what Levinas means by 'face to face', insofar as the 'face of the other' is not a sign, properly speaking – but this is the subject of another essay. Suffice it to say that the Pauline 'face to face' is not without relevance for Levinas; Schrader's approach, however, is grounded in a romantic, ultimately positive, assumption of representability.[58] Even if the sacred itself, as 'wholly other', escapes representation, for Schrader one's relation with the sacred is susceptible to representation that, from a Levinasian perspective, 'render[s] transcendence illusory'.[59] The close-up, *qua* close-up, remains within the realm of signification. As with affect, any theory of the sacred in relation to cinema, or of Schrader's 'transcendental' film style, will always run up against the *contradictions* of representing the sacred, or that which lies on the other side of transcendence, whether historically or in a contemporary, postsecular context. For Levinas, for instance, ethics *precedes* ontology; in his reading of Levinas, Brent S. Plate concludes that 'aesthetics *precedes* Ethics'.[60] According to this logic, therefore, aesthetics precedes ontology, if not literally then logically, which is to say epistemologically – or, as Plate puts it in another context: 'We only exist insofar as we exist with others, and to be with others means we must communicate and do so through, and in, media; *there is nothing outside media*.'[61] Opponents of the radical constructivism informing this claim should note that Plate defines both cinema and religion as forms of media, each of which survives and thrives through a rich mutual transmediation.[62]

This salutary emphasis on the medium and the process of mediation leads us back to the question of how to make sense of all the different meanings of 'face' in various critical-theoretical contexts. For Deleuze and Guattari, for instance, in a discourse distinct from Deleuze's cinema books, situated at the intersection of 'significance' and 'subjectification, the "face" is the consummately Eurocentric object/event/structure, and therefore not necessarily something for the non-western "primitive" to covet'.[63] In the 'Year Zero: Faciality' plateau of *A Thousand Plateaus*, they write:

> The face is a politics [. . .] Certain assemblages of power require the production of a face, others do not. [. . .] The reason is simple. The face is not a universal. It is not even that of the white man: it is White Man himself, with his broad white cheeks and the black hole of his eyes. The face is Christ. The face is the typical European. . . . [I]n other words, your average ordinary White Man.[64]

In this postcolonial critique *avant la lettre*, for Deleuze and Guattari, 'to be "Christianized" is to be "faceified" (*visagéifiée*) [sic]' – insofar as one may so easily elide the distinction between the two Deleuzes.[65] To be 'faceified', therefore, is to be subjectivized, turned into or recognized as a subject that, while radically pre-psychoanalytic is also emblematic of the most deeply entrenched Eurocentric, colonizing and racist metanarrative.[66] As Doane explains, in her discussion of 'the politics of the close-up', '[t]he semiotic of capitalism, of what Deleuze and Guattari call modern White Men, requires the face as a mixed semiotic of *significance* and subjectivity, both of which work to annihilate, or at a minimum constrain, polyvocality.'[67] In this formulation, the face is the locus of a Christo-hellenic humanist-colonialist-imperialist paradigm.[68]

In his elaboration of what he calls 'anatheism',[69] Richard Kearney invokes Levinas and the 'epiphany of the face' of God in the (all-too-human) face of the stranger, in which 'another before me becomes utterly unique and irreplaceable'.[70] Kearney foregrounds the 'ethical encounter with the stranger, who, Levinas argues, bears the face of the wounded, the destitute, the naked – "the widow, the orphan, the stranger" – which is itself, for Levinas, the "trace of God"'.[71] By 'other' Levinas refers to what Derrida once described as 'the other than self, the other that opposes self-identity . . . not something that can be detected and disclosed within a philosophical space'.[72] The category of the other as it is used here came into being, for very good reasons, out of the prior eradication, in a supposedly secularized Western modernity, of the ground of authentically radical alterity. This is the other principal meaning of 'other': an *other* other, or 'Other', that exists as such (in theory) outside the determinate horizon of Western signifying practices, beyond the limits of representation. Alterity therefore means: not the all-too-human 'other' of much contemporary theory (e.g. postcolonial critiques), but the radical unknowability of genuine difference – an other with whom the self can only be in asymptotic and radically asymmetrical relation. This is a way of reintroducing to cultural, philosophical and historical inquiry, through the back door, the problem of the other as absolute Other – 'God', for example. Historically, the occlusion or erasure or, at best, marginalization, of this category of alterity is a move with potentially wide-ranging political, ethical and aesthetic ramifications. Non-anthropomorphic, transcendent, invisible, silent, absconded or 'sublime' – this Other sets an extreme problem for any mode of representation, and has engendered a broad range of responses, whether discursive, cinematic or mystical. Ostensibly, this Other, in its presence and potential 'universality', is the ground of a particular logocentric metaphysics; in its absence, of the various negative theologies.[73]

From its inception, cinema has had to negotiate a relationship with the biblical prohibition articulated in Exod. 33.20: 'You cannot see my face, for no one shall see me and live', anticipating the spirit of the second commandment's prohibition on the fashioning of idols, the fetishistic sacralization of objects, whose postsecular corollary in the realm of aesthetics is the anthropomorphization of the non-human. There is a gap or tension between a reading, in the most extreme example, of the Levinasian face, on the one hand, as asymmetrical relation between self and other – not a sign properly speaking because it is a *trace* of an Other who has passed absolutely – and, on the other hand, as impossible *interface* between a viewer and whatever it is that cinema both mediates and obscures. Despite the apparent theoretical impasse suggested by these different viewpoints, I approach the cinematic close-up (as affection-image + 'face') as a potential starting point in addressing Deleuze's contention in *Cinema 2* that the task or capacity of 'modern cinema' is to restore not our belief in God or another life but 'our belief in the world'.[74] It should be noted that Levinas does not militate against images so much as he advocates a relation – the face to face – that transcends or otherwise escapes mediation or representation. What we have, in other words, is a distinction or contradiction between the immanent and eminently representable *cinematic* face of the other, in an utterly human sense,[75] versus the negatively transcendent *Levinasian* 'face of the Other', which escapes visual or other representation. At this juncture, I would again invoke the distinction that Coates identifies between the 'Jewish' and the 'Christo-Hellenic' Levinas: between the philosopher of the unrepresentable face of radical alterity and the thinker of a genuinely ethical relation that one might want to try to represent, if only as an object lesson; for, insofar as this relation is predicated upon the radical abnegation of self to the other, to the other's absolute primacy over the self, it is in practical terms a wholly impractical model: a model that is simply too difficult to follow, in the same way that Christ's example of self-sacrifice in the Passion narrative is always already too difficult to imitate. And yet the unattainability of the example has not precluded its countless remediations in other narrative contexts.

Film is well-suited to explore these issues, given that the cinematic realisms that emerge out of the postwar art film counter-tradition – precisely what Deleuze identifies as the cinema of the time-image – have furnished subsequent filmmakers with the stylistic tools and strategies to explore questions for which a more mainstream cinematic realism has no time. This fundamental difference at the intersection of form and content is well illustrated in the uses to which the close-up has been put in an early twenty-first-century art film vernacular. I have space here for only a single example, Xavier Beauvois's *Of Gods and Men* (2010), a film that maximizes the expressive and thematic potential of the close-up to address the kinds of fundamental ethical questions under consideration; what results, however, is a turn away from the 'impossible' Levinasian ethical model towards the model of dialogue as communion, articulated in the mid-twentieth century by German-Jewish theologian Martin Buber.[76] In its anti-metaphysical, dare I say 'posthuman' materialism, the latter may be more readily reconciled with the immanentism that underscores Deleuze's approach.

Of Gods and Men: Communion as 'dialogue'

In his most famous work *I and Thou* (1923), Buber elaborates what he calls the 'I/thou' (*ich/du*) formation as another way of talking about the *self-other* relation; or rather, another way of talking about the self without putting the self *before* the other.[77] To this extent Buber is aligned with Levinas. Unlike the more iconophobic Levinas, however, Buber's 'I/thou' maps more readily onto filmic examples insofar as the 'other' in the equation is not conceived in such a radically negative fashion; while never reducible to the self, the point is not to highlight the other's infinite unknowability but rather to emphasize the primacy or precedence of the intersubjective/interpersonal/interhuman (*zwischenmenschliche*[78]) dimension of human relationships over the individuals at either end. 'In the beginning is *relation*', begins Buber (*I and Thou* 32): what he calls the *I-thou* 'primary word' *precedes* the 'I' in the 'originary *twoness*' of dialogue.[79] Much later in his life, Buber turned away from his earlier openly theological approach, however, embracing a more radical, human-centred conception of the self-other relation as dialogue.[80] This was not a move towards the secular so much as a good example of what we mean by the postsecular. To cite Buber from one of his last published texts, titled 'Dialogue': 'living means being addressed', an address that implies an obligation – an ethical *responsibility* – to respond.[81] Unlike Levinas, for instance, Buber writes here with no theological overlay; his discourse is direct and practical, even practicable. He differs from Russian theorist Mikhaïl Bakhtin as well, insofar as the latter 'posits the necessity for an active answerability on the part of the reader or spectator, which serves to animate and bring the work of art to life'.[82] Buber's notion of 'response' is a component in an act of unmediated interhuman communication; it is nevertheless susceptible to representation in the close-up, whose 'content' cannot be reduced to its affective dimension, insofar as a genuine ethics can never be reduced to an affectively grounded position vis-à-vis the world.

The title *Of Gods and Men* is taken from Ps. 82.6-7:[83] 'I said, "You are gods, sons of the Most High. But you shall die like men and fall like princes"'.[84] According to Wendy M. Wright, '[t]he theological anthropology that supports normative Catholic theology echoes this scriptural phrase: succinctly stated it is that human beings are created in the divine image but that image is wounded through sin, thus the task of human life is to heal that wounded image by cooperating with grace so that the true image will be revealed.'[85]

In this case, however, the theological masks the significance of a secular scholarly reading unbeholden to church doctrine. The title in French in fact reads *Des hommes et des dieux*, literally 'of men and gods'. The plural form begs the question: *which* 'gods'? Whose? This psalm uses the polytheistic conceit of the 'council of gods' to figure 'the God of Israel standing up in the midst of this council and pronouncing judgment upon all the other members', who, he says, will 'die' just like mortal human beings despite their 'divinity', because they are not 'true' deities, but merely cultural constructions.[86] The potential clash of divergent religious cultures is therefore inscribed in the title and epigraph, at the very outset of the film. One of its most impressive features, ultimately, is how it manages to present not only Christianity but also Islam in a favourable light, presenting the real possibility of deep mutual understanding across the gulf of faith.

Beauvois's film dramatizes the true story of a group of French Trappist monks, who, during the Algerian Civil War in the mid-1990s, were abducted from their monastery in a remote region of the Atlas Mountains by the fundamentalist faction who, in opposing an oppressive regime, sought to forcefully impose a harsher form of Islam. The film's entire plot is driven by the emergence of this threat to the monastery's peaceful and well-integrated existence in a small mountain village; as the story progresses, the monks' individual and collective fears are explored as each man gradually comes to the same realization: that it is not possible for them to leave and save themselves; that it is their religious and moral duty, in fact, to stay and risk almost certain death at the hands of the terrorists.[87] They gradually arrive at this collective decision because of the ethical obligation they feel towards the local villagers, whose collective identity has also come to be defined in relation to the monastery, not despite but because of their divergent religious traditions. More importantly, though, they reach this decision out of a wordlessly expressed commitment to one another, not only as fellow-monks or brothers but as human beings who stand to meet the same fate together. The latter point is made in an extraordinary scene late in the film that is constructed almost entirely of a series of close-ups.

In this scene, the brothers are gathered for what turns out to be their final meal together, their 'last supper' – an allegorical association with the Passion narrative that is explicitly invoked and transformed within this specific context. After a scene showing the communion ceremony, made up of symmetrically composed medium shots and medium close-ups, the monks gather for dinner. Their abbot, the aptly named Christian (Lambert Wilson), intones the pre-meal blessing: 'Lord, blessed art thou for this meal which unites us as brothers.'[88] As he finishes, Brother Luc (Michael Lonsdale) enters carrying two bottles of red wine and a cassette tape, which he inserts into a tape player. As he opens the wine, the strains of the finale from Act 4 of Tchaikovsky's *Swan Lake* (1875) fill the soundtrack, the only such instance of intra-diegetic music in the film. The thematic purpose of this particular choice seems to relate to the general themes of resignation in the face of imminent death and the ultimate promise of some form of redemption. The actual visual structure of the scene, however, emphasizes far more the immanent, emphatically *human* dimension of the story at this point. As the music builds slowly to its melodramatic climax, the scene progresses wordlessly, one last medium shot of the whole group around the U-shaped table giving way to a series of ever-closer framings, linked either through fluid back and forth horizontal camera movement, or discrete close-ups of each man, in sequence round the table. First the camera tracks left, past each monk on one side of the table, as he sips his wine and smiles. Cut to Christian, who smiles in response. The camera tracks back to the right, past Christian to the men on the opposite side, as they drink and smile in turn. As the camera begins its return journey, from right to left, the mood around the table visibly shifts, the monks' faces grow sober, registering the gravity of their situation. From Christian again, in the middle, there is a straight cut to a tighter close-up of only his face, as if to underline this affective shift. The tracking shot gives way to a series of close-ups of each monk around the table, as each ponders what lies ahead. Then the tracking recommences, from the left moving rightward, pausing at Christian again, who has tears in his eyes. Cut to and pause on Brother Amédée (Jacques Herlin) (as the oldest monk, one of only two who will escape death at the hands of the terrorists), also quietly weeping, and then to the others in turn, always in the same close framing. With another straight cut there is a shift to an even closer framing on Brother Christophe's face (Olivier Rabourdin), who had undergone the greatest struggle with personal fear, and whose expression now combines tears with a smiling acceptance. This look echoes round the table, in a series of extreme close-ups of each monk, their final, communal glance expressing a mutual, unspoken understanding. The scene culminates in an extreme close-up on the upper half of Christian's face, focused on his eyes, which almost seem to meet the viewer's.

As Buber writes, we live in the 'night . . . of an expectation' of 'a theophany of which we know nothing but the place, and the place is called community. . . . [T]here is no single God's Word which can be clearly known and advocated, but the *words* delivered are clarified for us in our human situation of being turned to one another.'[89] Buber makes clear that the form of expression – the 'words' in question – need not be literal, audibly spoken words but may come in any form of human communication, as in this sequence where an entire scene's worth of dialogue is replaced by a series of intensely meaningful glances round a communal dinner table. 'Two men bound together in dialogue must obviously be turned to one another, they must therefore – no matter with what measure of activity or indeed of consciousness of activity – have turned to one another.'[90] Moreover, 'for a conversation no sound is necessary, not even a gesture. Speech can renounce all the media of sense, and it is still speech.'[91] It is a cliché as old as negative theology itself that silence – or rather wordless gesture, facial expression, affective glance – is still within the order of language, a form of communication.[92] In this one scene, the monks neither quote scripture nor sing in antiphonal harmony, as periodically happens throughout the film. Here the 'body and blood' of the communion ceremony, in which the men have just participated, is replaced by the wine of conviviality (Plato's *Symposium* is not far away) and the human face in close-up, as the Christological metaphorization of the Eucharist gives way to the literal dialogue of communion as shared human experience. 'What does he now "know" of the other? No more knowing is needed. For where unreserve has ruled, even wordlessly, between men, the word of dialogue has happened sacramentally.'[93] It is worth recalling here Deleuze's contention that it is the task or capacity of 'modern cinema' to restore 'our belief in the world.'[94] Not only in terms of content but formally as well, Beauvois's film represents one form of the 'modern cinema' Deleuze seems to call for. *Of Gods and Men* also represents a hybrid of the time- and movement-image, in a manner typical of contemporary transnational art cinema. More specifically, in scenes such as this the film addresses the 'political' issues raised by Deleuze and Guattari's proto-postcolonial critique of the 'face of Christ' as 'average, ordinary White Man.'[95] The faces turned each to the other are all eminently white and European; the film's convincing portrait of 'the life of authentic religious faith' has the face of the White European male,[96] in the highly specific context of French postcolonial Algeria. The face of the other is conspicuously absent; and what of the face of the non-human Other? How much can the image be asked to bear?

The ethics of the image

As an example of postsecular cinema, the scene from Beauvois's film might be said to substantiate Massumi's apophatic reconceptualization of affect as 'primary, non-conscious, asubjective or presubjective, asignified, unqualifying and intensive'.[97] What is easy to forget, however, is that in any such specific cultural-textual example, the affective dimension identified therein can only come into existence through a reflective act of critical reading. That is, one can see in this scene the act of bearing witness to something inexpressible in words, and to this extent the Deleuzian analysis from *Cinema 1* breaks down: the perception-image (medium shot of monks gathered together for dinner) leads to the affection-image (close-ups of their faces) that structures the rest of the scene, in a manner reminiscent of Dreyer's *The Passion of Joan of Arc* (1928), a film famously made up almost exclusively of close-ups of the characters' faces.[98] In other words, it is too easy to overlook the difference between the cinematic staging of affect and its reception by the viewer. This example from *Of Gods and Men* is especially telling in this light as the viewer is privy to a non-verbal exchange in which a group of men recognize their mutual responsibility to one another – a responsibility replicated at one remove for the viewer, who is then free to choose whether or not to try to understand what has transpired. In any case, for the viewer it is never only about affect, an affective response, whether pleasurable or otherwise. This is something that is never completely clear in either the kind of affect theory popularized by Massumi, or in Deleuze's affection-image: how does the filmic image function to produce an *ethical* response in the viewer? Or rather, why is it that some recourse to an understanding of ethics grounded in a pre-Deleuzian, humanist position seems unavoidable in this kind of analysis? And: what is the role of the close-up in this process? In the foregoing discussion I have tried to show that the visible face in itself may be, in Buber's words, 'nothing but physiognomy',[99] but Buber is talking about relatively unmediated encounters, such as the one dramatized in Beauvois's film, which is itself irreducibly mediated. The face in close-up, as an element in a filmic narrative, is not a trace but a sign, and is therefore not merely susceptible to representation but is concrete evidence that representation has taken place. For Buber, 'living means being addressed' by the other, in expectation of a response.[100] The problem, with which I must conclude, is that such address, if it happens at all, does so in a radically mediated fashion, the possibility of an authentic face-to-face encounter always already short-circuited by our engagement with not the face but its image, not a face but an interface, in a relation in which our relations with other humans are always already posthuman.[101]

It should be clear from the foregoing analysis that the cinematic 'posthuman' may not lead us beyond a certain conception of the human, at least insofar as narrative film and the close-up are symptomatic of the medium's ongoing exploitation of its anthropomorphic potential. This does not necessarily mean, however, that this type of cinema or image cannot lead us beyond the received discourses of a humanist model that can no longer sustain the kind of intense ethical pressure being brought to bear upon it by a posthumanist approach that desires to salvage those aspects of a so-called secular humanism – often lost on humanism's more enthusiastic critics – as the source of both the worst of occidental culture and also of its most promising alternatives.[102]

Notes

1 In an essay on the Dardenne brothers' *Two Days, One Night*, Sarah Cooper connects Levinas's 'face to face' to the biblical injunction to 'love thy neighbour', warning that '[t]he possibility of loving the neighbor as oneself is perhaps too close to the mirroring and reductive move to bring others into our orbit and domesticate them, rather than leaving their alterity intact. Indeed, Levinas emphasizes the asymmetrical nature of the command implying that loving our neighbor does not come naturally to us' (2018, 231).

2 See also Emmanuel Levinas. In what might be described as a lapse in an ethical philosophy suspicious of mimesis and the visual image, Levinas, in *Existence and Existents* (1978), claims for the cinematic close-up the 'positive aesthetic function' of revealing the 'particular and absurd nature' of a small piece of reality, laying bare 'the coexistence of worlds that are mutually alien and impenetrable' (55). Echoing Walter Benjamin's notion of the 'optical unconscious', a hallmark of the cinematic image as symptomatic of modernity's media of mass reproduction, Levinas's claim here for

the close-up complicates the thinking of the 'face', as trace of the other, as not a sign properly speaking.
3 For Mary Ann Doane, '[t]he classical close-up assures us that we can indeed see and grasp the whole, in a moment rich with meaning and affect' ('The Close-up', 109).
4 See, for example, Žižek for a convincing account of the two Deleuzes, the one who co-authored books with Félix Guattari versus the other Deleuze, who I read as much more significant, and who is 'much closer to psychoanalysis and Hegel' (Slavoj Žižek, *Organs Without Bodies*, xxi).
5 See Jean-Luc Nancy's introduction to *Who Comes After the Subject?*
6 About the impact of Derridean deconstruction and Levinasian ethics on contemporary theorists of the postsecular and posthuman moment, see, for example, Richard Kearney and Catherine Keller, and also the recent work of Judith Butler.
7 Gilles Deleuze, *Cinema 1*, 65.
8 Ibid., 87.
9 Ibid., 88.
10 Eric Shouse, 'Feeling, Emotion, Affect'.
11 Brian Massumi, *Parables for the Virtual*, 27.
12 Steven Shaviro, *Post-Cinematic Affect*, 3.
13 Mary Ann Doane, 'The Close-up', 91.
14 'The face in the cinema inherits certain tendencies of the portrait in its reflection/production of the concept of the bourgeois subject' (Ibid., 106).
15 Arguably, the 'selfie', as a 'close-up' that one takes of oneself, represents a kind of closed, narcissistic loop that is the very opposite of the close-up in the classical sense.
16 Paul Coates, *Screening the Face*, 24.
17 Ibid., 35.
18 Ibid., 26–8.
19 Ibid., 26.
20 Hugo Münsterberg, *The Photoplay* 87; italics in the original.
21 Gilles Deleuze, *Cinema 1*, 87.
22 Ibid., 88. Cf. Mary Ann Doane, 'The Close-up', 107; cf. also Gilles Deleuze and Félix Guattari, who state that the 'face' 'is by nature a close-up . . .' (*A Thousand Plateaus*, 171).
23 Gilles Deleuze, *Cinema 1*, 88.
24 Paul Coates, *Screening the Face*, 24. According to Coates, in the heyday of early Soviet cinema, 'Kuleshov's experiment combat[ed] bourgeois individualism by denying expressivity to that primary signifier of individuality, the face' (Ibid., 17). Bálasz describes as 'typically American the acting practices that allegorically over-inscribe one emotion on a performing body' (quoted in Ibid., 16), an evaluation which applies equally well to German Expressionist acting style. In terms of American film acting, one of the major changes that would manifest with the emergence of classical Hollywood style is that from long to medium shots showing the whole of the actor's body to an increasing employment of the close-up within the syntax of a conventional scene structure.
25 See Mary Ann Doane, 'The Close-up', 105–8.
26 See also: Balász, 'The Close-up'. Cf. Mary Ann Doane, 'The Close-up', 107.
27 Paul Coates, *Screening the Face*, 26. Historically, the Russian avant-garde of the 1920s provided 'the seminal ideological and aesthetic connection with Brecht's work' (Martin Walsh, 'The Complex Seer', 14–15). 'A committed Marxist, Brecht saw art as inevitably political. Impressed by Eisenstein's *Potemkin*, he also believed that

playwrights would cease to focus on individuals and would eventually represent mass movements' (David Bordwell and Kristin Thompson, *Film History*, 562). Brechtian 'alienation-effects' are the basis of what Brecht calls 'epic theatre', or, in this context, 'epic cinema'. According to Martin Walsh, '[t]he generic focus of epic replaces the individualist focus of most dramatic and lyric art; intellectual activity replaces emotional involvement; the audience becomes the co-creator of the work, rather than its receptacle' ('The Complex Seer', 14).
28 See Mary Ann Doane, 'The Close-up', 92; Paul Coates, *Screening the Face*, 21.
29 Cf. Paul Coates, who connects Griffiths' 'allegorical' faces with Eisenstein's 'typage' (*Screening the Face*, 17–21).
30 Ibid., 21.
31 Massumi's formulation of affect is radically negative in logical and grammatical and therefore ontological terms. See Steven Shaviro: 'For Massumi, affect is primary, non-conscious, asubjective or presubjective, asignified, unqualifying and intensive; while emotion is derivative, conscious, qualified, and meaningful, a "content" that can be attributed to an already-constituted subject' (*Post-cinematic Affect*, 3).
32 Richard Grusin, *The Nonhuman Turn*, xvii.
33 Gilles Deleuze, *Cinema 1*, 88.
34 Which he refers to as 'Lulu', the title of the 1904 Frank Wedekind play upon which it based.
35 Gilles Deleuze, *Cinema 1*, 97; quoted in Richard Grusin, *The Nonhuman Turn*, xvii–xviii.
36 Gilles Deleuze, *Cinema 1*, 90. As Coates remarks of films featuring psychotic knife-wielding murderers, 'each knife inevitably stands for the phallus (its metaphorical status intimating real absence) and seeks to undo inadequate relationships with women. [. . .] [M]an's turn toward the audience indicates the definitive disappearance of the expected other (who need not be the Other), of woman' (Paul Coates, *Screening the Face*, 30). Cf. also Gilles Deleuze and Félix Guattari, *A Thousand Plateaus*, 184.
37 In the negative theological context God is 'posthuman' in the sense that 'God' as 'absolute Other' – or any *other* 'absolute Other', for that matter, as 'being beyond being', is by definition *both* pre- *and* posthuman, in the most radical sense.
38 As one of the most radical pre-modern understandings of the relation between ontology and language, negative theology already understood that there is no escaping a basic anthropocentrism as long as one is speaking of the human, even in a negative fashion. A 'non-anthropocentric ethical orientation' *qua* ethical orientation is inevitably anthropocentric, and the non-human always conceals the human, in the end, just as the word itself conceals the 'human', hiding in plain sight. See, for example, Max Hantel, who attempts to marshal Levinas to the cause of animal studies ('Bobby Between Deleuze and Levinas', 105).
39 Gilles Deleuze, *Cinema 1*, 70.
40 Ibid., 65.
41 Ibid.
42 Ronald Bogue, *Deleuze on Cinema*, 76.
43 Gilles Deleuze, *Cinema 1*, 65.
44 Ronald Bogue, *Deleuze on Cinema*, 38.
45 Gilles Deleuze, *Cinema 1*, 66; see also Ibid., 87.
46 Ronald Bogue, *Deleuze on Cinema*, 76.
47 Gilles Deleuze, *Cinema 1*, 87.

48 Ronald Bogue, *Deleuze on Cinema*, 71. In Peircean semiotics, iconicity describes 'those signs in which there is a relatively convincing or believable', visual-structural, '*resemblance* between the signifier (word/image) and the thing signified' (Marita Sturken and Lisa Cartwright, *Practices of Looking*, 357). Indexicality, on the other hand, indicates 'those signs in which there is a physical causal connection between the signifier (word/image) and the thing signified, because both existed at some point within the same physical space' (Ibid., 358).
49 Deleuze says, 'The face is this organ-carrying plate of nerves which has sacrificed most of its global mobility and which gathers and expresses in a free way all kinds of tiny local movements which the rest of the body usually keeps hidden' (*Cinema 1*, 87).
50 Paul Coates, *Screening the Face*, 32.
51 See Ibid., 31-2.
52 'Leaving something unseen makes concessions to the temporality that will cause its disclosure later' (Ibid., 33).
53 Ibid.
54 Ibid. As an example of this interplay of gazes in close-up, Coates cites Godard's *Two or Three Things I Know About Her*, in which, as in several of Godard's mid-1960s films, actors oscillate between averting the face and thereby remaining in character, and facing the camera and addressing the viewer directly 'in a Brechtian separation of actor and role' (32). In the parlance of the theatre, the latter strategy is referred to as 'breaking the fourth wall', underlining the violence of the gesture and the shock entailed for the viewer – a shock that has been severely weakened by sheer repetition of this and similar self-reflexive strategies in contemporary commercial cinema.
55 Gilles Deleuze, *Cinema 2*, 157.
56 Gilles Deleuze, *Cinema 1*, 70. Cf. Gilles Deleuze and Félix Guattari, *A Thousand Plateaus*, 176.
57 *The New Oxford Annotated Bible*.
58 'The concept of transcendental expression in religion or art necessarily implies a contradiction. Transcendental expression in religion and art attempts to bring man [sic] as close to the ineffable, invisible and unknowable as words, images, and ideas can take him' (Paul Schrader, *Transcendental Style in Film*, 8).
59 Emmanuel Levinas, *Totality and Infinity*, 80. For Levinas, the relation is itself radically negative, escaping representation, it is a 'relation without relation' (Ibid.).
60 Brent S. Plate, *Religion and Film*, 67.
61 Brent S. Plate, *Representing Religion*, 4.
62 Ibid., 3-4.
63 Gilles Deleuze and Félix Guattari, *A Thousand Plateaus*, 167. The term is Deleuze and Guattari's (e.g. 178).
64 Ibid., 176-8.
65 Gilles Deleuze, *Cinema 1*, 88.
66 Putting aside its cultural and racial specificity, this 'face' corresponds to the concept of the self against which Levinas, in a radically different philosophical framework, reacts, a self predicated upon a subject that continues 'to affirm being as identical with itself' ('The Trace of the Other', 346), denying the other its alterity and bringing it into the fold of the same. For example, 'European racism as the white man's claim has never operated by exclusion, or by the designation of someone as Other. . . . Racism operates by the determination of degrees of deviance in relation to the White-Man face. . . . From the viewpoint of racism, there is no exterior, there are no

people on the outside. There are only people who should be like us and whose crime it is not to be' (Gilles Deleuze and Félix Guattari, *A Thousand Plateaus*, 178).
67 Mary Ann Doane, 'The Close-up', 105.
68 On this point my reading of each theory is the exact opposite of Hantel in his reading of Deleuze and Guattari's critique of the 'Christ-face' in this section of *A Thousand Plateaus*: although 'Deleuze and Guattari do not mention Levinas by name in . . . "Year Zero: Faciality" . . . the latter's monotheistic description of the face-as-commandment, exposed to us in destitute vulnerability, is clearly their target' ('Bobby Between Deleuze and Levinas', 111). Choosing to read the Levinasian face this way, as an essentially positive quantity, is to overlook its non-semiotic status as trace; its determining quality of infinite unknowability.
69 Glossed by Jean-Luc Marion as 'the death of the death of God' (Richard Kearney, *Reimagining the Sacred*, 176).
70 Ibid., 16.
71 Ibid., 262n6.
72 Ibid., 18.
73 This *other* Other is also at the basis of the Levinasian notion of the face, and of the face-to-face encounter. In the 1963 essay 'The Trace of the Other', Levinas shifts register, from the Neoplatonic to the literally Judeo-Christian (See Paul Coates, *Screening the Face*, 40). 'The God who passed is not the model of which the face would be an image. To be in the image of God does not mean to be an icon of god, but to find oneself in his trace' (Emmanuel Levinas, 'The Trace of the Other', 359). The Levinasian trace thus directs our gaze as it were back down, to the face of the other, the trace par excellence, which, Levinas insists, is *not* an anthropomorphic semblance, or *prosopopeion*, of divinity. The trace in Levinas is a notion derived ultimately from Plotinus tempered by a Judaic subordination of self in the face of the transcendence immanent in the scriptural text. For Levinas, the 'face' of the other is the other in its irreducible alterity, inassimilable to the self/same or to semantic totalization. This 'face' is primordial, as is the relation; therefore, it is not a sign but the ground, in the face-to-face, of signification, which in turn makes the sign, and therefore language, representation, signification and communication, possible. On this basis, finally, the conditions emerge for the subject's coming-into-being.
74 Gilles Deleuze, *Cinema 2*, 172.
75 See Plate about film's capacity for revealing *different kinds* of faces (*Religion and Film*, 68).
76 Robert Bernasconi first broached the question of the relation between the two thinkers in 1988, with respect to the question of dialogue ('Dialogue and the Lack of Dialogue').
77 On the significance of Buber and the *I-thou* relation in the context of contemporary European law and politics see Jürgen Habermas, *The Lure of Technocracy*.
78 *Mensch*: 'person'; 'human being' – *not* 'man' in the sense of a masculine human subject; Yiddish: 'a person of integrity and honour'.
79 Charles Lock's phrase (personal communication). Re 'primary' or 'first word' as shorthand for the first of the mosaic laws or commandments, see Paul Coates, *Screening the Face*, 39.
80 Martin Buber, 'Dialogue', 51–3.
81 Ibid., 49. One finds similar language in Levinas, who in an interview remarks that 'the first language is the response' (Robert Bernasconi, 'Dialogue and the Lack of Dialogue', 174), and also in the Russian literary theorist M. M. Bakhtin, as well as

Judith Butler; for example, Emmanuel Levinas, *Totality and Infinity*; Mikhaïl Bakhtin, *Art and Answerability*; Judith Butler, *Giving an Account of Oneself*.
82 Miriam Jordan and Julian Jason Haladyn, 'The Art of Answerability'.
83 The citation in the film, in French, gives Psalm 81.
84 *The New Oxford Annotated Bible*.
85 Wendy M. Wright, '*Of Gods and Men*', 12.
86 *The New Oxford Annotated Bible*, 720.
87 'It seems unique to see a film . . . where both individual and communal dynamics are held in creative tension. Each of the monks reacts differently to the felt sense of impending peril. But viewers are not treated to a story of one individual against many but to a story about genuine community in which individual struggle is honored and at the same time the integrity and deep bonds of the whole are acknowledged' (Wendy M. Wright, '*Of Gods and Men*', 7).
88 *Of Gods and Men* (*Des hommes et des dieux*). Directed by Xavier Beauvois.
89 Martin Buber, 'Dialogue', 47.
90 Ibid.
91 Ibid., 43.
92 'The underlying silence experienced throughout the film is, of course true to foundational Trappist practice. Silence is meant to create a space where attentive listening to the depths of the heart, to the whisper of the Spirit, and to the longing of the world, becomes possible. . . . Space and time apart, both literal and interior, is cultivated. All this is designed to foster the capacity to listen attentively and to plumb the depths of the spacious, receptive heart to which the divine is understood to speak most clearly' (Wendy M. Wright, '*Of Gods and Men*', 4–5).
93 Martin Buber, 'Dialogue', 44.
94 Gilles Deleuze, *Cinema 2*, 62.
95 Gilles Deleuze and Félix Guattari, *A Thousand Plateaus*, 178.
96 Wendy M. Wright, '*Of Gods and Men*', 10.
97 Steven Shaviro, *Post-Cinematic Affect*, 3.
98 See Gilles Deleuze, *Cinema 1*, 70. On Dreyer's film in this context see: Paul Schrader, *Transcendental Style in Film*; Deleuze; Paul Coates, *Screening the Face*.
99 Martin Buber, 'Dialogue', 48. That said, for Buber, as for other philosophers of the face, the face need not be literally a human one: 'it by no means needs to be a man of whom I become aware. It can be an animal, a plant, a stone. . . . Nothing can refuse to be the vessel for the Word. The limits of the possibility of dialogue are the limits of awareness' (Ibid., 49).
100 Ibid.
101 I thank Terrance McDonald for this insight.
102 See Rosi Braidotti, *The Posthuman*, 34.

Bibliography

400 Blows. Directed by Francois Truffaut. 1959. Paris and France: MK2 Éditions, 2001. DVD.

Alphaville: The Strange Adventure of Lemmy Caution. Directed by Jean-Luc Godard. 1965. New York: The Criterion Collection, 1998. DVD.

Bakhtin, Mikhaïl M. *Art and Answerability: Early Philosophical Essays*. Edited by Michael Holquist and Vadim Liapunov. Translated by Vadim Liapunov and Kenneth Brostrom. Austin: University of Texas Press, 1990.
Balász, Béla. *Theory of Film*. Oxford and New York: Berghahn Books, 1978.
Bergstrom, Anders. 'In Search of Lost Selves: Memory and Subjectivity in Transnational Art Cinema'. (PhD Dissertation, Wilfrid Laurier University, 2016).
Bernasconi, Robert. 'Dialogue and the Lack of Dialogue between Buber and Levinas'. In *The Provocation of Levinas: Rethinking the Other*, edited by Robert Bernasconi and David Wood, 100–35. London: Routledge, 1988.
Bogue, Ronald. *Deleuze on Cinema*. London and New York: Routledge, 2003.
Bordwell, David and Kristin Thompson. *Film History: An Introduction*, 2nd ed. Boston: McGraw-Hill, 2003.
Braidotti, Rosi. *The Posthuman*. Cambridge: Polity Press, 2013.
Brecht, Bertolt. 'A Short Organum for the Theatre'. In *Brecht on Theatre*, translated by John Willet, 179–208. New York: Hill and Wang, 1977.
Buber, Martin. 'Dialogue'. In *On Intersubjectivity and Cultural Creativity*, edited by Shmuel N. Eisenstadt, 70–80. Chicago: University of Chicago Press, 1992.
Buber, Martin. *I and Thou*. Translated by Walter Kaufmann. New York: Touchstone, 1970.
Butler, Judith. *Giving an Account of Oneself*. New York: Fordham University Press, 2005.
Coates, Paul. *Screening the Face*. New York: Palgrave Macmillan, 2012.
Cooper, Sarah. '"Put Yourself in My Place": Two Days, One Night and the Journey Back to Life'. In *Immanent Frames: Postsecular Cinema Between Malick and Von Trier*, edited by John Caruana and Mark Cauchi, 229–44. Albany, NY: SUNY Press, 2018.
Cooper, Sarah. 'Time and the City: Chris Marker'. In *Cities in Transition: The Moving Image and the Modern Metropolis*, edited by Andrew Weber and Emma Wilson, 113–22. London: Wallflower Press, 2008.
The Conformist. Directed by Bernardo Bertolucci. 1970. Hollywood, CA: Paramount Home Video, 2006. DVD.
Deleuze, Gilles. *Cinema 1: The Movement-Image*. Translated by Hugh Tomlinson and Barbara Habberjam. Minneapolis, MN: University of Minnesota Press, 1986.
Deleuze, Gilles. *Cinema 2: The Time-Image*. Translated by Hugh Tomlinson and Robert Galeta. Minneapolis, MN: University of Minnesota Press, 1989.
Deleuze, Gilles and Félix Guattari. *A Thousand Plateaus: Capitalism and Schizophrenia*. Translated by Brian Massumi. London and New York: Continuum, 1987.
Doane, Mary Ann. 'The Close-up: Scale and Detail in the Cinema'. *Differences: A Journal of Feminist Cultural Studies* 14, no. 3 (Fall 2003): 89–111.
Eisenstein, Sergei. 'The Cinematic Principle and the Ideogram'. In *Film Theory and Criticism*, 7th ed., edited by Leo Braudy and Marshall Cohen, 13–24. New York and Oxford: Oxford University Press, 2009.
Gray, John. *Straw Dogs: Thoughts on Humans and Other Animals*. London: Granta Books, 2015.
The Great Train Robbery. Directed by Edwin S. Porter. 1903. New York: Kino Video, 2002. DVD.
Grusin, Richard, ed. *The Nonhuman Turn*. Minneapolis, MN: University of Minnesota Press, 2015.
Habermas, Jürgen. 'A Post-Secular Society – What Does That Mean?'. *Reset: Dialogues on Civilizations* (16 Sept. 2008): 1–11.
Habermas, Jürgen. *An Awareness of What is Missing: Faith and Reason in a Post-Secular Age*. Cambridge: Polity Press, 2010.

Habermas, Jürgen. *The Future of Human Nature*. Cambridge: Polity Press, 2003.
Habermas, Jürgen. *The Lure of Technocracy*. Cambridge: Polity Press, 2015.
Hantel, Max. 'Bobby Between Deleuze and Levinas, Or Ethics Becoming Animal'. *Angelaki: Journal of the Theoretical Humanities* 18, no. 2 (2013): 105–26.
Jay, Martin. *Downcast Eyes: The Denigration of Vision in Twentieth-Century French Thought*. Berkeley, CA: University of California Press, 1994.
Jordan, Miriam and Julian Jason Haladyn. 'The Art of Answerability: Dialogue, Spectatorship, and the History of Art'. https://www.academia.edu/2320854/The_Art_of_Answerability_Dialogue_Spectatorship_and_the_History_of_Art. Accessed 5 May 2016.
Kearney, Richard. *Anatheism (Returning to God After God)*. New York: Columbia University Press, 2011.
Kearney, Richard and Jens Zimmerman, eds. *Reimagining the Sacred*. New York: Columbia University Press, 2016.
Keller, Catherine. *Cloud of the Impossible: Negative Theology and Planetary Entanglement*. New York: Columbia University Press, 2015.
La Dolce Vita. Directed by Federico Fellini. 1960. Los Angeles, CA: Koch Lorber Films, 2004. DVD.
Levinas, Emmanuel. *Existence and Existents*. Pittsburgh, PA: Duquesne University Press, 1978.
Levinas, Emmanuel. 'The Paradox of Morality: An Interview with Emmanuel Levinas'. In *The Provocation of Levinas: Rethinking the Other*, edited by Robert Bernasconi and David Wood, 168–80. London: Routledge, 1988.
Levinas, Emmanuel. *Totality and Infinity*. Translated by Alphonso Lingis. Pittsburgh, PA: Duquesne University Press, 1969.
Levinas, Emmanuel. 'The Trace of the Other'. Translated by Alphonso Lingis. In *Deconstruction in Context*, edited by Mark Taylor, 345–59. Chicago: University of Chicago Press, 1986.
Massumi, Brian. *Parables for the Virtual: Movement, Affect, Sensation*. Durham, NC: Duke University Press, 2002.
Mulvey, Laura. 'Visual Pleasure and Narrative Cinema'. In *Film Theory: An Anthology*, edited by Robert Stam and Toby Miller, 483–94. Oxford: Blackwell, 2000.
Münsterberg, Hugo. *The Photoplay: A Psychological Study and Other Writings*. Edited by Allan Langdale. New York and London: Routledge, 2004.
Nancy, Jean-Luc. *Who Comes After the Subject?* Edited by Eduardo Cadava, Peter Conner and Jean-Luc Nancy. New York: Routledge, 1991.
The New Oxford Annotated Bible, 4th ed. New Revised Standard Version, With Apocrypha. Edited by Michael D. Coogan, Bruce M. Metzger, Carol A. Newsom and Pheme Perkins. New York: Oxford University Press, 2010.
Of Gods and Men. Directed by Xavier Beauvois. 2010. Montreal, QC: Métropole Films, 2010. DVD.
Pandora's Box. Directed by G.W. Pabst. 1929. New York: The Criterion Collection, 2006. DVD.
The Passion of Joan of Arc. Directed by Theodor Dreyer. 1928. New York: The Criterion Collection, 2004. DVD.
Persona. Directed by Ingmar Bergman. 1966. Beverley Hills, CA: MGM Home Entertainment, 2004. DVD.
Plate, Brent S. *Religion and Film*. London: Wallflower Press, 2009.
Plate, Brent S, ed. *Representing Religion in World Cinemas: Filmmaking, Mythmaking, Culture*. New York: Palgrave Macmillan, 2003.

Schrader, Paul. *Transcendental Style in Film*. Berkeley, CA: Da Capo Press, 1972.
Shaviro, Steven. *Post-Cinematic Affect*. Winchester: Zero Books, 2010.
Shouse, Eric. 'Feeling, Emotion, Affect'. *M/C Journal* 8, no. 6 (2005). http://journal.media culture.org.au/0512/03-shouse.php. Accessed 10 August 2016.
Sturken, Marita and Lisa Cartwright. *Practices of Looking*. Oxford: Oxford University Press: 2003.
Walsh, Martin. 'The Complex Seer: Brecht and the Film'. In *The Brechtian Aspect of Radical Cinema*, edited by Keith M. Griffiths, 5–21. London: BFI, 1981.
Wright, Wendy M. 'Of Gods and Men'. *Journal of Religion and Film* 15, no. 2: 1–12. Article 10. http://digitalcommons.unomaha.edu/jrf/vol15/iss2/10.
Žižek, Slavoj. *Organs Without Bodies*. New York: Routledge, 2004.

8

'Subaltern' imaginings of artificial intelligence

Enthiran and *CHAPPiE*

William Brown

Filmmaker Alex Rivera writes that '[s]cience fiction in the past has always looked at Los Angeles, New York, London, Tokyo... [but that w]e've never seen São Paulo, or Jakarta, or Mexico City. We've never seen the future of the rest of the world, which happens to be where the majority of humanity lives.'[1] While Rivera suggests that the Global South does not feature in science fiction cinema, I shall in this chapter examine the way in which characters from the Global South do indeed feature in science fiction narratives, with the chapter focusing in particular on three films about artificial intelligence (AI) and which prominently feature characters of South Asian/Indian origin. These are *Enthiran/The Robot* (Shankar, India, 2010) and *CHAPPiE*(Neill Blomkamp, USA/ Mexico, 2015), which both also are set in the Global South (respectively in India and South Africa), with the US-based *Short Circuit* (John Badham, USA, 1986) providing a third example with which I shall engage briefly.

The reasons for looking at films about AI that feature the relatively uncommon trope of South Asian/Indian characters are various and intertwined. First, it is my hypothesis that such films give expression to a phenomenon occulted in many/most other films about AI, namely that the global computing industry – both in terms of hardware and software – is upheld by (often invisible) labour carried out by 'subaltern' peoples from Asia and other parts of the world. Second, I wish to relate this 'return' of an otherwise repressed 'subaltern' contribution to our globalized economy to discourses of posthumanism. For, while there have historically been links between posthumanism and, for example, postcolonialist and subaltern discourses, these links have on the whole themselves undergone something of an occultation. As a result, strands of posthumanism – especially those that celebrate the would-be technological prowess of humanity in that we can, at least in fiction films, create intelligent life forms/AI – offer a Eurocentric (and thus all-too-human) understanding of what posthumanism is or might be. Finally, I wish to suggest that a 'posthumanism through Deleuze' might help us to get around such a Eurocentric conception of posthumanism, even though Gilles Deleuze himself is or was guilty of Eurocentric thought, especially in his considerations of cinema. By challenging its historical Eurocentrism, films like *Enthiran* and *CHAPPiE* can help us to create a more inclusive understanding of the posthuman and of posthumanism as a whole. In order to do this, let us start by looking at historical and recent definitions of posthumanism.

What is posthumanism?

Broadly speaking, posthumanism is a critique of the humanist project of modernity. If modernity has through industrialization entailed incredible advances in technology and afforded great amounts of wealth for many people, posthumanism wishes to point out that such advances have not taken place in a bubble. That is, advances in technology are linked to a history of colonialism and imperialism, whereby materials that have been used in making those advances have been acquired cheaply/exploitatively from colonized countries. Furthermore, the ensuing accumulation of wealth has been wealth only for a tiny minority. Much of the planet has otherwise been consigned to material misery – not just in comparison to but also for the purposes of the wealth of the few. Those few have tended to be white European or North American men. If modernity calls itself humanist, therefore, then 'humanism' becomes a byword for a patriarchal and Eurocentric project called capitalism. This project has not only historically excluded non-white, non-European and non-male humans, both separately and in combination, but it also has overlooked/neglected the cost of the contribution made to modernity by non-humans, including animals, the environment in general, and perhaps also those machines that we have fabricated in the name of progress.

If this sounds like an overstatement, then we need only look at two foundational thinkers in the West, namely Plato and his student Aristotle. In *The Republic*, Plato suggests that neither women, nor slaves nor foreigners could belong to the state of Athens since they were as good as mere barbarians.[2] Meanwhile, in his *Politics*, Aristotle equally suggested that women, slaves and animals were inferior to men, who could and should use them as they see fit, that is, without regard for consequences.[3] In other words, from its earliest treatises on politics and the management of daily life, Western culture has been about the exploitation and deliberate exclusion of others. If the reader feels that references to philosophers writing in the fourth century before the Christian era are unfair because humanity has greatly progressed since such times, then we need only point to the ongoing existence of feminist, postcolonial, queer, subaltern, animal rights, environmentalist and other 'minor'/minority discourses in order to demonstrate that 2,500 years later similar exclusions are (perceived as) taking place.

It is not that all feminist, postcolonial, queer and other discourses adopt the figure of the posthuman, or that they sit easily under the branches of posthumanist debate. However, if the 'human' and by extension humanism have been bywords for exploitation and slavery, or what I am broadly terming capitalism, then the desire to expand the definition of the human in order to include those otherwise excluded and/or marginalized groups seems naturally to lead to the term 'post-humanism'. For, it involves moving 'beyond' humanism as historically it has been defined, while also demonstrating how the human is dependent on (and not merely able to dispose of) a non-human world including animals and the environment. This is, for example, Rosi Braidotti's argument in her recent book *The Posthuman*, to which I shall return shortly.[4]

However, while I have suggested that posthumanism is a discourse that allows us to bring together various different strands of thought that each in their own way constitute a critical reaction on the part of the dominated to the dominant practices of capitalism, this has not always been the case. That is, posthumanism could incorporate feminist, postcolonial, queer, ecological, animal rights and other discourses, but more often than not it fails to do so. Let us examine how this is so by looking at two classic posthumanist texts, before also looking more closely at Braidotti's *Posthuman*.

In 1985, Donna J. Haraway published her renowned *Cyborg Manifesto*, in which she posits a move away from essentialism, or the notion that different things can be easily defined, or have an essence, positing instead that all things are mixed, or hybrid, or what she terms a 'cyborg'. That is, 'a hybrid of machine and organism, a creature of social reality as well as a creature of fiction'.[5] I shall return to the issue of social reality and fiction later. At present, however, I wish simply to emphasize the way in which Haraway advocates for a breakdown of the traditional boundary between technology and nature; these are not easily separated realms, and the human is certainly constituted by both. As Thao Phan writes in her introduction to a thirtieth anniversary re-examination of Haraway's essay, the *Cyborg Manifesto* can be considered feminist because it broke down the typical binary associations between nature-woman and technology-man, positing instead that both men and women are technological and natural and that indeed the difference between men and women can (and perhaps should also) be undermined.[6] What is more, even though Haraway does not use the term, we might consider the text to be posthumanist because of its call for us to consider ourselves part of an ecology that extends beyond simply the human and into the technological and natural realm. Meanwhile, Phan suggests that Haraway acknowledges 'postcolonial feminism' in the manifesto.[7] However, while the essay does decry 'the terrible historical experience of the contradictory social realities of patriarchy, colonialism, and capitalism',[8] this acknowledgement comes primarily in the form of footnotes that make mention of work by postcolonial writers like Trinh T. Minh-ha and Edward W. Saïd. In other words, while Haraway declares kinship between her conception of the cyborg and postcolonial discourses, it is a muted one at best.

In a similar vein, N. Katherine Hayles mentions early on in her seminal book, *How We Became Posthuman*, how 'postcolonial theorists have taken issue not only with the universality of the (white male) liberal subject but also with the very idea of a unified, consistent identity, focusing instead on hybridity'.[9] Hayles has in mind the work of Homi K. Bhabha, but this is her only real reference to postcolonial theory throughout her otherwise considerable tome.

Finally, Rosi Braidotti does make a far greater number of references to postcolonial theory in *The Posthuman*, charting how Saïd did indeed critique the Eurocentrism of humanism as it had historically been defined in the West,[10] through to final declarations that the posthuman has its roots in the work of '[Baruch] Spinoza, Deleuze and [Félix] Guattari, plus feminist and post-colonial theories'.[11] The 'creative dimension' of posthumanist discourse that seeks not simply to critique the status quo but also to redefine and thus create afresh the terrain of debate 'constitutes the affirmative and innovative core of the radical epistemologies of feminism, gender, race and post-colonial studies'.[12] This last sentence is worth discussing in greater detail. For, while Haraway and Hayles pay lip service to postcolonial discourse as being influential upon their work, Braidotti lets slip an assertion not that posthumanist discourse is influenced by postcolonialism, but the reverse (posthumanism constitutes the 'core . . . of postcolonial studies'). This slip also comes across when Braidotti posits that '[t]he work of post-colonial and race theorists displays a situated cosmopolitan posthumanism that is supported as much by the European tradition as by non-Western sources of moral and intellectual inspiration'.[13] That is, we might again accuse Braidotti of suggesting that posthumanism influences postcolonial discourse, and not the other way around. Does this reversal undermine postcolonial discourse, reinforcing its position as subaltern? If, as we shall see later, postcolonial discourse involves a desire to be recognized as human, then does this reversal not also risk denying the humanity of the postcolonial subject? No matter how laudable Braidotti's intention, the claim for the posthumanism of postcolonial discourse is fraught with danger; the post in posthumanism is not necessarily the same as the post in postcolonial theory.

If posthumanism is a sort of 'cyborg' *à la* Haraway, then in some respects it is fine that posthumanism and postcolonialism are conflated in this way, such that the history of the relationship between the two becomes confused. After all, it is not as if both discourses do not have at their core an anti-hegemonic ambition in the sense of expanding thought beyond the patriarchal Eurocentrism of 'humanism'. However, if Hayles, Haraway and Braidotti all seek to reassert the embodied nature of the posthuman as a result of the way in which that embodiment has been 'systematically downplayed or erased',[14] then to conflate the histories of posthumanism and postcolonialism is to deny precisely the lived or embodied history of the latter discourse, instead uniting the two in an ideal, or disembodied realm.

Is the post- in posthumanism the same as the post- in postcolonial?

While Haraway and Hayles attribute postcolonialism as being at least a peripheral influence on their work (relegated to passing comments and footnotes), Braidotti seems to assert that posthumanism has influenced postcolonial thought. However, in texts like Bhabha's *Location of Culture* (1994) and Saïd's *Orientalism* (1978), as well as in works by Trinh T. Minh-ha such as *The Digital Film Event* (2005), the term 'posthumanism' is not mentioned at all. Indeed, discussion of the two terms side by side seems relatively rare, with Western scholars putting the terms together, often in the name of feminism, far more regularly than postcolonial scholars do in the name of what we might term 'subaltern studies'.

In 1988, Gayatri Chakravorty Spivak borrowed the term 'subaltern' from Antonio Gramsci in order to write her influential text, 'Can the Subaltern Speak?' This essay is a critique of, among other things, strands of Western scholarship (including the work of Deleuze and Michel Foucault), while at the same time trying to make clear the pitfalls of the very act of speaking itself. That is, if to speak is shorthand for 'to speak the language of domination' (such that the dominant person understands the dominated one), then the issue becomes whether the subaltern can speak without losing their identity as subaltern. In some senses, to cease to be a subaltern is probably desirable; one does not want to continue to be dominated. However, when being subaltern coincides with, say, being a woman, then if to cease to be a subaltern is also to cease to be a woman, then this is potentially problematic.[15] Indeed, in Spivak we might find a critique of Haraway, in that for the latter becoming a cyborg involves no longer respecting traditional gender boundaries or definitions, definitions that for Spivak may nonetheless be key to the identity of the person who is trying to assert (themselves in spite of) their subaltern status. That is, being a woman is (in some senses) not the result of domination, but the cause. To 'speak', therefore, is not only to transcend one's status as dominated/subaltern, but it is also to cease in some respects to be a woman if woman and subaltern are in fact synonymous. Learning to speak, then, is not simply casting off a subaltern identity imposed by the dominating power, but also in part losing the identity that provoked the domination in the first place – and yet which one might want (rightfully) to retain, since it is indeed part of one's identity. As Spivak concludes: '[t]he subaltern cannot speak.'[16]

Now, Spivak does not quite fit into, but nevertheless is not far removed, from a history of thinkers who take negative terms like 'subaltern' and reappropriate them for political purposes. Postcolonial Argentine philosopher Enrique Dussel, for example, challenges Plato directly by putting forward a 'barbarian' philosophy of 'liberation' in which those humans consigned historically to non-being proactively use that non-being in order to assert their presence in the world.[17] Similarly, Hamid Dabashi has recently rephrased Spivak's question in order to ask provocatively whether non-Europeans can think.[18] However, while Spivak critiques the subaltern position, and while Dussel reappropriates barbarianism and Dabashi queries thought as a Eurocentric project in its entirety, there is no history in postcolonial studies of appropriating terms like 'cyborg' or even the posthuman, perhaps because both speak of technological empowerment and (post)modernization. If historically one has been recognized as subhuman, then perhaps it would be odd to progress immediately from the sub- to the post-, without ever really stopping at the human along the way.

Indeed, in a brief essay on precisely this issue, Monirul Islam argues that the 'basic objective' of posthumanism 'remains to be the realization of the human potential through the extension of the field of science and technology. As it happens to be the case with many other postmodern discourses the discourse of posthumanism seems to be a corollary of neo-colonialism'.[19] That is, '[t]oday's subaltern is tomorrow's human or pre-posthuman. In the posthuman world the movement of the subaltern will become foreclosed since in the technologically advanced civilization there will be no human error.'[20] Since the subaltern will have graduated to become human, but will not be posthuman, the fact that they will likely commit human error remains, for Islam, a conceptual stumbling block. In effect, 'the question is not . . . [that] the subhumans are asking for old-fashioned humanism and hence are hopelessly anachronistic – but [the issue is] about priority within the same historical moment shared and lived by all.'[21] If Islam potentially presents a limited definition of posthumanism (potentially overemphasizing technological empowerment), he nonetheless presents a credible case for arguing that the post- in posthumanism is not the same as the post- in postcolonialism. For in the posthuman moment, that which previously was subhuman (subaltern, barbarian, non-thinking, non-being) will not enjoy a world democratically 'shared and lived by all'. As per the film *Elysium* (Neill Blomkamp, USA, 2013), some humans might well be living on perfect and beautiful space stations in orbit, but the multitude of people will continue to be struggling on an ever-more arid earth.[22] Meanwhile, Joseba Gabilondo (1995) presents a similar case not against posthumanist discourse but against cyborg theory. For Gabilondo, cyborg theory furthers the divide between First and Third World nations, since the cyborg expresses a position of technological privilege.

Short-circuiting posthumanist discourse

In light of Islam and Gabilondo's arguments, we might begin to read Braidotti's (presumably unintended) placement of posthumanism as central to postcolonial thought (as opposed to vice versa) as a quite literal expression of how posthumanism involves a kind of neocolonial mining of postcolonial ideas. It re-presents them not only as its own, but as if postcolonialism had taken from posthumanism ideas that posthumanism in fact took from postcolonialism. Turning our attention to fiction films that are about the posthuman, we can in many respects see this Eurocentric process reaffirmed, while also seeing reasons as to why posthumanism has been adopted in feminist and not postcolonial discourse. This latter point will require some further theorization, before we can look at the films themselves.

It is Cary Wolfe who draws the distinction between transhumanism and posthumanism. Transhumanism is, Wolfe explains, the quasi-science fictional dream of humans transcending their bodies and uploading their consciousnesses into computers and/or machine bodies – as per the theories of someone like Hans Moravec. Transhumanism is thus a concept that derives from the 'cyborg' strand of posthumanism,[23] but which in fact is diametrically opposed to posthumanism as Wolfe and others, including Braidotti, Haraway, Hayles and Robert Pepperell,[24] understand it. Transhumanism might aspire to perfect rationality, an absence of emotion and thus freedom from the supposed obstruction that is the body, but posthumanism 'proper' (as represented by the authors discussed here) is precisely the realization of an embodied presence in the world, such that our connection with others, including non-humans and the environment as a whole, is taken into account – rather than others and our environment assumed as unthinking objects that we can treat as we please, as evinced by Plato and Aristotle's attitude towards women, slaves and animals.

Numerous films, from *Metropolis* (Fritz Lang, Germany, 1929) and *The Stepford Wives* (Bryan Forbes, USA, 1975; Frank Oz, USA, 2004) through to *Weird Science* (John Hughes, USA, 1985), *TRON: Legacy* (Joseph Kosinski, USA, 2010), *Her* (Spike Jonze, USA, 2013) and *Ex Machina* (Alex Garland, UK, 2015), all imagine AI as feminine. Here we can see the relevance of posthumanism for feminist theory. For if these transhumanist tales basically propagate the sexist myth that woman is or should be created/controlled by man, then it is correct for feminist theory to critique this myth – not simply via a rejection of technology, but in such a way that woman remains connected to technology (Haraway's cyborg), while at the same time positing that we cannot transcend our bodies, but remain embodied and enworlded, which would be posthumanism 'proper' instead of the transhumanist version of posthumanism.

While this feminist critique is important, however, these and other films involving depictions of AI – we might add *Transcendence* (Wally Pfister, USA/China, 2014) and the celebrated *Terminator*, *RoboCop* and *Matrix* franchises to the list – in their Western settings all present to us how the transhumanist myth about transcending one's body – either by disappearing into the virtual ether, or by entering a new, highly technologized body – is a Eurocentric one. Perhaps this is made most clear by a film about AI that features a seemingly 'subaltern' character, namely *Short Circuit*.

Short Circuit tells the story of a military robot, Number Five, which comes alive after being struck by lightning. The robot's inventor, Newton Crosby (Steve Guttenberg), finds it living with animal carer Stephanie (Ally Sheedy) and tries to return it to the military. However, Number Five escapes, convincing Newton and his assistant Ben Jabituya (Fisher Stevens) that Number Five is indeed alive. There ensue various scrapes as the army tracks down Number Five, which fools them by building a decoy that they destroy. Number Five then reveals himself to Newton and Stephanie as they leave Oregon (where the film is set) for Montana to start over again.

Short Circuit can be read as suggesting various things. First, it is critical of the military industrial complex, while also suggesting that it is only through divine intervention (lightning), as opposed to through human labour, that robots can come alive. Having mistaken Number Five for an alien, Stephanie's instinct is then to look after the robot as she does her animals. This might suggest a 'posthumanist' care for others and other species (Number Five also regrets nearly killing a grasshopper). However, Number Five clearly becomes an ersatz child for Stephanie and Newton by the film's end, suggesting that its potentially dangerous or disruptive otherness is negated, or sacrificed, for the heteronormative couple, with Stephanie's care becoming thus a stereotypical expression of the motherly in all women.

More important for this chapter, though, is the character of Ben, whom Fisher Stevens plays wearing a fake tan, coloured contact lenses and adopting a broad Indian accent – even though at one point his character claims to be from Bakersfield (with his ancestors supposedly from Pittsburgh). Ben is of course Newton's assistant (i.e. in the subservient role), and he spends most of the film making a mixture of sexual innuendos, spoonerisms or both – coming across thus as a hapless, sex-obsessed nincompoop. When he first meets Stephanie, she wearisomely asks herself 'what planet is this guy from?'[25] In other words, Ben like Number Five is an alien or an animal, but where Number Five graduates from alien to animal to son, Ben undergoes no such transition. Indeed, while Number Five learns to control itself, Ben seemingly cannot, hence his constant references to sex.[26] Perhaps it is for this reason that Ben cannot be incorporated into the nuclear family at the film's end, while even a robot can. In other words, *Short Circuit* reveals that posthumanism can incorporate animals as equals,[27] and perhaps even by extension all matter, in that the metal that constitutes Number Five contains the potential for life[28] – provided that it simply remains cute or is socialized. However, the posthumanism of *Short Circuit* seemingly cannot incorporate the postcolonial subject, who through his libidinous difference here 'short circuits' the posthuman.

And yet, it is Ben who is perhaps the real mathematical/computing genius behind Number Five, something affirmed especially in *Short Circuit 2* (Kenneth Johnson, USA, 1988), where Ben (now renamed Ben Jahveri) is making toy robots with minimal resources on the streets of New York, before being reunited with Number Five (prompting adventures to ensue). In other words, while it is problematic that a non-Indian actor plays Ben in such a stereotypical way (Indians are aliens/animals), the film(s) nonetheless also suggest(s) that Ben is an exploited worker with a high level of technological expertise, who must be subservient to mainstream white society, into which he otherwise barely fits – and yet without whom mainstream white society would not be able to make its technological advances. By no means a paragon of postcolonial filmmaking, *Short Circuit* (and its sequel) nonetheless establish problematically the link between a posthuman world of AI (all matter can come or is alive; humans might transcend their bodies) and the way in which this is based upon neocolonial labour in or from the 'former' colonies.

The globalized film industry

According to Indian information technology (IT) organization NASSCOM, India's IT services and business process outsourcing (BPO) industries brought in US$147 billion to India in 2015 (NASSCOM 2015). Thirteen per cent greater than the revenue created in the same sector in 2014, clearly IT services and BPO are growth industries in India. In addition, India is also regularly the recipient of outsourced labour in software development, as various studies have made clear.[29] Bangalore is considered the hub of the Indian IT industry, but while Bangalore has been dubbed India's Silicon Valley, Balaji Parthasarathy contends that as Bangalore struggles to progress from developing the software of others to defining its own products and technologies, it is perhaps better known as Silicon Valley's India.[30] In other words, while India clearly plays a major role in the global IT industry, it is paid only through contract work and not necessarily in terms of profit share, with major profits being retained by the international companies that employ the Indian contractors. While clearly profitable to various local entrepreneurs, on a global scale the Indian IT industry is arguably one based, therefore, on ongoing exploitation, not least because the major reason for foreign companies to invest in Indian IT services is cheapness of labour.

What is true of the IT industry more generally is perhaps also true of the role that computing plays in the contemporary film industry. Nitin Govil has written, for example, about how Hollywood's special effects industry is itself now thoroughly globalized, such that many Hollywood companies employ special effects programmers based in India as part of their production process.[31] Furthermore, as programming for the film industry is outsourced, and thus in part based upon exploitation, so too might a Western cinema that depicts a posthuman world also be exploitative. To offer a provocative example, it is relatively widely acknowledged[32] that Satyajit Ray's proposed film *The Alien*, due to be made with Columbia Pictures in Hollywood, heavily influenced *E.T.: The Extra-Terrestrial* (Steven Spielberg, USA, 1982). Furthermore, in addition to *Short Circuit*, more recent films like *The Transformers* (Michael Bay, USA, 2007) and *Slumdog Millionaire* (Danny Boyle and Loveleen Tandan, UK/USA, 2008) both feature Indian call centres (a standard BPO operation) that link respectively to American and British callers. In both films, the scenes set in the call centre are played for laughs, especially through the strength of the employee's accent, their less-than-professional tone and/or their attempts to conceal the fact that they are in India. Similarly, while American, Divya Narendra was nonetheless surprised not to see himself played by an Indian actor in *The Social Network* (David Fincher, USA, 2010) since he is the son of two Indian doctors (he was played by Max Minghella).[33] In other words, we see Indian identities and labour being concealed in all three films, and problematically for the sake of humour in the former two (we do see the workers, but they are included for laughs rather than for the purposes of being depicted as human).

Now, my intention is not to suggest that it is all one-way traffic as profit leaves India and goes elsewhere in the developed world, and as India's contribution to the global IT and filmmaking industries is rendered invisible. As mentioned, the IT services and BPO industries are enormously lucrative. Furthermore, with regard to cinema, many ideas and images from Hollywood are taken in an unlicensed fashion and recycled in many parts of the world, including India.[34] If *E.T.* borrows ideas from Ray's proposed *Alien* film, the Indian film industries similarly take ideas back and rework them there. Furthermore, it would simply be wrong to assert that the Indian film industries do not play a major role in contemporary cinema around the world, especially Bollywood. Indeed, in the era of globalization, perhaps nothing less than a complex intertwining of ideas and products moving in different directions is to be expected.

Nonetheless, despite such mitigations, across various levels there has been and perhaps continues to be an ongoing history of exploitation as ideas and products leave the periphery for the benefit of the centre. If posthumanist discourse has at its core technology and depictions of technology, then not only does posthumanism take from and not really give back to postcolonial discourse (Braidotti's slip), but so, too, do the IT industries, the IT industries as applied to filmmaking, and a film industry that depicts posthumanist visions of the world (films about aliens) take from and not really give back to the periphery. It would seem that posthumanism is utterly the remit of the privileged centre and not that of the postcolonial periphery – and that posthumanism involves not the redistribution of power but the perpetuation of old imbalances of power – as per Islam's analysis.[35]

Postcolonial science fiction and *CHAPPiE*

That said, there is a growing history of postcolonial and/or Third World science fiction literature and film, in which we read/see/hear stories both about humanity's relationship with technology and about its technologized relationship with the material world more generally. This trend can be seen in Latin America,[36] India,[37] and other places.[38] Arguably, this growth speaks of the general ubiquity of digital technology, which allows filmmakers to create the kinds of science fiction images that formerly were the preserve of Hollywood special effects departments – a ubiquity that in turn speaks of globalization and a possible decentring of power from Western countries/ the Global North. Indeed, accepting that this might be the case, the empowerment involved in the use of computers for filmmaking – when not done as outsourced labour for someone else – might possibly also open up the door for posthumanist discourse finally to become useful for a postcolonialism that, as suggested earlier, otherwise struggles to find it relevant. We can begin to see how this is so in relation to *CHAPPiE*.

In *CHAPPiE*, young programmer Deon Wilson (Dev Patel) creates an AI that he runs on a police robot as crime soars in a near-future Johannesburg. Kidnapped by debt-ridden crooks Ninja (Watkin Tudor Jones), Yolandi (¥o-Landi Vi$$er) and Amerika (Jose Pablo Cantillo), Deon saves his own life by offering to train the robot, referred to as Chappie, to help them in their bid to pay off their debts. Chappie thus is encouraged to adopt a criminal and destructive approach to the world, even though this seems to go against the pleasure that it derives from creating things. When Deon's rival AI developer Vincent (Hugh Jackman) disables the police robots designed by Deon and instead sends out his significantly weaponized MOOSE robots in order to prove that they provide more effective (i.e. violent) law enforcement, it comes down to Chappie to save the day – as well as to help Ninja, Yolandi and Amerika with their issues. During their battle with the MOOSE robots, Amerika and Yolandi die, the latter in trying to save Ninja, while Deon is badly injured in the crossfire. However, with the MOOSE robots disabled, Chappie then attacks Vincent before using the latter's MOOSE-controlling headgear to transfer Deon's consciousness into a spare police robot, before the now-robot Deon then does the same for Chappie before his current robot body expires/runs out of battery. The film ends with Chappie and Deon also transferring Yolandi's consciousness, stored on a pen drive, into a third police robot – thereby creating a robot family.

In that the film tells the story of humans transcending their bodies and being uploaded into robot bodies, *CHAPPiE* presents to us a transhumanist fantasy, one that likely is impossible in the real world, our embodied relationship with which posthumanism 'proper' is keen to emphasize. However, whereas most Hollywood transhumanist fantasies suggest the transcending of the body as an act of empowerment, here we might read this narrative trope differently. In part this is because of the setting of the film, as well as because of the ethnicity of lead actor Dev Patel, who plays Deon.

Even though Deon Wilson is not obviously an Indian name, British actor Patel is nonetheless well known for his roles as Indian characters in the aforementioned *Slumdog Millionaire* as well as in *The Best Exotic Marigold Hotel* (John Madden, UK/ USA/United Arab Emirates, 2011) and its sequel (John Madden, UK/USA, 2015). In this way, his persona represents on screen another Indian IT wiz – like Ben in *Short Circuit* – who this time is not a clown played for laughs, but rather the object of envy for rival (and white) programmer Vincent. In other words, *CHAPPiE* makes visible the contribution of Indians/South Asians in the global computing industry – and has as part of its plot the occultation/suppression of that contribution.

In a similar way, this is not a film that takes place in the West, but in Johannesburg. It might be problematic that Blomkamp's film presents to us a crime-ridden

Johannesburg (confirming the city's negative stereotype). Furthermore, the film has a relatively homogeneous cast with regard to race (even though set in South Africa, the film does not have any prominent black characters, with white and Hispanic actors, together with Patel, being foremost in the *mise-en-scène*). Nonetheless, *CHAPPiE* offers to us an unusual setting for a film about AI. Artificial intelligence is not developed in Los Angeles, New York or London, but rather in Johannesburg. It is not that the development of AI could not happen in somewhere like Johannesburg, assuming that to create AI is even possible. But as per his earlier *District 9* (USA/New Zealand/Canada/South Africa, 2009), there is a sense here of Blomkamp rewriting the conventions of science fiction, since the genre tends to depict technological advances as taking place in the West/Global North. What is more, while not impossible for AI to be developed by someone with identifiable associations with India in a place like Johannesburg, *CHAPPiE* also gives expression to the aspiration for technological advancement in somewhere like South Africa. In other words, while a film about empowerment, the film is also in part an expression of disempowerment.

This functions on several levels. First, Deon's fantasy of transcending his body can be read racially as a dream to enter into the 'colour blind' world of the robot – where he might stand a greater chance of uniting with a white woman like Yolandi. That is, in reality (i.e. not in the robot realm), Deon's body carries cultural signifiers (he is subaltern), as made clear by the signifiers also carried by actor Dev Patel (although British, he is associated with a Western version of 'Indianness'). Second, *CHAPPiE* in some respects is a fantasy of being able to shrug off oppressive legal regimes (both Chappie's police robot brethren and Vincent's MOOSE robots) and to escape the debt that cripples Ninja, Yolandi and Amerika. In other words, the fantasy is one of escape from the signifiers of class that certain bodies carry with them. Indeed, as much is signified by the presence of Ninja and Yolandi, who outside of the film are famous for being members of *zif* (lower middle class and uncouth) rap group Die Antwoord. Finally, in the creation of a nuclear family comprised of Deon, Yolandi and Chappie, we see a fantasy of union that seems not to be possible in the physical, embodied realm. Unlike *Short Circuit*, in which the family union sees Newton and Stephanie get together and adopt Number Five (latterly referred to as Johnny), here it is only in the robot realm that any union can take place, thus bespeaking its impossibility in the flesh world. What *CHAPPiE* helps to reveal through its fantasy of disembodied transhumanism, then, is the fact that mainstream versions of the same fantasy tend to rely upon the patriarchal white body as 'normalized' to the point of invisibility – that is, it is in some respects always already 'disembodied' as a result of its privileged (white, patriarchal) position.[39] It may be that posthumanism wishes to remind us of our very embodied existence in the world, but in some senses this task is not necessary for the postcolonial subject, since their body is always already inescapable. Nonetheless, the insistence on the body in posthumanist discourse (as well as posthumanism's interest in human-animal relations, which also feature prominently in the film) might help us to understand aspects *of CHAPPiE* – even if critically in relation to the transhumanist fantasy that is presented to us. Indeed, as mentioned earlier, Haraway asserts that the cyborg straddles social reality and fiction. Rather than being a white fantasy regarding disembodied transhumanism, *CHAPPiE* demonstrates the situatedness, or the embodied nature, of Third World science fiction (it is fiction from a specific social reality). As a result, cyborg theory, and by extension posthumanism, might not be entirely irrelevant to or unsuitable for helping us to understand the film – not as a replacement of, but in addition to theories of the postcolonial and/or the subaltern.

Finally, while set and primarily shot in Johannesburg, *CHAPPiE* is classed as an American-Mexican co-production. While it might constitute a fantasy of empowerment in terms of filmmaking (and in terms of computing as far as the film's diegesis is concerned), nonetheless, we arguably see with the film the ongoing disappearance of profits (via the failure to own one's own products) away from the creators and towards the would-be neocolonial American film industry. As *CHAPPiE* presents to us a fantasy of transcending the body on several levels (race, class, aspiring to the 'white' nuclear family and a life free from debt), we can read the film itself as a fantasy of self-empowered autonomy when in reality the film's fiction is itself a cyborg also grounded in the social reality of a global film industry, the domination of which continues to be carried out by American production and distribution companies (here Columbia Pictures, a subsidiary of Sony).

However, am I insisting on 'subalternity' where in fact there is none? Am I insisting upon the significance of the 'Indianness' of Dev Patel, the social class of Die Antwoord, and the impossibility of the mixed family – thereby Eurocentrically imposing on the film that which it does not merely attempt to, but perhaps actually does shrug off? Are there examples of more 'empowered' posthumanist and postcolonial cinemas? It is with these questions in mind that I shall end this chapter by examining *Enthiran*.

Enthiran

A 'Kollywood' film (named after the Kodambakkam district of Chennai, the hub of Tamil filmmaking), *Enthiran* is about a computer scientist, Dr Vaseegaran (Rajinikanth), who develops a robot called Chitti (also played by Rajinikanth), which may or may not possess AI. Rival scientist Professor Bohra (Danny Denzongpa) initially fails Chitti's AI exam. However, he then passes it when Chitti helps to deliver the child of Latha (Devadarshini), the sister of Vaseegaran's girlfriend, Sana (Ashwarya Rai Bachchan). Chitti falls in love with Sana, and deliberately fails a test with the Indian military when she rejects its advances. Bohra then implants into Chitti a disc giving it psychopathic tendencies. Chitti goes on a rampage, producing numerous copies of itself, before Vaseegaran defeats Chitti and its clones with the use of magnets. With Vaseegaran facing a death sentence, Chitti reveals that Bohra was responsible for its psychopathic tendencies. The film ends in 2030 with Chitti in a museum explaining that it was dismantled because it started thinking.

Enthiran is a film that recycles iconography from various Western science fiction films, in particular *The Terminator* (James Cameron, USA, 1984), when we see the skin removed from half of Chitti's face and a robotic eye shining forth from its metal skeleton. But while we might read into such references the hegemony of Hollywood cinema, such that *Enthiran* feels compelled to imitate it, the film also differs enormously from Western films, not least through its length (nearly three hours) and its structure.

For example, as an Indian film, *Enthiran* features song and dance sequences that are highly unusual in Western science fiction. The famous 'masala' aesthetic of Bollywood cinema applies also to this Kollywood film,[40] in that it mixes comedy, science fiction, drama, musical and various other genres in an original blend. More than this, though, the film can also be read through a Deleuzian frame, in such a way that we see that it is not merely a reaffirmation of the centrality of Hollywood, but a more nuanced film.

For Deleuze, the movement-image and the action-image broadly define mainstream Hollywood cinema. Movement-image cinema consists of easy-to-follow stories, in which the editing is designed in such a way that as little as possible that exceeds the narrative is included; it is a cinema without ambiguity and defined by action (hence action-image[41]). While there are various American science fiction films that are not so easy to follow (because of a convoluted storyline involving various parallel universes, for example, *Looper*, Rian Johnson, USA/China, 2012), we can argue that *Short Circuit* and even *CHAPPiE* are movement-image films. The above synopsis of *Enthiran* might give the impression that it also has a clear narrative. However, the film equally is full of moments that 'exceed' the narrative in many ways, especially the musical numbers. Indeed, the songs lend to the film not simply a movement-image quality, but also what Deleuze[42] might call a time-image one: the film suddenly cuts from Chennai to Machu Picchu during a song sequence – with no explanation as to how or why it has relocated there. Given the lack of explanation, we are not sure whether there is any reality to these moments, or whether they are fantastical dream sequences. In other words, at such moments, there is much more ambiguity in the film; structuring the film around external action (the movement-image) is displaced by structuring the film around internal experience (the time-image).

David Martin-Jones has outlined the way in which Bollywood cinema is not quite a movement- or a time-image cinema, but 'another-image' that is a combination of the two.[43] The same might apply to *Enthiran*; as a hybrid film that combines aspects of the movement-image and the time-image, the result is a different kind of cinema. This can be seen in the film's ultimate triumph over but rejection of AI: Chitti is entered into a museum rather than incorporated into the family as per *Short Circuit* and *CHAPPiE*. Chitti is not a child in need of a mother as per *Short Circuit*, *CHAPPiE*, or *A.I.: Artificial Intelligence* (Steven Spielberg, USA, 2001), nor an idealized woman as per *TRON: Legacy*, *Her* and *Ex Machina*. Chitti rather is a sexually aggressive and masculine machine who wants to steal its creator's partner.

Not only is Chitti a machine created by an Indian genius whose talent is recognized (unlike Number Five and in some respects Chappie), but it also is a machine that is Indian in appearance and which is not co-opted into white majority culture. Not only is this unusual in science fiction, but it equally suggests a complex postcolonial or 'subaltern' take on AI. Chitti is the colonial subject brought into being by the colonizing powers of science and rationalization, as is made clear by the fact that he will have military applications. However, rather than fight, the machine really wants to love. As a result, Chitti must in effect be castrated and put into a museum. In this way, Chitti is not assimilable into society, nor able to form a new family. Instead, like the colonial Indian subject who starts to think, Chitti must be disempowered and its libido must be tamed. *Enthiran* might positively show Indian genius creating Indian AI, but

Chitti also speaks to the impossibility of the postcolonial subject being or becoming fully accepted by 'human' society – just as his consignment to the museum represents the impossibility for the Indian computer labourer to gain the profits from their AI creation. In other words, *Enthiran* suggests that the subaltern must remain subaltern, since he will be punished for thinking, punished for loving, punished for anything except accepting servility/subalternity in an ongoing fashion.

If posthumanism is, as I have argued, Eurocentric and not compatible with postcolonialism, then in *Enthiran* we arguably have a film that tells a posthumanist tale in order to make precisely this point; there is no fantasy AI ending for Chitti. Meanwhile, David Martin-Jones has criticized Deleuze for being Eurocentric in his views on cinema (he almost exclusively discusses North American and European cinema in his two *Cinema* books).[44] Nonetheless, when we consider that *Enthiran* is not just a movement-image film, but a time- and movement-image film ('another – image'), we can see how the Deleuzian framework of the hybrid movement-/time-image film helps to bring out the difference between *Enthiran* and other, more conventional science fiction films like *Short Circuit* and even *CHAPPiE* (which ultimately is an American-backed film).

This 'posthumanism through Deleuze' arguably opens up space for us finally to put posthumanism and postcolonialism into contact with each other. This is a matter of form – how the story is told – and not just of story. A hybrid movement- and time-image film not only recalls Bhabha's conception of the postcolonial hybrid subject,[45] but in the case of *Enthiran* it also allows us to identify a postcolonial aesthetic that in its own way both appropriates Western posthuman (transhumanist) iconography (*The Terminator*), and critiques the Eurocentrism of that transhumanist myth. In its validation of 'excessive' moments (e.g. musical numbers) and in its ability to see the potential for life in all matter (metal can live), *Enthiran* affirms a 'proper' posthumanist conception of how the human and non-human are co-dependent and connected; nonetheless, it also speaks of a political reality in which the subaltern-ness of the subaltern is also brought forcefully into view. Through Deleuze, posthumanism and postcolonialism speak – even if the message that emerges is that much more political work needs to be done in order for posthumanism to get past its Eurocentric roots and thus to help realize a more egalitarian world.

Notes

1 Quoted in Dennis Lim, 'At the Border between Politics and Thrills'.
2 Plato, *The Republic*.
3 Aristotle, *The Politics*.
4 Rosi Braidotti, *The Posthuman*.
5 Donna J. Haraway, *Simians, Cyborgs and Women*, 149.
6 Thao Phan, 'Introduction', 4.
7 Ibid.
8 Donna J. Haraway, *Simians, Cyborgs and Women*, 155.
9 N. Katherine Hayles, *How We Became Posthuman*, 4.

10 Rosi Braidotti, *The Posthuman*, 14.
11 Ibid., 188.
12 Ibid., 191.
13 Ibid., 46.
14 N. Katherine Hayles, *How We Became Posthuman*, 4.
15 See Gayatri Chakravorty Spivak, 'Can the Subaltern Speak?'.
16 Ibid., 104.
17 See Enrique Dussel. *Philosophy of Liberation*.
18 Hamid Dabashi, *Can Non-Europeans Think?*
19 Monirul Islam, 'Posthumanism and the Subaltern'.
20 Ibid.
21 Ibid.
22 One of the problems with *Elysium* is that Blomkamp has a white male (Matt Damon) star as the hero of his film, thereby occulting the correlation between race, ethnicity and poverty that clearly plays a role in determining who goes to (the practically all-white) luxury space station. Nonetheless, at least *Elysium* addresses the issue of who gets to be saved, unlike *Interstellar* (Christopher Nolan, USA/UK, 2014) and *2012* (Roland Emmerich, USA, 2009).
23 Cary Wolfe, *What Is Posthumanism?*, xiii.
24 Robert Pepperell, *The Posthuman Condition*.
25 *Short Circuit*. Directed by John Badham.
26 In a text that precedes his *What Is Posthumanism?*, Cary Wolfe quotes Gayatri Chakravorty Spivak in suggesting that making distinctions between species, especially between what constitutes human and not human, is part of the historical problems that are slavery and exploitation (Cary Wolfe, *Animal Rites*, 7). As per the implied association between Ben and animals in *Short Circuit*, it seems problematic to me to imply, as Wolfe does, that subalterns are equal to dogs – even if Wolfe's claim (but seemingly not that of *Short Circuit*) is that dogs and subalterns are also equal to humans (the latter precisely because human). Nonetheless, perhaps we can permit Wolfe this curious comparison since his intentions seem to be good (if good intentions can count for anything). In turn, Indian theorist Pramod K. Nayar tellingly refers to the same passage from Spivak in his treatment of posthumanism – although he barely makes reference to postcolonialism in what is ultimately a critical overview of the former (Pramod K. Nayar, *Posthumanism*, 80).
27 See Donna J. Haraway, *When Species Meet*.
28 For more on this, see Karen Barad, *Meeting the Universe Halfway*, and Jane Bennett, *Vibrant Matter*.
29 See, for example, Brian Nicholson and Sundeep Sahay, 'Some Political and Cultural Issues'.
30 Balaji Parthasarathy, 'India's Silicon Valley or Silicon Valley's India?'.
31 Nitin Govil, 'Hollywood's Effects, Bollywood's FX'.
32 See Somdatta Mandal, 'The Curious Case of *The Alien*', and Martin Scorsese, 'Ray Influenced *E.T.* says Martin Scorsese'.
33 See Katherine Zhu, 'Divya Narendra on Being a Wildcat'.
34 For more on this, see Iain Robert Smith, '*Memento* in Mumbai'.
35 The purloining of posthumanist ideas from the periphery for the benefit of science fiction films about posthumanism in the centre is not restricted to India. For example, Eliseo Subiela's film, *Hombre mirando al sudeste/Man Facing Southeast* (Argentina, 1986) was seemingly remade in Hollywood – without credit being given – as *K-PAX*

(Iain Softley, USA/Germany, 2001). See Robert Koehler, 'Review: *K-PAX*', and Everett Hamner, 'Remembering the Disappeared', 63.
36 For considerations of Latin American science fiction film, see Mariano Paz, 'South of the Future'; Geoffrey Kantaris, 'Buenos Aires 2010'; Alfredo Suppia, 'The Quest for Latin American Science Fiction & Fantasy Film'.
37 See Dominic Alessio and Jessica Langer, 'Nationalism and Postcolonialism in Indian Science Fiction'; Suparno Banerjee, 'Melodrama, Mimicry, and Menace'.
38 See Ericka Hoagland and Reema Sarwal, *Science Fiction, Imperialism and the Third World*; Masood Ashraf Raja, Jason W. Ellis and Swaralipi Nandi, *The Postnational Fantasy*.
39 If the white body is paradoxically 'disembodied' already, this disembodiment is a myth – albeit one that has gained validity as a result of the myths peddled in films and other media products about the power of the white body. To explain: humans believe that they are as intelligent as their machines, if not more so. Alan Turing famously developed his 'test' whereby the sign of AI would be the ability of a machine to converse with a human without them realizing. While humans obsess about whether or not a machine can or would pass this test (I assume it could happen if it has not happened already, especially depending on precisely with whom the machine is talking), what is perhaps more telling is to ask how many humans would *not* pass the test. That is, we hubristically pronounce our intelligence, all the while forgetting that we are not that smart – because even a white body is limited by its fact of being a body.
40 See Jigna Desai and Rajinger Dudrah, 'The Essential Bollywood'.
41 See Gilles Deleuze, *Cinema 1*.
42 Gilles Deleuze, *Cinema 2*.
43 See David Martin-Jones, 'Towards Another " - Image"'.
44 See David Martin-Jones, *Deleuze and World Cinemas*.
45 For how Indian science fiction subversively mimics Western cinema as per Bhabha's work, see Suparno Banerjee, 'Melodrama, Mimicry, and Menace'.

Bibliography

Alessio, Dominic and Jessica Langer. 'Nationalism and Postcolonialism in Indian Science Fiction: Bollywood's *Koi Mil Gaya* (2003)'. *New Cinemas: Journal of Contemporary Film* 5, no. 3 (November 2007): 217–29.
Aristotle. *The Politics*. Translated by T. A. Sinclair. London: Penguin, 2000.
Banerjee, Suparno. 'Melodrama, Mimicry, and Menace: Reinventing Hollywood in Indian Science Fiction Films'. *South Asian Popular Culture* 12, no. 1 (2014): 15–28.
Barad, Karen. *Meeting the Universe Halfway: Quantum Physics and the Entanglement of Matter and Meaning*. Durham, NC: Duke University Press, 2007.
Bennett, Jane. *Vibrant Matter: A Political Ecology of Things*. Durham, NC: Duke University Press, 2009.
Braidotti, Rosi. *The Posthuman*. Cambridge: Polity Press, 2013.
Dabashi, Hamid. *Can Non-Europeans Think?* London: Zed Books, 2015.
Deleuze, Gilles. *Cinema 1: The Movement-Image*. Translated by Hugh Tomlinson and Barbara Habberjam. London: Continuum, 2005.
Deleuze, Gilles. *Cinema 2: The Time Image*. Translated by Hugh Tomlinson and Robert Galeta. London: Continuum, 2005.

Desai, Jigna and Rajinder Dudrah. 'The Essential Bollywood'. In *The Bollywood Reader*, edited by Jigna Desai and Rajinder Dudrah, 1–17. Maidenhead: Open University Press, 2008.
Dussel, Enrique. *Philosophy of Liberation*. Translated by Aquilina Martinez and Christine Morkovsky. Eugene: Wipf & Stock, 1985.
Gabilondo, Joseba. 'Postcolonial Cyborgs'. In *The Cyborg Handbook*, edited by Chris Hables Gray, Heidi Figueroa-Sarriera and Steven Mentor, 423–32. New York: Routledge, 1995.
Govil, Nitin. 'Hollywood's Effects, Bollywood's FX'. In *Contracting Out Hollywood: Runaway Productions and Foreign Location Shootings*, edited by Greg Elmer and Mike Gasher, 92–116. Lanham: Rowman & Littlefield, 2005.
Hamner, Everett. 'Remembering the Disappeared: Science Fiction Film in Post-dictatorship Argentina'. *Science Fiction Studies* 39 (2012): 60–80.
Haraway, Donna J. *Simians, Cyborgs and Women: The Reinvention of Nature*. New York: Routledge, 1991.
Haraway, Donna J. *When Species Meet*. Minneapolis. MN: University of Minnesota Press, 2008.
Hayles, N. Katherine. *How We Became Posthuman: Virtual Bodies in Cybernetics, Literature, and Informatics*. Chicago. IL: University of Chicago Press, 1999.
Hoagland, Ericka and Reema Sarwal, eds. *Science Fiction, Imperialism and the Third World: Essays on Postcolonial Literature and Film*. Jefferson: McFarland & Company, 2010.
Islam, Monirul. 'Posthumanism and the Subaltern: Through the Postcolonial Lens'. *India Future Society: 2014*, 4 May. http://indiafuturesociety.org/posthumanism-subaltern-postcolonial-lens/. Accessed 29 October 2015.
Kantaris, Geoffrey. 'Buenos Aires 2010: Memory Machines and Cybercities in Two Argentine Science Fiction Films'. In *Memory, Culture and the Contemporary City: Building Sites*, edited by Uta Staiger, Henriette Steiner and Andrew Webber, 191–207. Basingstoke: Palgrave Macmillan, 2009.
Koehler, Robert. 'Review: *K-PAX*'. *Variety*, 25 October 2001. http://variety.com/2001/film/reviews/k-pax-1200553165/. Accessed 29 October 2015.
Lim, Dennis. 'At the Border Between Politics and Thrills'. *The New York Times*, 15 March 2009. www.nytimes.com/2009/03/15/movies/15denn.html. Accessed 14 June 2015.
Mandal, Somdatta. 'The Curious Case of *The Alien*: Satyajit Ray vs. Steven Spielberg'. *Asian Cinema* 10, no. 2 (Spring/Summer 1999): 116–29.
Martin-Jones, David. *Deleuze and World Cinemas*. London: Continuum, 2011.
Martin-Jones, David. 'Towards Another ' – image': Deleuze, Narrative Time and Popular Indian Cinema'. *Deleuze Studies* 2, no. 1 (2008): 25–48.
McHugh, Susan. *Dog*. London: Reaktion, 2004.
NASSCOM. 'India IT-BMP Overview'. *NASSCOM*, 2015. http://www.nasscom.in/indian-itbpo-industry. Accessed 29 October 2015.
Nayar, Pramod K. *Posthumanism*. Cambridge: Polity, 2014.
Nicholson, Brian and Sundeep Sahay. 'Some Political and Cultural Issues in the Globalisation of Software Development: Case Experience from Britain and India'. *Information and Organization* 11 (2001): 25–43.
Parthasarathy, Balaji. 'India's Silicon Valley or Silicon Valley's India? Socially Embedding the Computer Software Industry in Bangalore'. *International Journal of Urban and Regional Research* 28, no. 3 (September 2004): 664–85.
Paz, Mariano. 'South of the Future: An Overview of Latin American Science Fiction Cinema'. *Science Fiction Film and Television* 1, no. 1 (2008): 81–103.

Pepperell, Robert. *The Posthuman Condition: Consciousness Beyond the Brain*. Bristol: Intellect, 2003.
Phan, Thao. 'Introduction'. *Platform: Journal of Media and Communication* 6, no. 2 (2015): 4–7.
Plato. *The Republic*. Translated by Desmond Lee. London: Penguin, 1987.
Raja, Masood Ashraf, Jason W. Ellis, and Swaralipi Nandi, eds. *The Postnational Fantasy: Essays on Postcolonialism, Cosmopolitics and Science Fiction*. Jefferson: McFarland & Company, 2011.
Saïd, Edward W. *Orientalism*. New York: Pantheon, 1978.
Scorsese, Martin. 'Ray Influenced E.T. Says Martin Scorsese'. *The Times of India*, 19 May 2010. http://timesofindia.indiatimes.com/entertainment/english/hollywood/news/Ray-influenced-E-T-Says-Martin-Scorsese/articleshow/5944881.cms. Accessed 29 October 2015.
Short Circuit. Directed by John Badham, written by S. S. Wilson and Brent Maddock. United States of America: TriStar Pictures, 1986.
Smith, Iain Robert. '*Memento* in Mumbai: 'A Few More Songs and a Lot More Ass Kicking''. In *Storytelling in the Media Convergence Age: Exploring Screen Narratives*, edited by Roberta Pearson and Anthony N. Smith, 108–21. Basingstoke: Palgrave Macmillan, 2015.
Spivak, Gayatri Chakravorty. 'Can the Subaltern Speak?' In *Colonial Discourse and Post-Colonial Theory: A Reader*, edited by Patrick Williams and Laura Chrisman, 66–111. New York: Harvester, 1994.
Suppia, Alfredo. 'The Quest for Latin American Science Fiction & Fantasy Film'. *Frames Cinema Journal*, 6 December 2014. http://framescinemajournal.com/article/the-quest-for-latin-american-science-fiction-fantasy-film/. Accessed 29 October 2015.
Trinh, T. Minh-ha. *The Digital Film Event*. London: Routledge, 2005.
Wolfe, Cary. *Animal Rites: American Culture, the Discourse of Species and Posthumanist Theory*. Chicago, IL: University of Chicago Press, 2003.
Wolfe, Cary. *What is Posthumanism?* Minneapolis, MN: University of Minnesota Press, 2010.
Zhu, Katherine. 'Divya Narendra on Being a Wildcat, *The Social Network* and His Suit against Facebook'. *North by Northwestern*, 10 November 2010. http://www.northbynorthwestern.com/story/divya-narendra-on-being-a-wildcat-the-social-netwo/. Accessed 29 October 2016.

9

Becoming-squid, becoming-insect and the refrain of/from becoming-imperceptible in contemporary science fiction

David H. Fleming

Introduction

Across his two *Cinema* books,[1] Deleuze contends that because cinema puts movement into the image, films can be understood as autonomous thinking machines that provide viewers with the material conditions for thought. This is to say, thinking occurs courtesy of the more-than-human assemblage of the biological brain and an agential non-human thinking machine. In *Cinema 2*, Deleuze further maintains that the cinema's essence 'has thought as its higher purpose, nothing but thought and its functioning'.[2] As arguably *the* most 'philosophical' of all the cinematic genres,[3] science fiction has long harnessed cutting-edge industrial techniques and adopted a futural (or parallel) narrative tense to provoke viewers to think *through* the technological and sociopolitical issues relevant to the present. By so doing, the genre is often acknowledged as a valuable 'barometer of our times',[4] granting audiences an opportunity to see the operations of contemporary sociotechnical practices and technocratic politics in a novel light.[5] Beyond telling speculative stories, the science fiction genre in general, and the Hollywood Blockbuster iterations in particular, are also renowned for their technophilic embrace – and pushing the capabilities – of the latest industrial effects and imaging techniques, which often result in crowd-pulling spectacles that likewise surface as barometrical signifiers indicative of the broader technological assemblages the wider culture has entered into, or else have caught up the cinema, and can be understood recreating and refashioning it. As such, the double articulation of science fiction fantasies with the industrial realms of science and technology help to highlight the genre's privileged position for philosophically exploring the nature, politics and potential of present technologies and sociotechnical practices.

Deleuze himself commented upon the importance of emerging cinematic techniques and technological forms, which he saw directly impacting cinema's ability to think. Longer takes, the addition of sound, colour, mobile cameras or an increased depth of field were all 'in some sense *theorematic*'; in that they served to make new forms of 'thought immanent to the image'.[6] Accordingly (and to momentarily take Deleuze 'from behind' and make him say what I need him to say), the material form cinema takes at any given historical moment 'becomes capable of revealing to us [a] higher determination of thought', which at once 'demands a new conception of the role of the actor but also of thought itself'.[7] And because Hollywood products still technologically remain the dominant and dominating image of (neocolonial) cinema today, it becomes important to critically engage with the images it disseminates globally – particularly with regard to the content of its so-called posthuman imaginary in the era that W. J. T. Mitchell playfully calls our 'age of biocybernetic reproduction'.[8]

Of course, cerebral Hollywood science fiction films concerned with higher determinations of thought are rare. Gregory Flaxman lists Stanley Kubrick's *2001: A Space Odyssey* (1968) as an exceptional example, linking this cerebral 'sci phi' (a portmanteau combining sci-fi and philosophy) film's production of enigmatic images that outstrip thought to the praxis of Deleuzian philosophy.[9] Admittedly, few of the examples explored below fall into this highfalutin *sci phi* category. For, I predominantly look to examples of what Deleuze would likely classify as cretinoid sci-fi, using this broader contemporaneous assemblage to gain an impressionistic picture of today's evental becomings (or de- and reterritorializations) – as understood from the perspective of the molar centre. And while many films do admittedly peddle clichéd and conservative 'all-too-human' (*qua* Eurocentric) images of (non-)thought, it becomes possible to raise consciousness en passant about how their outwardly universal stories try to occult or obscure various economic, racial, geopolitical, gender and techno-political asymmetries (as are explored from the flip side by William Brown elsewhere in this collection).

Accordingly, this chapter pays attention to recurrent posthuman themes and vectors that become thought or expressed by the form and content of digital era science fiction films produced within the dark heart of the molar machine. And to best explore the processes of becoming these Eurocentric films think, I here engineer a productive encounter between Deleuze and Guattari's immanent concept of 'becomings' and the provocative writing of Vilém Flusser and Roger Caillois upon the art, practices, and 'politics' of inhuman creatures. In combination, these complimentary conceptual models make tangible the extent to which modern digital and electromagnetic technologies 'molecularly' connect Hollywood humans to, and ignite strange forms of becoming *with*, the 'alien' kingdoms of squids, insects and digital software. Before proceeding, however, we should first take pause to recall how in *Metamorphoses: Towards a materialist theory of becoming*, Rosi Braidotti upholds that the stratified sexes necessarily undergo asymmetrical forms of becoming: especially with regard to the 'unholy marriage of *bios* and *zoe* with *technos*'.[10] Certainly, the more conservative Hollywood products explored below appear to bear out Braidotti's arguments; not least within their representational narratives, which, as we will see, still appear to think the posthuman becomings of woman slightly differently to those of molar man.

If recognition of such differences offers us a convenient structure with which to organize this investigation, it becomes important to stress that as we explore the sexed becomings and lines of flight that appear to be opened up by narratives that foreground the ever-intensifying congress of the biological and technological, I also aim to keep one eye upon the inorganic technological forms and industrial formats of the films themselves: paying heed to how different digital aspects and theorematic arrangements likewise immingle, interfere with, and impact what it is, and how, these films think. To begin, I turn to one of the most popular science fiction stars of the moment, Scarlett Johansson, using her wide body of science fiction and science fictive work as a convenient focalizer. Therein, I initially expose how Johansson's star image *and* the characters she plays help make palpable peculiar animalistic lines of flight opened up by the triangulated congress of the human, the cinema and the digital that fit with feminist posthumanist scholars such as Donna J. Haraway and Braidotti, who celebrate technology's ability to break down gender and species binaries. Thereafter, I move on to explore how strange processes of becoming-insect evoked by several Johansson films expose further lines of escape that gesture towards the bewildering thresholds of what Deleuze and Guattari term 'becoming-imperceptible'. Finally, in lieu of a corresponding man of the moment or definitive male science fiction star, the final sections of the chapter pick up on comparable expressions of inhuman becomings that appear to be thought and expressed by four D3D (Digital 3D) Hollywood blockbusters featuring male leads and characters. There, I maintain it becomes possible to detect divergences in the way these big budget films think through their male actors' and masculine characters' relationship to the intensifying congress of the digital with the biological and the psychological.

Starlet Johansson

Scarlett Johansson's on-screen star identity is clearly raced and racialized, sexed and sexualized in a variety of complex ways, which finds certain parallels in her online meme-etic parameter-personae, which exhibits the modulating characteristics of what Deleuze calls 'dividuality'.[11] For Adam Knee,[12] as digital technologies are fully implicated in all aspects of her celebrity personality, especially her online mutability and dividuated simulated nature (as per the reams of ScarJo memes), she perfectly reifies the deconstruction or discombobulation of the classical celebrity image; in essence becoming a 'post-cinematic' star that although perfectly adapted to new online media ecosystems, is still found steering these increasingly 'old school' vehicles that constitute Hollywood blockbusters.[13]

While in agreement with such observations, I would add that from a 'media archaeology' perspective, Johansson's changeling star image also paradoxically surfaces as a somewhat 'timeless' and enduring one. Recall here that Johansson has famously embodied a pre-cinematic 'star' in the period film *Girl with a Pearl Earring* (2003), where she plays the muse of Johannes Vermeer (Colin Firth): the Flemish master that captures her image through his proto-photographic *camera obscura* machine. More recently, Johansson has also played a quintessential 1940s femme fatale in Brian De Palma's nostalgic neo noir *The Black Dahlia* (2006), and an archetypal 1950s blonde bombshell in Joel and Ethan Coen's meta-cinematic ode to the golden era studio system, *Hail Caesar* (2016). Johansson's on- and off-screen celebrity image has likewise witnessed her morphologically actualize two or three of the twentieth century's most famous on-screen 'blondes'; at once realizing an iconic Marilyn Monroe-cum-Madonna image for her Dolce and Gabbana lipstick commercials, and personifying Janet Leigh in *Hitchcock* (2012), another meta-cinematic film about Hollywood filmmaking. Meanwhile, Johansson became a bona fide star and muse in her own right, as can be evidenced by her appearance in a string of millennial Woody Allen films including *Match Point* (2005), *Scoop* (2006), and *Vicky Christina Barcelona* (2008). Beyond these, Johansson has also played a series of prominent science fiction roles in what some have coined the 'post-cinematic' digital era. In tandem with her dividuated online celebrity attributes, these aforementioned performances grant Johansson's star image a certain cinematic timelessness and hypermutability, which at once appears to encompass and invoke pre-, past-, present- and even post-cinematic thresholds.

In this latter grouping, Johansson's sexed and sexualized modular image has often been harnessed to help realize a series of 'post-human' or inhuman roles in science fiction films that include *The Island* (2005), *Her* (2013), *Under the Skin* (2013), *Lucy* (2014), and a growing number of science fictive-themed films in the Marvel cinematic universe including *The Avengers* (2012), *Captain America: The Winter Soldier* (2014), and *Avengers: Age of Ultron* (2015). Elsewhere Brown and I also explore her troubled and troubling turn in the US live action appropriation of the cyberpunk Japanese anime *Kôkaku Kidôtai/The Ghost and the Shell* (1995), where Johansson plays a Caucasian cyborg slave, whose white body houses the brain and rebooted consciousness of a Japanese technology terrorist (Brown and Fleming 2019). Seeing how this production became embroiled in debates surrounding Hollywood 'whitewashing' (see, for example, Rose 2017), in another essay we also foreground how Johansson essentially operates as the poster child for the largest military-entertainment complex in the world, and that her racialized and sexualized image become complicit in a greater project of, what we call after Vilém Flusser, 'cybernetic Nazism' (see Flusser 2012: 71, and Brown and Fleming 2020a: 127).

As is the case with Johansson's *Ghost in the Shell* (2017), in the majority of her other Hollywood science fiction films, her fictional characters can be bound together by their deceptive appearances, which are typically employed to conceal a 'true' identity or nature behind a misleading façade or body form.[14] By keeping an eye on the role technology plays both within and beyond the frame—as Brown and I also do in our recent engagement with 'Deepfake' Johansson pornography elsewhere (Brown and Fleming 2020b) —we can see that Johansson's multiple science fiction outings help make many of the contemporary hopes and fears bound up with our current transformative embrace of new technological forms tangible. That is, her characters and actorly performances collectively betray a feeling that the present congress of digital software and biological wetware disturbs everyday identity politics and signals an ontological breakdown in our understanding of the divisions between the human and the inhuman, biology and technology, nature and culture.

Deleuze and Guattari's dynamic non-linear models of *becoming* can aid us in describing the various forms of creative transformation and evolution probed into, or indexed by, Johansson's science fiction performances and characters. In the first instance, Deleuze and Guattari's models offer an antidote to fixed and stagnant notions of 'beings' and 'identity', replacing them with fluid and dynamic non-linear processes of becoming, which appear better equipped to express the forms of evolution and involution ignited by forming assemblages with digital technologies. In their co-authored work Deleuze and Guattari describe humans in terms of machinic-assemblages through which desire flows, or else in terms of territories that are in constant processes of de- and reterritorialization with their surrounding environments and ecosystems, with all the necessary rhizomatic flows and connections. The human is here immanently entangled within a dynamic ecological flux and is subject to ongoing processes of change and becoming, which is to say *becoming-different*. Or again, the human organism is immanently embedded within a vibrant plane, wherein 'everything stirs, slows down or accelerates', and a shimmering emission or transmission of 'molecular' vibrations can be perceived passing across, and in-between the different levels of organization. The human body here becomes akin to a sedimentalized territory, formed by layers and layers of physiological memory, like geological strata; albeit within a wider nexus of ever-shifting assemblages with which it must respond and interact as they become different together.

In replacing nominal notions of 'beings' and 'identity' with flowing models of 'becomings', we are accordingly obliged to pay attention to the contingent borderings embedding the human at any given moment, and to the various *fibres* that crossover these thresholds, historically establishing what Deleuze and Guattari term 'lines of flight'. As Cliff Stagoll explains, rather than pointing towards notions of fixed or essential beings, final products or even an interim stage, these processual models highlight 'the very dynamism of change, situated between heterogeneous terms and tending towards no particular goal or end-state'.[15] Although there may be no teleological destination, Deleuze and Guattari insist that all becomings do rush towards a *becoming-imperceptible*, with this serving as 'the immanent end of becoming, [or] its cosmic formula'.[16] The authors also outline a quasi-hierarchy, or cascading range of entangled and interleaving thresholds through which all human becomings necessarily pass. These are arranged upon a plane of consistency and outlined in terms of: becoming-woman (the initial departure point from the historical 'man' standard), becoming-animal, becoming-molecular, becoming-particles, becoming-imperceptible. All these strata are ultimately enmeshed, however, and all becomings constantly zigzag across and in-between these various levels. Of course, we all know our bodies are made up of millions upon millions of microscopic cells, and we all know that these are in turn composed of billions upon billions of particles. But the point is we do not always know what these are reacting to or interacting with, or what might trigger their becoming-different. As such, becomings can sweep us up and take us away from above or below the 'all-too-human' levels of perception, affect, thought and action.

After forming an embodied assemblage with the synthetic drug technology CPH4 in *Lucy*, for example, Johansson's eponymous character undergoes a series of transformations and becomings that pass through all these interleaving vectors: taking us from the human to the animal, from the animal to the molecular, from the molecular to particles, and from particles towards the imperceptible. Lucy's becomings here serve to update and expand upon similar forms of drug experiences explored in Carlos Castaneda's mescaline-inspired novels, which Deleuze and Guattari similarly argue helped to reveal this expanded immanent plane.[17] Like drugs, digital electromagnetic technologies also overlay and interconnect all these material and temporal substrata, and after moving into composition with the human body and brain, equally begin to open up this plane of consistency, at the same moment as novel forms of becoming-different are ignited. Space dictates that I predominantly focus upon the median-region of becoming-animal inculcated by these processes today, and to two specific forms of becoming-animal: a becoming-cephalopod, and becoming-insect, with these being the two thresholds that Johansson's science fiction films appear to make the most dramatically perceptible.

Adopting such dynamic approaches to the 'unnatural nuptials' forged between humans, technologies and animals also helps expose certain limitations in traditional (technologically or socially determinant) approaches to technologies, which often foreground the effects of these assemblages upon pre-existing human minds and preformed social subjectivities, or egos. Instead, and in taking inspiration from modern media archaeologists and philosophers such as Jussi Parikka, Nicholas Carr, Rosi Braidotti, Steven Shaviro, Patricia Pisters and N. Katherine Hayles – who increasingly demand we focus upon the reciprocal relationships technologies have with our bodies, brains, nerves and neurons – I pay heed to how we sense and 'nerve with'[18] our supersaturated media(ted) world, which now increasingly includes smart cities, intelligent environments and interactive media ecosystems.

Importantly, as Parikka has it, media theory here becomes transformed into a form of 'ethology', which allows us to conduct a radical 'media-studies of a nonhuman kind'.[19] One consequence of this is that we must also discard traditional gnomic distinctions between the normal and the abnormal, or between the so-called natural and artificial, and recognize our *actual* world 'as a specific kind of assemblage of technology + biology + nature + politics + economics + n'.[20]

Indeed, in our contemporary world of ubiquitous computing, human actors increasingly find themselves immersed in, and penetrated by high frequency waves of electromagnetic signals and information, at once passing in-between our communicative machines, as well as through our eyes, bodies and brains. Taking inspiration from Flusser's essay on 'The City as Wave-trough in the Image-Flood' (2005), Anna Greenspan observes how contemporary electrified cities are now so flooded by these waveforms that we should increasingly image and imagine our 'Oceanic' habitat in terms of an alien 'liquid topology'.[21] Similar ideas undoubtedly find concrete visual expression in *Lucy*, where the nominative hero suddenly tunes into these electromagnetic frequencies, not only becoming able to perceive the supersaturated flows of digital data surging around her but also interfering with them from within the immersive volume.

All Johansson's science fiction films become interesting from this vantage, particularly as their diegetic (fictional of futural) and extra-diegetic (visual effects) embrace of technology makes it possible to perceive how the conglomeration of human and technology suggests processes of becoming-animal. It becomes important to stress that I am not being metaphorical here, for as Deleuze and Guattari remind us, these processes should not be mistaken for symbolic metaphors or resemblances. Neither am I claiming that there is a transformation in our molar species, as if one really did become another animal.[22] Instead, I am simply arguing that collectively, Johansson's science fiction films allow us to detect molecular vibrations shimmering across the plane of consistency, and to perceive intensive eruptions of the animal within our contemporary digital culture.

I will commence by exploring the two aforementioned forms of becoming-animal that are made most overt by Johansson's science fiction films, and the broader glut of contemporary science fiction more generally: beginning with a becoming-cephalopod, which is a fitting animal for our oceanic times. This initial threshold is best illuminated by taking a brief detour through Flusser's speculative (and spectacular) writing upon the art and politics of the deep sea creature *Vampyroteuthis Infernalis* (the Vampire Squid from Hell), which can help us account for the peculiar forms of transformation that Johansson undergoes as a digitally augmented (posthuman) actress, *and* the various inhuman lines of flight her characters often take within the fictional universes.

The vamp becoming Vampyroteuthis

In *Vampyroteuthis Infernalis: A Treatise, with a Report by the Institut Scientifique de Recherche Paranaturaliste* (2012), respectively by Vilém Flusser and Louis Bec, the former provocatively and imaginatively engages with a 'hellish' alien organism that dwells in the deepest darkest abysses of earth's oceans. Synthesizing a Heideggerian notion of being-in-the-world with a Spinozian-esque model of mind and body parallelism, Flusser initially suggests that Vampyroteuthis can be fruitfully approached as the perverted inverse reflection of the human being. Why so? Our peculiar mode of being variously sedimentalizes (and indeed sentimentalizes) around our upright bipedal skeletal frame, the arrangement of our forward-facing stereoscopic eyes (which are pointed towards an enlightened terrestrial horizon), the symmetrical and lateral arrangements of our extended bodies, and our opposable thumbs. In assemblage, these various properties and configurations instil a certain form of extended and embodied gestalt spatio-temporal perception and thought. Against this, Flusser contrasts the boneless gelatinous cloak-like body-brain and aggregated betentacled nerve-net intelligence of the cephalopod, who ostensibly sucks its dark watery world into its mollusc foot, which is also its cerebralized mouth and anus.[23]

Throughout his biophilosophical treatise, Flusser thereafter imagines the divergent forms of 'art' and 'politics' that would result from this immersive mode of being with a dark watery medium and world; as well as the strange intersubjective relations the creature shares with its mates, predators and prey. Of primary importance here is the squid's art of display and deception, which arrive courtesy of its unparalleled abilities to transform its shape and texture at will; alongside its capacity to secrete bioluminescent chromataphore pigments upon its skin's surface so that it can performatively display, distract, startle or confuse other animals within the pitch blackness. Between members of its own species, for example, Vampyroteuthis' expanded-cinema-like skin performances are used to directly and transsubjectively affect and stimulate the body-brain of his sexual (and predatory) other.

Although on first blush Vampyroteuthis may appear to be our opposite, by also tracing the phylogenetic tree back to a common ancestor of which the human and the squid were each latent or virtual evolutionary possibilities, Flusser maintains that this inhuman creature always-already lurks deep within the darkest depths of our own hominid psyche and culture. In particular, modern screen culture reveals a 'return' or eruption of the squid's dark art and politics in our own cultural expressions. Originally penned in the 1980s when computer and video technologies began to explode onto the scene, Flusser noted that humans presently 'create chromatophores (television, video, computer monitors transmitting synthetic images) with whose help the senders deceitfully seduce the receivers'.[24] He thus pronounced that humanity was almost 'at the point of Vampyroteuthising our own art'; and that we were becoming 'noticeably more Vampyroteuthian'.[25] Thirty years hence, things appear to have intensified and crystallized, or so N. Katherine Hayles suggests when she considers the parallels emerging between the squid's transpiercing liquid bio-aesthetics and our current informatic imaging technologies and glowing liquid-crystal displays.[26]

Johansson's science fiction films can help make this intensive quantum of cephalopod-ness even more palpable I argue, particularly as they exaggerate these Vampyroteuthian-like vibrations at the level of both form of content and form of expression. Or put more plainly, Vampyroteuthis's shape-shifting morphological form and chromatophoric skin performances demonstrate intensive molecular resonances with various of Johansson's technologically assisted shape-shifting performances, at the same time as the squids' dangerous and deceptive sexual 'politics' increasingly become reflected by her diegetic inhuman and posthuman roles.

Let us recall that squids primarily employ their morphogenetic body and pigmented surface displays for acts of deception and seduction and are known to cannibalize their mates directly after copulation. Interestingly, almost all of Johansson's science fiction characters assume deceptive forms and disguises as a tactic to fool, entrap, mislead, or do violence to other (predominantly male) characters. In *Captain America 2*, for instance, Johansson's Black Widow wears a hologrammatic masking unit to disguise herself as Councilwoman Hawley (Jenny Agutter), allowing her to trick and overpower enemy agents. The titular Lucy is able to morphologically assume any shape or form she needs in order to elude, deceive or overpower her enemies.[27] A slower form of devious shape-shifting is also evidenced in Johansson's *Under the Skin*, which witnesses the inhuman character dissolve and digest its (hu)man prey in a manner that resonates with the post-coital cannibalism of the Vampire squid. There, not only are the alien's mates tellingly lured into the depths of a dark watery abyss after a deceitful sexual seduction, but the fleshless and boneless skin-bags that she leaves suspended in the oceanic after-life visually resemble squid-like beings. These flailed fleshless membranes also evoke the hollow simulacral 'skins' of modern digital actors or 'cyberstars'.[28] That is, they simultaneously utilize and pass comment on contemporary digital animation techniques, highlighting how viewers of photorealistic CGI movies (such as *Ghost in the Shell*) increasingly watch characters that are, ontologically speaking, little more than hollow skin renderings or shadings.

The cephalopod vectors of Johansson and her characters' digital becomings mark mere thresholds however, which in both *Lucy* and *Under the Skin* appear to be undergirded by more radical and rapid processes of becoming-insect; which as we will shortly discover, move us in turn one step closer towards a becoming-imperceptible.

Becoming-digital, becoming-insect, becoming-imperceptible

Certain insect lines of flight are suggested and signalled by several of Johansson's science fiction films. Although not an insect in the strictest sense, our acquaintance with the conduct of Black Widow spiders help erect venomous arachnid vectors with Johansson's namesake assassin in the Marvel universe.[29] In *Under the Skin*, her alien also becomes fascinated by an ant, which on first viewing is granted a puzzling lingering close-up upon her finger. This sequence is best understood retroactively after the film's main conceit is revealed, and Johansson's character is exposed as a black shiny ant-like alien that disguises itself beneath a white sexualized human-skin decoy. The final stages of Lucy's immanent becomings also witness her meld with digital computer technologies, only to emerge as a black and shiny discombobulated molecularized insectiod multiplicity, which swarms like a colony of nanobot ants. These thresholds of Johansson's becomings force us to again rebound and interrogate these animal thresholds of our contemporary ethnographic congress with digital and electromagnetic computing technologies.

Among others, Steven Shaviro, Braidotti and Parikka recognize insects surfacing as the 'totem animal' of our contemporary digital era, and as *the* organisms most relevant to our contemporary technological becomings. In *Insect Media* (2010), for example, Parikka engages with 'media as insects' and 'insects as media', in a political manoeuver designed to unconceal the 'becoming-insect' of our contemporary culture.[30] There, although insects are framed as literal 'aliens' on earth, Parikka reminds us how our precious digital machines made their greatest quantum leaps only after human designers ceased attempting to emulate human forms of intelligence *qua* centralized 'automata', and instead embraced a distributed insect logic of 'antamata', which is to say, an 'alien' mode of being that operates through swarms, mobs and distributed 'dumb' intelligence.[31]

Insects necessarily become the last threshold of our animal-becomings, though, particularly as in both the Johansson films and in reality, these aliens predominantly serve to point beyond themselves towards a bewildering worlds of becoming-chemical, becoming-matter, becoming-imperceptible. To this end, Roger Caillois (2003) argues that space and matter become dangerously seductive and infectious for insects, forever threatening to devour them in an irresistible block of becoming. This is because insects erect fibrous lines of connection *with* their environments and engage in radical forms of 'psychasthenia', whereby they topologically aggregate or distribute themselves onto and into space, while concomitantly mapping their environments into and onto themselves, while developing incredible forms of mimicry and disguise that seemingly move beyond mere utilitarian camouflage. Entomologists certainly inform us that the environment is utilized as an expanded chemical memory or brain for insects, who use their chemoreceptors to pick up information or memories left or deposited there (sometimes over generations). Tracing a reverse line, even the 'nonvisible' internal organs of insects at times appear to mimic or become like the things their outer armour camouflages or blends with, at a level that appears to go beyond that which their predators can perceive. On account of these extreme forms of 'depersonalisation through assimilation into space', Caillois ultimately argues that disappearing into their environments becomes both a tactic of, and threat to, insect existence.[32]

Arriving at these blurred boundaries of the insect body-milieu-continuum helps to unconceal yet another molecular line of flight that is indexed by and relevant to our reading of Johansson's technologically assisted roles, and science fiction characters. For here, we might recall that Lucy's assemblage with CPH4 initially serves to magnify the range of affectations and affects her body is able to move into composition with. Echoing Patricia Pisters's work on becoming-animal in the modern cinema,[33] the first threshold of Lucy's transformations is here manifested as an intensification of her human senses: 'I *feel* everything. Space. The air. The vibrations. The people. I can feel the gravity. I can feel the rotation of the Earth.'[34] As the drug doses increase, however, her sensory-motor perceptions expand and hurtle towards the affective perception of *n* dimensions, until she forms an assemblage with the realms of our digital machines and transforms into a swarming electromagnetic insect-like multiplicity. After the explosion of her human self, she then begins to move into composition with immanent space itself, encountering the expressive universe as a form of informatic computer brain, before she perceptively enters what Deleuze and Guattari term the 'Hypersphere', the 'Mechanosphere', or the 'abstract cosmic machine' that reveals the intersection of all planes.[35]

Lucy's becoming-digital-insect thus rapidly leads to her becoming-molecular, becoming-particles and then slipping into the cracks and wave-troughs in-between matter-energy and time-space. During her controlled slippage between different sheets of past, the white Lucy even comes face to face, and finger to finger, with her namesake Lucy the Australopithecus, so that Lucy the ('Ethiopian') pre-human meets Lucy the posthuman in a pre-post-erous iconic (Eurocentric) recreation of Michelangelo's *The Creation of Adam*. Lucy finally vanishes in a becoming-imperceptible of the posthuman body, which is matched by a concomitant unmaking and remaking of the world (or a worlding wherein she insists – rather than exists – and enters in-between, or overlays, the entire plane in its own process of becoming-different). Lucy here arguably gestures towards Deleuze and Guattari's three virtues of 'imperceptibility, indiscernibility, and impersonality'.[36] But, while the film's final gesture appears to reduce the human to the impersonal abstract line of pure becoming, to a pure haecceity, and an immanent being *with* the universe and 'the creator',[37] Lucy thereafter sends the humans that remain stranded in the chronological movement-image world a quasi-text message that reads: '*I* am everywhere',[38] with this 'I' trying, but essentially failing, to function as a fully depersonalized one/One. Among other things, I would note that the plication or superimposition of a white 'Hollywood action-babe' (O'Day 2004) atop the pre-human fossil found in Ethiopia, and thereafter the universe or creator itself, leaves an indelible racial trace upon human history and the Absolute which, pace Brown, is not nearly posthuman enough.

No doubt, this final threshold of Lucy's becoming somewhat recalls, but significantly contrasts, another of Johansson's personified and anthropomorphized posthuman electromagnetic *Übermensch* characters from *Her*, which offers up another Johansson science fiction outing that gestures towards, but ultimately refrains from entering, the posthuman forms of becoming-imperceptible. There, Johansson the actress and Samantha the character (an artificially intelligent Operating System) once again become articulated with digital electromagnetic technologies that push each towards the thresholds of the infinite and imperceptible. In this instance, the alien phenomenological worlds of software algorithms, electromagnetic signals, digital informatics, vibrant matter and the contracted durational timelines of oscillating electrons. However, the human nature of Johansson's voice on this occasion ensures that as both a character and star she again falls shy of posthuman indiscernibility.

For one thing, Jenna Ng and Brown indicate that Johansson was a late addition to *Her*, being chosen by Spike Jonze at the eleventh hour to revoice the original performance given by Samantha Morton (who had performed Samantha's voice on set from within a wooden box).[39] For Ng, far from offering the film a disembodied voice, Johansson's was chosen precisely because of the corporeal immediacy that *her* voice makes palpable to the viewers' senses. Ng reminds us that we ultimately have voices because of the physical arrangement of our corporeal bodies, and the performative coming together of the lungs, voice box, tongue, cheeks, lips, etc. Johansson's voice performance thus deliberately endows Samantha with a sensual human physicality and presence. Thinking back to the final text message sent in *Lucy*, then, we can better recognize how the use of a text message perhaps does deterritorialize Lucy and Johansson a smidgen more. But arguably both films highlight the inability of rationalized Hollywood industries to fully let go of individualistic humanistic and star personality politics. However, as we will shortly discover, the ideological limitations evidenced by *Lucy* and *Her* appear even more restricted in Hollywood science fiction films starring male actors and characters, whose stratification and abilities to morphogenetically transform appear far more bounded and constrained.

The good 'all-too-human' bad boys

Big budget science fiction films featuring male leads such as *Ender's Game* (2013), *Big Hero 6* (2014), *Transcendence* (2014) and *Ant-Man* (2015) similarly invoke and index empowering and dangerous concepts of becoming-squid, becoming-insect and becoming-imperceptible. However, it remains noticeable that these appear to operate differently – both diegetically and extra-diegetically – when a male actor and character pilot the film. To take but one prominent example worth mentioning with regard to the squid-like body shape-shifting use of CGI upon the star body, it is interesting to observe how in *Ant-Man's* historical flash back to 1989, the actor Michael Douglas appears to undergo a miraculous digital 'face lift' in two and a half dimensions: comparable to the age reduction processes pioneered by Digital Domain for *The Curious Case of Benjamin Button* (2009), wherein digital imaging technologies were used to reduce Brad Pitt's seam lines, eye droop and treat his face to reinvigorating virtual skin grafts.[40] Consequently, the technophilic spectacle applied to the male star body in these examples is not so much used for the purposes of modulation or deception, but more precisely for restoration and authentication. Which, in the case of *Ant-Man*, is applied to nostalgically return Douglas to his former 1980s Gekko-like glory.

In all four of the science fiction films listed above, we can also locate tropological scenes and sequences that utilize visual effects comparable to the ones showing Lucy discombobulating into a swarming digi-insectoid multiplicity after merging with computer technology. Arguably, the triangulated congress of humans, computers and insects is made most overt in the (somewhat insipid and sentimental) adaptation of Orson Scott Card's science fiction epic *Ender's Game* onto the big 'Z-screen' (new matte silver digital screens that boast a 'xyz axis'[41]). There, in a futuristic earth apparently threatened by an alien species called the formics (named after formic acid, the chemical compound found in ant venom), a militarized mankind is pitted against an alien *Other* that viewers are dutifully informed is 'most often compared to ants'.

Within the narrative, a young Ender Wiggin (Asa Butterfield) inhabits a universe where human bodies and digital technologies have fully merged and converged. He is, therefore, raised in a militaristic boot camp on an embodied diet of violent video games and propagandistic media. After earning a place in the battle academy, Ender quickly becomes adept at neurally controlling militaristic software. In the film's climactic scenes, he is moved inside an entirely immersive D3D simulation suite where he assumes control of a fleet of battleships strategically positioned around the formics' home planet. Thereafter, in what he falsely believes is a 'photoreal simulation' of war, Ender acts as the centralized intelligence controlling a hive of drone-like warships. Assuming the role of a quasi-insect queen, Ender becomes responsible for relaying hierarchical commands to his team leaders, who in turn cascade his orders to their squadrons of drones. With rather broad strokes, the film thus depicts a technologized and militaristic humanity that is ultimately made insect-like, on account of embracing digital technologies and engaging with an insectoid enemy.

Comparable tech-insect vectors are also made evident by the other three films under examination here. The digitally animated Hiro Hamada (voiced by Ryan Potter) of *Big Hero 6* (another Hollywood appropriation of Japanese anime-aesthetic predating *Ghost in the Shell*) becomes the remarkable inventor of a revolutionary new 'microbot' technology: whereby millions of semi-autonomous electromagnetic machines harbour an ability to swarm together and form into any shape, structure, or motile conglomerate their operator can imagine: courtesy of a neurotransmitter attached to their scull. Tellingly, for creating the visual effects for these micro-technologies, the Disney animators professedly drew inspiration from studying the movements and connective logic of 'fire ants and other insects building structures atop each other'.[42] A comparable technofantasy is also evident in *Ant-Man*, this time created by the exceptional scientist-inventor Dr Hank Pym (Douglas), who fashions a neural transmission device capable of translating its operator's brain waves into electromagnetic signals that allow them to manipulate swarms of ants. This becomes particularly useful when used in conjunction with a chemical gas called the Pym Particle, which is able to 'reduce the distance between atoms'.[43] When this gas technology is pumped into Ant-Man's rebreather suit, it allows its wearer to scale-shift down to nearly any size and take control of ant armies.

It becomes interesting to consider here how the Pym gas technofantasy – which its inventor claims literally 'transforms the texture of reality'[44] – finds its inverse reflection in the latest visual forms outputted by digital imaging software. This is to say, far from the digital technology being harnessed to allow filmmakers to keep up with Ant-Man (Paul Rudd), we can conversely recognize the growing popularization of (what Brown and I elsewhere call after Deleuze) these latest 'gaseous' digital imaging techniques triggering the desire for ever-more conceited Hollywood stories like these to become actualized. Or to speak *theorematically*, the technophilic affordances offered by these *gaseous* imaging technologies – which were pioneered and perfected in films such as *Fight Club* (1999) and *Enter the Void* (2010) to allow filmmakers to scale-shift at will and pass their ephemeral skeuomorphic digital 'cameras' effortlessly through solid matter, and move seamlessly 'through psyche to physics' – increasingly determine what and how modern cinema thinks, and consequentially the forms of stories it tells.[45]

Another associated result of embracing these modes of digital imaging has witnessed the emergence, or cinematic thinking of, increasingly novel forms of 'space-image'.[46] Arguably, these are further technologically enabled and enhanced when released in Z-screen and IMAX D3D (and 4D) formats, which in and of themselves signal space becoming an ever-more tangible and marketable aspect of these affective economy cinemas of *attractions*. In a technologically intensified manner, these digital forms of gaseous space-image synthesize with the Z-screen entertainment facilities to blur any rigid distinction between the on-screen diegesis and the overlapping off-screen auditorium. By utilizing and exploiting the formal potentials of these expanded image forms, all four of the science fiction films considered here contain D3D 'cinema of attractions',[47] sequences that derive their spectacle from suspending human bodies within an expanded and immersive spaced-out plane. As with *Gravity* (2013), these are often coded as dangerous and hostile spaces that threaten to devour, freeze or turn the human body inside out.

An illustrative example of one of these space-images can be located in *Ant-Man*. Therein, and as if updating Deleuze and Guattari's discussion of Richard Matheson's *Incredible Shrinking Man*, we find our deflated hero collapsing downwards in a rapid scale-shifting arc, so that he 'passes through the kingdoms of nature, slips between molecules, to become an unfindable particle in infinite meditation of the infinite'.[48] As Ant-Man drags viewers down below and beyond the realms of Newtonian mechanics and human perception, descending through Euclidean geometry into the quantum abyss, he is finally left suspended in the negative parallax plane 'outside' the screen-frame, within a spaced-out modulating Mechanosphere that is equal parts geometric psychedelic trip and abstract algorithmic screen-saver programme. Here, viewers are reminded by an extra-diegetic voice-over of the dangerous and devouring nature of this plane, which previously swallowed the life of Dr Pym's wife. In contradistinction to the helpless Mrs Pym, however, Ant-Man is able to engineer an escape from this infinite plane (back to the action-image), thanks to his own mental and physical agility, and some new McGuffin tech conveniently devised by Dr Pym in the interim.

An analogous story also plays out in *Big Hero 6*. Predictably, it again becomes the role of a female character to reveal the devouring and perilous nature of this abstract and alluring space, by getting trapped in it. There, it is the young female test pilot Abigail (voiced by Katie Lowes) – the daughter of Professor Callighan (voiced by James Cromwell) – who becomes stranded in the otherwise inaccessible and imperceptible hypersphere dimension. Ultimately, it takes Hiro and his beetle-like robot Baymax to enter this space and rescue her from her abstracted hypersleep indiscernibility.

Intriguingly, at another level of register, the male heroes entering into these spaced-out planes begin to reveal certain 'molecular' resonances and reflections with the embodied D3D viewers in the auditorium. In *Ender's Game, Big Hero 6* and *Ant-Man*, for example, the male heroes are all forced to wear embodied tech (often with helmets and visors or glasses) in order to enter into these liminal gaseous realms. If we trace the reverse line (as with insects that appear to mimic their environments), we can observe how the auditorium bound D3D viewer is likewise compelled to wear their own embodied technology in order to access these spaced-out perceptual zones.[49] As such, during D3D screening events technologically unassisted (or 'all-too-human') eyes can only perceive an impoverished and fuzzy double vision image upon the flat screen's surface, signalling that at the extra-diegetic level, these modern spaced-out blockbusters demand actual (plastic) posthuman spectacles in order to optimally and optically achieve their on-screen posthumanist (Z-screen) *spectacles*.

Another associated theme that links together the form, format, and content of these films can be teased out by briefly returning to a common narrative thread running throughout all four stories. For, all these male heroes typically display healthy problems with (certain forms of) authority, inasmuch as they strive to keep their empowering biocybernetic technologies away from corrupt power-hungry corporations and militaristic forces. Of course, as is so often the case with Hollywood action cinema, scratching below the surface immediately serves to undermine these facile moral and ideological interpretations. With specific regard to the 'evil' militaristic and corporate themes the films purportedly critique, for example, it proves beneficial to momentarily reconsider Thomas Elsaesser's eye-opening discussions of James Cameron's *Avatar* (2009), particularly where he introduces the director's musing upon 'the multiple origins and uses' of the very D3D technologies that allow viewers to become immersed in his blockbuster's seeming critique of economic and military exploitation of 'nature'. Indeed, Elsaesser hones in on one particular scene – that bears strong resemblances to the one already discussed in *Ender's Game* – wherein the fictional US humans employ D3D informatic imaging technologies to probe and gather information at a distance from the alien planet they are about to plunder. Importantly:

> The instruments that identify and locate the deposits of unobtanium are shown to rely on 3-D imaging (the holographic model of the 'Tree of Life' makes this evident), and thus draw attention to the fact that the exploitation of Pandora's 'natural resources' (and by implication, the natural resources on Earth, too) depends heavily on the technology of digital 3-D as developed for non-entertainment uses, such as land surveying, geo-tagging, weather prediction, not to mention the many military or medical uses of 3-D. These, of course, are precisely the applications which benefit from the same research and development that underlies digital 3-D in the cinema where we are watching the film, reminding us of the tight mutual interdependence between military and engineering 3-D, and movie-making and computer-gaming 3-D.[50]

Elsaesser argues that what *Avatar* ultimately 'thematizes – in a form that testifies to, critiques and embodies its own contradictions – is the alliance that the high-tech Hollywood has entered into with the US military and defence sector, and vice versa': to such an extent, in fact, that the film bears out Tim Lenoir and Henry Lowood's notion of a 'military-entertainment complex' having succeeded the famous 'military-industrial complex'.[51] With its exclusive focus upon 3D war games and military simulations, *Ender's Game* appears to intensify these themes, throwing up Ender as the sympathetic Xenocidal hive mind product of a morally bankrupt futuristic military-entertainment complex. When Ender finally learns that he was a pawn made queen for a day, the lesson he takes away is comparable to those learned by Hiro and Ant-Man, and conveniently verbalized by Dr Pym: 'You can't destroy power. You can just make sure it is in the right hands'.[52]

Tellingly, in all of these films it is predominantly (white)[53] rational male scientists and/or exceptional geniuses that create and determine who deserves these transformative technologies. Narrative conventions ensure that they also suffer, and are forced into action when irrational feminine forces, sinister Machiavellian powers, or evil/alien others covet or desire these technologies. In this sense all these male-piloted science fiction films appear decidedly conservative, trying to have their cake and eat it by sticking to a somewhat banal and traditional Eurocentric humanist morality. That is, by explicitly celebrating and embracing world-changing technologies, while attempting to ensure that they stay in the hands of traditional sites of hegemonic power, so that things will ultimately remain the same as before.

Transcendence arguably betrays the conservative sexual politics of this brand of science fiction most overtly, not least because it can be superficially conceived of as a riff on *Lucy*'s themes played by a male star: Jonny Depp. In the first place we might note that if Johansson's Lucy was a drug mule that was unwittingly catapulted into her posthuman imperceptible-becomings, Depp's character is (surprise, surprise) an exceptional scientist wholly responsible for creating a new superhuman technology. Depp here plays Dr Will Castor, a computer scientist that specializes in Artificial Intelligence (AI) and the neurobiology of the mammalian brain. His desire is to upload a human consciousness onto a quantum computer, so that he can create a posthuman 'singularity'. However, his utopic visions for a neutrally networked techno 'God' occasions an attempt on his life by an anti-technocratic terrorist cell, led by his disillusioned graduate student. Failing their attempt, Castor is left with just enough time to upload his own brain onto the quantum drive. Somewhat repeating Lucy's journey, Castor thereafter accesses the internet, and by degrees begins devising new swarms of nanobot technologies that allow him to repair, reshape, and enhance various material bodies (including humans), and to take control of an army of superhuman hybrids via earth's satellite systems and the immersive electromagnetic oceans they orbit above.

Castor's ever-increasing God-like power and intelligence is gradually framed as a monstrous (Frankenstein-esque) threat to humanity, to the extent that the US military covertly assists the terrorists in taking down the networked assemblage that Castor's distributed consciousness inhabits. Somewhat divulging its own biased sexual politics, it is finally revealed that in and of himself Castor was never really a dangerous and evil threat to humanity but became so only on account of desiring to realize his wife's dreams. Indeed, in an early Ted Talk-style speech, Castor earns a cheap laugh by explaining to his audience that as a scientist he only wants 'to understand the world', unlike his wife Evelyn (Rebecca Hall), who 'wants to change it'.[54] (She previously discussed harnessing technology to make the planet a better place.) Castor thus ultimately crosses the line because of his all-too-human love for a woman, and his desire to transform and heal the ecosphere as per her wishes. Or put differently, it is what Evelyn would have done with these powers that the film frames as a problem, with Castor merely surfacing as the vanishing mediator for her monstrous will. Politically speaking, then, in this film's ideological universe we could imagine that the might of the US military would also have been mobilized against a Lucy-like being, in order to make right her abhorrent imperceptible-becomings and worlding.

This fairly trite ethos highlights just how conservative and old-fashioned many of these commercial military-entertainment complex products are. For in the last analysis, these are old school action films draped in the cloaks of science fictive technophilic attractions. Beneath or behind these modal drapes, we discover the same old threadbare reactionary beliefs and conservative clichés: that white male heroes should take control of empowering technologies and sublimate their deterritorializing potentials in order to better act, and save the day. That is, the sorts of thoughtless inadequate ideas that Deleuze identified as the hallmarks of 'bad cinema'.[55]

Conclusions

If Johansson films like *Lucy* and *Her* illustrate that imperceptible-becomings can be seductive and empowering, on the whole the science fiction films featuring male leads were more sentimental, or else expressed a desire to slow down and control our posthuman becomings, if not to back them up somewhat (like the CGI age reduction of Michael Douglas). Of course, this can never really happen, for as Deleuze and Guattari point out, there are no processes of becoming-man: with man being a stratified molar segment, which increasingly appears from the vantage of our agential machines like an old petrified fossil.[56] Against such nostalgia for the centrality of human actors and agency, Johansson's science fiction films (which might serve as a barometer for female characters in science fiction more generally) allow us to detect a celebration of more emancipating forms of becoming. And while we might argue that these are perhaps still not 'posthuman' enough, by attempting to make the bewildering abstract thresholds of becoming-imperceptible palpable to the senses, they may just, in a Deleuzian sense, make the thinking of these as yet unthought horizons a more likely future possibility.

Notes

1 Gilles Deleuze, *Cinema 1* and *Cinema 2*.
2 Gilles Deleuze, *Cinema 2*, 163. Deleuze takes pains to distinguish between the classical movement-image cinema that functioned as a 'spiritual automaton' capable

of '*producing a shock to thought, communicating vibrations to the cortext, touching the nervous and cerebral systems directly*' (emphasis in original 2004b, 151), and the postwar time-image cinema, that he saw introducing 'mental relations' and a 'dissociative force' into the image: so that viewers were confronted by the *unthought* that precedes thought (158, 162).

3 Such notions are implicit in the writing of many film scholars. See, for example, Stephen Mulhall's *On Film* (2015) and Daniel Shaw in *Film and Philosophy* (2008). Deleuze too often commented upon the important role that science fiction played for philosophy and philosophers. For example, Deleuze spoke of David Hume's work as a form of science fiction. 'His empiricism is, so to speak, a kind of science fiction: as in science fiction, the world seems fictional, strange, foreign, experienced by other creatures: but we get the feeling that this world is our own, and we are the creatures' (2004, 162).

4 Geoff King and Tanya Krzywinska, *Science Fiction Cinema*, 1.
5 See Todd McGowan, 'Hegel and the Impossibility of the Future', 19.
6 Gilles Deleuze, *Cinema 2*, 168.
7 Ibid., 172.
8 William J. T. Mitchell, *What Pictures Want*.
9 Gregory Flaxman, *Gilles Deleuze and the Fabulation of Philosophy*, 299.
10 Rosi Braidotti, *Metamorphoses*, 150.
11 Gilles Deleuze, 'Postscript'. In 'Deleuze's Objectile', David Savat explains that dividuality 'is the effect and experience of on the one hand being made into a flow, an event, a fluid or formless state. Dividuality is precisely the experience of being neither this nor that', 58–9.
12 Adam Knee, 'The Future is Scarlett'.
13 See also Amy Herzog, 'Star Vehicle'.
14 This theme is also in evidence in Johansson's recent digitally animated performance as the spellbinding python Kaa in *The Jungle Book* (Jon Favreau, 2016). Reflecting her star image, Kaa initially appears as a disorienting and echoic voice that emanates from different points and places simultaneously. On the creature's slithering emergence from a dark ancient tree, the erotic reptile immediately begins seducing and hypnotically incapacitating the young male hero, transporting him to another world via her eyes (which project film-like images wherein past and present, reality and fantasy merge) while she deceptively coils her constricting serpentine length around his body, binding him within the folds of her predatory flesh, which simultaneously encodes sex and death.
15 Cliff Stagoll, 'Becoming', 26.
16 Gilles Deleuze and Félix Guattari, *A Thousand Plateaus*, 308.
17 Ibid., 274, 311.
18 Jussi Parikka, *Insect Media*, 160.
19 Ibid., xxv.
20 Ibid., 160.
21 Anna Greenspan, 'Wireless Waves'.
22 Gilles Deleuze and Félix Guattari, *A Thousand Plateaus*, 302.
23 Vilém Flusser (and Louis Bec), *Vampyroteuthis Infernalis*, 57.
24 Vilém Flusser, '*Vampyroteuthis* Infernalis', 5.
25 Ibid., 4–6.
26 N. Katherine Hayles, 'Speculative Aesthetics and Object-Oriented Inquiry (OOI)'.

27 It is worth remembering here that the pioneering iterations of this shape-shifting CGI technology were found in James Cameron's underwater science fiction film *The Abyss* (1989). Of poetic and political relevance to this argument, the very first technophilic encounter with this inhuman spectacle takes place in the dark diegetic depths of the ocean. What is more, at the meta-cinematic level, this first contact with these forms of CGI effects manifest themselves as a fluid technologically advanced shape-shifting spectacle that mimics and doubles the head and face of a female Hollywood star (in this case Mary Elizabeth Mastrantonio) on-screen. We might, therefore, take pause to consider what these commonalities reveal about the enduring sexual politics of Hollywood science fiction cinematic spectacles.
28 Barbara Creed, 'The Cyberstar', 79–86.
29 In light of our previous discussion, it is interesting to note that in *Staying with the Trouble* Donna J. Haraway remarks that 'Octopuses Are Called Spiders of the Seas', 55.
30 Jussi Parikka, *Insect Media*, xiii–xiv.
31 Ibid., xi–xxxiv, 129. We can witness the analogue grandfather of these distributed dumb computational intelligence machines being conceived and built by Alan Turing (Benedict Cumberbatch) in *The Imitation Game* (2014).
32 Roger Caillois, 'Mimicry and Legendary Psychasthenia', 100.
33 Patricia Pisters, *The Matrix of Visual Culture*, 142–52.
34 Scarlett Johansson, performer. *Lucy*.
35 Gilles Deleuze and Félix Guattari, *A Thousand Plateaus*, 278.
36 Ibid., 309.
37 Gilles Deleuze and Félix Guattari, *A Thousand Plateaus*, 309.
38 Scarlett Johansson, *Lucy*.
39 Jenna Ng, 'Falling in Love with an OS', and William Brown, 'The Digital Female Body'.
40 See David H. Fleming, 'Digitalising Deleuze', 204–5.
41 The 'xyz axis' pertains to D3D imaging techniques that increasingly allow for the simultaneous rendering and interleaving of 'negative parallax' images (which penetrate into the auditorium space), more traditional converged 'frame' plane images, with embedded 'positive parallax' images (spatially located within the depths of the screen). For more, see Ray Zone, *3-D Revolution*.
42 Disney, 'Microbots'.
43 *Ant-Man*. Directed by Peyton Reed.
44 Ibid.
45 See William Brown and David H. Fleming, 'Deterritorialisation and Schizoanalysis', 'A Skeuomorphic Cinema', and 'Voiding Cinema'.
46 See David H. Fleming, William Brown and David H. Fleming, 'Voiding Cinema'.
47 See Tom Gunning, 'The Cinema of Attractions', and 'An Aesthetic of Astonishment'.
48 Gilles Deleuze and Félix Guattari, *A Thousand Plateaus*, 308.
49 For the D3D viewer their tech amount to cheaply manufactured plastic glasses equipped with divergent 'circular polarizing filters', that when positioned at 'interocular distances' serve to screen out 'different visual elements in the same shot' and allow for the simultaneous rendering of multiple planes of parallax imaging. See Ray Zone, *3-D Revolution*, 261–70.
50 Thomas Elsaesser, 'James Cameron's Avatar', 259.
51 Ibid.
52 *Ant-Man*. Directed by Peyton Reed.

53 The Disney character of Hiro is perhaps the exception to this rule, being a US-Japanese cartoon hybrid, albeit a Westernized one that moves into composition with what Koichi Iwabuchi describes as a culturally and ethically 'odourless' Japanese aesthetic that is often phenotypically awash with Caucasian characteristics (see Iwabuchi's *Recentering Globalisation*, 24–9, 94–5).
54 *Transcendence*. Directed by Wally Pfister.
55 Gilles Deleuze, *Cinema 2*, 152.
56 Perhaps *Ender's Game* highlights this conservative preposterousness best, when the young hero is informed, as if he were an old Western gunslinger, that when targeting his space weapons, the 'difference between half a second and a tenth of a second' will make all the difference. Meanwhile, in the real world beyond the screen, today's fastest computers are already capable of making up to 10 quadrillion calculations per second, while other considerably slower militaristic machines have rendered the glacial durations of human perception-action and cognitive decision making nearly obsolete. *Ender's Game*. Directed and written by Gavin Hood. United States of America: Summit Entertainment, 2013.

Bibliography

Ant-Man. Directed by Peyton Reed, written by Edgar Wright, Joe Cornish, Adam McKay and Paul Rudd. United States of America: Marvel Studios, 2015.

Braidotti, Rosi. 'Animals, Anomalies and Inorganic Others: De-Oedipalising the Animal Other'. *Publications of the Modern Language Association of America (PMLA)* 124 (2009): 526–32.

Braidotti, Rosi. *Metamorphoses: Towards a Materialist Theory of Becoming*. New York: John Wiley & Sons, 2002.

Brown, William. 'The Digital Female Body: ScarJo as Inhuman'. Paper presented at Screening Animals and the Inhuman: 25th Annual Screen Studies Conference, University of Glasgow, Scotland, 26–28 June, 2015.

Brown, William and David H. Fleming. 'A Skeuomorphic Cinema: Film Form, Content and Criticism in the 'Post-Analogue' Era'. *The Fibreculture Journal* 24 (2015): 176.

Brown, William and David H. Fleming. 'Deterritorialisation and Schizoanalysis in David Fincher's *Fight Club*'. *Deleuze Studies* 5, no. 2 (2011): 275–99.

Brown, William and David H. Fleming. 'Voiding Cinema: Subjectivity Beside Itself, or Unbecoming Cinema in *Enter the Void*'. *Film-Philosophy* 19 (2015): 124–45.

Brown, William and David H. Fleming. *The Squid Cinema From Hell: Kinoteuthis Infernalis and the Emergence of Chthulumedia*. Edinburgh: Edinburgh University Press, 2020a.

Brown, William and David H. Fleming. 'Celebrity headjobs: Or oozing squid sex with aframed-up leaky {Schar-JØ}'. *Porn Studies* 7, no. 4 (2020b): 357–66.

Brown, William and David H. Fleming. 'What We Do Defines us': ScarJo as war-machine'. In *Screening Scarlett Johansson: Gender, Genre and Celebrity*, edited by K. Stevens, W. Monaghan and J. Lorecky, 183–203. Palgrave Macmillan, 2019.

Caillois, Roger. 'Mimicry and Legendary Psychasthenia'. In *The Edge of Surrealism*, edited by Claudine Frank, 91–103. Durham, NC: Duke University Press, 2003.

Carr, Nicholas. *The Shallows: What the Internet Is Doing to Our Brains*. New York: W. W. Norton & Co, 2011.

Creed, Barbara. 'The Cyberstar: Digital Pleasures and the End of the Unconscious'. *Screen* 41, no. 1 (2000): 79–86.
Deleuze, Gilles. *Cinema 1: The Movement-Image*. Translated by Hugh Tomlinson and Barbara Habberjam. London: Continuum, 2005.
Deleuze, Gilles. *Cinema 2: The Time-Image*. Translated by Hugh Tomlinson and Roberta Galeta. London: Continuum, 2005.
Deleuze, Gilles. *Desert Islands and Other Texts, 1953–1974*. Edited by D. Lapoujade. Translated by M. Taormina. London: Semiotext(e), MIT Press, 2004.
Deleuze, Gilles. 'Postscript on the Societies of Control'. In *Negotiations: 1972–1990*, translated by Martin Joughin, 177–82. New York: Columbia University Press, 1995.
Deleuze, Gilles and Félix Guattari. *A Thousand Plateaus: Capitalism and Schizophrenia*. Translated by Brian Massumi. London: Continuum Books, 2004.
Disney. 'Microbots'. 2015. Accessed 23 December 2015. http://disney.wikia.com/wiki/Microbots
Elsaesser, Thomas. 'James Cameron's Avatar: Access for all'. *New Review of Film and Television Studies* 9, no. 3 (2011): 247–64.
Flaxman, Gregory. 'Sci Phi'. In *Gilles Deleuze and the Fabulation of Philosophy*, edited by Gregory Flaxman, 292–324. Minneapolis, MN: University of Minnesota Press, 2011.
Fleming, David H. 'Digitalising Deleuze: The Curious Case of the Digital Human Character, or 'What Can a Digital Body Do?'. In *Deleuze and Film*, edited by David Martin-Jones and William Brown, 192–209. Edinburgh: Edinburgh University Press, 2012.
Flusser, Vilém. 'The City as Wave-Trough in the Image-Flood'. Translated by Phil Grochenour. *Critical Enquiry* 31 (2005): 320–8.
Flusser, Vilém. '*Vampyroteuthis* Infernalis: His Art'. *Flusser Studies* 9 (2009): 1–6.
Flusser, Vilém (illustrated by Louis Bec). *Vampyroteuthis Infernalis: A Treatise*. Translated by Valentine A. Pakis. Minneapolis, MN: University of Minnesota Press, 2012.
Greenspan, Anna. 'Wireless Waves'. Paper presented at ICDC Seminar Series, The University of Nottingham Ningbo, China, 13 March 2015.
Gunning, Tom. 'An Aesthetic of Astonishment: Early Film and the [in]credulous Spectator'. In *Viewing Positions*, edited by Linda Williams, 114–13. New Brunswick: Rutgers University Press, 1989.
Gunning, Tom. 'The Cinema of Attractions: Early Film, its Spectator and the Avant-Garde'. *Wide Angle* 8 (1986): 3–4.
Haraway, Donna J. *Staying with the Trouble*. Durham, NC and London: Duke University Press.
Hayles, N. Katherine. 'Speculative Aesthetics and Object-Oriented Inquiry (OOI)'. *Speculations: A Journal of Speculative Realism*, 2014. Available at http://speculations-journal.org.
Herzog, Amy. 'Star Vehicle: Labor and Corporeal Traffic in *Under the Skin*'. *Jump Cut* 57 (2016). https://www.ejumpcut.org/currentissue/-HerzogSkin/index.html.
Iwabuchi, Koichi. *Recentering Globalisation: Popular Culture and Japanese Transnationalism*. Durham, NC and London: Duke University Press, 2002.
Johansson, Scarlett, performer. *Lucy*. Directed and written by Luc Besson. France: EuropaCorp Distribution, 2014.
King, Geoff and Tanya Krzywinska. *Science Fiction Cinema: From Outerspace to Cyberspace*. London and New York: Wallflower, 2006.
Knee, Adam. 'The Future is Scarlett'. Paper presented at Imagining the Future, Shanghai Theatre Academy, China, 14 November 2014.

McGowan, Todd. 'Hegel and the Impossibility of the Future in Science Fiction Cinema'. *Film-Philosophy* 13, no. 1 (2009): 16–37.
Mitchell, William J. T. *What Pictures Want: The Life and Loves of Images*. Chicago: University of Chicago Press, 2005.
Mulhall, Stephen. *On Film*, 3rd ed.. London: Routledge, 2016.
Ng, Jenna. 'Falling in Love with an OS: Imagining the Future with Things in Spike Jonze's Her'. Paper presented at Imagining the Future, Shanghai Theatre Academy, China, 14 November 2014.
O'Day, Marc. 'Beauty in Motion: Gender, Spectacle and Action Babe Cinema'. In *The Action and Adventure Cinema*, edited by Yvonne Tasker, 201–18. London: Routledge, 2004.
Parikka, Jussi. *Insect Media: An Archaeology of Animals and Technology*. Minneapolis, MN: University of Minnesota Press, 2010.
Pisters, Patricia. *The Matrix of Visual Culture*. Stanford, CA: Stanford University Press, 2003.
Pisters, Patricia. *The Neuro-Image: A Deleuzian Film-Philosophy of Digital Screen Culture*. Stanford, CA: Stanford University Press, 2012.
Popiel, Anne. 'The Art of Vampyroteuthis'. *Flusser Studies* 09 (2009). http://www.flusserstudies.net/sites/www.flusserstudies.net/files/media/attachments/popiel-vampyrothuetis.pdf.
Rose, Steve. '*Ghost in the Shell*'s Whitewashing: Does Hollywood Have an Asian Problem?' *The Guardian*, 31 March 2017. https://www.theguardian.com/film/2017/mar/31/ghost-in-the-shells-whitewashing-does-hollywood-have-an-asian-problem.
Savat, David. 'Deleuze's Objectile: From Discipline to Modulatin'. In *Deleuze and New Technology*, edited by Mark Poster and David Savat, 45–62. Edinburgh: Edinburgh University Press, 2009.
Stapleton, Erik K. 'BAD COPIES: The Experience of Simulacra in Interactive Art'. *Rhizomes* 26 (2014). http://www.rhizomes.net/issue26/stapleton.html.
Shaw, Daniel. *Film and Philosophy: Taking Movies Seriously*. London and New York: Wallflower, 2008.
Stagoll, Cliff. 'Becoming'. In *The Deleuze Dictionary*, edited by Adrian Parr, 25–7. Edinburgh: Edinburgh University Press, 2010.
Transcendence. Directed by Wally Pfister, written by Jack Paglen. United States of America: Warner Bros. Pictures, 2014.
Wabuchi, Koichi. *Recentering Globalisation: Popular Culture and Japanese Transnationalism*. Durham, NC and London: Duke University Press, 2002.
Zone, Ray. *3-D Revolution: The History of Modern Stereoscopic Cinema*. Lexington: University Press of Kentucky, 2012.

Part Three

The politics of Deleuze, Guattari and posthumanism

10

The biopolitics of posthumanism in *Tears in Rain*

Sherryl Vint

One of the most powerful figurations in the contemporary cultural imagination is envisioning the future of our species as posthuman. Rosi Braidotti argues that figurations are 'not figurative ways of thinking, but rather more materialistic mappings of situated, or embedded and embodied, positions'.[1] While much of the imagery attached to posthuman figurations envisions it as a kind of transcendence of human limitation through enhanced embodiment or uploading our minds into virtual realms where we might live forever, there is an equally vibrant critical discussion that argues that we urgently need to imagine another kind of philosophical identity for the human, whether or not we modify human embodiment. Responding to descriptions of our era as the Anthropocene and to a sense that humanist definitions of our species have disconnected us from other life on the planet – to the peril of all life – feminist materialist conceptions of the posthuman stress a more porous understanding of the boundaries between the human and other beings. Figurations are more than just abstract images but, in Braidotti's words, offer ' a cartography [that] is a theoretically-based and politically-informed reading of the present'[2] (*Metamorphosis* 2).

Recent critical work on the biopolitical, that is, on thinking through the implications of a mode of governance that takes as its object the living experience of its subjects, which it manages through normalizing bodies and pleasures, is fundamental to the widespread interest in the posthuman. Foucault asserts the invention of 'the human' as a category of knowledge and practice has a specific and contingent history, an invention of 'recent date . . . perhaps nearing its end'.[3] Crucial to Foucault's concept of the biopolitical is an interest in managing the health of the population as a resource of the state and thus the rise of institutions dedicated to monitoring, managing and policing bodies and their productivity. As he notes in *Discipline and Punish*, the accumulation of capital that transformed political and social life in the West was enabled by the 'accumulation of men' through new 'subtle, calculated technology of subjection'.[4] Indeed, as Eduardo Mendieta powerfully argues, 'biopolitics then is a more proper name for the political economy that enables capitalism',[5] that is, the management of the health of the population, often Foucault's way of framing this strategy, is a management based on the profitability of those bodies. This management of life was inevitably also the management of death, as the state increasingly became involved in decisions of resource distribution, birth and death rates, access to employment, and other quotidian matters of thriving or dying. Foucault tells us that while 'the right of sovereignty was the right to take life or let live', the new right established with the rise of modern governance is 'the right to make live or to let die'.[6] One of the ways of fostering the 'making live' of the valued body politic is by expelling or excising that which is deemed unhealthy.

Thus economics, liberal governance and discourses of health became entwined. Giorgio Agamben, another key biopolitical thinker, sees the central operation of this state power as being the decision on a line that separates the life that is part of the political – *bios*, the life of the citizen, the definition we attach to 'the human' in liberal discourses such as 'human rights' – and life that is mere living matter, *zöe*, the life we share with other living species, the bare existence of those who have not been granted the status of liberal humanist subjects. The human, Agamben argues, 'is neither a clearly defined species nor a substance; it is, rather, a machine or device for producing the recognition of the human'.[7] This distinction between life that is fostered and that which is devalued is key to feminist materialist definitions of the posthuman. Posthumanism, then, needs not merely to transcend humanism and anthropocentrism, but to engage the 'uneven development' of the human, a terrain that is continually shifting with changes in economics, immigration and technology. While the goal is to move beyond humanism, we must keep in mind that humanism and 'the human' are moving targets. Posthumanist risks being constitutively blind to its own exclusions, its own production of the non-human, if it fails to recognize this fragmented terrain.

This chapter situates the posthuman within the tension between the becoming-more-than-human of certain kinds of posthumanist discourse that celebrates our power to 'control' our own evolution, and the struggle-to-be-recognized-as-human that is the experience of vulnerable and politically dispossessed groups. Crucial to this exploration, which seeks ultimately to find a more affirmative but not transcendent figuration of the posthuman, is the biopolitical context that requires us to recognize the constitutive relationship between the 'making live' of valued life and the 'letting die' of life deemed unproductive to the economic ends of the state. Thinking through a more positive vision of the posthuman begins with the materially embedded position of those subjects who are marginalized and often seen as less-than-human in current political discourse: the migrant workers whose labour is desired but whose human subjectivity is overlooked by discourses of nationalism; the impoverished, underemployed and perhaps homeless individuals who populate city streets. Pheng Cheah's *Inhuman Conditions: On Cosmopolitanism and Human Rights* examines the lives of 'guest' or foreign workers, present in a country as legalized labour power but absent any civil protection or status beyond this limited framework, to illuminate ongoing reconfiguration of what it means to be human via an analysis of the consequences to those who fail to be so recognized. Cheah points out that Enlightenment humanity is always troubled by the inhuman from which the recognition of the human is produced: 'As a product-effect of the inhuman, the human is always haunted and possessed by it. But because we intuitively grant priority to the human, this original contamination has always been viewed as a fall from a prior presence, whereby our humanity is threatened or eroded by the inhuman.'[8] It is critical that we keep in mind how the dialectic between making live and letting die maps onto a discourse that would vehemently defend those deemed human precisely by attacking those who fall outside this designation.

Braidotti notes the value of science fiction (sf) as a place for figuration that can 'subvert the construction and consumption of pejorative differences',[9] and I would stress as well the genre's affinities to her own, Deleuzian definition of feminist knowledge. Such knowledge, she argues, 'estranges us from the familiar, the intimate, the known, and casts an external light upon it'.[10] This is the core technique of sf, a genre that allows us not only to imagine 'what if' questions that push us towards seeing the given world as only one among many possible worlds but also that conveys its central ideas precisely through the meanings that such changes generate. Although seemingly about worlds far different to and distant from our own, sf is one of the most astute ways of mapping, grasping and perhaps changing what seems given about contemporary reality. How then might we figure the posthuman in the twenty-first century? My analysis will centre on Rosa Montero's sf novel *Tears in Rain*, a text that not only uses posthuman figurations to reveal something about contemporary biopolitics but one that also embeds another sf text within it – Ridley Scott's *Blade Runner* (1982), a film adaptation of Philip K. Dick's novel *Do Androids Dream of Electric Sheep?* (1968).

Let us begin briefly with Dick's novel, one of the most influential depictions of humanity's relationship with its non-human creations. Dick imagines a future world overrun with what he calls kipple, the detritus of a consumer civilization, 'useless objects, like junk mail or match folders after you use the last match or gum wrappers'.[11] The kipple stands in for the forces of entropy and thus reveals an anxiety about disorder as an erasure of the human: in Dick's future, most of humanity has left an ecologically devastated earth for Mars and other off-world colonies; animals are almost extinct, and the world is populated only by those humans who could not afford to leave, and by androids, humanoid beings designed for labour in harsh space environments. The androids have a limited, four-year lifespan, and it is illegal for them to be on earth; being across a border they are not entitled to cross is a death sentence, and any android found on earth is 'retired' by a bounty hunter whose sole purpose is to hunt and kill these out-of-place entities. Since androids are biologically manufactured, one cannot differentiate humans from androids easily and a complicated protocol of measuring 'empathy' through autonomic embodied responses has developed to enable this sorting. Androids are deemed incapable of empathy, while humans have developed an extensive religion centred around collective empathy by vicariously participating in the experiences of their martyr-saviour Mercer. Care of animals is a crucial sign that one is sufficiently empathic, and in a context in which almost all animals have become extinct, most must make do with nurturing less costly electric animal substitutes.

Ridley Scott's more widely known film dubs these bounty hunters blade runners and takes its title from this coinage. The religion of Mercerism recedes into the background, as do the animals, but questions of empathy remain central. Both texts explore something of a crisis of conscience for Deckard, who struggles to continue to feel sufficiently human – that is, empathetic – when his job is to kill beings who seem human and clearly want to live. The film more strongly focuses on Deckard's sexual relationship with one of the androids, Rachel, a being raised to believe that she was the niece of the founder of the Tyrell Corporation who manufacture them. Unlike other androids, Rachel was implanted with memories of human childhoods, and her confusion about her ontological status draws into question both whether there is a meaningful difference between humans and androids – beyond lifespan – and whether Deckard himself may also be an android who does not know his own identity. Continuity of memory is one of the anchors of a sense of stable human identity, after all, and so if memories can be implanted and changed, subjectivity is more fluid and open than liberalism would have it: subjectivity in Dick's fiction is closer to Deleuzian notions of fluid becoming.

As Dick stresses in numerous interviews and other commentary on his work, his figuration of the androids opens up questions about ethics and responsibility. In his essay 'Man, Android, and Machine', he argues, '"Man" or "human being" are terms that we must understand correctly and apply, but they apply not to origin or to any ontology but to a way of being in the world.'[12] Responding to a contemporary social order increasingly informed by the technocratic values that would eventually give us neoliberalism, Dick envisioned the machine-like android as what humanity might become in a culture that put efficiency before compassion. An android, he contends, is 'someone who does not care about the fate that his fellow living creatures fall victim to'.[13] Scott's film depicts the androids, called replicants in the film, with more sympathy than Dick imagines, drawing stronger connections between them and other socially marginalized subjects, but at the same time also makes them monstrous, tapping into the deep fear of the non-human that Cheang links to the fragility of the category 'human'. Whereas Dick uses the androids to embody the worst qualities he feared humanity was rapidly embracing, Scott presents them as similarly detached and potentially dangerous to humans but able to form deep bonds with one another. Yet, at the same time, his narrative still ties into a 'human' fear of otherness, a sense of our vulnerability and transience in the face of more powerful alternatives.

The leader of the replicants, Roy Baty, is not defeated by Deckard in Scott's film but rather dies as his lifespan runs out near the end of their confrontation. Before he dies, Baty offers a poetic assessment of the wonders that he has seen with his different embodiment, briefly stepping outside of the abject status of the non-human to gesture towards the possibilities inherent in another kind of embodiment and subjectivity: 'I've seen things you people wouldn't believe. Attack ships on fire off the shoulder of Orion. I watched c-beams glitter in the dark near the Tannhäuser Gate. All those moments will be lost in time like tears in rain. Time to die.' Allowed this brief moment of poignancy, Baty nonetheless must disappear from the narrative because *Blade Runner* remains a humanist story; our point of identification is with Deckard, and even if he may be another replicant, this possibility points only towards the inclusion of replicants within the category of valued subjects of *bios*, indistinguishable from the human (as is suggested by the erasure of the relations with animals from the film). A truly posthuman and Deleuzian-inflected perspective demands something more radical, as Braidotti indicates when she makes their work the foundation for her nomadic ethics:

> [Deleuze and Guattari] rethink continuities between the subject and his or her context both socially (power-relations) and ethically (contiguity with the Earth).

They do so without reference to humanistic or holistic worldviews, in so far as these are the pillars on which the humanist subject used to stand, dialectically opposed to His 'others'. In this respect, I see in these philosophies of radical immanence a shift of emphasis away from anthropocentrism in favour of biocentric egalitarianism.[14]

Rosa Montero's *Tears in Rain* begins with what Deleuze and Guattari would call the 'minoritarian' position of the other, the deterritorialization of the liberal humanist subject, and thus has more promise for a figuration of the vital posthuman. Montero's title comes from Baty's speech, and in the future, she imagines a class of technohumans, manufactured from stem cells, occupy a tenuous position in a social order that only recently saw them as things. *Blade Runner* is a film known in this world as well, and the technohumans – called replicants as a slur – see it as a tragic story of their inevitable marginalization. Yet as technohuman protagonist Bruna Husky dryly notes when discussing this scene, Roy's tranquil death as 'he lowered his head and died so easily. So easily. Like an electric machine that someone unplugs' is quite different from the reality of technohumans who inevitably die at age ten of Total Techno Tumour, an eruption of cancer across their bodies as their engineered cells simultaneously stop. Yet although Roy dies 'without suffering the nightmare of TTT', nonetheless, 'his powerful words reflected wonderfully the inconsistency of life, of that subtle, beautiful insignificance which time was unraveling without leaving a trace'.[15] By centring her novel on the technohuman experience of the humanist world, Montero opens up human-non-human relations to new possible meanings that move beyond conventional visions of androids and robots aspiring to be human, or behaving in such a way that we are compelled to recognize their humanity. Montero is interested in telling a different story, one in which being human is not the superlative achievement. *Tears in Rain* is thus a Deleuzian vision of the posthuman that opens up different lines of flight.

As in the antecedent texts, Montero's technohumans are created for their labour, designed precisely so that they could be required to do things that humans find demeaning, distasteful or dangerous. After the initial success of the process, 'specialist versions began to be developed, and by 2057 there were already four distinct types of androids available, for mining, computation, combat, and pleasure'.[16] Like many working-class people, technohumans are trapped in circumstances of debt, and after the Rep War, which ended with them being granted civil status, they are compelled to spend four of their ten years working for their manufacturers to pay the cost of their production. The Law of Artificial Memory of 2101 required that all technohumans be given artificial memories of a human childhood because it was found that 'humans and technohumans coexist and integrate socially far better if the latter have a past, and that androids are more stable if they are furnished with mementos';[17] although they are attached to their memories, technohumans know the circumstances of their origins. While this might on the surface seem to reinforce the gap between the subjectivity of humans and that of technohumans, Montero takes care to show us how much of human memory is also the product of desire and construction through two narrative strands: one about a father, Yiannis, who begins to forget aspects of his deceased child precisely because he spends so much time meditating upon the few photos he has, artefacts that displace any 'organic' memory; another about illegal editing of the historical archive to produce a new public consciousness that is anti-technohuman, a storyline clearly influenced by George Orwell's *Nineteen Eighty-Four*.

Both *Tears in Rain* and its sequel *Weight of the Heart* (2016) are fusions of sf and detective fiction: Bruna is a former military technohuman who has become a private investigator, and in each novel she solves a case. What is compelling about Montero's vision is less the particular details of such investigations and more the facts we learn about the social order through which Bruna moves as we follow her on these investigations. It is an often-harsh world, especially for those marginalized by poverty and species (technohumans, aliens). The novel opens with Bruna attempting to get medical assistance for a neighbour who has been stabbed, but emergency services 'prioritized humans, of course, a practice that wasn't legally acceptable, but it was what happened', a choice that Bruna muses is justified precisely by the kind of biopolitical governance of maximizing productivity that Foucault diagnosed as characteristic of modernity:

> When a medical service was overloaded, maybe it was sensible to give priority to those who had a much longer life expectancy – to those who weren't condemned to a premature death, like the reps. Was it more beneficial to save a human who might still live another fifty years or a technohuman who might have only a few months to live?[18]

We see examples of damage to those who are not recognized as central to the health of the state in numerous incidents throughout both novels: no research is done to end or mitigate TTT because technohumans are not a sufficiently wealthy healthcare market; Yiannis's child dies of a treatable disease because of shortages caused by diverting resources to the Rep War; there is a plan to make air a commodity that is narrowly defeated, but nonetheless 'zones' are established where rents are pegged to air quality, ensuring that those with the most capital also have the best health. A fundamentalist group called Ultra-Darwinists maintains that earth cannot sustain the population that it has, 'a fact that in one sense was self-evident', but they twist this into a logic that concludes that deaths from disease and environmental contamination are 'a process of natural selection of benefit to Earth, given that the highest mortality rates were occurring in the overpopulated, economically disadvantaged zones that, on the whole, were inhabited by individuals whose racial origins were non-Caucasian, and whom the Ultras viewed as defective and dispensable human material'.[19] Ultra-Darwinists thus seek to exacerbate rather than mitigate the worse aspects of a militarized, patriarchal and species-ist culture in order to speed up this process of the earth 'healing' itself from overpopulation.

In contrast to a human culture that passively endorses the hierarchical model of the subject that supports such ideologies, even if not all humans embrace this most extreme rhetoric, Bruna offers a posthuman model of subjectivity that transforms social and environmental relations as well. Aware of how she is positioned outside of human culture and ethics, she makes common cause with other socially marginalized subjects, who are often discriminated against because of their non-normative embodiment: the woman-of-size, Oli, who owns the bar Bruna frequents; RoyRoy, a woman reduced to earning her living by being a billboard, that is, by wearing clothing that continually spews advertising at anyone within her proximity; and the alien, Maio, an Omaá refuge from religious wars on his own planet, 'the poorest aliens precisely because they were stateless',[20] whose non-normative sexuality and partly translucent body serve as targets for human harassment. Extra-terrestrials are officially called 'Other Beings' but they are more commonly referred to by the slur 'bichos', that is, 'creeps'.[21] Bruna also adopts Bartalo, a talking animal from Omaá kept as a domestic pet, a crucial inclusion that crosses species lines to indicate that Montero's transformed ethical vision is not merely about humans and their alien figurations but about human and non-human relations in the reader's world as well. This is one of many sensibilities Montero shares with Braidotti, who argues:

> My situated position as a female of the species makes me structurally serviceable and thus closer to the organisms that are willing or unwilling providers of organs or cells as spare parts than to any notion of the inviolability and integrity of the human species. . . . I want to think from within the awareness that the market price of exotic birds and quasi extinct animals are comparable, often to the advantage of the plumed species, to that of the disposable bodies of women, children and others in the global sex trade and industry.[22]

Mapping such connections among disposable bodies and lives among those not categorized as human is a shared project of nomadic ethics and Montero's fiction. The world Montero creates is also populated by 'mutants' whose deformities are the result of too-frequent use of teleportation technology, individuals who are often compelled to take this risk of teleporting for their employment, and those dubbed 'moths', who illegally abandon their contaminated cities and live without permit in Clean Air Zones, 'attracted by the sunlight and the oxygen' but often going up in flames when they are caught, facing 'arrest, deportation, and a fine', even 'up to six years in jail'.[23] In *Weight of the Heart*, when caught in the riot suppression of an overly zealous security force policing the checkpoint out of Zone Zero, 'one of the most contaminated'[24] on the planet, Bruna rescues and provides papers for a young girl, Gabi, who becomes something like her ward. Gabi is suffering from curable leukaemia, but within Zone Zero she will not be treated, and even outside it, Bruna must do a favour for one of the wealthiest citizens to gain access to sufficient healthcare for Gabi. Montero's vision of the future is deeply aligned with Foucault's theorizations of the biopolitical, seeing clearly that fostering the health of some comes at the cost of the neglect of others and recognizing that capital accumulation, that is, class status, is a central determinant of one's circumstances.

Starting from her minoritarian position, Bruna builds community with those she sees as similarly excluded from the status and protection of middle-class human identity rather than aspiring to secure such status for herself and other technohumans. She is almost as suspicious of the Radical Replicant Movement as she is of the Human Supremacist Party, seeing in both a deadlock of fixed identities and zero-sum-game postures that impoverish the world for both humans and technohumans. Montero's vision is thus aligned with Dick's original depiction of the androids in that, in the midst of various kinds of species or ontological differences, what matters is not origin but a way of being in the world, an openness – or not – to difference, flow, becomings instead of fixed being. Bruna is posthuman not as a measure of her ontology, her birth via stem-cell manufacture, but because of her refusal to invest in the differentiations and boundaries that are the heritage of liberal humanism.

Bruna is a posthuman rooted in an embrace of *zöe* and its generative, proliferating power, as celebrated in Braidotti's nomadic ethics:

> the breakdown of species distinction (human/non-human) and the explosion of *zöe*-power, therefore, shifts the grounds of the problem of the breakdown of categories of individuation (gender and sexuality; ethnicity and race). This introduces the issue of becoming into a planetary or worldwide dimension, the earth being not one element among others, but rather that which brings them all together.[25]

Bruna's life and choices, helping humans who are economically marginalized, embracing aliens and animals into her community, is one example of a compelling figuration that helps us understand the present, politically and theoretically, and opens us up to more inclusive futures. She embodies Braidotti's argument that it is 'impossible on the cognitive plane and irresponsible on the ethical level actually to uphold categorical distinctions between human and other-than-human subject positions'.[26]

Montero's characterization of Bruna evokes but also moves beyond sf's history of using non-human characters to explore what it means to be human and a history of how the 'human' has been an exclusionary category. Like many of her sf predecessors from Isaac Asimov's robots to *Blade Runner*'s replicants, Bruna and her kind were created for labour only, as beings that would exist outside the political order, that is, outside *bios*. While this is a site of vulnerability in Agamben's theory, Braidotti sees something more hopeful. Often posthumanist figures in sf, such as Bruna, push us towards expanding the zone of *bios*, the categories of beings recognized as deserving the protection of 'human' rights: we see this in popular sf figures such as *Star Trek: The Next Generation*'s Data, an android who aspires to be like the humans he admires and works among. Bruna, in contrast, consistent with Braidotti's Deleuzian idea of nomadic subjectivity, does not long to be recognized as human because she perceives that the concept of the human that forms the horizon of such desires 'was colonized by phallogocentrism, it has come to be identified with male, white, heterosexual, Christian, property-owning, standard-language-speaking citizens'; in contrast, '*zöe* marks the outside of this vision of the subject, in spite of the efforts of evolutionary theory to strike a new relationship to the non-human.'[27]

This historical trajectory of those who were once excluded from full participation in the liberal state and who petitioned for and secured inclusion – those without property, colonized subjects, women – forms the background for Montero's world. We learn that technohumans were granted the same rights as humans in the Constitution of 2098 which unified the earth under one government. Montero is careful to show us, however, that such formal and legal protection is not sufficient to transform social relations or to ensure a liveable future on a planet still struggling with so many economic and environmental crises. Moreover, as we see from work such as Cheah's, the limitation of rights discourse in a biopolitical context is a significant ethical issue in the material realm as well, aptly captured by Montero's sf figuration. Montero envisions the inclusion of technohumans into the Constitution as an outcome of the establishment of global government, and Cheah situates her work as speaking to the condition of globalization. The human is not a given and stable ontological category, Cheah argues, but nor is it 'a myth or mere ideological abstraction'.[28] The human of human rights discourse, she suggests, is a 'product-effect' of discourses of the self and technologies of production, and the urgent task of the humanities is to situate 'such humanity-effects in terms of their conditions of possibility and actuality, and also their limits. How do these effects constrain lives? What do they necessarily exclude in a given conjuncture?'[29] Cheah asks:

> In an uneven world, how can struggles for multicultural recognition in constitutional-democratic states in the North be brought into a global alliance with postcolonial activism in the periphery? The possibility of realizing a global civil society or an international public sphere capable of representing or mediating the needs and desires of humanity's radically different constituencies through cross-identifications stands or falls here.[30]

Drawing on sf's capacity to estrange our quotidian perspective and thus cast a new light on the familiar, Montero situates Bruna's technohuman struggles for a liveable existence within a world peripherally filled by economically marginalized humans whose vicissitudes are similar to her own. We find in Bruna's example, then, a figuration that responds to Cheah's call for a political discourse of solidarity that moves beyond the limitations of human rights.

The first step is imagining political subjectivity without the human, clear in Bruna's lack of interest in aspiring to a subjectivity based on humanist *bios*. Instead, her desires and alliances resemble Braidotti's model of a posthumanism that can emerge from *zöe*. Refusing to accept the hierarchies that would conceptualize *zöe* only through its vulnerability outside the protections of the biopolitical state, Braidotti champions a posthuman that flows from the affirmative possibilities of *zöe*, a nomadic posthuman. New ways of imagining the social flow are made possible by these new ways of theorizing subjectivity. Like other technohumans, Bruna has a set of implanted memories that give her a core sense of who she is. Most technohumans receive only a minimal and non-contradictory set of memories and impulses, but Bruna receives the full human memories of her memory technician, Nopal, a man whose early life was shaped by abuse and isolation. Like all technohumans, Bruna is aware that her memory is constructed, but because she is simultaneously aware that she shares these memories with Nopal who lived them, she develops a curious kind of non-unitary identity. She is always more than just herself, but at the same time she and Nopal are not identical either. They are neither one nor two but rather a dyad whose shared but also contradictory desire can enable 'the affirmative mode of becoming' that sustains Braidotti's nomadic posthuman: 'encounters between multiple forces and the creation of new possibilities of empowerment', embodying desire that 'is outward-directed and forward-looking, not indexed on the past of a memory dominated by phallocentric self-referentiality'.[31] Although it is the past, memory, that unites them, these memories necessarily become detached from the self-referential because they are memories shared identically between two distinct personalities who, paradoxically, both remember them as individual experiences and forge an alliance through them.

We see Bruna's commitment to another kind of subjectivity in her struggles not to feel resentful or cheated by her ten-year lifespan. Although in both novels Bruna continually counts down the time she has left (four years, plus dwindling months and days in *Tears in Rain*; down to three-years-plus in *Weight of the Heart*), she also finds ways to see death as something other than the enemy of life, a posture that is consistent with Braidotti's commentary on another way of thinking vitality. For Braidotti, '*zöe* refers to the endless vitality of life as continuous becoming',[32] to a 'reinvention of nature' that is not merely the opposite of *bios*. Although Bruna is often angry about the grief she experiences through the loss of loved ones due to economic inequities and the structure of technohuman lifespans, Nopal reminds her that pain is also life: 'that's how it is. Life hurts'.[33] Although Bruna continues to contest the inequitable way in which chances of life and death are distributed in a biopolitical regime, she also comes to see death as a becoming, a transformation of vitality that can continue to flow into other configurations, rather than the opposite of life. Braidotti argues that an ethics of dying can also be a kind of vitality, a vision of sustainable life, pointing out – as does Nopal – 'the traumatic elements of this same life in their often unnoticed familiarity', and prompting us to recognize that life 'is at best compelling, but it is not compulsive'.[34] From this nomadic and estranged perspective, life is intense energy that 'reaches its aim and then dissolves' and thus dying can be 'another expression of the desire to live intensely'.[35]

Bruna learns to value how she lives rather than lose the pleasures of life in an obsession with how long she will live. She comes to identify with Melba, a polar bear produced from stem cells in a technique similar to Bruna's own manufacture, a clone of the last living bear who drowned because climate change meant she could not reach another ice floe before exhaustion set in. From one point of view, Melba has a rather macabre existence, destined to die of TTT after a short lifespan, only to be replaced by another Melba, in an endless chain. The zoo enclosure where she lives is augmented by projections of the 'real' Melba in the wild, footage captured by drone cameras who were able to watch her in her final days, although no one could reach her in time to save her. Yet from moment to moment, Melba also has a vital existence, 'diving and playing with a ball and happily frolicking while relaxing a trail of bubbles from her snout'.[36] Near the end of *Tears in Rain*, Bruna has a moment of bonding with Melba through the glass of the enclosure:

> And for an instant, she saw herself next to the bear, the two of them floating in the blue of time, in the same way that Bruna had floated in the night and the rain nearly two years ago, next to the dying Merlín [her lover, another technohuman]; floating on that bed like a piece of flotsam in the midst of a shipwreck. All of which was very painful but very beautiful, too. And beauty is eternity.[37]

Shortly afterward, Bruna and her friend Yiannis, who also experienced a significant loss, exchange quotations from Cicero that emphasize that the mere fact of living is not what is significant about one's life, but rather the connections one forms, the positive changes that one may leave in the world that can persist beyond the death of the body.

This new orientation towards finitude and a politics of sustainability, which is not the same as a politics of immortality, is crucial to the path that Bruna charts towards overcoming the conspiracy and solving the case in *Tears in Rain*. Tensions between human supremacist and technohuman activists have been exacerbated by a research scientist, Ainhó, who is bitter about the loss of her teenaged son, who was shot by technohuman security guards when he broke into her office as part of an activist protest.[38] Ainhó creates a virus that infects technohuman memories, convincing them that they are human and that they must commit some act of murder to save a child they love or else convincing them that their failure to do so requires their suicide. This memory of the grief caused by the loss of a child or of a child in peril is based on Ainhó's own experiences, and when Bruna is infected with the virus, we see how powerful and real it feels through her. This virus thus ties into a common narrative of human futurity, the reproduction of self through child, a narrative that invites a narrow and solipsistic sense of ethics and sustainability that would sacrifice all others for the sake of one's own. This is the logic that sustains a hierarchical and exclusionary sense of ethics that places human life above all other life and that rationalizes one's complicity in global patterns of inequity, because one's sense of ethics is narrowly focused on the survival of one's own biological family (or community, or country). To refuse a politics that attaches so strongly to 'the child' is not to deny that children should be nurtured or that they are important to a sustainable future, but it is to counter the idea that the self or the child can survive in isolation, that either the self or the child have meaning outside a network of flows and exchanges with other beings.

Bruna refuses to be seduced by this fiction of the child, to commit to an emotional investment in a future in which what is 'hers' is privileged beyond what is collective. Although her memory tells her that this child, Gummy, is in peril and she must kill in his name, Bruna refuses to indulge this 'debilitating memory of the child'.[39] Instead, she forces herself to inhabit her memories of him but also continually tells herself that they are not true, that he doesn't exist, until she 'managed to erase the image bit by bit, like the pixels of a defective graphic'.[40] In Bruna's case, of course, the child truly does not exist, it is simply a false memory planted by the virus. At the same time, however, her grief over losing him is very real, experienced both in the false memory in which he is in peril *and* in her deliberate deconstruction of that memory by refusing to allow herself to inhabit it. The novel establishes that, official ideology notwithstanding, from the point of view of subjective experience human and android memory are the same – selective, fallible, affective and always being rewritten. Thus although Bruna does not sacrifice a real child, we can take something valuable from her sacrifice of the fantasy of the child, especially when Bruna's choices are contrasted with the destruction wrought by Ainhó, who allows grief over her lost child to multiply into damage to the world around her and other beings.[41] Bruna refuses to indulge an understanding of the self and her child (as extension of self) that reinforces humanist hierarchies, and her pain in giving up this fantasy is emphasized by the fact that technohumans cannot reproduce at all. Yet it is only by refusing to play out this narrative of the child in peril that Bruna is able to survive infection by the virus, something that killed all others.

In Bruna's choice, we see another kind of subjectivity, a vital posthumanism that can embrace new and alternative modes of political and ethical agency that dismantle and resist an ethics focused too narrowly on the self. Ainhó emblematizes the kind of thinking that puts oneself, one's child, one's narrow community ahead of other life, whereas what is needed is what Braidotti calls a 'mutation' of cultural values, one that

> redefines what it means to be human through nomadic practices of transpositions of differences in the sense of practices of the not-One, of affinities and viral contaminations, interdependence and non-entropic economies of desire. . . . [A mutation that] moves towards the construction of possible and hence sustainable futures by enforcing the notion of intra-species and intra-generational justice.[42]

Bruna's commitment to intra-species justice is evident in the community she forms and in her act of refusing the false memory of *her* child to instead foster an ethical future of interdependence. It is important to stress that this is not an 'anti-child' position: Bruna demonstrates a commitment to intergenerational justice that seeks to make the world more equitable for *all* children, something reinforced in *Weight of the Heart* when she rescues and begins to care for Gabi. This deprogramming of the virus memory, then, is aligned to a deprogramming of conventional cultural values endorsed by the liberal humanist subject position. Bruna literally deprograms her memory as a figuration of how nomadic posthuman subjects might deprogram our subjectivities.

Braidotti argues that 'the proper object of ethical inquiry is not the subject's moral intentionality, or rational consciousness, as much as the effects of truth and power that his or her actions are likely to have upon others in the world. This is a kind of ethical pragmatism, which is attuned to the embodied materialism of a non-unitary vision of the subject.'[43] This focus on effects rather than consciousness can be understood as in some ways analogous to the ethical distinctions Dick sought to make in his vision of the difference between human and android consciousness, although Dick expressed his ideas in humanist language. Dick's advocacy of empathy as that which ensures one remains human opens a door to the nomadic posthuman. Braidotti points out that 'the dominant vision of the self we have institutionalized in the West, that of liberal individualism, serves the purpose of a vampire-like economic system based on stock and exchange, common standards and unjust distribution, accumulation and profit.'[44] This is where we see the connection between the way we construe our subjectivity and the biopolitics of life and death so tightly woven with capitalist economic systems and the liberal governance that sustains them. Much of the power of Montero's work, then, comes from her recognition that these politics of resource distribution – especially the uneven distribution of chances to thrive or risks of withering – are deeply enmeshed in the ethics of how subjectivity is imagined and lived. Dick's androids live in a world of kipple that indicates the ethical and material depletion of their world, but Montero paints a more nuanced picture of the hierarchical forces that create such zones of devastation within islands of plenty.

By refusing the hegemony of individual reproduction and the future as embodied in one's own child, Bruna exemplifies an ethics of accountability, the production of sustainable futures that resist the territorializing of the future with the reproduction of oneself. This is a 'nomadic subjectivity [that] critiques liberal individualism and promotes instead the positivity of multiple connections'.[45] It is a vision of the posthuman that is not about transcendence or escaping embodiment and intrasubjective connection. If we wish to move beyond the exclusions and violence that accompanied the humanist project, we must remain attentive to posthumanism's own moments of 'letting die' as much as to its possibilities for 'making live'. This is not a complete deterritorrializing of the subject or a celebration of its absence, but a continual push towards a more empathetic, more connected, more dispersed subject, a subject that refuses and resists the liberalist logic that invented the human as a kind of capital.

Such a vital posthumanism has the potential to shift political discourse in several registers that are relevant to ongoing issues of social and economic justice that mirror those depicted by Montero in her imagined future. A vital posthumanism can conceptualize ethics outside of the framework of nation states and their distinctions about who is within or without the scope of the citizen/bios. Such ways of theorizing subjectivity and community will become increasingly vital as climate change, and other environmental factors continue to move people and other living beings to new locales, and as related factors such as changes in sea levels create climate refugees alongside economic refugees. Instead of imagining a posthuman as a transcendence of the human body and its limitations of fragility and mortality, this is a posthumanism that can embrace finitude and another kind of ethics in which the human is only one among species, this generation only one among those to live on this planet. More importantly, perhaps, such a posthumanism offers us a way to think beyond the zero-sum games that dominate so much of the political imagination, in which mitigating the damage for one group is believed to come at the expense of another. The structures of humanism with its hierarchies, its liberal notions of property ownership, including in one's self, and its investment in individualism are not adequate for dealing with the crises that face us in the Anthropocene. A posthumanism based on transcendence and augmented ability simply intensifies these problems of humanism. A vital posthumanism, thinking in planetary and generational dimension, refuses impasse of this uneven development of the human, and thus opens us up to other ways of thinking about sustainable futures.

Notes

1 Rosi Braidotti, *Metamorphoses*, 2.
2 Ibid.
3 Michel Foucault, *The Order of Things*, 387.
4 Michel Foucault, *Discipline and Punish*, 220.
5 Eduardo Mendieta, 'Biopolitics', 40.
6 Michel Foucault, *Society Must Be Defended*, 241.
7 Giorgio Agamben, *The Open*, 26.
8 Pheng Cheah, *Inhuman Conditions*, 230-1.

9   Rosi Braidotti, *Metamorphoses*, 182.
10 Ibid., 13.
11 Philip K. Dick, *Do Androids Dream of Electric Sheep?*, 65.
12 Philip K. Dick, 'Man, Android, and Machine', 212.
13 Ibid., 211.
14 Rosi Braidotti, *Metamorphoses*, 63.
15 Rosa Montero, *Tears in Rain*, 208.
16 Ibid., 10.
17 Ibid., 15.
18 Ibid., 8.
19 Ibid., 195.
20 Ibid., 113.
21 Ibid., 44.
22 Rosi Braidotti, *Transpositions*, 100.
23 Rosa Montero, *Tears in Rain*, 179.
24 Ibid., 2.
25 Rosi Braidotti, *Transpositions*, 97.
26 Ibid., 131.
27 Ibid., 37.
28 Pheng Cheah, *Inhuman Conditions*, 10.
29 Ibid.
30 Ibid., 42.
31 Rosi Braidotti, *Metamorphoses*, 99.
32 Rosi Braidotti, *The Posthuman*, 41.
33 Rosa Montero, *Tears in Rain*, 76.
34 Rosi Braidotti, *The Posthuman*, 133.
35 Ibid., 133.
36 Rosa Montero, *Tears in Rain*, 160.
37 Ibid., 405.
38 Space precludes a lengthy plot summary, but there is also a subplot regarding how Ainhó hid her identity as RoyRoy and thus gained access to Bruna's inner circle. When the truth is finally revealed, there is this added sense of personal betrayal.
39 Rosa Montero, *Tears in Rain*, 362.
40 Ibid.
41 We might note here as well that Yiannis also loses a child – indeed, this shared grief is what bonds he and Ainhó when he knows her in her RoyRoy persona – but he does not let his loss turn him against other living beings.
42 Rosi Braidotti, *Transpositions*, 274.
43 Ibid., 14.
44 Ibid., 111.
45 Rosi Braidotti, *Metamorphoses*, 266.

Bibliography

Agamben, Giorgio. *The Open: Man and Animal*. Translated by Kevin Attell. Stanford, CA: Stanford University Press, 2003.

Braidotti, Rosi. *Metamorphoses: Towards a Materialist Theory of Becoming*. Cambridge: Polity, 2002.
Braidotti, Rosi. *The Posthuman*. Cambridge: Polity, 2013.
Braidotti, Rosi. *Transpositions: On Nomadic Ethics*. Cambridge: Polity, 2006.
Cheah, Pheng. *Inhuman Conditions: On Cosmopolitanism and Human Rights*. Harvard: Harvard University Press, 2007.
Dick, Philip K. *Do Androids Dream of Electric Sheep?* New York: Del Rey, 1996.
Dick, Philip K. 'Man, Android, and Machine'. In *The Shifting Realities of Philip K. Dick: Selected Literary and Philosophical Writings*, edited by Lawrence Sutin, 211–32. New York: Vintage, 1996.
Foucault, Michel. *Discipline and Punish: The Birth of the Prison*. Translated by Alan Sheridan. New York: Vintage Books, 1977.
Foucault, Michel. *The Order of Things: An Archaeology of Human Sciences*. Translated by Alan Sheridan. New York: Vintage, 1970.
Foucault, Michel. *Society Must Be Defended. Lectures at the College de France 1976-1976*. Translated by David Macey. Edited by Arnold I. Davidson. New York: Picador, 2003.
Mendieta, Eduardo. 'Biopolitics'. In *The Cambridge Foucault Lexicon*, edited by Leonard Lawlor and John Nale, 37–43. New York: Cambridge University Press, 2014.
Montero, Rosa. *Tears in Rain*. Translated by Lilit Zekulin Thwaites. AmazonCrossing, 2012.
Montero, Rosa. *Weight of the Heart*. Translated by Lilit Zekulin Thwaites. AmazonCrossing, 2016.

11

Dis/abled reflections on posthumanism and biotech

Martin Boucher

Technomedicine and disability

In the following, I will be offering a few reflections on what disability can show us about our relationship to emerging biotechnologies. In doing so, I must discuss the case of *technomedicine* as it has profound implications on how we perceive the body today. By technomedicine, I mean the broad shift towards technologically mediated diagnostic techniques and interventions. As Lewis writes, 'New biotechnologies – including advanced imaging techniques, genetic manipulations, organ transplantation, artificial limbs, expanding cosmetic surgeries, and an array of new psychopharmaceuticals – are rapidly turning medicine into technomedicine.'[1] As we shall see, the types of discourse and the types of subjects that emerge as a result of this technomedicine will have a negative impact on disability politics.

However, we must keep in mind that medicine has always had a difficult relationship with disability. This is nothing new. One could argue that the entire discipline of disability studies has been an attempt to overcome the 'medical model' of disability. First, this model places the cause of disability in the body itself – while disability studies scholars locate the cause of disablement in society – and second, in approaching disability in this way, there is seldom any large-scale mobilization of assistive technologies that happen outside of its industries (pharmaceutical, home-care, accessibility devices, etc.) and the societal role of medicine (economics, global governance, national politics, benefits/insurance, etc.). Because of this relationship, any discussion of emerging technologies and disability has to account for the major changes (or mutations) in the life sciences.

In addition to the changes in medicine's relationship to the body, which will be discussed shortly, we must remember that medicine, since the eighteenth century, has entrenched itself in the systems of governance in Western nations. In the eighteenth and nineteenth centuries, a discourse appears which concerns itself with hygiene, epidemics, birth and death rates and with potentially problematic – normal/pathological – social patterns in relation to child rearing, family planning, breastfeeding, etc. These discourses of truth materialize through various professions and institutions that are tasked with the understanding and policing of these phenomena.[2] Labour medicine, the standardization of health officers in urban and rural areas, the top-down administration of medicine all represent what Foucault would call a 'state medicine'.[3] This administrative structure is concretized in a certain state responsibility after the Second World War, first in the UK with the Beverage plan and soon after in most Western nations.[4] Health, having entered the realm of government, required an extensive system of surveillance and control for its constant regulation.[5] The primary means of regulation are social-medical interventions on populations and regulatory policies; but there is also a parallel mechanism of self-regulation emerging from the discourse of neoliberalism that creates an image of the individual as autonomous and rational that makes them responsible for their own health choices and personal competitiveness.[6] Not only are governments responsible for the administration of health (through hospital services, public health initiatives, insurance and benefit systems etc.), but also individuals are responsible to society for making choices that limit their dependence and increase their productivity (including choices about health, family, education and work). This *politicization* of social and individual health underlies much of the discussion in this chapter. Disability is one site that has historically been the target of both social medicine and individuation through pathologization. As Bill Hughes puts it, 'the history of impairment throughout modernity has been a history of pathologization and supervision'.[7] The above is only a sketch of how a system of supervision and control could be established. This history continues today, as we shall see, in the neoliberal-able discourse of the body and is compounded further by the advancements of technomedicine.

Technomedicine and vital politics

There are three distinct medicines that need to be discussed here. First, there is a rupture between a medicine of symptoms, aimed at the experience of bodies, and a technological medicine of signs, aimed at functions, systems, organs and limbs (i.e. molar medicine[8]). We can then identify a mutation from that molar medicine to a medicine of molecular mechanisms aimed at the vital functions of life and its most minute building blocks (i.e. from molar to molecular medicine). The first medicine is a Hippocratic medicine, where the patient is an expert on his/her experience and, in discussing symptoms, asks the doctor to play the role of interpreter and healer.[9] He/she must interpret the symptoms and return some balance to the body. The systems and practices developed in this period of medicine, according to Canguilhem and Foucault, no longer make sense in the scientific and objective medicine of modernity.

A different kind of medicine emerged in modernity, a medicine that used the methods and discourses of the scientific revolution. It was no longer about symptoms per se, but about objective signs. From this perspective, the body is a machine. This body has an understandable structure from which empirical knowledge can be gathered. It gives us some objective basis on which informed clinical decision can be made. Importantly, the mechanical view was supported by the development of the scientific perspective in a variety of disciplines, the wider practice of dissection, the invention of the stethoscope and the availability of microscopes in the eighteenth and nineteenth centuries. These early devices allowed us to codify the body – as tissues, organs, kinetic functions – into an objective discourse on health and disease.[10]

The further development of this perspective led to the invention of technologies far beyond the simple stethoscope or even the ordinary X-ray. Increased computational capacity gave us the ability to look inside the body with CAT scans and MRIs. In addition to these, we developed technologies to look at the *living body* in real time with ultrasounds and fMRIs. All these taken together make up what we call technomedicine. The practice of medicine would be impossible without technologically mediated information about *signs* of disease. This changes the relationship of the doctor to his/her patient from the interpretation of experience to the interpretation of signs, data and images.

In the third kind of medicine, a mutation from the above, Nikolas Rose proposes that with the mapping of the human genome and the ever-evolving possibilities of genetic screening and manipulation, in conjunction with the development of increasingly complex pharmaceutical agents, we have entered a period of *neuro-molecular* medicine.[11] We have developed technologies that allow us to understand and intervene on disease at the level of the minute building blocks of life, its molecular functions, its neuro-chemical processes, and its system of information (genes, protein coding, DNA, mRNA, tRNA, rRNA, Neuro-transmitters, transporters and receptors, etc.); simply put, it is a medicine of the body as *vital information*. With this new medicine, an abnormality can be found in an individual before any symptom is experienced and before any sign can be found.[12] It is a medicine that still refers to materiality but to a materiality of a different kind. It refers to the real and immanent existence of a probable future. Responsibility is extended beyond the present into our personal future, the future of our families and friends (and society as a whole), and the future of our descendants (and their future, that is, intergenerational biosecurity). If before we could talk of a biopolitics at the level of individuals and populations, now we can also speak of a *vital politics* where medicine is concerned with the predictive powers of information at a much smaller level *within* the individual or population. It is concerned with the future through the monitoring and control of a collection of factors and risks (often in genetic terms, but also in terms of 'risky brains', dangerous compounds, or behaviours) where the primary goal is prevention.[13]

Deleuze was quite forward looking in noticing the sociopolitical danger of what would become a defining feature of technomedicine: 'The new medicine "without doctor or patient" that singles out potential sick people and subjects at risk, which in no way attests to individuation – as they say – but substitutes for the individual or numerical body the code of a "dividual" material to be controlled.'[14] The patient is reduced to risk factors, and the goal is to prevent or mediate a future that has not yet come. Deleuze had seen this coming as society was switching from a primarily disciplinary form of power to one of control,[15] but the full extent of this shift was not yet perceptible. The new strategies of regulation and control, according to Castel, 'dissolve the notion of a *subject* or a concrete individual, and put in its place a combinatory of *factors*', contact with individuals is replaced by the collection of data centred on establishing '*flows of populations* based on the collation of a range of abstract factors deemed liable to produce risk in general'.[16] Moreover, medical knowledge itself is shared with and developed by industry; it exists in universities and engineering laboratories outside of the clinic. At the cutting edge of medical science is a shift away from its two primary actors, the doctor and the patient. At the extreme, 'clinicians are in danger of becoming glorified distributors of the new technologies for the giant transnational biotech corporations – sort of like new car dealers with a medical certificate'.[17] This is certainly an exaggeration – doctors still play an important and semi-independent role – but the caricature is informative in warning us about some dangers inherent in the relationship between industry, research and medical practice.

Though this medicine is projecting into the future and concerns itself with dividual units as opposed to individual bodies, within the context of biopolitics and neoliberalism, it is individualized through personal choice and responsibility. It is in this complex interplay between the propagation of economic cost/benefit thinking, risk and preventability, and responsibility for the future that an individual makes decisions regarding biotechnologies and their bodies. In this context, the *difference* from the norm inherent in the 'disabled' body is conceived in the negative and represents a deeply moral and political pressure to normalize. The desirable person is a good *neoliberal-able*[18] subject, so technologies are developed to *cure* or *repair* bad neoliberal subjects. This places the disabled subject squarely in the negative – objectively, politically and morally. This is precisely what disability studies urges us to avoid and resist. The term 'neoliberal-able subject' captures this very well. It challenges both the normalizing demands that neoliberal society places on the subject, and points to its reinforcement of ableist social and political perspectives. Neoliberalism and normality are historical discourses that cause a great deal of concern for many individuals in today's society. Not only has posthumanism troubled these foundational discourses, it also captures the ways in which individuals do, or attempt to, go beyond the fixed positions afforded to them by this way of thinking. We will see how, in our case in critical disability studies, the ways we use and understand biotechnology is always informed by the above problematizations.

Dis/ability

The basic assumption of orthodox disability studies is that disability does not reside in the individual, but that it is a result of social organization. The individual may have an impairment, but the fact that that impairment plays out in a disability is because of the social and political environment that surrounds that individual.[19] This idea has recently been criticized by post-structuralist disability theorist Shelley Tremain on the basis that, much like in feminism, this division of impairment and disability – like sex and gender – is only momentarily politically useful. One's disability is *caused* by society, but one's participation in this identity is contingent on having some impairment – it is still an identity based on some essentialist version of the body.[20]

The post-structuralist critique, in theorizing disability in its discursive construction, served as a more solid ground on which to criticize normalizing discourses and ableism; however, by rejecting the materiality of impairment, it excluded people's experience of embodying impairment and minimized the importance of the material reality of our fleshy bits – that is, our bodies. We cannot attribute anything to the individual or the social body that is essential, concrete or natural in the traditional sense, but it remains that social organization, historicized discourse *and* the diversity of human experience are in some way linked to the material body. The material body may not be the locus of disability, but one's embodiment in the world *is* affected by one's point of access to the world.[21] What makes human experience diverse is always in some way mediated through language, but it is, after all, a physical body that is in the shadow of its functional discursive constructions.

For this reason, there has been a recent turn towards phenomenology and new materialisms in disability studies. This has been very useful in giving experience – through the lens of embodiment – a useful position in thinking about disability. For our purpose, the embodiment of people living with disability is important, but I acknowledge that its experience *cannot* serve as the exhaustive foundation for political resistance because experience itself happens in the context of constitutive discourses that challenge its *a priori* status.[22] Furthermore, bringing a new focus to materiality cannot mean bringing back some conception of a pre-discursive body because we would again fall into the trap that defining this pre-discursive body is itself a discursive formation. Experience and the body simply serve as guides as we navigate the embodiment of disability, but it offers nothing like an essence, truth, universality, etc.

One particularly useful philosophy in overcoming these problems and honouring the lived-embodiment of marginalized subjects and their political struggles is a certain posthumanism that has been emerging in contemporary feminism (e.g. Haraway, Braidotti and Shildrick among many others). In understanding materiality as both immanent and relational, these perspectives do not give the body (or embodied assemblage) the status of an ahistorical material *a priori*, but it does imbue it with a kind of materiality that is dispersed, fluid and interconnected.

In formulating a posthuman disability position, I rely heavily on Dan Goodley and his use of Rosi Braidotti's recent work. Goodley and his colleagues have recognized the problems in early disability studies that emerge from the participation in liberalism (law, rights, human dignity, identity politics, etc.), but have also seriously considered the dangers for disability studies of a complete rejection of these practices (given its current importance in social justice). Their theory, which they call *dis/humanism*, is a response to this difficult situation where:

'People with intellectual disabilities seek to be recognized as human: ontologically, materially and politically' while at the same time seeking to keep the 'radical potential [of disability] to trouble the normative, rational, independent, autonomous subject that is so often imagined when the human is evoked, social policies are made, social and human sciences are developed and forms of activism are enacted'.[23]

This is clear in the *dis/human* manifesto[24] where, in some situations, modernist concepts such as normalcy, autonomy and choice can be desirable, but when they are mobilized it is always accompanied by the fact that we must allow disability to destabilize and shape what is meant by these, and that the focus must always be on affirming the positivity of difference. This is important when discussing normalizing technologies and devices as in many cases recipients and consumers of these devices welcome them into their lives. One can certainly show, philosophically, how the integration of these technologies and the *hopes* for inclusion or normalcy they generate, even if they are grounded in experience, are often constructed through the very discourses we wish to critique – normalizing biopolitical and neoliberal discourses. However, we must not, on the other hand, use the result of critique as a means of imposing and limiting the legitimacy of the choices and hopes of those living with disabilities. Alternatively, we must encourage people to *live critically* – and the experience of disability has something to teach us about how this is to be done.

It is precisely here that I see a great potential for what Goodley et al. call 'becoming dis/human'. To 'dis', they explain, is a slang term that means putting something down, to fail to show respect for something, to show contempt for something – 'to *dis* is to trouble'.[25] Too often critique is black and white (read *polemical*); however, if we take seriously the critique of Truth passed down from post-structuralism to posthumanism, we have to acknowledge that it is the potential for resistance that makes critique useful and not its ability to *fix* something (as in to concretize an alternative 'Truth'). The posthuman condition demands that we take into account the flux and flow of things. Our relationship to ethico-political *truths* cannot be based on something concrete, transhistorical or necessary but on something that is fluid, immanent and contingent. There is, in the dis/human, the possibility of using categories like autonomy, normalcy, or humanness while at the same time actively and perpetually troubling what these things are to us (and in relation to us). The goal of developing a posthuman dis/ability theory, then, is not to discourage all claims to humanist concepts – autonomy, rights, dignity, etc. – but to judiciously and purposefully modify them for our needs with the critical understanding that this 'humanism' will never be what it was historically intended to be, and can never serve the function it once attempted to serve. In other words, in its iteration it is not an elaboration of the concepts but a constant and purposeful alteration.

This confusing affirmation-confrontation paradox is expressed through what Kuppers calls 'the crip dance' between the fixed category of *disabled* and the interconnections of the personal, the social, the cultural, etc.[26] As she puts it, '[w]e (this group so heterogeneous in experience, identity formation, allegiance, or medical labeling) are not malingerers, fakes, of unclear provenance, unspecified or unknown. But the uncertainty inherent in the political use of the word *disabled* easily gives rise to a deterritorialization that needs to be reclaimed, reterritorialized strategically, but not essentially.'[27] There is no universal essential core of disability generally – like we would find in medicine, that is, abnormality/dysfunction, in community, that is, pitiable/ brave, or in political discourse, that is, dependent/accommodated – but a myriad of experiences that need to give rise to strategic de- and reterritorializations. Living differently and affirming one's life in incongruent ways deterritorializes the subject, the space they occupy and the network within which they find themselves. One can ask to be helped with a difficult (for them) task without affirming some ineptitude; one can accept social assistance without affirming some personal failure. These events do not materialize from a singular subject but emerge in an interconnected space. They are seen as moments of interdependence or dis/independence – new configurations and assemblages. These new configurations deterritorialize modernist concepts and reterritorialize them in the idiosyncratic networks formed in immanent experience.

In Goodley and Runswick-Cole's dis/humanism, we find a common example in a person called Matt. Matt is described as a person with significant communication difficulties and so requires social assistance and round-the-clock community supports. With these things in place, Matt becomes *Matt*, a complex assemblage of a person extended outside of himself and connected to others, which is already a challenge to the classical idea of a community member. He is *dis*/independent in his own way. But at the same time, he is also seen to claim his independence: he is a homeowner, holds a job, and has 'his "own life"' so he is 'dis/*independent*'.[28] Notice the conscious choice of italicization by Goodley and Runswick-Cole. There is again, as in the Kupper's example, a friction between affirming and challenging (or *dissing*) given concepts. In one case, Matt is showing a different way to *be* in the community, and in the other, he is strategically claiming something without negating aspects of his difference. He is not *fixed* in the concept itself.

In dis/humanism, when these concepts are evoked, it is done so *equivocally*, where what is claimed in one instance is different than another, and is surely different than its original historical meaning – this is where its potential resides.[29] In our posthuman times, many of the foundational concepts of modern humanism are undermined, and our claims to these concepts for our own purposes represent a discontinuity with the historical progress of these ideas. As Goodley and Runswick-Cole explain, the *fallacy of equivocation* is a good metaphor for this natural ambivalence to humanness, and accounts for those resistances and experiences that challenge the assumed univocal nature of normality in humanism.[30] The *difference* is what destabilizes, troubles, resists and ruptures the traditional ideas of acceptable life; the presence of infinitely different embodiments leading to what can only be described as a becoming-dis/human. In philosophical terms, this becoming is a Deleuzian *becoming-minoritarian*.[31] It is the formation of new paths without affirming or creating a model of what *ought to* or *must be* done (i.e. not becoming-majoritarian). For example, what is right for Matt cannot be imposed onto others and become a new standard or norm aimed at fixing something that is essential in Matt's disability or situation. In the same way, a technology cannot be assessed once and for all and given an essential ethical or utilitarian standing – outside the assemblages where these technologies become integrated.

We then have a very complex job to do in evaluating the role of technology. The goal is not to put forth an idea of our relationship to technology and, on that basis, tell individuals with disabilities what they ought to do or avoid doing. This is akin to a certain fascism that both Deleuze and Foucault were actively trying to avoid. Our goal is more complex, and it is a matter of making visible the possibilities that are opened up by posthumanism and disability in order to avoid some of the dangers of modernity that, for disability studies, could not be overcome by simple *inclusion* or by stopping at the level of discourse analysis. Taking disability seriously, and adopting the critical attitude that enables it, poses a challenge for modernist notions of the human. This is best understood through a posthumanist framework that contests the individualism and limited relationality of the modern subject and substitutes for it a radically relational and interconnected assemblage. A dis/ability experience, whatever it may be in its infinite plurality, is a Deleuzian becoming in the sense that nothing is ever fixed, but new possibilities emerge in the immanent field of experience. This results in new assemblages between people, environment, and technology that challenge the modernist notions we try to resist without substituting them for equally unwavering and fixed ways of being.

In the following sections, I will be looking at some technologies that have, or will soon have, some significant effect on individuals living with disabilities. Foucault had something very useful to say about the task that this troubled relationship asks of us when, in one of his last interviews, he said: 'My point is not that everything is bad, but that everything is dangerous, which is not exactly the same as bad. If everything is dangerous, then we always have something to do. So, my position leads not to apathy but to a hyper- and pessimistic activism.'[32] It is with this ethico-political vision in mind that I will be exploring contemporary biotechnologies. I look at the dangers they may entail and how critical disability studies may help us understand them.

Whose technology?

As discussed above, technomedicine brings with it a real danger in that perceiving ourselves in increasingly biotechnical and neuro-molecular ways does not lead to a critical re-evaluation of our relationship to technology and of its role in our lives. The goal of technomedicine is to normalize and cure, and the technologies developed have this as their primary goal. We should be very sceptical of their emergence and development *within* technomedicine (with the aim of cure) and the technophilic obsession with overcoming challenges solely by means of technology. This technological optimism – curing the blind, the mute, the lame – imbues science with a telos of biblical proportions founded on the idea of disability as *lack* and the desirable body as an independent and productive one. It denies people the ability to identify *what they need* within their very complex internal and external networks, needs which often challenge what technomedicine and society offer the individual living with a disability. The demands that individuals living with disabilities place on these networks trouble the idea that their body is *lacking* and shows that their relations with the external world – with experts, helpers, technologies – are unevenly/unjustly problematized. The contemporary posthuman perspectives mentioned above, especially those that rest in part on Deleuzian assemblage theory, account for interdependence (between the human, the non-human, and the inorganic) as a matter of course, not as something that we *ought to* strive for.

In the neoliberal-able perspective though, certain forms of dependence are invisible ('normal' dependence on social institutions and services, or 'normal' technologies) and others are marked as problematic (such as a dependence on social *assistance* and *assistive* technologies). The disabled subject is a bad neoliberal subject by definition because he/she is dependent on society for its needs, and in many cases, their needs are seen as constraints to their productivity and potential. This, of course, is the result of ableist ways of thinking that fail to account for their own dependence on human and non-human networks and so fail to see the extent of their own interdependence. Goodley cautions us to 'be careful not to be seduced by shiny technology when, on a more mundane level, we are already potentially enhancing our humanity through a myriad of inter-relationships'.[33] One's relationship with assistants, guide dogs, support systems and groups are themselves posthuman assemblages through which one lives out their different bodies. Enhancement is not only a matter of biomechanical/ bionic prosthetics, technologically mediated communications or pharmaceutical technologies.

We can certainly understand the tendency to problematize or exceptionalize the experience of disability for those on the outside. It seems obvious, from the point of view of common experience, where the difference between normality and abnormality, enhancement and therapy, desirable and undesirable forms of life are. It is a problem of perspective and of subjugated experiential knowledge. Thinking from the typical and given position, 'it is easy to miss the point that for the person with a variation/disability [. . .] it is *this* experience and not the "normal" one that is normative'.[34] The dominant discourse confirms the truth of the normal body, and the experience of navigating the world *as it is* confirms – at least in large part – the naturalness of navigating the world in the typical way. Buying into this illusion, it is reasonable to think that people with un-accommodated variations *naturally* suffer, and the reasonable thing is to *fix* them.

Troubling needs

The experience of disability, as described by those who live it, is often diametrically opposed to the descriptions of disabled experience in popular consciousness. All too often disability is equated with suffering in popular, medical and policy discourses. Certainly, disability can lead to pain, suffering, awkwardness, feelings of inadequacy, moments of frustration, but these are most often than not due to ableist ways of thinking and disabling social structures. By and large, people living with disabilities adapt to their impairment (the exact same way an 'able-bodied' individual learns to navigate his/her environment) and live not in spite of them but with them. Eli Clare expresses this very well in his foundational text *Exile and Pride* when he discusses a question he is sometimes asked by non-disabled others. They ask if he could take a magic pill and wake up 'normal' would he do it. He answers that having cerebral palsy is for him the same as having blue eyes or red hair, 'I don't know my body any other way'. His frustration comes from the fact that 'no one gives me grief, denies me employment, treats me as if I were ten years old, because I have blue eyes'.[35] What he is looking for is not a cure – a magic pill – but a certain type of collective relationship. He goes on to say that the technologies that he uses to live the body he has 'can be found in a computer catalog, not a hospital'.[36] This second point is also important for our purposes, as someone who is very critical of most discourses of 'cure', he also makes clear that technologies are an important and integrated part of his embodiment. His frustration towards charities and research groups is that they would rather look for cures 'but won't buy respirators for those who need them; big money on the next genetic breakthrough, but not on lift bars to make bathrooms accessible."[37] This is important when looking at the development of new technologies in the biotech fields because most of the attention and money is being spent on *cure* and not on the actual concerns of people. Money is invested at the cutting edge of advanced technological research, but not in the simple social goal of making the world accessible and liveable for people with different bodies and needs. This situation is supported by the perception of suffering. If disability *is* suffering, then the primary goal is to eliminate the cause; assistive technologies only alleviate the situation (symptom) and so are not a suitable end goal. It is precisely this that Clare criticizes, and any critical evaluation of biotechnology needs to understand this problematic logic.

Casting disability in an affirmative and positive light is an important step in resisting the imposition of passivity and normalization, but it too needs to be qualified by some negativity. As Scully notes, some forms of negativity may be inevitable, and 'no amount of social transformation will take it away' but 'this irreducible negative may be much smaller than generally supposed, or it may be larger, or it may consist in entirely unanticipated aspects of the experience of impairment'.[38] What is left over, what needs to be addressed – for the purpose of this chapter, what needs to be addressed by biotechnology – cannot be deduced or inferred by medical science or ideas of normal/abnormal bodily function/structure. There is no one answer, we must be aware of the real plurality of different lives so as to not problematically promote or discredit certain technologies – it is a matter of being a bit more critical about how these technologies can be integrated in an affirmative way. The discourse of biomedicine sees bodily difference as automatically in need of fixing, which does not reflect the needs of all people and denies the affirmative ways in which they navigate their lives. The lay perspective of *disability as suffering* that technologists and researchers accept is very distorting. Speaking of her own experience, Scully notes that 'although people assume that the worst thing about hearing impairment is not being able to hear, for me by far the most disabling aspect of having a damaged cochleae is the intermittent bouts of tinnitus I get'.[39] Figuratively speaking, if there was some technology (surgery, pill, or implant) that would stop her experience of tinnitus, we would be hard-pressed to interpret her decision to use it as an act of normalization. It is by no means the same thing as a 'magic normal pill'. The difference is a matter of a situated perspective whose complexities go beyond reductive biomedical understandings. There is no other way to know what legitimate uses of technologies are *other than actively seeking and integrating the perspectives of people living with disabilities*. It is not discernible from an understanding of typical bodily functions or rationalizations derived from general diagnostic categories.

These examples show why it is important to have a critical, affirmative, dis/abled perspective on the role of technology as opposed to a bioconservative/technophobic (anti-tech), technophilic or technomedical (cure/correction) perspective. It must be thought *through* the immanent potential that it opens up for the individual. Individuals living with disabilities refuse to submit to a discourse of suffering – this clearly shines through in the history of disability activism and thought – so the challenge, then, is to find ways of integrating technologies in order to expand the possibilities of living an ethics of affirmation[40] instead of submitting one's body to the normalization of cure and the demands of neoliberalism.

Assistive devices and prosthetics

It is understood that individuals today are some of the most technologically integrated of any generation that has ever come before. We use computers and information technologies in every aspect of our daily life and work. Cell phones and portable computers only scratch the surface of the sheer amount of info-tech in the background of a functional Western society. For this reason, individuals with disabilities need, and fight for, assistive devices that help them access these technologies in the same way they do for hearing aids and wheelchairs. We can say that they are dependent on these technologies, but in saying this we cannot mean anything different than the fact that we are all dependent on 'assistive' devices. Who among us did not need to learn to use a computer mouse or keyboard? To use the internet or navigate library databases? Could I have written this chapter *like I have* without them? The issue is that assistive devices, because of disability's status as a medical condition, are tied up in a whole system of medical/educational expertise, engineering and insurance. They are seen as *different* because other means of access are 'normalized' and become invisible. This is why, in claiming that people living with disabilities represent posthuman assemblages and embodiments, we can mean nothing other than the fact that their status as posthuman is simply more obvious because it *does things differently.*[41]

One great example is that of Jason Becker, guitar virtuoso, whose ALS forced him to change the ways in which he could write music. Without getting into the discourses surrounding his condition – a discourse of overcoming and suffering[42] – what is most striking from the perspective of a posthuman disability studies is seeing how he writes. To create his music, he depends on a complex assemblage consisting of his father recording notes on guitar while he gives him instruction using a (physical) eye-controlled communication interface. Once the notes are recorded, Becker makes his composition by communicating how to arrange the song – note for note – through an assistant using a music editing software (LogicPro). Following this he works with other musicians and producers to polish the mix in a complete mastered track. Using this complex array of intermediaries (eye, father, guitar, computer, musicians, producers, etc.), Becker is able to write music in a way that challenges the traditional notion of 'composer' – a posthuman composer, we might say. Perusing any studio and looking at the acknowledgement section of any music album attests to the fact that only a complex network of assemblages between human and technology can lead to a completed musical project. All composers are posthuman; Becker is but one very interesting example.

The same could be said about Oscar Pistorius,[43] whose prosthetic limbs allowed him to compete in both the Paralympics and IAAF (able-bodied) sanctioned competitions in 2005 and 2007. I do not mean to suggest that Paralympians are not athletes, or that they do not show us something about posthuman possibilities. They certainly do this. However, the case of Pistorius is interesting because, in crossing over to able-bodied competitions, the myriad of social and institutional reactions shows us something about how the challenge is received. In 2007, during Pistorius's rise, the IAAF amended a rule concerning athletic advantages regarding prosthetic devices.[44] Pistorius was a very able runner, but his running times and the trajectory of his career were not atypical of any future Olympian; however, his *difference* necessitated the international regulatory body to probe into the mechanics of his *running differently*.

Given Pistorius's wish to compete in the Olympics, an expert report was commissioned. The report found three things, that (1) the energy loss through ankle motion versus prosthetic gave a significant advantage to Pistorius, that (2) the artificial limb does not offer a mechanical disadvantage because of its weight, and that (3) the 'bouncing' motion is 'significantly different to sprinting of able-bodied athletes on hard surfaces' which leads to a lower metabolic cost.[45] On that basis he was deemed ineligible to compete.

Though we may sometimes think of his prosthetics as relatively simple in contrast to highly technological body enhancements, we see in the case of Pistorius how this line of imagination can be quite blurred. Complex as they may be – being heavily dependent on advance material science and biomechanical engineering – Pistorius's limbs are not necessarily what we would consider highly technological (in relation to imaginations of sci-fi bionic super humans), but they do transform his body into a kind of *enhanced* body. He becomes, through the authority of the IAAF, a super-able posthuman. He is 'enhanced' in relation to the able-bodied athlete, but only identified as such through a very detailed scientific analysis. He was not a superhuman prior to this analysis, he was an individual with a disability. What this example shows us is that the line between disabled and able bodied, assistive device and human enhancement, is quite murky. Though he didn't win any medals, Pistorius was finally allowed to compete in the 2012 Olympic games. As Braidotti discusses in the conclusion of her book, his inclusion in the Olympics is equally complex. On what basis are we to judge what counts as human ability? What counts as our 'common reference' point? Did Pistorius cease to be super-abled when he was allowed to compete in the Olympics, or did he only cease to be when he failed to secure a medal? His disability (as Paralympian), enhanced super-ability (as subject of scientific scrutiny), and return to normality (as a rank-and-file Olympian) are all contingent on the fact that he is judged through a still modernist-ableist framework of the human. But his body did not change in the process; he was simply a (posthuman) sprinter the entire time.

As Braidotti tells us, 'we now need to learn to think differently about ourselves and to experiment with new fundamental schemes of thought about what counts as the new basic unit of common reference for the human.'[46] The experiences of Clare, Scully, Becker and Pistorius show us that this frame of reference has not yet been successfully challenged, that we still consider different bodies as somehow *lacking* or *exceeding* an already failing metric of 'humanness'. The idea of humanness that not only singles out their embodiment as problematic but also cast their complex assemblages and relational networks as something additional, as if the typical person did not represent an assemblage or were not dependent on relational networks in order to navigate the world.

Highly technical robotic/cybernetic limbs that connect to the nervous system are currently being developed, some that even go beyond opening the signals from brain to limb, but of limb back to brain. Myoelectric limbs (that function through muscle contraction at the connection of limb and body) are already in use, nerve connected limbs (functioning through surgically inserted pathways between remaining nerve endings), and neurologically controlled limbs/organs/exoskeletons (through electrodes connected directly or indirectly to the brain) are nearing completion. How these technologies will be implemented and interpreted depends on our capacity to think differently, and to consider, as the somewhat rudimentary technologies mentioned above, what ability, disability and enhancement really mean.

Certainly, issues of social justice and capitalism do arise. Because neoliberalism begins from the perspective of equality (equal responsibility and choice), and not that of equity, the responsibility of individuals with disabilities to be good neoliberal subjects happens outside the reality of their disadvantaged position within Western societies. It is well understood that poor health and poverty are linked, as well as increased levels of poverty among individuals living with disabilities. This is important for any discussion of prosthetics since, as we can imagine, advances in robotics and cybernetics make for expensive devices. As Shakespeare reminds us, the solution for most people is not a $25,000 iBot wheelchair – allowing the user to navigate stairs and lift themselves up to eye level when talking to someone – it is a basic $200 wheelchair.[47] The scale of the problem goes beyond what we can attribute to the novelty of highly technological innovations and all its practical and cultural challenges. Currently, only 5–15 per cent of people needing *basic* assistive devices worldwide receive those devices – basic devices meaning wheelchairs, hearing aids, crutches, etc.[48] It is likely that the same disparities will be replicated with successive generations of more technologically complex prosthetics. Neoliberal-able normalization, profit-driven technomedicine and research monetization threaten to replicate in bionic and robotic prosthetics the same – or even greater – divide between rich and poor, Western and non-Western, and increase the accessibility gaps. There are avenues of hope, however, as we have seen a certain kind of collectivity form within our technological worlds. Open source software,[49] open source development and affordable prosthetic initiatives,[50] and new trends such as crowd-sourcing, and 3-D printing do hold some promise of an equitable future. The technologies themselves cannot solve the issues discussed here; we can only do that together. I do share Braidotti's optimism when she states, we 'are perfectly capable of rising to the challenge of our times, provided we make it into a collective endeavor and joint project'.[51] We have to look at alternative routes of development, distribution, and cooperation in biotechnological innovation while continuing to support the resistance of people whose potential embodiments are most problematically tied to these technologies. Without this, we risk (a) continuing the development of technologies based on biomedical concepts as opposed to actual lived experience, (b) falsely marketing novel prosthetics as solutions to the 'problem' of disability while in actuality only resting on the trope of *disability as suffering* to develop luxury products for a privileged few, and (c) ignoring the important insights of people with alternative adaptive embodiments on the potentials and dangers of biotechnological prosthetics.

Self-governance and genetic normalization

One technological sphere that brings together our discussion of technomedicine and neoliberalism is that of genetic technology. Neuro-molecular medicine does not only represent a change in clinical understandings of disease but also represents a change in how subjects are constructed (and construct themselves) as subjects. Novas and Rose would call the subject of medical genomics the neuro-molecular self (which is part of the larger concept of somatic individuality),[52] that is, an individual who is understood and understands themselves (their behaviours, social existence, indentity and body) in genetic or neuro/biochemical terms. We live in a time where any individual can order a genetic test over the internet and send it in through the mail – that is, without the involvement of doctors or medical laboratories. For $249 (CAD), I can get a report on 'over 100 health conditions and traits', find out about my 'inherited risk factors [. . . and how I] might respond to certain medications', and discover 'my lineage' and 'DNA relatives'.[53] Essentially, I can start to make decisions about my health with *more information* than my family doctor. That is something quite unique to our period in time, and something that comes with its own challenges. As a consequence of conceiving of health primarily in genetic terms, the exercise of choice 'has become familial, a matter both of family histories and potential family futures . . . it reshapes prudence and obligation, in relation to marriage, having children, pursuing a career, and organizing one's financial affairs'.[54] Since this type of medicine deals with *information* one does not necessarily need to be sick (or ever become sick) in order to be subjected to it. One only needs to have its *potential* in one's genes.[55] As we discussed in the section above on technomedicine, the choices we make (self-regulation) are a matter of managing *risk* at the level of our own life course, that of our children and, sometimes, the species in general. This is a huge amount of responsibility. So, when looking at the choices we make, we ought not be surprised that they do not necessarily *affirm* the possibilities of posthuman dis/ability. I argue with Rose and Novas that in most cases, though it is never explicit, neoliberal-somatic logic would imply that passing on risky genes is *irresponsible*.

The case of Huntington's disease is an often-referenced case in discussions of bioethics and genetic testing because it is an identifiable condition that can remain asymptomatic for a great deal of a person's life. Since a test can be done at any age, it raises interesting ethical questions related to the predictability of untreatable diseases. Who gets to order the test (parents, child)? At what age? Who gets to see the results? When do you disclose your risk to your partner? etc. Once one gets the results (most cases a clear yes/no confirmation of the disease), questions about life choices inevitably follow. In almost all cases, genetic tests can only operate at the level of risk, not of confirming the expression of a certain gene (a certain level of uncertainty), but the limit case of Huntington's disease shows what kinds of things that somatic individuals need to grapple with. To illustrate this further, let us look at the situation of expectant mothers.

In the clinical situation, the risk of expecting mothers is calculated based on family history of genetic conditions and age. These *risk factors* form the baseline for the potential of having a child with a birth defect. In addition to these, we can count the triplet test (a computational hormone/protein test that factors in age) and, if a high level of risk is found, it can then lead to further (relatively riskier) tests such as umbilical blood sampling or amniocentesis. At every step, genetic councillors do not actively push the option of abortion but speak in statistical terms about possible risk. However, in a society that values able-bodied and productive neoliberal subjects, it is no wonder what choice is expected of the mother.[56] As Goodley puts it, 'our contemporary times are development times. . . . We want our children to mature into rational young people, to exercise choice, to compete educationally and to succeed through labour. We know society shares these values.'[57] Flowing from these values there is a risk of a sort of 'self-imposed eugenics', where disability is seen as something to be avoided. Again, these choices are made based on the current ideas of what lives are worth living, what kind of individuals we need to be in society, and of what makes a successful society – that is, a competitive one. 'It is not the case that disabled people are hated . . ., it's just that *they* don't fit the world's (ableist) demands.'[58] It is no surprise then that in one meta-analysis of data between 1980 and 1998, 92 per cent of prenatal Down's syndrome diagnoses led to termination,[59] and in another study of 833 mothers, 86 per cent of autosomal trisomy led to termination and 60 per cent in cases of sex chromosome aneuploidy.[60] And a recent meta-study found a range between 60 per cent and 93 per cent in different settings.[61] There is a great danger that we may usher in a new form of eugenics, but this time by weaponizing choice, and by creating a society where disabled voices are not silenced but rendered moot by the very fact of their *preventability*.

The above is the result of a technomedicine that can *observe* and *see* issues in the genome, but new technologies are not only rapidly expanding our ability to do that but are nearing the possibility to do 'edits' to the genome. The Human Genome Project was certainly a significant leap in the scientific understanding of human life, and it serves as one of those events that precipitated a great deal of discussion and critical work. As we have seen above, just the act of mapping genetic defects leads to a change in understanding (genetic/somatic individuality), to submit this understanding to the dominant biological understanding of normality (able bodiedness) and the pressures to act in accordance with these norms (the norm of the neoliberal-able subject). As of yet, abortion, embryo selection (in IVF), and risk mitigation (i.e. choosing not to have children, not to have this or that career because we carry a 'faulty' gene, not accepting a partner who has risky genes, etc.) are the only available options. But with the very recent invention of genetic manipulation techniques, there will be, in the very near future, the possibility of actually changing one's genetic make-up *in utero* or *in vivo* after birth.

At the horizon of this was the invention of Zinc Finger Nuclease (ZFN, first used in 2002) and Transcription Activator-Like Effector-Based Nucleases (TALENs, first used in 2010). These technologies work by cleaving DNA at specific sites and either letting them repair themselves through regular cell mechanisms or by inserting exogenous DNA at the site of cleavage. In the case of TALENs, which are still very much part of the research arsenal today, proteins need to be coded and the technical challenge of implementing the technology requires very complex knowledge and brings with it very high costs. Researchers working with bacteria in the food sciences have recognized an ability of certain bacteria to protect themselves from viruses. Part of this mechanism is the bacteria's ability to copy exogenous DNA as part of their defence. From this finding, the CRISPR-Cas9 system for gene editing was invented, which made it easier to code the gene and to deliver it precisely where it was intended (because it has a built-selection mechanism). First used in 2012, by 2015 CRISPR-cas9 was named by the journal *Science* as the scientific 'Breakthrough of the Year'.[62] In 2015 alone, there were well over a thousand CRISPR-related research papers published[63] – about three papers a day – because it is effective, cheap (and relatively easy to use). The main use of this technology at the moment is research on gene mechanisms by way of *reverse genetics* (which means inserting a gene sequence into an organism and studying the result). Actual gene therapy in humans, however, is not far off in the horizon. The first clinical trials for therapeutics are already underway. Though they are typically accompanied by lively debate, these are centred on traditional biomedical and bioethical concerns. What concerns us here is the much broader effect that these new technologies will have *in a neoliberal-able society* with regard to disability.

In the above example of genetic screening, we can see that the neoliberal-able subject is expected to seek normalization. When this is accompanied by greater and greater preventative measures, it brings up the possibility of an even more widespread eugenics practice; an intensification of what Couser calls a 'stealth eugenics – a kinder, gentler eugenics carried out by supposedly free agents, pregnant women and elderly and disabled people'.[64] If disabilities can be prevented *in vitro*, then policies and funds ought not be invested in supportive social structures, but in preventative genetic technologies. This is increasingly becoming the case in bioethical debates about prevention, but even more so in transhumanist discourses that actively defend more 'humane' forms of eugenics.[65] In such a system, where preventability is easier, more acceptable, and more fiscally responsible, one cannot expect anything different than the proliferation of a self-propelled eugenic practice. However, these self-normalization practices on the individual level, and the system level diversion of funds away from the actual social needs of people with disabilities are borne out of fantasy. The development of preventative therapeutics is hampered by the debunked one-gene-one-disease model (the relationship between genes and their manifestation in a disability are more complex than non-experts realize); genetic selection practices only apply to IVF births, otherwise the only option is termination of pregnancy; and the focus on preventing genetic-linked disabilities ignores the reality that most disabilities are acquired after birth (through injury, illness and ageing). We can add to this the fact that significant numbers of individuals born with pathologized variations do not see them as such, for example, the lively 'Deaf culture' or activism by self-labelled 'neuro-atypicals'. These are fundamental practical problems to the ideal of eliminating disability that ought to dampen optimism for genetic solutions and end the almost totalizing focus on this supposed silver bullet. But alas they do not; it remains an important focus of the dominant discourse because it resonates so well with how we see life today (i.e. the lens of molecular technomedicine). For those without disabilities, though, this tendency is not inconsequential.

As Rose would tell us, 'At the genomic level . . . none of us – none of you – are "normal". . . . We are all asymptomatically, presymptomatically ill – and perhaps all suitable cases for treatment.'[66] If we take seriously the precarity of human life itself, the 'normal' of technomedicine is an impossible illusion. All of our bodies are frail, weak, prone to breaking down and in need of support.[67] Rose again: 'we are all at risk . . . all of us harbour, in those three billion base pairs that make up our 23 chromosomes, multiple minor variations that are potentially knowable, and which appear (although I would like to stress that word) to render our future risks of everything, from Alzheimer's disease to obesity, knowable and calculable.'[68] The dangers that Dis/ability thinkers see in these genetic technologies should be of concern for us all. Our heart health, risk of cancers and mental disorders, undesirable behaviours such as addiction, criminality, sexual behaviours are all being linked to genetic factors. As seen above, these can have significant sociopolitical effects even in the absence of definitive causal links or concrete therapies; the suggestion of a link is enough to trigger social effects. Beyond that, and following the same logic, we find the desire to improve ourselves or to select and enhance yet unborn children to better compete in our society. There will always be (and are) individuals wishing to change their future children (which is already possible to a limited extent through embryonic selection) or their own bodies (already shown through 'smart drugs' and steroids, for example) in order to reach this insidious neoliberal-able norm. So from disability to previously 'normal' human differences to human enhancement and engineering, we can imagine that 'physicians, geneticists, and biotechnology companies will not run out of customers'.[69] The example of dis/ability is important in itself, but it also shows something that is relevant for all individuals in modern society.

Genetic technologies may be called for in many cases, but as was the case in biotech/bionic prosthetics, without a re-evaluation of what life is beyond the narrow definition of modernity, we are heading towards a very dangerous period of experimentation and normalization. We can never do away with disability, though the attempts to do so may lead to a disastrous period of time where disability (and in many cases, hitherto 'normal' lives) will be once again pushed to the margins.

Conclusion

The relationship between the able-body versus incapacity/suffering, the social norms of autonomy and productivity, and technomedicine represents the greatest challenge and introduces the gravest dangers with regard to biotechnologies – not the technologies themselves. Goggin and Newell put our troubled relationship with technology quite well when they say:

> The tragic life of an individual or several devalued individuals is portrayed in a way designed to elicit maximum effect; A technology is portrayed as delivering a person from disability, provided society legalizes, funds, or embraces such a solution; securing the technology means that disability has been 'dealt with'; after deploying such rhetoric there is to be no more appeal to emotion and the solution lies in the rational pursuit of the technology identified in step 2; disability as a political issue goes away, until the next time it is needed in the powerful politics of media representation.[70]

And the cycle continues! Such a mechanism does not serve individuals but only supports the normalizing structures of society (to keep others in line) and benefits the profit-making endeavours of the bio-techno/technomedical fields. What I have shown in this chapter is that posthuman disability studies demand that we think differently about both disability and biotechnologies.

Clare shows us that one can find ways to live different bodies that may appear problematic to others, but from the perspective of that individual – within assemblages that include very rudimentary technologies – it is a perfectly fine life. In the case of Scully, we are reminded that though disability does have some negatives that we may wish to mediate through medical or technological means, we do not necessarily need to refer to a logic of *cure*. Like all individuals, we can legitimately seek to incorporate technologies into our lives. These cannot be inferred from the medical logic quoted above[71] but emerge from the navigation of actual bodies in society. The example of Becker shows us that very complex networks of individuals and technology can enable affirmative embodiments that both challenge our received ideas – of what a composer is in this instance – and shows us how these too can be considered posthuman. But the example of Pistorius also problematizes the challenge that is levelled against these received ideas. In mis-fitting the category of an 'athlete', he is considered disabled, able and super-able at different moments and in relation to different aspects of the dominant discourse. It illustrates that the narrow concept of the modernist subject cannot possibly describe the reality of posthuman embodiments.

Finally, because of real and imagined (fiction/sci-fi) fears, in the case of what is often the most vilified technology – genetic manipulation – we are cautioned against considering the lives of individuals with disabilities as pure suffering, as this error leads to a justifiable consideration of termination, prevention or cure. This logic can, and to a certain extent does, lead to a 'soft' eugenic practice. Concurrently, understanding that the majority, if not all, of us have potentially problematic DNA, and that a genetically informed risk adverse society affects us all, it begs us to learn from the limit case of disability in order to better understand the dangers of the technology more generally. On the other hand, it does open up posthuman possibilities that are quite desirable, but these cannot be separated from its negative effects without turning away from technomedical and neoliberal-able frames of reference.

The realization of our interdependence and creative relationality (between people, technologies, and the world) that critical posthumanism posits and that the disability experience exemplifies ought to serve as a roadmap for a posthuman critique of technomedicine. It represents a critical and affirmative voice contra the all-encompassing search for cures or transhumanist utopia of a perfected posthuman race. In many ways, disability activists and people living with disabilities engage in what Braidotti calls an ethics of *affirmation*, because they do not dwell on the very fact of acquiring or having their *different* bodies,[72] but would rather look at their potential (as desiring machines, but also in their ability to be affected and affect others), and the assemblages that would enable these potentials to be actualized. Think here of the Spinozist idea that we do not yet know what the body can do – people living with disabilities explore this in real terms on a daily basis. Building an enabling society, based on affirmative ethics, would mean harnessing the creative possibilities of different bodies and experiences of embodiment by creating networks of interconnected posthuman subjects that encourage or favour possibility and creativity (*potentia*), and where there is collective resistance to those ideologies, institutions, and interconnections that disable the expressions of difference and posthuman becomings (*potestas*). Dis/ability is about exploring possibilities, blazing new paths, living with others, affecting them and being affected by them in new and creative ways. Technomedicine and new technologies can either play an affirmative role in this or lead to a destruction of new possibilities of life. I did not, however, propose a general model through which to judge if a technology is good or bad; if it leads to normalization or opens up new possibilities. This is because such a model cannot exist. We must find our ground in the fluid and immanent – but critical – moments of becoming.

Notes

1. Bradley E. Lewis, 'Prozac and the Post-Human Politics of Cyborgs', 52.
2. Michel Foucault, 'Confessions of the Flesh', 226.
3. Michel Foucault, 'The Birth of Social Medicine', 141.
4. Michel Foucault, 'The Crisis of Medicine', 7.
5. Michel Foucault, *The History of Sexuality. Volume 1*; Michel Foucault, 'Society Must be Defended'.
6. Michel Foucault, *The Birth of Biopolitics*.
7. Bill Hughes, 'What can a Foucauldian Analysis Contribute to Disability Theory?', 80.
8. The term 'molecular medicine' is widely used today. Molar medicine is a term that is used to differentiate the earlier clinical medicine that dealt with 'body parts' and the medicine of microbiology. It is used in this way by Nikolas Rose to illustrate this very point (in *The Politics of Life Itself*).
9. Georges Canguilhem, *Écrits sur la médecine*, 200.
10. Georges Canguilhem, 'Epistemology of Medicine'; Michel Foucault, 'Open up a Few Corpses', and 'The Visible Invisible', in *Birth of the Clinic*.
11. Nikolas Rose, 'Biopolitics in the Twenty-First Century', in *The Politics of Life Itself*.
12. Nikolas Rose, *The Politics of Life Itself*, 107.
13. Nikolas Rose, 'Screen and Intervene'; Nikolas Rose, 'The Human Sciences in a Biological Age'; Nikolas Rose, 'In Search of Certainty: Risk Management in a Biological Age'.
14. Gilles Deleuze, 'Postscript on the Societies of Control', 3–7.
15. Ibid.
16. Robert Castel, 'From Dangerousness to Risk', 281.
17. Bradley E. Lewis, 'Prozac and the Post-Human Politics of Cyborgs', 52.
18. Dan Goodley, 'Dis/ability', 21–35.
19. This idea can be found in the work of the UPIAS (Union of the Physically Impaired Against Segregation), 'Fundamental Principles of Disability', 20, but it is given its theoretical backing in the book that can arguably be said to launch the discipline, Michael Oliver, *The Politics of Disablement*, and discussed in Dan Goodley, *An Interdisciplinary Introduction*, 8.
20. Shelley Tremain, 'On the Government of Disability'; Shelley Tremain, 'The Subject of Impairment', 32–47; Shelley Tremain, 'This Is What a Historicist and Relativist Feminist Philosophy of Disability Looks Like'.

21 For an interesting exchange on the topic see Carol Thomas and Mirian Corker 'A Journey Around the Social Model', 18–31.
22 Shelley Tremain, 'This Is What a Historicist and Relativist Feminist Philosophy of Disability Looks Like'.
23 Dan Goodley and Katherine Runswick-Cole, 'Becoming Dishuman', 2; Dan Goodley, *Dis/ability*; Katherine Runswick-Cole, Dan Goodley, Rebecca Lawthom and Kirsty Liddiard, 'Dis/human Manifesto'.
24 Katherine Runswick-Cole, Dan Goodley, Rebecca Lawthom and Kirsty Liddiard, 'Dis/human Manifesto'.
25 Dan Goodley and Katherine Runswick-Cole, 'Becoming Dishuman', 5.
26 Petra Kuppers, 'Toward a Rhizomatic Model of Disability: Poetry, Performance, and Touch', 231.
27 Ibid, 231.
28 Dan Goodley and Runswick-Cole, 'Becoming Dishuman', 11.
29 Dan Goodley and Katherine Runswick-Cole, 'Becoming Dishuman', 7ff, 13.
30 Ibid., 13.
31 Gilles Deleuze, *Negotiations*, 173.
32 Michel Foucault, 'On the Genealogy of Ethics', 231–2.
33 Dan Goodley, Rebecca Lawthom and Katherine Runswick-Cole, 'Posthuman Disability Studies'.
34 Jackie Leach Scully, 'When Norms Normalize', 93.
35 Eli Clare, *Exile and Pride*.
36 Ibid.
37 Ibid.
38 Jackie Leach Scully, 'Drawing Lines, Crossing Lines', 270.
39 Ibid.
40 Rosi Braidotti, 'Affirmation versus Vulnerability', 12.
41 And, of course, that also means that the victories and challenges in *their* resistance to neoliberalism and humanism are also useful in developing resistance strategies to these things *in general and for everyone*.
42 I don't mean to minimize his experience, but I mean to focus on the affirmative. He didn't choose to have ALS, but he chose to remain a composer. There is no reason to dwell on the negativity – which is not to deny its existence – but to learn from the affirmative possibilities of his deciding to compose and the ways in which he does. I find Braidotti very informative here: 'In a nomadic, Deleuzian-Nietzschean perspective, ethics is essentially about transformation of negative into positive passions, that is, about moving beyond the pain. This does not mean denying the pain but rather activating it, working it through' (Braidotti, 'Affirmation versus Vulnerability', 12). See also, Not Dead Yet; The Jason Becker Movie (2012), http://www.jasonbeckermovie.com/.
43 Volumes have been written on Pistorius, but I focus here on one specific aspect. I intentionally steer away from the controversy surrounding his murder trial, and the discovery of steroids in his home. I make the narrow argument that in scrutinizing his ability within the sport at that period in his career his classification moved from 'disabled' to 'super-abled' to 'normal'. This shift is very important as it centres on his body and performance as something that is objectifiable based on some standard of normality, and more specifically, on the classification of his device as enhancing or assistive.
44 IAAF rule 144.2 'use of any technical device that incorporates springs, wheels or any other element that provides the user with an advantage over another athlete not using such a device'.

45 Gert-Peter Brüggemann, Adamantios Arampatzis and Frank Emrich, 'Biomechanical and Metabolic Analysis'.
46 Rosi Braidotti, *The Posthuman*, 196.
47 Tom Shakespeare, 'Five Thoughts About Enhancement', Location 134.
48 World Health Organization, 'Unmet Global Need for Assistive Technologies'.
49 For example, Fullmeasure website: http://fullmeasure.co.uk/.
50 For example, Open Bionics website: http://www.openbionics.org; Low Cost Prosthesis website: http://www.lowcostprosthesis.org.
51 Rosi Braidotti, *The Posthuman*, 196.
52 Carlos Novas and Nikolas Rose, 'Genetic Risk and the Birth of the Somatic Individual'.
53 23 and Me Website: www.23andme.com/en-ca/.
54 Nikolas Rose, *The Politics of Life Itself*, 108.
55 Ibid.
56 One must clarify here that this is not an anti-abortion argument. A woman's right to choose what happens to her body was a long fought (and still unfinished) project that itself is an important political move for one of modernity's largest marginalized populations. My discussion here focuses solely on abortion as a medical technique and the effects of discourse on what choices are being made and what that shows us about how we think of and treat disability as a society. It is not a condemnation of women who have had abortions (even in cases where the reason was a possible genetic anomaly). I want to make it clear that given how society deals with disability, one can certainly understand the choice to abort. See Anne Waldschmidt, 'Who Is Normal? Who Is Deviant?' Anne Waldschmidt, 'Normalcy, Bio-Politics and Disability'; and my discussion of these texts in Martin Boucher, 'The Normalizing Society and Disabilities'. See also Shelley Tremain, 'Reproductive Freedom, Self-Regulation, and the Government of Im-pairment In Utero'.
57 Dan Goodley, *Dis/ability*, 28.
58 Ibid.
59 Caroline Mansfield, Suellen Hopfer and Theresa M. Marteau, 'Termination Rates'.
60 Brian L. Shaffer, Aaron B. Caughey and Mary E. Norton, 'Variation in the Decision to Terminate Pregnancy', 667–71.
61 Jaime L. Natoli, Deborah L. Ackerman, Suzanne McDermott and Janice G. Edwards, 'Prenatal Diagnosis of Down Syndrome'.
62 John Davis, 'Making the Cut', 1456–7.
63 Anna Quinlan, 'CRISPR'.
64 G. Thomas Couser, 'What Disability Studies has to Offer Medical Education', 26, quoted in Dan Goodley, *Dis/ability*, 28.
65 E.g. Julian Savulescu, 'Procreative Beneficience'; Julian Savulescu, *New Breeds of Humans*; John Harris, *Enhancing Evolution*; Daniel Wikler, 'Can We Learn from Eugenics'.
66 Nikolas Rose, 'Normality and Pathology in a Biomedical Age', 73.
67 Judith Butler, 'For and Against Precarity'.
68 Nikolas Rose, 'Normality and Pathology in a Biomedical Age'.
69 Ruth Hubbard and Elijah Wald, *Exploring the Gene Myth*, 70–1. This specific book is part of the reaction to the beginning of the real explosion of genomic medicine and so certainly has different concerns than our current situation. What remains true, though, is that the existence of genetic technologies is, even today, accompanied by a whole system of monetization.

70 Gerard Goggin and Christopher Newell, *Disability in Australia*, 108, quoted in Dan Goodley, *Dis/ability*, 5.
71 Ibid.
72 Certainly, some do, and I do not mean to say that those people ought not feel or react in whatever way they happen to feel or react to their situation. I am not making a moral statement about what individuals ought to do but am acknowledging the fact that individuals living with disabilities do adapt to their situation and do find ways of becoming that challenge the received view that they are passive dependents locked in perpetual suffering.

Bibliography

Boucher, Martin. 'The Normalizing Society and Disabilities'. In *Studies in Disability; Human Monograph Series No. 12*, edited by Moira Ferguson and Alain Beaulieu, 21–38. Sudbury: HSMS, 2013.
Braidotti, Rosi. 'Affirmation Versus Vulnerability: On Contemporary Ethical Debates'. *Symposium: Canadian Journal of Continental Philosophy* 10, no. 1 (2006): 235–54.
Brüggemann, Gert-Peter, Adamantios Arampatzis and Frank Emrich. 'Biomechanical and Metabolic Analysis of Long Sprint Running of the Double Transtibial Amputee Athlete O. Pistorius Using Cheetah Sprint Prostheses'. *Institute of Biomechanics and Orthopaedics German Sport University Cologne* (2007). http://www.aipsmedia.com/allegati/Pistorius_Final_Report.pdf.
Butler, Judith. 'For and Against Precarity'. *e-Flux*, 2013. http://www.e-flux.com/wp-content/uploads/2013/05/7.-Butler_Precarity.pdf.
Canguilhem, Georges. *Écrits sur la Médecine*. Paris: Éditions du Seuil, 2002.
Canguilhem, Georges. 'Epistemology of Medicine'. In *A Vital Rationalist; Selected Writings*, edited by François Delaporte, translated by Arthur Goldhammer. 129—57. New York: Zone Books, 2000.
Castel, Robert. *The Foucault Effect*. Chicago, IL: Chicago University Press, 1991.
Clare, Eli. *Exile and Pride*. Durham, NC: Duke University Press, 2009.
Couser, G. Thomas. 'What Disability Studies has to Offer Medical Education'. *Journal of Medical Humanities* 32 (2011): 21–30.
Davis, John. 'Making the Cut; CRISPR Genome Editing Technology Shows its Power'. *Science* 350 (2015): 1456–7.
Deleuze, Gilles. *Negotiations*. Translated by Martin Joughin. New York: Columbia University Press, 1995.
Deleuze, Gilles. 'Postscript on the Societies of Control'. *October* 59 (Winter 1992): 3–7.
Foucault, Michel. *The Birth of Biopolitics. Lectures at the Collège de France, 1978-1979*. Translated by Graham Burchell. New York: Palgrave, 2008.
Foucault, Michel. *Birth of the Clinic*. Translated by Alain Sheridan. New York: Taylor & Francis, 2003.
Foucault, Michel. 'The Birth of Social Medicine'. In *Power; the Essential Works of Foucault (1954-1984). Volume 3*, edited by James D. Faubion, 134–56. New York: New Press, 2000.
Foucault, Michel. 'Confessions of the Flesh'. In *Power/Knowledge; Selected Interviews and Other Writings*, edited by Colin Gordon, Leo Marshall, John Mepham and Kate Soper, 194–228. New York: Pantheon Books, 1977.

Foucault, Michel. 'The Crisis of Medicine or the Crisis of Antimedicine'. *Foucault Studies* 1 (2004): 5–19.
Foucault, Michel. *The History of Sexuality*, Vol. 1. Translated by Robert Hurley. New York: Vintage, 1990.
Foucault, Michel. 'On the Genealogy of Ethics: An Overview of Work in Progress'. In *Michel Foucault: Beyond Structuralism and Hermeneutics*, edited by Hubert L. Dreyfus, 227–52. Chicago, IL: Chicago University Press, 1983.
Foucault, Michel. *'Society Must be Defended'. Lectures at the Collège de France 1975–1976*. Translated by David Macey. New York: Picador, 2003.
Hughes, Bill. 'What can a Foucauldian Analysis Contribute to Disability Theory?'. In *Foucault and the Government of Disability*, edited by Shelley Tremain, 78–92. Ann Arbor: Michigan University Press, 2008.
Goggin, Gerard and Christopher Newell. *Disability in Australia – Exposing a Social Apartheid*. Sydney: UNSW Press, 2005.
Goodley, Dan. *An Interdisciplinary Introduction*. London: Sage, 2011.
Goodley, Dan. *Dis/ability; Theorizing Disableism and Ableism*. New York: Routledge, 2014.
Goodley, Dan and Katherine Runswick-Cole. 'Becoming Dishuman: Thinking about the Human Thought Dis/ability'. *Discourse: Studies in the Cultural Politics of Education* 37, no. 1 (2014): 1–15.
Goodley, Dan, Rebecca Lawthom and Katherine Runswick-Cole, 'Posthuman Disability Studies'. *Subjectivity* 7, no. 4 (Dec 2014): 342–61.
Harris, John. *Enhancing Evolution; The Ethical Case for Making Better People*. Princeton, NJ: Princeton University Press, 2007.
Hubbard, Ruth and Elijah Wald. *Exploring the Gene Myth; How Genetic Information is Produced and Manipulated by Scientists, Physicians, Employers, Insurance Companies, Educators, and Law Enforcers*. Boston: Beacon Press, 1999.
Kuppers, Petra. 'Toward a Rhizomatic Model of Disability: Poetry, Performance, and Touch'. *Journal of Literary & Cultural Disability Studies* 3, no. 3 (2009): 221–40.
Lewis, Bradley E. 'Prozac and the Post-Human Politics of Cyborgs'. *Journal of Medical Humanities* 24, no. 1/2 (2003): 49–63.
Mansfield, Caroline, Suellen Hopfer and Theresa M. Marteau. 'Termination Rates after Prenatal Diagnosis of Down Syndrome, Spina Bifida, Anencephaly, and Turner and Klinefelter Syndromes: A Systematic Literature Review'. *Prenatal Diagnostics* 19, no. 9 (1999): 808–12.
Natoli, Jaime L., Deborah L. Ackerman, Suzanne McDermott and Janice G. Edwards. 'Prenatal Diagnosis of Down Syndrome: A Systematic Review of Termination Rates (1995–2011)'. *American Journal of Medical Genetics* 167, no. 4 (April 2015): 756–67.
Novas, Carlos and Nikolas Rose. 'Genetic Risk And The Birth Of The Somatic Individual'. *Economy and Society* 29, no 4 (2000): 485–513.
Oliver, Michael. *The Politics of Disablement*. New York: St. Martin's Press, 1992.
Quinlan, Anna. 'CRISPR: The Hopes, The Fears, and the Biology'. *Bioradiations Database* (August 2015). http://www.bioradiations.com/crispr-the-hopes-the-fears-and-the-b iology/.
Reardon, Sara. 'First CRISPR Clinical Trial Gets Green Light From US Panel'. *Nature* (June 2016). http://www.nature.com/news/first-crispr-clinical-trial-gets-green-light-from -us-panel-1.20137
Rose, Nikolas. 'The Human Sciences in a Biological Age'. *Theory, Culture and Society* 30, no. 1 (2013): 3–34.

Rose, Nikolas. 'Normality And Pathology In A Biomedical Age'. *Sociological Review* 57 (2009): 66–83.
Rose, Nikolas. *The Politics of Life Itself; Biomedicine, Power and Subjectivity in the Twenty First Century*. Princeton, NJ: Princeton University Press, 2007.
Rose, Nikolas. 'Screen and Intervene; Governing Risky Brains'. *History Of The Human Sciences* 23, no. 1 (2010): 79–105.
Rose, Nikolas. 'In Search of Certainty: Risk Management in a Biological Age'. *Journal of Public Mental Health* 4, no. 3 (2005): 14–22.
Runswick-Cole, Katherine, Dan Goodley, Rebecca Lawthom and Kirsty Liddiard. 'Dis/human Manifesto'. www.dishuman.com/dishuman-manifesto/.
Savulescu, Julian. 'New Breeds of Humans: The Moral Obligation to Enhance'. *Ethics Law and Moral Philosophy of Reproductive Biomedicine* 1, no. 1 Supplement 1 (2005): 36–9.
Savulescu, Julian. 'Procreative Beneficience: Why we Should Select the Best Children'. *Bioethics* 15, no. 5 (2001): 413–26.
Scully, Jackie Leach. 'Drawing Lines, Crossing Lines: Ethics and the Challenge of Disabled Embodiment'. *Feminist Theology* 11, no. 3 (2003): 265–80.
Scully, Jackie Leach. 'When Norms Normalize: The Case of Genetic Enhancement'. *Human Gene Therapy* 12 (2001): 87–95.
Shaffer, Brian L., Aaron B. Caughey and Mary E. Norton. 'Variation in the Decision to Terminate Pregnancy in the Setting of Fetal Aneuploidy'. *Prenatal Diagnostics* 26, no. 8 (2006): 667–71.
Shakespeare, Tom. 'Foreword: Five Thoughts About Enhancement'. In *The Human Enhancement Debate and Disability*, edited by Miriam Eilers, Katrin Grüber and Christoph Rehmann-Sutter, Location 86–146. New York: Palgrave, 2014.
Thomas, Carol and Mirian Corker. 'A Journey Around the Social Model'. In *Disability/Postmodernity*, edited by Mairian Corker and Tom Shakespeare, 18–31. New York: Continuum, 2006.
Tremain, Shelley. 'On the Government of Disability'. *Social Theory and Practice* 27, no. 4 (2001): 617–36.
Tremain, Shelley. 'Reproductive Freedom, Self-Regulation, and the Government of Im-pairment In Utero'. *Hypatia: A Journal of Feminist Philosophy* 21, no. 1 (2006): 35–53.
Tremain, Shelley. 'The Subject of Impairment'. In *Disability/Postmodernity*, edited by Mairian Corker and Tom Shakespeare, 32–47. New York: Continuum, 2006.
Tremain, Shelley. 'This Is What a Historicist and Relativist Feminist Philosophy of Disability Looks Like'. *Foucault Studies* 19 (2015): 7–42.
UPIAS (Union of the Physically Impaired Against Segregation). *Fundamental Principles of Disability*. London: Leeds, 1994 [1976], 20. http://disability-studies.leeds.ac.uk/files/library/UPIAS-fundamental-principles.pdf.
Waldschmidt, Anne. 'Normalcy, Bio-Politics and Disability: Some Remarks on the German Disability Discourse'. *Disability Studies Quarterly* 26, no. 2 (2006). http://dsq-sds.org/article/view/694/871.
Waldschmidt, Anne. 'Who is Normal? Who is Deviant? 'Normality' and 'Risk' in Genetic Diagnostics and Counseling'. In *Foucault and the Government of Disability*, edited by Shelley Tremain, 191–207. Ann Arbor: Michigan UP, 2008.
Wikler, Daniel. 'Can We Learn from Eugenics'. *Journal of Medical Ethics* 25 (1999): 183–94.
World Health Organization. 'Unmet Global Need for Assistive Technologies'. *Fact Sheet* (2018). https://www.who.int/news-room/fact-sheets/detail/assistive-technology.

12

Deleuze after Afro-pessimism

Claire Colebrook

At first glance, there would seem to be nothing at all worthy in reading Deleuze and Guattari in the aftermath or wake of Afro-pessimism. There are a few scholarly connections where writers like Jared Sexton and C. Riley Snorton have briefly drawn on the work of Deleuze and Guattari,[1] and there is also the common debt to Franz Fanon.[2] This seeming convergence is eclipsed when one looks at the details. At the simplest level, Deleuze and Guatarri are often hailed[3] (and derided[4]) as writers of joy and affect, while Afro-*pessimism* goes well beyond critique and suspicion to an insistent refusal of 'the human'. For Calvin Warren, Black being, anti-Blackness and 'the human', are equiprimordial, with the humanity of free and world-forming affectivity being grounded on the non-being of Black existence:

> This is to say that the problem of black being, as both a form of ontological terror for the human and a site of vicious strategies of obliteration, remains. To ask the (un)asked question 'How is it going with black being?' is to inquire about the resolution of the problem of black and nothing, ontometaphysically, as it imposes itself onto the Negro. The answer to the Negro Question, then, is that the ritualistic and repetitive murder of the flesh, the primordial relation, is absolutely necessary and indispensable in an antiblack world. And as long as the world exists, this murder must continue.[5]

This is one of the key, complex, and subtly varying claims of Afro-pessimism: humanism and its world cannot be adjusted to include Black existence, because Black existence comes into being with the slavery that makes 'the human' possible. One might see this constitutive anti-Blackness as bound to the free modernity of the metaphysical subject, as Warren suggests, or as grounded more in the geopolitics of slavery. For Frank B. Wilderson, this is why Blackness is not, and cannot be, one identity among others, nor understood by way of analogy with other forms of dehumanization:

> Blackness cannot be separated from slavery. Blackness is often misconstrued as an identity (cultural, economic, gendered) of the Human community; however, there is no Black time that precedes the time of the Slave. Africa's spatial coherence is temporally coterminous with the Arab, and then European, slave trade. The time

of Blackness is the time of the paradigm; it is not a temporality that can be grasped with the epistemological tools at our disposal. The time of Blackness is no time at all, because one cannot know a plenitude of Blackness distinct from Slaveness. The prior references of the worker, a time before the Enclosures, for example, or of the postcolonial subject, a time before the settler, are simply not available to Black people.[6]

Even if one were to narrow constitutive anti-Blackness to the United States and not more broadly to the slavery and metaphysics of modernity, the Afro-pessimist project cannot be aligned easily with posthumanism. Indeed, without confronting the force and inescapability of the human there cannot be a reckoning with the composition of the world. This much was already accepted in the crucial critical work of writers like James Baldwin, who at once recognized whiteness as an occluding force that could never confront the history of slavery, and who insisted that the denial and negation constitutive of the human could not be overcome with gestures of feeling and sentiment. If posthumanism wills away human exceptionalism in a gesture of joyous affirmation, Afro-pessimism insists on 'the human' as constitutive of the anti-Blackness that composes the world. To confront 'the human' as real, forceful, not at all bound to any natural essence, and the effect of the geopolitics of modernity—this is where Afro-pessimism connects with Deleuze and Guattari's work.

Deleuze and Guattari may well refuse a simple humanism, but their ultimate project – especially as articulated in *What Is Philosophy?* – amounts to an affirmation of the high modernist tradition of Western Art as an intuition of the cosmos, thereby intensifying the counter-humanism that has always accompanied humanism. Even *Anti-Oedipus* and *A Thousand Plateaus*, in different ways, explore the distinction of the human – not as the simple unfolding of a natural kind, but as a shift in register, or a different way in which nature deterritorializes. To say that the hand is the deterritorialized paw[7] is to recognize that bodies have the capacity to create new strata, new modes of relation that break with prior relations. Without confronting the distinction and geopolitical formation of the human and (ultimately) 'the subject', it is possible to miss one of the most fruitful consequences of Deleuze and Guattari's thought. As Ian Buchanan has recently argued:

> The most important function of the strata I would argue is that they problematize and map the terrain of human existence in a very particular way that can perhaps be visualized along the lines of three dimensional chess, providing we modify the rules so that only the pieces on the top level are capable of moving across all the planes. It amounts to saying, 'we' humans depend on the properties of the earth for our existence (geology) and 'we' depend on the properties of our bodies for what 'we' can do on the earth (biology), but 'we' constantly exceed those limits in the outpourings of our minds. This is the essential difference between geological and biological strata and the techno-semiological stratum – the production of signs (both symbols and language) enables the third stratum to translate the other two and in a sense range beyond them.[8]

In a different manner, and with a focus on Deleuze, Keith Ansell-Pearson has also provided a counter-posthumanist reading of Deleuze: 'What cannot be upheld, though, is the idea that Deleuze flattens ontology in such a way that he is seen to have little concern, if any, with issues of normativity and as they pertain to what is distinctive about the existence of the human animal.'[9]

Afro-pessimism, in its many forms, knows all too well that posthumanism's affirmations of life and vitality provide yet one more occlusion of the anti-Blackness that has founded both rational humanism and its aftermath. For Afro-pessimism, the primordial anti-Blackness that is constitutive of the world generates an imperative to end the world, beginning with Aimé Césaire and Franz Fanon, and continuing into twenty-first-century demands for the destruction of the humanism and posthumanism of the present. For Calvin Warren:

> Black freedom, then, would constitute a form of world destruction, and this is precisely why humanism has failed to accomplish its romantic goals of equality, justice, and recognition. In short, black humanism has neglected the relationship between black(ness) and nothing in its yearning for belonging, acceptance, and freedom. The Negro was invented to fulfill this function for metaphysics, and the humanist dream of transforming invention into human being is continually deferred (because it is impossible).[10]

By contrast, within *A Thousand Plateaus* the world already harbours the potentiality for intuiting the cosmos. Even if Deleuze and Guattari are as critical as the Afro-pessimists of the average white man who constitutes humanity, it is possible to see the history of humanism in *A Thousand Plateaus* as a *felix culpa*. They trace a history of the miserable contraction of life into the bourgeois man of opinion, and yet they also see the affirmative exit and higher deterritorialization of this same tradition in its own artworks – Virginia Woolf, Paul Klee or D. H. Lawrence. In this chapter, I will explore what *A Thousand Plateaus* looks like after the end of the world or after the end of a specific mode of posthumanism. That is to say, if there is no world in the phenomenological sense – no shared horizon of meaning and coherence – then we can read both Afro-pessimism and Deleuze and Guattari's philosophy as exploring a deep fracture that undercuts any sense of 'the human' as a ground or ideal.

Although Deleuze and Guattari are more often than not associated with the claims of posthumanism and affirmation, it is quite possible to read the trajectory of their corpus as a pessimism with regard to a restricted humanism, and affirmative *only* as a hyper-humanism. The problem is not that humans have taken themselves to be exceptional, but rather that they mistake the mode of their difference as being grounded on nature rather than through an event of deterritorialzation. Humanity is an event of inscription and stratification and needs to be understood geologically. This would include understanding the lure of the natural moral subject, its intimate relation to colonization, and its structural whiteness. As long as 'the human' forms a moral foundation for thought and action – or worse, action grounded on an impoverished image of thought – then the very forces that make the human possible are curbed or turned back upon their own potentiality. There would be an essential misery or neuroticism attached to 'the human', a certain joylessness that follows from being attached to *who we are*. There would also be a joy made possible by intensification, taking the potentiality that makes the human possible and allowing it to take flight. One way to think about this relation between joy and misery of 'the human' would be through the history of whiteness, a history that is hinted at but not fully explored in *A Thousand Plateaus*. Deleuze and Guattari theorize the whiteness of face as crucial to the formation of interiority – the white face as a screen that is capable of being read, with the black holes of the eyes that look out upon the world.

> Significance is never without a white wall upon which it inscribes its signs and redundancies. Subjectification is never without a black hole in which it lodges its consciousness, passion, and redundancies. Since all semiotics are mixed and strata come at least in twos, it should come as no surprise that a very special mechanism is situated at their intersection. Oddly enough, it is a face: the white wall/black hole system. A broad face with white cheeks, a chalk face with eyes cut in for a black hole. Clown head, white clown, moon-white mime, angel of death, Holy Shroud.[11]

Whereas Emmanuel Levinas regards the face as a transcendental – the very condition for personhood that inaugurates my ethical being as a relation to otherness – Deleuze and Guattari situate the face within a history of colonization and whiteness. The average white man of private property is formed by way of a contraction: from relations among bodies in tribal societies that forge identities by selecting qualities from non-human forces, the 'man' of reason increasingly attaches himself to interiority.[12] One could make a broad contrast between indigenous cultures that negotiate relations according to different modalities of personhood, and the oddly parochial Western sense of 'the human' that is produced through a relation to the interior. Eduardo Viveiros de Castro, picking up a mode of perspectivism that he finds in Deleuze and Guattari's work, contrasts a Western reduction of all relations to variations of the human, with indigenous worlds that are able to imagine the perspectives and relations that unfold from non-human persons.[13] This radical perspectivism would be quite different from anthropological perspectivism, where the master anthropologist translates all observed relations back to variations of 'the human', and where the human is bound up with a certain image of thought – the good and common sense that subtends all relations and enables recognition of the same across various cultures.

In both *Anti-Oedipus* and *A Thousand Plateaus*, Deleuze and Guattari describe the formation of the human as the effect of a particular mode of relations, and in this respect, they need to be contrasted with certain forms of posthumanism that relinquish the singularity of the human. On the one hand, and this is the strand of Deleuze and Guattari's thought that is taken up by Viveiros de Castro, 'man' is a specific modality of a broader potentiality of the human, and what is required – in order to understand man and his others – is a political, racial and sexual history of the 'humanity' that has become the transcendent figure for human life in general. 'Man' would be bound up with capitalist social formations, where there is no transcendent authority – no despot or law – and only the axiom of maximizing the flows of labour and property. In *Anti-Oedipus* they mark out the three formations of primitivism, despotism and capitalism, where relations among bodies that are formed by the selection of qualities, become subjected to a single body as the origin of the law (despotism) and then becomes further deterritorialized with the single capitalist axiom of maximizing flows: there is no overarching body of law other than the capacity to exchange. However, when one thinks about neoliberalism one can at least acknowledge, by its own admission, that it is the 'end of man':[14] no norm or ideology rules the whole, in a world that is nothing more than the free flow of capital – where capital includes affects, data and apparent resistance. Being a good subject does not amount to adopting the norms of the man of reason, nor does it entail obeying the morals of the upright soul. Foucault argues in *Discipline and Punish* that the soul is the prison of the body; discipline is achieved by way of techniques that turn attention and care inwards.[15] In neoliberalism, the discipline enabled by technologies of the self shifts towards the control mechanisms that quantify and maximize life. The subject becomes nothing more than a point of flow; the corporations that manage big data know all too well the value of a certain flat and affect-laden posthumanism. Be nothing more than the feels and resistances of one's screen time: one can purchase pussy hats, 'Black Lives Matter' merchandise and copies of Franz Fanon on Amazon. The neoliberal university wants nothing more than public impact of research, which amounts to quantifying citations and more inventive outputs. It does not matter what is said, so much that one's output is circulated – where impact is measured in keeping the flows going; grants beget grants, projects beget projects and impact delivers the further funding that will then be measured in terms of impact. One might think of this type of posthumanism as seemingly ontologically flat but ultimately equivocal: everything flows in the same mesh or web of relations, and yet everything is thought of according to an overarching conception of life (or affect or relationality). What *cannot* be thought of is either differences of register *or* a radical perspectivism. What if one were to admit that there are different – radically different – ways of thinking about perspective? What if each aspect of the word unfolded with its own sense of the infinite? Rather than the lofty gaze of the anthropologist who understands all others as human 'just like me' one might consider that there are other-than-human conceptions of the whole, points of view for whom the grand inclusiveness of 'humanity' might appear oddly parochial. Univocity would demand that relations be liberated from 'the human', and this would include liberating relations from posthumanism's faux humanisms – where everything is part of one vital domain of life or affect.[16] Deleuze's *Difference and Repetition* concludes with the radical affirmation of univocity; such a thought would require that *no* term or set of relations provides a privileged way to think the whole; each aspect of the whole opens to its own infinite:

> Opening is an essential feature of univocity. The nomadic distributions or crowned anarchies in the univocal stand opposed to the sedentary distributions of analogy. Only there does the cry resound: 'Everything is equal!' and 'Everything returns!'. However, this 'Everything is equal' and this 'Everything returns' can be said only at the point at which the extremity of difference is reached. A single and same voice for the whole thousand-voiced multiple, a single and same Ocean for all the drops, a single clamour of Being for all beings: on condition that each being, each drop and each voice has reached the state of excess – in other words, the difference

which displaces and disguises them and, in turning upon its mobile cusp, causes them to return.[17]

It is important to think of the difference between neoliberal posthuman vitalisms and affects, and the more radical and singularly hyper-human Deleuze and Guattarian modes. Foucault's claim, in *The Order of Things*, that 'life itself did not exist'[18] prior to the eighteenth century is not at all in conflict with Deleuze and Guattari's apparent vitalism in *A Thousand Plateaus*. What Foucault would be critical of is life as an explanatory ground, a way of reducing all relations to a single register. In *The Order of Things*, he would also be critical of anthropology and ethnography, along with the general modality of the human sciences – where 'the human' would become a being to be explained within a general paradigm that would increasingly allow for the expertise of biopolitics. Foucault's resistance to an explanatory and managerial conception of life met its limit with his own relation to neoliberalism,[19] but one thing was clear: life enables a shift from normativity to normalization. As long as life is maximized (and increasingly managed and quantified), there is no external limit or subjection, only the imperative to be fruitful and multiply. What cannot be tolerated is saying 'no' to a life that should be forever in a condition of difference and becoming. The media's embrace of highly normalized queer, trans and Black lives makes this apparent. *Queer Eye for a Straight Guy* markets queer as a form of super-stylized consumption. *I Am Cait* allows trans life to be a personal journey of finding one's self, valorizing the trajectory of self-acceptance while leaving the terrain of monetarized, pathologized and intensely normalized procedures out of the frame. Race, perhaps more than any other political force, demonstrates the shift from the morality of man to the normalization of life. There is a plethora of feel-good morality tales about race, where the production of sympathy and affect overcomes the rigidity of prejudice. These contemporary conceptions of a post-racial world of potential harmony, in which race is but one predicate among others, are haunted by archaisms – especially in philosophy. One might nevertheless mark a transition between the faux-post-racial present in which one can claim not to see colour, and a more explicit past of denying humanity to Blackness. Hegel could claim that Africans are a 'race of children that remain immersed in a state of naiveté'[20] and in so doing continued a long philosophical history of placing racial differences within the history of man as a rational animal. Even Heidegger, despite his resistance to the metaphysics of life and *bios*, saw *thinking* as a potentiality that would fulfil its journey of revelation in Europe.[21] Where Foucault locates the shift to biopolitics in the eighteenth century, race remains as one of the archaisms that haunts philosophy. Kant may well have argued that subjectivity was transcendenta – not a thing within the world, but the condition for the possibility of the world – and yet he could also argue that 'The Negroes of Africa have by nature no feeling that rises above the ridiculous.'[22] Theories of reason in general held on to racist archaisms, subtended by what Deleuze and Guattari refer to as racial delirium:

> The first things to be distributed on the body without organs are races, cultures, and their gods. The fact has often been overlooked that the schizo indeed participates in history; he hallucinates and raves universal history, and proliferates the races.

> All delirium is racial, which does not necessarily mean racist. It is not a matter of the regions of the body without organs 'representing' races and cultures. The full body does not represent anything at all. On the contrary, the races and cultures designate regions on this body – that is, zones of intensities, fields of potentials. Phenomena of individualization and sexualization are produced within these fields.[23]

The generic race-free subject emerges from a history of colonization in which 'man' is produced from desiring attachments to the figure of the colonizer. The unconscious is not, for Deleuze and Guattari, a merely private history – the dream of the father is already a dream of the tax-collector, the cop, the judge. This is a point that Deleuze and Guattari take from Fanon; insofar as one seeks to attain to the status of 'the subject' the terrain of desire is populated with figures from a history of colonization:

> what a grotesque error to think that the unconscious-as-child is acquainted only with daddy-mommy, and that it doesn't know 'in its own way' that its father has a boss who is not a father's father, or moreover that its father himself is a boss who is not a father....
>
> The father, the mother, and the self are at grips with, and directly coupled to, the elements of the political and historical situation – the soldier, the cop, the occupier, the collaborator, the radical, the resister, the boss, the boss's wife – who constantly break all triangulations, and who prevent the entire situation from falling back on the familial complex and becoming internalized in it.[24]

It is not surprising then when philosophers speak of reason in general there is nevertheless something inassimilable about Blackness, for man in his most generic and properly race-free form is not simply white, but the white colonizer; the generic subject is a contraction and abstraction from a racial history. With late capitalism and the shift away from the morality and normativity of man, racism can either 'ground' itself on the pseudo-science of genetics – as it did with eugenics – or can take the more progressive path of affirming that we are all members of the family of man, in one grand web of life. All we need is to overcome our ugly feelings and recognize each other. Race and racism are reduced to feelings and attachments – so much so that some philosophers have argued that if one can choose one's gender one might also choose one's race,[25] thereby affirming the neoliberal outcome of late biopolitics. Life is utterly malleable, and who we are is a matter of free choice. As long as we fashion ourselves and are allowed to do so freely, without the impediment of imposed norms we can be who we want to be. Racism – rather than being structural and constitutive of the subject – becomes an affective impediment, enslaving us to petty prejudices that preclude us from being our properly flourishing selves.

To think of race as an affect that impedes a subject's full and affective flourishing is not simply an error, but constitutive of posthuman humanism. 'We' become nothing more than an ongoing extirpation of prejudice; without our moral judgement of the racist 'we' might have to confront the more existential anti-Blackness that is constitutive of humanity, *especially* in its posthumanist neoliberal mode. This is where the tradition of Afro-pessimist thought enriches and tempers Deleuze and Guattari's theorization of race and its relation to humanizing desire. One of the crucial manoeuvers of *Anti-Oedipus* was to shift the terrain of desire outside the subject; subjects do not have desires but are the effect of desiring relations (or desiring machines, brought into being through connections that produce relatively stable bodies.). In the stratification that forms human history, desire is sexual and racial, but what has come to be known as sexuality – the relations between stable genders – is the effect of racial history. There can only be the familial relation of mother-father-child if complex social formations are reduced to the generic family unit, and that happens by way of colonization and the generation of the Oedipal subject. Desires and affects do not belong to subjects; subjectivity is made possible by the privatization of desire. From the desiring relations that join bodies through attachments to the inhuman – such as indigenous cultures and their cosmologies of a richer world of animal spirits – the 'subject' turns inwards, understanding themselves through the bourgeois family drama. The 'father' becomes the figure for authority in general, contracting the broader range of historical figures and relations that lead up to the nuclear family. The more desire becomes privatized, the more affects become reduced to the lived and to feeling.

In *What Is Philosophy?* Deleuze and Guattari seek to open thought away from the lived towards affects that stand apart from the human. Rather than opinion, which is grounded in the subject – where one passes from feeling to judgement – they seek to free thought from the lived. One might imagine the contrast in terms of racial affect. Should we think about the politics of race in terms of changing how we feel? If this were so, then feel-good narratives and microaggression trainings would be crucial to a just future. Alternatively, one might argue that a certain mode of affect – anti-Blackness – is constitutive of the human. Here, the subject of fine feeling would be the effect of racial affect. There would be something white and upright about the bourgeois subject, capable of recognizing all others as just like himself. The human – or more specifically 'man' as the form of humanity that takes itself as the ground for all becomings – is a racial-sexual form produced through the social machine of the nuclear family and its reduction of all differences to the domain of interiority.

There is, in Deleuze and Guattari, no becoming-man because 'man' is the being in command of all he becomes, the subject for whom the world is a rich array of differences to be felt and lived. By contrast, becoming-woman and becoming-animal are transformations through attachments and encounters. Rather than the unfolding of a potentiality that is typical of the liberal subject, Deleuze and Guattari's use of becoming is always attached to a noun, with becoming-woman marking the first or 'key' transformation of the putatively generic subject. Becoming-animal is a transformation according to the apprehension of those traits that bring a body into being: I watch a dog roll joyfully in the snow, and then come to feel snow as if it were a sensuous cooling bed of bliss; I see a chipmunk dart away from a patiently stalking and pouncing cat and intuit the different rhythms and ways of moving that occupy my human domestic space. Becoming-animal is a way of taking up a different unfolding of the world, of seeing and feeling another body's richness in world. Becoming-woman *can* be read as indebted to a rather tired trope of high modernism where beginning with the human subject's other is the key to all becomings; one could tie Deleuze and

Guattari's becoming-woman to Luce Irigaray's insistence on the primacy of sexual difference, and an affirmation of the maternal materiality that is constitutive of the subject's psyche.[26] But in a project of *schizo*analysis, which situates the formed psyche within a geopolitics of desire, becoming-woman is a move away from man as the ground of becoming. *Becoming*-woman is an intuition of those traits that compose a body, that mark out a difference; becoming-woman takes sexuality and desire out of its familial frame and opens onto a thousand plateaus. Becoming-woman, occurring as it does within a broader geopolitical theorization, no longer allows race to be a predicate that covers over the underlying unity of man. On the contrary, becoming-woman is the beginning of the end of the equivocal subject, the subject for whom all differences are tolerable, and where no difference really makes a difference. Univocity precludes a difference – such as sexual difference – being the difference upon which all others are grounded. Male-female would be but one relation among others, as would human-non-human. The difference of the human register – which is significant – would be one stratification among others. Becoming-woman takes desire and sexuality away from the familial and Oedipal complex towards the intense germinal influx, from extensive difference (or relations between male and female) to intensive differences (or the differences from which relations emerge). If the generic subject has been formed by contracting the complex formations of difference and relation into the 'subject' (who is made possible by a long history of colonization), becoming-woman is a rendering multiple of difference. Deleuze and Guattari often refer to high modernism to mark their difference from the psychology of humanism, but non-Western thought offers far more fruitful examples. Recent mobilizations of non-Western compositions of difference would include Alexis Wright's magisterial *The Swan Book* where dreams of swans disrupt the colonizing virus that has installed itself in the brain of the colonized.

> Upstairs in my brain, there lives this kind of cut snake virus in its doll's house. Little stars shining over the moonscape garden twinkle endlessly in a crisp sky. The crazy virus just sits there on the couch and keeps a good old qui vive out the window for intruders. It ignores all of the eviction notices stacked on the door. The virus thinks it is the only pure full-blood virus left in the land. Everything else is just half-caste. Worth nothing! Not even a property owner. Hell yes! it thinks, worse than the swarms of rednecks hanging around the neighbourhood. Hard to believe a brain could get sucked into vomiting bad history over the beautiful sunburnt plains.
>
> Inside the doll's house the virus manufactures really dangerous ideas as arsenal, and if it sees a white flag unfurling, it fires missiles from a bazooka through the window into the flat, space, field or whatever else you want to call life.[27]

Wright's book is not a retrieval of indigeneity as a pure origin that might save Western thought from itself, but instead something productive of a difference that is no longer grounded in a generic notion of the human. It does not take the European novelistic form of a journeying subject for whom the world is a rich array of difference to be consumed and mastered, but instead a powerful example of becoming-woman-becoming-animal-becoming-imperceptible. Dreams of swans by a young girl who has been 'born' from a tree allow for a space outside the colonial imaginary. The politics of race would no longer be negotiated at the level of feelings and attitudes (our relations to each other) but intensive; racial relations produce 'the subject'.

Finding a different mode of relating – through dreams of non-humans – overcomes the sovereignty of ownership, and its familial underpinnings. It is the organization of human bodies into small familial units that makes sex a familial condition and produces the white man of reason as the norm for humanity in general. This goes part of the way towards thinking of anti-Blackness as constitutive of the subject. Race is not an incapacity to see the underlying humanity of the other, not something that might fall away with more human sympathy, connectedness and feeling, but a quite specific and positive formation of a terrain. Race is bound up with a global history that forges *the human* by a withdrawal into a brain inhabited by a virus that wards off all intruders. Where Alexis Wright uses the figure of the virus to depict the colonizing imaginary that installs itself in an interior, and then wards off all others. N. K. Jemisin, in *The City We Became*, uses the figure of the invading white virus to describe a force that destroys the collective thinking of cities.[28] The challenge of the novel will be for cities and their collective and distributed imaginations to come together to overcome the dis-individuating force of the white virus that operates by marking out limited racial identities. (One manifestation of the virus takes the form of a white supremacist art collective seeking to save art in its ironic elevated form from identity politics, with critical white consciousness becoming the force that will bring down the multiple expressiveness of a community art centre.) Like Wright, Jemisin does not look back nostalgically to some moment of pre-racial purity but installs herself in a world of white invasion, and then asks how one might forge different modes of relation that no longer rely on some generic understanding of man. For both writers, coming from quite different traditions, new forms of relationality require thinking of the subject of whiteness as an invasive viral form that turns inward and precludes distributed and inhuman modes of relation. In her earlier *Broken Earth Trilogy*, Jemisin had imagined a mode of existence that intuited other beings *not* through recognition of a common humanity, but through a capacity to intuit the forces of the earth – *literally* the earth's vibrations and stony compositions – putting paid to the Heideggerian claim that the stone is poor in world. Poverty, in Jemisin's *Broken Earth Trilogy*, takes the form of seeking to destroy and enslave those whose intuitions exceed the range of 'stills' – those humans who are at war with the planet's energies. Alexis Wright also describes the weariness of those peoples who have dreamed and connected through the visions of inhuman beings – such as swans – but then had to deal with the colonizing imaginary that is at war with the earth. What *neither* author imagines is a future justice achieved by finding the humanity and sympathy that would sweep away racial affect. On the contrary – and here is where we can return to Deleuze and Guattari – one cannot understand the contraction of the present without understanding the formation of 'the human' as a history of white interiority constituted through anti-Blackness.

This is why the tradition of Afro-pessimist thought yields a far more critical and nuanced reading of Deleuze and Guattari's problem of humanism. Crucial to their global and intensive reading of the human – especially in *Anti-Oedipus* – is Franz Fanon's understanding of subjective desire as essentially colonialist: the desire to be the master is bound up with the violence and figures of the colonizer. This generates the critical and genealogical strand of *Anti-Oedipus*, where understanding the subject as a historical contraction – from intensive relations to the bounded individual – amounts to an opening out of the subject to its constitutive racial delirium. In *A Thousand Plateaus*, the project takes a more positive geological form, where each plateau explores one among many of the possible unfoldings of the infinite from certain points of relation – from music, metallurgy, the face, the signifier, war machines or rhizomes. Here is where the distinction of Afro-pessimism might add nuance to these two (genealogical and geological) forces of the history of capitalism. What if the pessimism of Afro-pessimism were not a sentiment that one might choose to feel – in the way that one might share a project's hope or optimism – but a refusal of the imperative of good feeling, of fellow-feeling? Sara Ahmed's work on happiness, in subtly different ways from the Afro-pessimist tradition, has suggested the important critical force of being a killjoy, of refusing the demand to be happy – which would be a demand to work within the current economy of affect.[29] Pessimism is not another sentiment but a refusal of the humanist domain of sentimentality that covers over the ways in which the subject of hopeful futurity is bound up with anti-Blackness.

There is no shortage of heart-warming stories that depict race and racism as unfortunate obstacles to the free flow of human good feeling. 2018's *Green Book* traces the journey of an Italian-American bouncer-chauffeur who works for an African American pianist, as they tour the US south in the 1960s. By the journey's end, the initially bigoted Tony Lip is reformed and redeemed. No longer racist and homophobic, he becomes capable of hugging his fellow (gay African American) man in a final scene of familial inclusion. The journey is typical of what James Baldwin diagnosed as the sentimentalism of anti-racism; we look with a redeeming liberal eye upon a past that is shrouded in prejudicial evil, comforted that we can rely on proper fellow-feeling to save us from the limits of our less-than-human past. What such feel-good redemption narratives do is repeat the Manichean affirmation of life against all its unfortunate impediments. The post-racial and neoliberal ethic is one of not seeing race, overcoming differences or arriving at a point where others can be included in the same flow of fellow-feeling. 'Humanity' is no longer bound to any specific ideal, and instead is defined *against* any form of rigid stereotype or identity; mentioning race and difference amounts to a faux pas.

What Baldwin's landmark essay on protest literature brought to the fore was both the mythic lure of 'the human', and the problem of humanity that humanism occludes. The ideal of human good feeling allows racism to be a surface affect that might be swept away through sympathy, covering over the existential trauma of the human.[30]

In this respect Baldwin's work anticipates the problematic posthumanism of later thinkers like Foucault, Bernard Stiegler and Deleuze and Guattari who also regard the human and its relation to life as a problem: life is neither a ground that seamlessly unfolds into a natural human existence, *nor* is it – as neoliberalism would have it – purely open to a becoming that is at our command. As recent work on Deleuze and Guattari has insisted, there *is* something essential about the human, and this lies in its difference of register, its peculiar torsion in relation to life.[31] Baldwin argued that humanist narratives that wallowed in sentimentality precluded examining the utterly existential force of racism; the racist horror directed at Blackness was a manifestation of an inability to confront an utterly *inhuman* otherness at the heart of the human.

There is something salutary and prescient in Baldwin's criticism of sentimental humanism. Like many versions of twenty-first-century posthumanism, Baldwin regards humanity *in its humanist form* – with its notion of a default goodness that one might retrieve if only one could sweep away contingent evil – as a lure. Unlike the flat posthumanisms that affirm a single domain of life where we could sweep away human exceptionalism, Baldwin sets humanity apart *not* because of any natural species difference given through material life, but precisely through the seductive illusion of the good moral subject. On the one hand, there is no such thing as the human that might give us a common moral grounding, and yet, on the other hand, 'the human', remains as a problem – an existential rather than metaphysical problem.

Those forms of contemporary posthumanism that would simply will away humanist moralism as if it were an idea or error repeat the humanist focus on politics as something cerebral, an idea that we might abandon or correct. The same would apply to psychoanalytic accounts of desire as mental content where certain images and objects organize the space of the subject. For Deleuze and Guattari desire exceeds and precedes the human, where the human is a quite specific form of stratification that is essentially bound up with racial delirium; the human is also a geological and geopolitical event. Only with the colonization of the globe does desire become deterritorialized; 'man' is formed through increasing privatization. In *Anti-Oedipus* Deleuze and Guattari describe the shift from bodies feeling affects in common – all eyes flinch as knife cuts flesh – to the privatization of desire, where one invests in the secrecy and setting apart of one's own organs. And one might think of Foucault's description in *Discipline and Punish* where premodern regimes use torture to display a festive cruelty of law that acts directly on the body so that observers feel the force of law. It would be important to bear in mind that this corporeal inscription of power does not at all go away in neoliberalism but remains as an archaism. In 2020, the visible and drawn out spectacle of the killing of George Floyd reinforced the sense in which there remained a libidinal enjoyment in the suffering of Black bodies that would then generate an authority of what remains, always at least in part, a police state.

The history of biopolitics shifts the law from outside the body towards interiority *and then life*; one might think of the shift from the moral subject obeying one's conscience to neoliberalism's imperative to maximize one's potential. From the soul and interiority there is now the command to be *other than* any fixed norm. Neoliberal marketing imperatives have seized upon the language of intensities, becoming and affect. From the Dove beauty campaign and the faux diversity of United Colors of Benetton to management trainings on how to avoid microaggression in the workplace, it is now mobility, fluidity and the capacity to reboot and reskill that is at the heart of the good citizen. The capacity to always be other than oneself, to be free of any rigid normativity is now the norm that is not one. The plaintive cry, 'Why can't we all just get along?' reduces differences to problems of ill-feeling, evading the very problem of centring the world on the feeling subject. Free self-formation, and the horror directed at an otherness that refuses to be fluid like me, is essentially intertwined with whiteness, and to a subjectivity that can purvey the world as so much affective difference. To think of race as a predicate, as an identity one chooses, or as something that is skin-deep that occludes our common humanity – especially when 'humanity' is nothing other than the flourishing of life – is utterly congruent with a certain form of 'flat' posthumanism.

To acknowledge the problem of the human would be to confront anti-Blackness – to accept that there is a point of view (the world of the man of reason *and* the world of the free neoliberal subject of pure affective malleability) where all others are ultimately white, or where one's world is composed around denying the humanity of Black life. Whiteness is the outcome of a long history of territorialization, deterritorialization and – with a certain conception of affect as emotion – reterritorialization. One of the crucial ways in which white interiority has been forged is through a form of heightened interiority and affect as sentiment. One might think both of the ways in which whiteness was produced as a form of pale sensitivity – with white femininity in particular being the figure of delicate subjectivity, *and* of the ways in which being sensitive to race amounts to unwarranted ill-feeling. Race *is* an affective assemblage but not because race is a problem of lack of sympathy. Rather it is the idea of race as a problem of feeling, a problem of us not all getting along, that precludes a radical pessimism, a pessimism that would not ask us to adjust our feelings so that we all get along, but one that demands an end of the world forged on familial feeling.

If one thinks of Afro-pessimism in light of Deleuze and Guattari's genealogy and geology of the white bourgeois subject of opiniated feeling, then one can see that pessimism would be destructive of this reterritorialized subject of sentimentality, opening political questions away from individual prejudices to the very composition of the world as premised on anti-Blackness. By the same token if we read Deleuze and Guattari in the wake and presence of Afro-pessimism we can grant far more specificity and force to the general project of schizoanalysis. One of the apparent weak points of Afro-pessimism might be the exclusive emphasis on anti-Blackness as the constitutive trauma that brings the world into being. In its most stringent form, anti-Blackness cannot be analogized with any other form of oppression; indigenous peoples can demand a return of sovereignty and recall a time prior to colonization, but anti-Blackness comes into being with Blackness and slavery, erasing any other possibility of being other than that of non-being. In a political rather than ontological register Baldwin had made the same claim regarding whiteness; it comes into being with the negation and constitution of Blackness: 'America became white – the people who, as they claim, "settled" the country became white – because of the necessity of denying the black presence, and justifying the black subjugation. No community can be based on such a principle – or, in other words, no community can be established on so genocidal a lie.'[32]

The refusal of analogy is one of Afro-pessimism's most compelling and inassimilable features. The refusal of analogy makes perfect sense from within Afro-pessimism; there is a world in which Blackness has no being. It also makes perfect sense in the broader framework of schizoanalysis's geopolitical dimensions. To take politics away from the reterritorialization of the psyche – away from humanity in general – requires that race be thought of as prior to the subject *and* as bound up with the history that brings the modern psyche into being. Afro-pessimism in its various articulations, and especially in the singularity of anti-Blackness, can give force to this deterritorialization of the psyche.

First, one might see the history of slavery as the material requirement for the bourgeois spaces of private reflection and interiority that define modernity. In particular, one might see the fetish attached to privacy and freedom in the United States as bound up with slavery *and* its denial, with the insistence that one stop talking about race, heal the wounds and all get along with each other. The denial of humanity to Black life, the ongoing refusal to recognize Black suffering, *and* the public libidinal investment in Black suffering can only make sense if anti-Blackness is more than a feeling, and instead constitutive of the subject of feeling. This both applies to the dehumanization of Black life – the inability to attribute fine feeling to Black bodies – and to the assumption that race is a problem of sympathy rather than being constitutive of the world. It is schizoanalysis that enables an understanding of the composition of the psyche as bound up with racial delirium. The production of the white face with eyes that reveal the depths of the soul is a contraction from those forms of existence that are composed from affective attachments that open out to the cosmos. To be pessimistic would be to refuse the world, to seek its end, to decline the attachment to who 'we' are. Only with the end of the psyche might there be something other than anti-Blackness.

Second, and this is a more speculative point: there is a world in which anti-Blackness is completely constitutive and this world cannot be analogized with other forms of racism or sexism. When I have taught Afro-pessimist thought to graduate students, this has been the one claim that raises resistance, and not only the resistance that comes from the force of truth. To live in twenty-first-century America, to witness the resurgence of white militia groups (along with their endorsement and defence by law enforcement), and to see unprecedented voter turn-out in an election where one chose between flagrant white supremacy or candidates with small 'r' racist track records, is to live in a world overwhelmingly premised on anti-Blackness. One of the major philosophical contributions of *A Thousand Plateaus*, and Deleuze's corpus more generally, is the destruction of *the world* – the phenomenological unity and coherence of the lived – which would give way to the truth of worlds. This is not to say that the truth of Blackness is relative from some more general point of view, but that it is absolutely true once we understand the truth of the relative. There is a world – definitely the United States, but probably not reducible to that nation – where anti-Blackness is overwhelming, and structural to the world. It is also true that there are worlds where transphobia (to take just one other world) overwhelms all other forces, and there are certainly worlds where these two intersect. One of the many positive challenges of Deleuze and Guattari's work lies in their affirmation of multiple plateaus and in the notion of inclusive disjunctions. The world is founded on anti-Blackness, and heteronormativity, and the annihilation of indigenous peoples, and species chauvinism. This is not so much a claim for intersectionality, where all these predicates exist in the same person, but exclusive disjunctions where the claims are in fruitful and traumatic conflict. Afro-pessimism's foundational anti-Blackness does not sit happily with the strong claims of indigeneity and decolonization. Without industrialized slavery colonization would not have been possible, and while indigenous peoples can make a claim for their own land and sovereignty, Blackness – constituted through slavery – can make no such claim. *At the same time*, but not in the same world, the displacement of native peoples is the theft that nations such as Australia, the United States, Canada, South Africa and New Zealand cannot acknowledge without profound existential trauma. This is so much so that Western nations have developed theories of existential risk that are grounded solely on maintaining the forms of technological progress that have annihilated native peoples. Rather than thinking that one must begin an account of where 'we' are with race *or* sexuality, and rather than thinking that race, sex, indigeneity and ableism intersect in a single political horizon for 'us', it is necessary to note that even though 'the human', presupposes an underlying 'we' its fracturing requires and generates a series of incompossible universals.

What Deleuze and Guattari offer in their history of capitalism is a rendering parochial of the modern psyche, its dependence on a series of barbarisms that reduce desire to the interiority of 'the subject'. Reading Deleuze and Guattari after, and through, Afro-pessimism – recognizing their debt to Fanon in their theory of the white subject as bound up with the racial delirium of colonization – is to hear the voice and history of a desire as crucial to the history of the presupposed 'we' of humanity. The *incompossibility of worlds* – not their intersectionality – is what gives force to Afro-pessimism and schizoanalysis. I am not of your world; the world that unfolds from my life is destroyed by your desire. If the white subject of sympathy and fine feeling can only look back upon the history of colonization and slavery as an unfortunate step in an otherwise benevolent history, then only a voice that refuses affective affinity holds any chance of a new future. Rather than recognizing that 'we' are all one in some gesture of collective sympathy, the idea of politics as fellow-feeling meets the end of the world. The world of 'the human', of technological maturity, of a presupposed 'we' for whom history is on the path to a free and just future, encounters the refusal of pessimism.

Anti-racism is marketable when it focuses on human efficiency and affect, and when affect occurs at the level of manageable feeling. Today I saw a truck with a confederate flag and a bumper sticker, 'Trump 2020: Fuck Your Feelings'. What this bumper sticker knows only too well is that liberalism is constituted through fine feeling, even if it does not quite acknowledge that white supremacism also has its own drama of good and evil, rage and self-righteousness. To exit this war requires confronting what Deleuze and Guattari refer to as the war machine – the pre-human contestations from which the bourgeois citizen emerges. There is one sense, then, in which 'the human' is the effect of a history that requires a geology of morals. What appears to be unremarkable and transcendental – the subject who in various forms makes up the diversity of human culture – is the outcome of a long history of contraction, where bodies that once related to each other by marking out spaces and assembling qualities, now reduce all life to relations among subjects, *and* reduce all relations to flows within the arena of global capital. By contrast, Deleuze and Guattari tear affects from the lived, as qualities or forces that might be thought beyond the relations among humans, and beyond the human body. Pessimism is a refusal of this world of all-too-human affect, a demand for the end of the world. This raises the question of whether one might end this world for the sake of other worlds – those that are offered in other literary and cultural traditions – *or* whether one might do away with the concept of 'world' and the mode of humanism it brings in train. Rather than this being an 'either/or' cerebral question this leads to an exclusive disjunction at the very composition of 'the human'. The 'human', as rich in world has been defined against animality but this sense of animality, in turn, is always already racialized. Becoming-animal is at the centre of a more critical and *race-critical* form of posthumanism, where 'world' or having a rich horizon of meaningful possibility is made possible through the exclusion of 'the animal'. The world that is constituted through anti-Blackness is a world that is – to use Heidegger's phrase – 'rich in world'. This *Da-sein* – this being that is nothing more than the taking up of a space of existence and not at all reducible to anything so fixed as humanity – defines itself against the natural species being or essence of most humanisms, and it also defines itself against the world-poor being of animality. Animality and the non-being of Blackness are at the end of the world: both because 'world' is bound up with a humanity that is a horizon of possibility, and this is constituted through the negation of the non-human.[33] It is possible that ending the world requires not simply ending *this* world of late capitalism constituted by way of anti-Blackness but also the attachment to being 'rich in world' – being pure potentiality of existence.

We can conclude by marking a contrast between two tendencies in posthumanism. The first would be the flat ontology criticized by Ansell-Pearson, where the distinction of the human is an illusion or error that ought to be replaced by a single domain or mesh of life. One way to read the demand for becoming-imperceptible would be to vanquish the distinction of the human. The second would be the race-critical confrontation with the world-ending reckoning with anti-Blackness. Here, the posthuman lure of a single web of life covers over the long history of thinking all figures of life and becoming through the white man of reason for whom the world is so much free and open potentiality. Taking up the 'world' of anti-Blackness is at once a refusal or pessimism with regard to all that has marked the human, *and* in that moment of utter destruction a possible posthumanism that is out of this world.

Notes

1 Jared Sexton, *Amalgamation Schemes*; C. Riley Snorton, *Black on Both Sides*.
2 Amber Jamilla Musser, 'Anti-Oedipus, Kinship, and the Subject of Affect', 77–95.
3 Rosi Braidotti, 'The Ethics of Becoming Imperceptible', 133–59.
4 Alexander R. Galloway, 'Forget Deleuze!'; Frank B. Wilderson also makes a brief remark about the 'faux politics' of Deleuze in *Afropessimism*, 183.
5 Calvin Warren, *Ontological Terror*, 48.
6 Frank B. Wilderson, *Afropessimism*, 217.
7 Gilles Deleuze and Felix Guattari, *A Thousand Plateaus*, 61.
8 Ian Buchanan, *Assemblage Theory and Method*, 30.
9 Keith Ansell-Pearson, 'Deleuze and the New Materialism', 88–108, 93.
10 Calvin Warren, *Ontological Terror*, 6. For C. Riley Snorton, 'For some, including and following Fanon, that future effectively means the end of the world. And perhaps Black and trans lives' mattering in this way would end the world, but worlds end all the time.' *Black on Both Sides*, 198. For Jared Sexton (also following Fanon, following Césaire): 'The overriding question is, how do we create a world where black lives

matter to everyone? Put differently, how do we imagine the "only thing in the world that's worth the effort of starting: The end of the world"?' 'Unbearable Blackness', 159–78, 162.
11 Deleuze and Guattari, *A Thousand Plateaus*, 167.
12 Ibid., 105.
13 Eduardi Viveiros de Castro, *Cannibal Metaphysics*, 12.
14 Francis Fukuyama, *The End of History and the Last Man*.
15 'The soul is the effect and instrument of a political anatomy; the soul is the prison of the body.' Michel Foucault, *Discipline and Punish*, 30.
16 Viveiros de Castro, *Cannibal Metaphysics*, 87.
17 Gilles Deleuze, *Difference and Repetition*, 304.
18 Michel Foucault, *The Order of Things*, 128.
19 Magnus Paulsen Hansen, 'Foucault's Flirt? Neoliberalism, the Left and the Welfare State; a Commentary on La dernière leçon de Michel Foucault and Critiquer Foucault', 291–306.
20 Charles C. Verharen, '"The New World and the Dreams to Which It May Give Rise"', 456–93.
21 Robert Bernasconi, 'Race and Earth in Heidegger's Thinking in the Late 1930s', 49–66.
22 Immanuel Kant, *Observations on the Feeling of the Beautiful and Sublime and Other Writings*, 58.
23 Gilles Deleuze and Felix Guattari, *Anti-Oedipus*, 85.
24 Deleuze and Guattari, *Anti-Oedipus*, 97.
25 Rebecca Tuvel, 'In Defense of Transracialism', 263–78.
26 Luce Irigaray, *An Ethics of Sexual Difference*.
27 Alexis Wright, *The Swan Book*, 5.
28 N. K. Jemisin, *The City We Became*.
29 Sara Ahmed, *The Promise of Happiness*.
30 James Baldwin, 'Everybody's Protest Novel'.
31 Bernard Stiegler, *States of Shock*.
32 James Baldwin, 'On Being White . . . and Other Lies', 166–70, 167.
33 Zakiyyah Iman Jackson, *Becoming Human*.

Bibliography

Ahmed, Sara. *The Promise of Happiness*. Durham, NC: Duke University Press, 2010.
Ansell-Pearson, Keith. 'Deleuze and the New Materialism'. In *The New Politics of Materialism: History, Philosophy, Science*, edited by Sarah Ellenzweig and John H. Zammito, 88–108. London: Routledge, 2017.
Baldwin, James. *Collected Essays*. New York: Library of America, 1998.
Baldwin, James. *The Cross of Redemption: Uncollected Writings*. Edited by Randall Kenan. New York: Vintage, 2011.
Bernasconi, Robert. 'Race and Earth in Heidegger's Thinking in the Late 1930s'. *Southern Journal of Philosophy* 48, no. 1 (May 2010): 49–66.
Braidotti, Rosi. 'The Ethics of Becoming Imperceptible'. In *Deleuze and Philosophy*, Edited by Constantin Boundas, 133–59. Edinburgh: Edinburgh University Press, 2006.
Buchanan, Ian. *Assemblage Theory and Method*. London: Bloomsbury, 2021.

Deleuze, Gilles. *Difference and Repetition*. Translated by Paul Patton. New York: Columbia, 1994.
Deleuze, Gilles and Felix Guattari. *A Thousand Plateaus: Capitalism and Schizophrenia*. Translated by Brian Massumi. Minneapolis, MN: University of Minnesota Press, 1987.
Deleuze, Gilles and Felix Guattari. *Anti-Oedipus*. Translated by Robert Hurley, Mark Seem and Helen R. Lane. Minneapolis, MN: University of Minnesota Press, 1983.
Foucault, Michel. *Discipline and Punish*. Translated by Alan Sheridan. New York: Vintage, 1995.
Foucault, Michel. *The Order of Things* New York: Random House, 1970.
Fukuyama, Frances. *The End of History and the Last Man*. New York: Simon and Schuster, 1992.
Galloway, Alexander R. 'Forget Deleuze!'. http://cultureandcommunication.org/galloway/forget-deleuze. Accessed 23 November 2020.
Hansen, Magnus Paulsen. 'Foucault's Flirt? Neoliberalism, the Left and the Welfare State; a Commentary on La dernière leçon de Michel Foucault and Critiquer Foucault'. *Foucault Studies* 20 (2015): 291–306.
Irigaray, Luce. *An Ethics of Sexual Difference*. Translated by Carolyn Burke and Gillian C. Gill. Ithaca, NY: Cornell University Press, 1984.
Jackson, Zakiyyah Iman. *Becoming Human: Matter and Meaning in an Anti-Black World*. New York: New York University Press, 2020.
Jemisin, N. K. *The City We Became*. New York: Hachette, 2020.
Kant, Immanuel. *Observations on the Feeling of the Beautiful and Sublime and Other Writings*. Edited by. Patrick Frierson and Paul Guyer. Cambridge: Cambridge University Press, 2011.
Musser, Amber Jamilla. 'Anti-Oedipus, Kinship, and the Subject of Affect: Reading Fanon with Deleuze and Guattari'. *Social Text* 30, no. 3 (2012): 77–95.
Sexton, Jared. *Amalgamation Schemes*. Minneapolis, MN: University of Minnesota Press, 2008.
Sexton, Jared. 'Unbearable Blackness'. *Cultural Critique* 90 (Spring 2015): 159–78.
Snorton, C. Riley. *Black on Both Sides: A Racial History of Trans Identity*. Minneapolis, MN: University of Minnesota Press, 2017.
Stiegler, Bernard. *States of Shock*. Translated by Daniel Ross. Cambridge: Polity, 2015.
Tuvel, Rebecca. 'In Defense of Transracialism'. *Hypatia* 32, no. 2 (2017): 263–78.
Verharen, Charles C. '"The New World and the Dreams to Which It May Give Rise": An African and American Response to Hegel's Challenge'. *Journal of Black Studies* 27, no. 4 (1997): 456–93.
Viveiros de Castro, Eduardi. *Cannibal Metaphysics*. Translated by Peter Skafish. Minneapolis, MN: Univocal Press, 2014.
Warren, Calvin. *Ontological Terror: Blackness, Nihilism, and Emancipation*. Durham, NC: Duke University Press, 2018.
Wilderson, Frank B. *Afropessimism*. New York: Liveright, 2020.
Wright, Alexis. *The Swan Book*. New York: Washington Square Press, 2018.

13

Incorporeal transformations in truth and reconciliation

A posthuman approach to transitional justice

Mickey Vallee

On the efficacy of assemblage thinking

This chapter bears on a particular dimension of posthuman philosophy that theorizes how the body and bodies are entangled in technical systems. The system with which it engages is transitional justice. As a contemporary form of social control in conflicted societies, truth commissions operate according to the ontological necessity of transforming social relations. The chapter explores the relationships between testimony and truth commissions in the context of Deleuze and Guattari's conception of 'assemblage', and seeks to propose an *assemblage theory of social justice*. Truth commissions are usually taken as a point of transition between a nation's violent past and its better future, the lynchpin of an official apology offered by a nation to a subjugated social group. There have been many truth commissions, and many more are being proposed, but each one is context-specific. The South African Truth and Reconciliation Commission, for instance, very much hinged on its exposure through the channels of mass media and was subject to criticism of having become a spectacle for national trauma. Offering a perspective on some of these criticisms is certainly a goal of this chapter. But a greater challenge rests on incorporating truth commissions and 'assemblage thinking', the latter currently a favourable methodology within 'posthumanist' literatures. It remains the most important task to put the assemblage to work by using examples drawn from recent truth commissions about their successes, their failures and their attempts to reconcile national dreams with regional realities. Indeed, the purpose of exploring this human-based model of transitional justice is to experiment with new forms of social justice that could be of great benefit in a situation where the greatest victim of the modern era, the earth, has yet to be heard or taken seriously as a witness or a survivor.

Truth commissions, I argue, hinge on the social distribution of affects: in particular, the apology, which has less to do with a discourse and more to do with an orientation, a pre-specular, pre-individuated, pre-emotional orientation that incorporeally transforms a subject's relationships with pasts, presents and possibilities. However, an apology cannot do its work if it does not express contrition, the latter of which moves apology from a simple orientation to an affective possibility to produce an incorporeal transformation. The apology has been subject to much academic discussion, but here within the context of affect and assemblage, the apology has a majorly transformative role in the way a nation redefines its colonialist relations.

The chapter also argues that truth commissions require 'assemblage thinking'. 'Assemblage thinking'[1] has emerged as a middle-ground theory that uniquely synthesizes the historical contingencies that precipitate the formation of new social arrangements. Although the concept emerged through the collaborative writings of Gilles Deleuze and Félix Guattari,[2] it is not necessarily a concept that lives up to its authors' reputation for anarchic imagination. Made of a coupled axis of virtual matter (horizontal, collective assemblages of enunciation) and virtual movement (abstract machines), the concept retains all at once the values of modernity and of the resistances that unfold through them.[3] Indeed, while the concept still centralizes structure, it places more emphasis on the fact that assemblages *change*. Assemblages are historical contingencies in that they are occupied by social actors who are, in certain regards, performing roles, all the while exercising a certain degree of agency by creating something the assemblage was unable to prognosticate.[4] As structures of determinism prove less adequate for understanding micro- and macro-sociological change, assemblage appears as a meeting ground between structuration and resistance and presents the analyst with the opportunity to account for the palpable structures of contemporary life while respecting the manner in which minoritarian social groups and deviant individuals work *through* them, and how they are subject to unpredictable modalities of change.[5] To apply assemblage thinking then requires us to think *through* connections and relations and how these relations incorporeally transform one another's spatial coordinates according to temporal mutations; namely, assemblages capture an emergence, how one *state* emerges from its past and moves into an unknowable and ultimately discoverable future. Assemblage is a site of experience, but it allows the researcher to mediate between the ephemeral potentials of cultural change and the relative stability of modern social institutions.

The question of truth commissions, especially in their global exponential growth since the widely broadcast South African Truth and Reconciliation Commission, requires committing to a global modality of assemblage, a variety of assemblage identified already by Collier and Ong[6] out of an anthropological concern of how individuals come into relation with one another, and how those relations change. Though many contend the opposite, truth commissions, I argue, are not necessarily encapsulated by the laws of a global capitalist doctrine, which Connolly describes as one that 'encounters the rest of the world through the categories of superiority, mastery, terrorism, resource base, market utility, and military right'.[7] Global assemblages, as proposed by Collier and Ong, are far more malleable than are those assemblages connected to global economic dogmatisms, made of a variety of configurations that contribute to the formation of a global knowledge that exceeds the institutions we traditionally associate with twentieth-century modernity. For instance, preferring the term 'concrete elements' as a challenge to the tired notion of global/local, Collier asserts elsewhere that a global assemblage constitutes the global as but one actor in a series of actors that produce incorporeal changes.[8] Dunn argues that the global standardization of food forces local producers to turn to alternative markets and means of trade.[9] Ong, arguing elsewhere that 'the space of the "assemblage" . . . becomes the site of political mobilizations by diverse groups in motion',[10] offers us the most useful definition that extends with ease into truth commissions. Ong contends that any debate regarding the citizen's freedom from the tyranny of the state is really incompatible with the directions that state action and activism are assuming,[11] since they are taking unpredictable forms that include assimilation, neoliberal ideologies and opportunities for radical self-transformation. She writes:

> A simple opposition between territorialized citizenship and deterritorialized human rights is not able to capture the varied assemblages that are the sites of contemporary political claims by a range of residential, expatriate, and migrant actors. The confluence of territorialized and deterritorialized forces forms milieus in which problems of the human are crystallized and problems posed and resolved. Diverse actors invoke not territorialized notions of citizenship, but new claims – postnational, flexible, technological, cyber-based, and biological – as grounds for resources, entitlements, and protection. . . . In short, global assemblages crystallize specific problems and resolutions to questions of contemporary living, thus further disarticulating and deterritorializing aspects of citizenship.[12]

Following Ong, I frame truth commissions as global assemblages in the following way: truth commissions are constituted of a relational set that induces the public to defer to voices of the past to affront a commission inquiring into missing truths in the present, in order to set a precedent for the prevention of a relation between the victim and the accused in the future. The temporal dimensions of past/present/future require a novel way of thinking through their co-agency and thinking through the process in which they accommodate all actors simultaneously. This requires some exegesis of Deleuze and Guattari's philosophies of time and territory, concepts which account for such assemblages as a truth commission, which attempts to capture the interpenetrability of organizations, norms and objects, and practices.[13] The implications of the analysis will be to at once critique the efficacy of truth commissions, but to equally suggest that undertakings of the cultural practices associated with truth commissions are essential if we are to learn about their efficacy, rather than relying on them from above, and reifying them, as practices with an expected outcome.

In anticipation of the criticism that an assemblage theory of transitional justice serves anthro-centric ends, it must be remembered that posthumanism does not necessarily mean shifting our focus onto solely non-human actants in order to garner an entirely non-human world. Instead, transitional justice represents a posthumanist and anti-hierarchical restructuring of social relations, in a court system wherein which authority is slippery and ambivalent, allowing a wide range of citizens to sit in the seat of power. And while the current state of transitional justice does serve the goals for human societies, it is not far off to suggest that the model could be transferred to other contemporary social problems such as environmental degradation and the

Anthropocene. It is not entirely implausible, for instance, to suggest that we may rely on transitional justice as a model for productive social change as we transition towards a post-Anthropocene relation with the non-human.

On the achromatic deadlock of truth commissions

As a contemporary form of social control in conflicted societies, truth commissions operate according to the ontological necessity of transforming social relations by way of distributing affects. The most crucial component of a truth commission is the acknowledgement of *historical trauma*. Historical trauma has been largely applied to instances of racial tension, especially indigenous rights in such contexts as the United States, Canada and Australia. Historical trauma materializes along two axes: a horizontal axis of real actors in real time whose proximity to context-dependent stressors trigger deep historical wounds; and a vertical axis as a temporal dimension of ancestral grief, loss of language, culture and deep cuts from colonization. Historical trauma is a particular mode of traumatic knowing, as a virtual temporal pathway between generations for trauma to be transferred. There is a tendency, within the historically traumatized, towards self-destruction in such affects and behaviours as 'depression, self-destructive behaviour, substance abuse, identification with ancestral pain, fixation to trauma, somatic symptoms, anxiety, guilt and chronic bereavement'.[14] Historical trauma marks another difficulty for social scientists; because it is a condition determined by the actions of the state (it is the infliction of the governmental policy upon the displacement or genocide of a people), it remains manifest at the level of the individual in their micro-sociological interactions (through such behaviours as mentioned earlier). The point, moreover, is that distal cause and proximal cause encroach upon one another in the manifestation of the self-destruction of the individual. Some generalizations can be made: it is a state of embodiment; that is, it is an affective state between bodies and carried within the bodies of individuals, manifest as self-destructive behaviour with implications towards the self-destruction of a social group.[15] Second, the micro-level health effects social groups suffer can be linked to broader social processes in the economic and cultural systems that serve to dominate them.[16] In many contexts, such as the legacy of the Rwandan 100-day genocide, victims live so closely to the perpetrators, who under a state of distress acted out in non-normal violent ways, that reconciliation is more than simply an option, but a requisite for healing at the individual, communal, national, and international levels,[17] involving real people from the public, colleges and universities, media, policymakers, government, the private sector and so on. And while truth commissions are not called for in every case, it is generally held that South Africa established the model for truth commissions to follow, because their involvement of the public and the persistent coverage by the media distinguished their commission from all predecessors.

The lack of consensus over the efficacy of a truth commission should be taken less as a sign of inadequacy than as a sign of its function. After all, Derrida's (2005) well-received paradox regarding forgiveness,[18] that forgiveness can only forgive the unforgivable, is a dramatic backdrop to the philosophical issues that every truth commission raises and is a paradox that cannot be resolved but *reckoned* with by every subject that finds themselves in a situation of power over the confessor in front of the witness of the state and the public – for Derrida, forgiveness is the affective transformation that more properly situates the bureaucratic necessity of reconciliation.[19] And, so, the danger lies within the way in which the TRC would *use* instances of forgiveness to elevate the discursive importance of reconciliation in the service of nationalist healing. Every time the TRC reached a moment of forgiveness, the media would intently focus on the moment of apology, at which point the commission would raise again the virtue of reconciliation.[20] The push for forgiveness might be too much for victims who are not ready to forgive, nor who feel as though an appropriate enough apology was delivered to them in order for them to forgive.[21] The neglect of the local has an even further gendered dimension, in that in South Africa, the testimony of women had a restricted role. Whereas male victims were encouraged to identify injustices done to their persons, women were more or less permitted to speak on behalf of their community, but not about their bodies. As Driver explains:

> when they [women] testified as women-in-family or women-in-community to the abuses against the men close to them in order to elicit perpetrators' truths, and possibly to elicit also their apologies or at least their visible self-recognition, women were figured as participants in the complex processes of exchange produced through the TRC process. However, when they testified to abuses against 'themselves', as women-in-themselves, women were not able to participate in the complex staging. Therefore, in their speaking for others (and primarily for men), as women-in-community, women were included in the process of reconciliation as conceived in the TRC. In their speaking for themselves, as women-in-themselves, women were excluded.[22]

The axiomatic questions regarding the identification of victims and perpetrators are entangled by difficulties (albeit less entangled than the politics of identifying the dead and missing). While Argentina's commission decided to include the names of *some* perpetrators mentioned in testimony, and Chile not to publish any names given that the commission was not qualified to administer legal negative sanctions, Canada decided to entirely block the possibility of the names of the accused entering the public record. Yet, this decision is not necessarily against the will and intentions of truth commissions. Niezen describes the less legislative and more affective inhesion of truth commissions:

> Anyone who has seriously considered the acts of bearing witness in truth commissions will recognize that they can be simultaneously replete with possibilities of insight and ambiguity. Some might be initially drawn almost against their wills to the horrors that are the subjects of testimony, not the seemingly mundane act of *giving* testimony. The images and information we pay attention to first usually turn out to be less compelling than the perplexing fact that we are compelled by them. I am more interested in the things that are in the background of a survivor being in front of a microphone and saying what they have to say. They

are there because of something horrible that happened in the past, something that was done to them or that they did, something for which the state was ultimately responsible. The past tense here is important: it *happened*.[23]

Truth commissions have become gradually driven on interrogating past injustices with any number of transitional, restorative, retributive or other forms of justice to correct a past wrong. One could argue that the truth commission hinges on an incitement to discourse: in particular, the confession.

Michel Foucault cites the confession as having emerged in the nineteenth century as an incitement to discursively construct the inner self, or, in Foucault's earlier received maxim in *Discipline & Punish*, that which confirms that 'The soul is the prison of the body'.[24] In *The History of Sexuality*, Foucault delineates the confession as having drawn upon the utopian and exotic desires constructed through intersubjective relations in confession: between doctor and patient, teacher and student, analyst and analysand, witness and the public, and so on. Confessions invite us to cast the eyes on hidden intentions, to invite new interpretations to the transactions of history; confessions are never self-involved, but facilitators of transformation between bodies, they incite new modes of power of transformation into discourse. Truth commissions are impelled by procedures of transformation: the before-and-after vision of colonization, postcolonialism being the most affluent position that a nation can enter into in order to prove the nation's ability to apologize. Thus, truth commissions are consistently and can only be state imposed. The state with the power to apologize is the new state seen as embodying a new benevolence, offering collective actions for a nation's healing.

Though, while truth commissions invite citizens to reflect on the injustices of the past and to constitute out of individual memories a collective memory, archived for the purposes of constituting history, the performative dimensions of truth commissions proffer very complex operations. In contemporary culture, they provide a representation of the past as presented for the public record by way of the technology of recording, an acceptable archive: the apology. But, the apology cannot so easily be separated from the technology of the confession; whereas Foucault's idea for the confession regarded the acquiescence of the body under truth/power, the apology, as it is discursively produced throughout truth commissions, is a confession that has a multiplicity of directions, not necessarily towards those with official authority (in fact, truth commissions hold little authority in imposing state-sanction justice, but operate as a kind of transformative operative); the apology has an ideal dimension, that is, that an apology is an offering of renouncement of a quest for the personal retribution of the accused. This can be conceived in general as a kind of incorporeal transformation, contained in the orientation one has towards those who harmed them. Performative dimensions of the apology proliferate with telling effect. They are more than signs, the constructed question of restitution, but seek for confirmation, they cannot be made without the exteriorization of the object hurt, and impose upon the inner narratives of others a kind of sharing of the burden of the past, the past recognized. The apology is part of a signifying regime, but, perhaps more importantly, it is expressive and performative. It is to give, to forgive, to gift and so on.

But the apology is fragile. The apology may lose its ontological being, especially in the case where those coming forward are looking for amnesty. It is not taking consequences for individual action. The top-down apology is well known in public discourse that is an apology without contrition. Prime Minister Stephen Harper, it is well known, in Canada, for instance, apologized in 2008 for the Indian Residential Schools, but in 2010 boasted on an international stage that 'Canada has no history of colonialism'. Apologizing without contrition has become something of a celebrity trend: #imsorry, or t-shirt slogans, 'I'm sorry for what I said when I was HUNGRY'. There is an industry of apology in the works. *Huffington Post* recently declared 2013 'The Year of the (Non) Apology'. Even if the apology represents what Elazar Barkan notes as the 'new public morality', the age of the non-apology is one in which apologies are offered for legal purposes, which, according to Sara Ahmed (2004), makes 'the apology . . . unutterable and . . . the demand for an apology is refused'.[25] *Non-apology is the refusal to express shame, and shame must be expressed as the evidence for truth.*

Apology ultimately constitutes a transformation of sorts, and so Ahmed views the apology as an act that at once claims responsibility, expresses an emotional assemblage of shame, regret and hope, all the while constituting a transformation that ultimately rests on acknowledgement that the past can never itself be transformed. The difficulty, Ahmed claims, in issuing an apology hinges on the fact that its outcome is entirely unpredictable; although it is a technology for a self or a nation in healing, in acknowledging the past, it also opens the self to intense criticism, criticism that it is probably unwilling to acknowledge, in which case, it isn't necessarily an apology. The openness of the apology is key, no matter how difficult it is to accept, and so an apology is *always* context dependent as an unfolding actor. The nature of the apology, then, depends on how it is demanded, and how it is aligned with contrition, regret, shame, affiliation and individual and representative responsibility. Because apology requires this ever-shifting context, the emotional impact of an apology (or its lack thereof) bespeaks something peculiar about affect and emotion, at least in this case: that emotions and affect are not inner conditions but are drawn out through contextualized intersubjective interactions. It can be said, then, that apology *is* a measure or a sign of *true feelings*, especially since non-apologies and non-sincerity appear so easily detectable, but only in the context of intersubjectivity – and so it appears that affect is tied to a particularly political and intersubjective context, that the affective attributes of an apology move into a representative domain. Apology is thus entirely social, only social, just like the confession, since, Ahmed points out, an apology cannot be read on the body of the deliverer only, but must be registered in the body of the recipient as either 'accepted' or 'unaccepted', in any case *negotiated* or *opposed*.

We might certainly be tempted to read the apology as a sign, in the good old-fashioned arbitrary sense of a signifier that inscribes upon the body a signified that is ultimately negotiable, within a general framework of meaning. As a sign, the apology, Ahmed writes, resonates on several registers at once, not on the condition of an 'inner feeling'. The apology, simply, must *apologize*. That is, an apology signifies affect in its representational status for shame, but it also reveals emotion, while signifying the subjective positions of the apologized-to and apologizer; the emotion it signifies, Ahmed claims, can itself be another sign for the truth of the utterance.

Or it may represent the emotions of those to whom the apology is directed. It may also represent the emotions of the exchange, which might not necessarily be within the bodies of any of the individuals taking part but might arise as an effect of the apology itself as a summoning of a particular emotion. And, so, in retributive justice, if justice is measured by the vengeance taken upon the accused, in cases of transitional justice, justice is measured emotionally, by the equinity of the apology, or a technology that opens the possibility to begin working through trauma. Ahmed explains in the circulation of shame: '[T]he expression of shame does not return ourselves to ourselves, but responds to demands that come from a place other than where we are. The apology in this instance would be a return address, an address to another, whose place we do not inhabit.'[26]

What an apology *does* rather than what it *means* is ultimately of more interest to those concerned with the political mobilization of apologies, then. Politically, the apology can only be accounted for as valuable to the nation. If anything, the apology must thus be an opening, a *discoverable*, opening up the truth of the past and the unpredictability of the future. The archive is the emotional apparatus of the affective institution.

Putting the assemblage to work

The purpose of employing the concept of the assemblage is neither to essentialize the complex task of truth commissions, nor to reify their movements towards new relations, but instead to suggest the following: *as a contemporary form of social control in conflicted societies, truth commissions operate according to the ontological necessity of transforming social relations*. In presenting my adaptation of assemblage thinking below, I anticipate and welcome backlash from more 'victim-centred' (or 'survivor-centred') approaches that account for the techniques of cultural healing that circumvent the striated space of the truth commission. But the purpose is, exactly, to understand how the truth commissions operate from the top down *as an assemblage*. As demonstrated earlier, assemblage thinking is a middle-ground theory that accounts for the intersections of movements from above and from below. Given the limited space in this chapter, I am presenting a model from the top, with the intention of constructing a complementary assemblage from below in another context, which will account for strategies of cultural resilience.

Assemblages work according to specific spatial and temporal dynamics. The spatial dynamics are configured by affects, the temporal dynamics by forces. Some principles on the assemblage are as follows, practically articulated by McFarlane: first, assemblages are embedded between the traces of the past and the emergence of the future;[27] second, they are structured according to context-specific configurations of human and non-human actors;[28] third, they command attention of their own particular sites by resisting meta-theoretical constructions;[29] and, fourth, assemblages resist the division between concretion of activities at the actual site and the virtual actors from wider contexts that take part.[30]

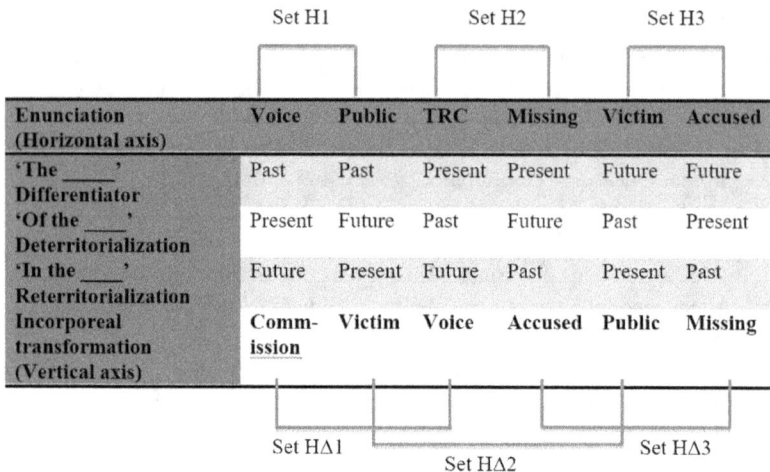

Figure 13.1 An Assemblage model for truth commissions.

'Assemblage-thinking' proffers a novel reconceptualization of emerging collectives and their transmutations. Arranged along two axes, assemblages distribute horizontal relations and vertical relations, the former of which constitutes an expressive spatial dynamic between quasi-molecular units (H relations, in Figure 13.1), the latter dynamics whereby each quasi-molecular unit undergoes a transmutation and enters a new relation along a new horizontal axis (HΔ relations, in Figure 13.1). The milieus I isolate are the voice, public, commission, missing, victim and accused. Because the truth commission is, in every instance, a commission intent on reassembling the past in the present for the future, I assign to these molecular units what, to me, appear to be their strongest temporal attributes during the commissions.

Along the vertical axis, assemblages are temporal and subject to the laws of territorialization, reterritorialization and deterritorialization, all of which circulate around the concept of the refrain: the refrain is the most consistent sonic block that occupies an assemblage, that binds its consistency, but that is itself subject to laws of transformation – we never 'hear' the refrain directly, but only through territorial processes of its deterritorialization and reterritorialization. We might think of the refrain as the most absolute form of habit, but the refrain is *not* habit per se; it is the non-habitual idiosyncrasy from which habit unfolds. I contend that the habit which binds the truth commission is that of what Walklate terms the 'imaginary victim', suggesting that truth commissions hinge on the presence of the victim, as the figure whom activists gather around, and so on, because it is the most tangible of figures in a truth commission (as opposed to 'the pursuit of justice', securing the future, or finding the truth). Habit coincides more broadly with Deleuzian vitalism. It is not a comprehensive uniform substance but rather an unabridged idiosyncrasy. A refrain is not the affirmation of life. Paradoxically, then, the essential building block of habit for Deleuze and Guattari in *A Thousand Plateaus* is *non-habitual*. Habit is always expressed in relation to *deterritorializing the refrain*, of cutting up the refrain and removing it from its positional security (its subjectivity, its identity), thus securing its inevitable course towards incorporeal change – that is, in Deleuze and Guattari's term, an absolute deterritorialization. Deterritorialization pertains equally to non-human, non-animal, and non-substantial phenomena when a refrain discharges from within the confines of its territory to become something other than itself. Deleuze and Guattari are radical de-contextualists, as context is one of many conceptual systems that enslave the transcendental subject in a territory. Therefore, continuous variation is the key to Deleuze and Guattari's philosophy of change, a secret language that 'places the public language's system of variables in a state of variation'.[31] We always think of territories in relation to one another, to their own deterritorializations, to their reterritorializations, the latter of which implies the deterioration of the refrain, the turning of habit into compulsive repetition. It is thus through the consistent deterritorialization of the refrain that we discover the inexpectations of incorporeal transformation.

When these milieus enter into the vertical axis of the assemblage, they (1) enter into new temporal dynamics that cause their own transmutation into other bodies, while (2) entering into new relations with other bodies that have themselves gone into temporal mutations into other bodies. The vertical axis is made up of the territorialization that Deleuze and Guattari delineate in the 'Refrain' chapter of *A Thousand Plateaus*.[32] It is my claim that, so long as the horizontal axis of a truth commission is composed of a spatial configuration of enunciations between milieus, the vertical axis is a particular working over of all temporal dimensions in order to offer new alternatives of time, history and memory: simply, the vertical axis is a particular working over of the past in such a territorialization *of the present of the past in the future*. But for every milieu along the horizontal axis, a permutation of this territorialization is operative:

- Milieu 1: Voice undergoes a transmutation along the *past of the present in the future* that incorporeally transforms the commission. That is, for the commission to discover truth, it hinges on the corporeal presence of the victim's testimony of truth.
- Milieu 2: Public undergoes a transmutation along the *past of the future in the present* that incorporeally transforms the victim. That is, for the victim to heal individually or collectively, they must be recognized by the public as having been victimized.
- Milieu 3: Commission undergoes a transmutation along *the present of the past in the future* that incorporeally transforms the voice. That is, if the voice is the affective quality of truth, it must be channelled through the truth commission in order to be registered as history.
- Milieu 4: Missing undergoes a transmutation along *the present of the future in the past* that incorporeally transforms the accused. That is, for the accused to stand before the potential for amnesty or justice, it must account for the missing as irrecoverable except through public memorialization.
- Milieu 5: Victim undergoes a transmutation along *the future of the past in the present* that incorporeally transforms the public. That is, for the public to move into a democratic state, it must understand its own role in creating, recognizing and contributing to the healing of victims.

- Milieu 6: Accused undergoes a transmutation along *the future of the present in the past* that incorporeally transforms the missing. That is, for the missing to re-present themselves, they must be accounted for as victims who are unable to speak because of their victimization.

The central point to Deleuze and Guattari's theory of incorporeal transformation is embedded in their philosophy of language, explicated in their 'Postulates of Linguistics' plateau of *A Thousand Plateaus*.[33] Briefly, the primary base of the linguistic utterance is not communication, nor is it information. Instead, incorporeal transformation is facilitated by the language's *capacity*, with the 'order-word' as its fundamental unit ('I hereby pronounce you . . .', or 'I sentence you to . . .'). Insofar as assemblages have some kind of content, they do not possess *properties* so much as they possess *capacities*: that is, bodies with capacities for facilitating incorporeal transformations. This doesn't mean that they *don't* have properties, but their ontological function as sites of incorporeal transformation rely greatly on their capacity and potential more than their property and certainty.[34] In other words, assemblages are multiplicities, but overlapping multiplicities, much like stereoscopic alignment of the horizontal and vertical axes, they constitute an unknowable whole out of parts, but they must be different to create a whole.[35]

Conclusion

Truth commissions are global assemblages insofar as they serve less the dimension of economic expansion or colonial acquiescence than the possibility of a previously disavowed truth which emerged from a condition of intense violence, something previously beyond our ability to imagine, though its components (forces, affects, etc.) have long been in place. Perhaps the best way to imagine the truth commission is as a communally spontaneous effort at mutually constructing a unique reality through the sudden and nearly accidental eruption of a happening that was entirely unforeseeable before its occurrence. At its most obvious, such events always contain a trace of the unforeseen: the denial of amnesty, the breach of forgiveness, the eruption of disapproval, the traces in cultural representations, and so on. These events become perceptible above and beyond the conflict society they are embedded within yet remain curiously determined by its various forces. If a truth commission is an event, it is a virtual one. 'With every event', Deleuze writes:

> there is indeed the present moment of its actualization, the moment in which the event is embodied in a state of affairs, an individual, or a person, the moment we designate by saying 'here, the moment has come'. The future and the past of the event are only evaluated with respect to this definitive present. On the other hand, there is the future and past of the event considered in itself, sidestepping each present, being free of the limitations of a state of affairs, impersonal, pre-individual, neutral.[36]

We are aware of the arrival of an event by announcing its arrival, yet the announcement can only say as much about the event that it is actually untouchable in colloquialisms – this is why, generally, the reports for truth commissions are written so matter-of-factly, because they do not need elaboration to be convincing, they are contained within a document which states that atrocities happened. But the untouchable aspect, the unbelievability of it, that which causes our fetishistic disavowal that civilization is capable of generating such global systematic human suffering, is what marks the central feature of the event, namely *the production of the New*. The New appears in the context of the familiar. The paradox in the event is that what is New can only emerge from within the coordinates of repetitions of the familiar. The event is thus not something we can hold onto, but something intangible, a process.

The past and future in truth commissions are stacked in a stratigraphic order where 'time' is experienced in place of *things in time* (we do not experience things through the mediation of time but rather mobilize things in order to access a pure becoming of time). An 'event' in the Deleuzian sense is the incorporeal sense-event out of which the new emerges through repetition, an immanent rule of emergence without consequence. To proceed further would require an exegesis of the *cultural* dimensions of truth commissions as they have occurred across a broad range of historical and cultural contexts. To certain extents, my theoretical disposition is aligned with a 'post-witness' model of reconciliation, one which doesn't see identification and understanding as a goal, but rather something we would prefer, conceptually at least, to avoid and evade: *for it is in the realm of understanding that the state is most justified in imposing*. Cole offers the most convincing account of what makes a truth commission with her study of the Truth and Reconciliation Commission of South Africa, which is its *performative* dimension, where cultural symbols are reinvented and identities in conflict are played out for the attention of the media.[37] The truth commission, as far as I can surmise, is an affective institution insofar as it is a topological zone that transforms affective enunciations into subject positions: it turns affect into a discourse – from subject to subjectivities. Truth commissions provide rich case studies for scholars willing to critically reflect on their own policies and consequences of embracing healing discourses that affect both individual and collective identities and images. They also enhance the understanding of the general context in which healing practices take place, a context profoundly characterized by the recent turn to truth.

Reframing transitional legal institutions, such as the truth commission, in a posthuman framework exposes the underlying forces that are causal agents in social transformation – particularly, the enunciations of the voice as itself an active agent in transformation, without the typically representative accountability to individuals or a subjectivity that it is often thought as reflecting. It is practically common sense that the voice represents an agency, or a reflexivity upon one's social actions, or cultural theory's favourite 'illocutionary acts' such as the speech acts involved in the dissemination of law. We might still think of the voice in such a way: to bring together the past, present and possibility of a just world. As the South African Truth and Reconciliation Commission and the Truth and Reconciliation Commission of Canada shows us, transformation is a multifaceted and complex undertaking that should let national images of benevolent domination and regional realities of counter-hegemonic resistance enunciate alongside one another. We might be tempted to live by the maxim that to prepare a just future, we must repair an unjust past. This is not a point lost on the Truth and Reconciliation Commission of Canada, especially now that the final reports have been published and are available to the public. Certainly, such a publication is where the 'voice' of transformation lies (as well as the proliferation of publications on the Indian Residential Schools), but if we are to abide by Deleuze and Guattari's favourite saying of the voice, that there are 'many voices in a voice', we are compelled to look within as well as beyond the official publications for the voice's echoes. Clearly, we are at a point when the study of a truth commission is not enough and are just beginning the necessary next steps in exploring an expanded definition of testimony, witness, voice and reconciliation.

Notes

1. See Ben Anderson and Colin McFarlane, 'Assemblage and Geography'; Manuel DeLanda, *A New Philosophy of Society* and *Philosophy and Simulation*; John-David Dewsbury, 'The Deleuze-Guattarian Assemblage'; Kim Dovey, 'Uprooting Critical Urbanism'; David Featherstone, 'On Assemblage and Articulation'; Michele Lancione, 'Homeless People and the City of Abstract Machines'; Colin McFarlane, 'On Context'; Dan O'Connor and Suzan Ilcan, 'Assemblages'.
2. Gilles Deleuze and Félix Guattari, *A Thousand Plateaus*.
3. See George E. Marcus and Erkan Saka, 'Assemblage'.
4. See Dan O'Connor and Suzan Ilcan, 'Assemblages'.
5. See Couze Venn, 'A Note on Assemblage'.
6. Stephen J. Collier and Aihwa Ong, eds., *Global Assemblages*.
7. William E. Connolly, 'The Christo-Capitalist Assemblage', 305.
8. Stephen J. Collier, 'Global Assemblages'.
9. Elizabeth C. Dunn, 'Standards and Person-Making in East-Central Europe'.
10. Aihwa Ong, 'Mutations in Citizenship', 499.
11. Ibid.
12. Ibid., 504.
13. See Manuel DeLanda, *A New Philosophy of Society*.
14. Maria Yellow Horse Brave Heart, 'Oyate ptayela', 111.
15. Karina L. Walters et al., 'Bodies Don't Just Tell Stories, They Tell Histories', 183–4.
16. Antonio L. Estrada, 'Mexican Americans and Historical Trauma Theory', 331–2.
17. See Linda M. Kreitzer and Mary Kay Jou, 'Social Work with Victims of Genocide'.
18. See Jacques Derrida, *On Cosmopolitanism and Forgiveness*.
19. Dorothy Driver, 'Truth, Reconciliation, Gender', 229.
20. Annelies Verdoolaege, 'Media Representations', 190.
21. Annelies Verdoolaege, 'Dealing with a Traumatic Past', 300.
22. Dorothy Driver, 'Truth, Reconciliation, Gender', 224.
23. Robert Niezen, *Truth and Indignation*, 14.
24. Michel Foucault, *Discipline and Punish*, 30.
25. Sara Ahmed, *The Cultural Politics of Emotion*, 117.
26. Ibid., 129.
27. Colin McFarlane, 'On Context', 380.

28 Ibid., 381.
29 Ibid.
30 Ibid., 383.
31 Gilles Deleuze and Félix Guattari, *A Thousand Plateaus*, 97.
32 Ibid., 310–50.
33 Ibid., 75–110.
34 Ben Anderson et al., 'On assemblages and Geography', 179.
35 Colin McFarlane, 'On Context', 377.
36 Gilles Deleuze, *The Logic of Sense*, 172.
37 See Catherine M. Cole, *Performing South Africa's Truth Commission*.

Bibliography

Ahmed, Sara. *The Cultural Politics of Emotion*. Edinburgh: Edinburgh University Press, 2004.
Anderson, Ben and Colin McFarlane. 'Assemblage and Geography'. *Area* 43, no. 2 (2011): 124–7.
Anderson, Ben, Matthew Kearnes, Colin McFarlane and Dan Swanton. 'On Assemblages and Geography'. *Dialogues in Human Geography* 2, no. 2 (2012): 171–89.
Cole, Catherine M. *Performing South Africa's Truth Commission: Stages of Transition*. Bloomington, IN: Indiana University Press, 2010.
Collier, Stephen J. 'Global Assemblages'. *Theory, Culture & Society* 23: 2–3 (2006): 399–401.
Connolly, William E. 'The Christo-Capitalist Assemblage'. *Theory, Culture & Society* 24, no. 7–8 (2007): 303–5.
DeLanda, Manuel. *A New Philosophy of Society: Assemblage Theory and Social Complexity*. New York: Continuum, 2005.
DeLanda, Manuel. *Philosophy and Simulation: The Emergence of Synthetic Reason*. New York: Continuum, 2011.
Deleuze, Gilles. *The Logic of Sense*. Translated by Mark Lester with Charles Stivale. New York: Columbia University Press, 1990.
Deleuze, Gilles and Félix Guattari. *A Thousand Plateaus: Capitalism and Schizophrenia*. Translated by Brian Massumi. Minneapolis, MN: University of Minnesota Press, 1987.
Derrida, Jacques. *On Cosmopolitanism and Forgiveness*. Translated by Mark Dooley and Michael Hughes. London: Routledge, 2005.
Dewsbury, John-David. 'The Deleuze-Guattarian Assemblage: Plastic Habits'. *Area* 43, no. 2 (2011): 148–53.
Dovey, Kim. 'Uprooting Critical Urbanism'. *City* 15, no. 3–4 (2011): 347–54.
Driver, Dorothy. 'Truth, Reconciliation, Gender: the South African Truth and Reconciliation Commission and Black Women's Intellectual History'. *Australian Feminist Studies* 20, no. 47 (2005): 219–25.
Dunn, Elizabeth C. 'Standards and Person-Making in East-Central Europe'. In *Global Assemblages: Technology, Politics and Ethics as Anthropological Problems*, edited by Stephen Collier and Aihwa Ong, 173–93. Malden, MA: Blackwell, 2005.
Estrada, Antonio L. 'Mexican Americans and Historical Trauma Theory; A Theoretical Perspective'. *Journal of Ethnicity in Substance Abuse* 8 (2009): 330–40.
Featherstone, David. 'On Assemblage and Articulation'. *Area* 43, no. 2 (2011): 139–42.

Foucault, Michel. *Discipline and Punish: The Birth of the Prison.* Translated by Alan Sheridan. New York: Vintage Books, 1977.
Heart, Maria Yellow Horse Brave. '"Oyate ptayela": Rebuilding the Lakota Nation Through Addressing Historical Trauma among Lakota Parents'. *Journal of Human Behavior in the Social Environment* 2 (1999): 109–26.
Kreitzer, Linda M. and Mary Kay Jou. 'Social Work with Victims of Genocide: The Alternatives to Violence Project (AVP) in Rwanda'. *International Social Work* 53, no. 1 (2010): 73–86.
Marcus, George E. and Erkan Saka. 'Assemblage'. *Theory, Culture & Society* 23, no. 2–3 (2006): 101–9.
McFarlane, Colin. 'On Context: Assemblage, Political Economy and Structure'. *City* 15, no. 3–4 (2011): 375–88.
Ong, Aihwa. 'Mutations in Citizenship'. *Theory, Culture & Society* 23, no. 2–3 (2006): 499–505.
Ong, Aihwa and Stephen J. Collier, eds. *Global Assemblages: Technology, Politics, and Ethics as Anthropological Problems.* Malden, MA: Blackwell, 2005.
Venn, Couze. 'A Note on Assemblage'. *Theory, Culture & Society* 23, no. 2–3 (2006): 107–8.
Verdoolaege, Annelies. 'Dealing with a Traumatic Past: The Victim Hearings of the South African Truth and Reconciliation Commission and Their Reconciliation Discourse'. *Critical Discourse Studies* 6, no. 4 (2009): 297–309.
Verdoolaege, Annelies. 'Media Representations of the South African Truth and Reconciliation Commission and Their Commitment to Reconciliation'. *Journal of African Cultural Studies* 17, no. 2 (2005): 181–99.
Walklate, Sandra. *Imagining the Victim of Crime.* New York: McGraw-Hill, 2007.
Walters, Karina L., Selina A. Mohammed, Teresa Evans-Campbell, Ramona E. Beltrán, David H. Chae and Bonnie Duran. 'Bodies don't Just Tell Stories, They Tell Histories: Embodiment of Historical Trauma among American Indians and Alaska Natives'. *Du Bois Review* 8, no. 1 (2011): 179–89.

Index

active joys   12, 63–8, 72–3, 77–9
actualization of latent power   95
adaxial-abaxial axis   98–9
adequate idea   64–8, 73, 76–8
aesthetics   12, 14, 17, 155–6, 195
affect   74–5
   and emotion   149–50
   and transcendence of
      representation   149
affection-image   14, 147–54, 156, 160–1
   close-up to   153
   difference between three-quarter and
      full-face close-ups   154
   face/close-up as   149
affirmative politics   31–6
   Bergsonian philosophy of time   33
   and contemporary capitalism   36
   as neo-materialism   34
   power-formations in   34
   structure of differentiation   32
Afro-pessimism   16, 250–65
   and anti-racism   264
   and capitalism   264
   constitutive anti-Blackness   250–2
   mode of relations   253
   and racial delirium   255–6
   racism   256, 260
   and sentimental humanism   261
   slavery   263
   territorialization and
      deterritorialization   262
   transformations in   257
Aftermath: Violence and the Remaking of a Self (Brison)   51
Agamben, Giorgio   212, 218
Ahmed, Sara   57, 149, 260, 274–5
A.I.: Artificial Intelligence (2001)   182
Alaimo, Stacy   45
   view of material self   45
Alphaville (1965)   154
alterity and face
   absolute art   155

aesthetics in   155
anatheism   156
biblical prohibition   156
and cinematic realisms   157
qua close-up   155
theory of 'transcendental' film
   style   154
amor fati, idea of   33
anatheism   156
Anderson, Bibi   154
androids, figuration of   213
animal ethics   90
animalesque nature of thought's
   body   89
   formal characteristics of   88
   and radial concentricity   88
   responding to climate change   89–90
   and right-left bilaterality   88
Ansell-Pearson, Keith   251, 265
anthropo/Euro-centric pseudo-
   cosmology   117
anti-Blackness   250–2, 256–7, 259–60,
   262–3, 265
anti-humanism   4, 6, 25–7
The Anti-Oedipus (Deleuze and
   Guattari)   26, 43, 251, 253, 257,
   259–61
anti-racism   29, 260, 264
Ant-Man (2015)   198–202
apical-basal axis   96–7
Apollo 13 (1995)   140
apology
   emotional impact of   274
   incorporeal transformation   273
   significance of   274–5
   top-down apology   274
Ark-Earth *(Ur-Archè)*   106, 120
Arnold, Magda B.   75
artificial intelligence (AI)   5, 14, 180,
   182, 202
assemblage
   assemblage-thinking   276

and concept of refrain 276
and habit 276-7
horizontal axis of 277-8
and model for truth
 commissions 276
spatial and temporal dynamics of 275
and theory of incorporeal
 transformation 278
vertical axis of 276-7
autopoiesis, principle of 31
The Avengers (2012) 191
Avengers: Age of Ultron (2015) 191
axes of asymmetry 99

Bachelard, Gaston 26
Bakhtin, Mikhaïl M. 158
Balász, Béla 151
Baldwin, James 16, 251, 260-2
Barad, Karen 45-6
 intra-activity 45
 matter 45
Baugh, Bruce 133, 136
Beauvois, Xavier 14, 147, 150, 157-8, 160-1
Bec, Louis 194
Becker, Jason 236-7, 243
becoming-active, stages for 66-70
 common notions/common sense ideas of 69-70
 composition and decomposition 67, 69
 effects of sadness 68-9
 genuine actions 66
 good encounters 69
 interaction between bodies 68
 poison and toxicity, concept of 68
Bekoff, Marc 91
Bene, Carmelo 118
Benjamin, Walter 89
Bennett, Jane 45-6
 vibrant matter, concept of 45-6
Bergman, Ingmar 151
Bergson, Henri 7-8, 112, 151, 153
Bergsonism 112
 Einstein's theory of relativity, critique of 112
 philosophy of time 33
 theory of affect 151, 153
Bernard, Claude 108

The Best Exotic Marigold Hotel (2011) 179
Bhabha, Homi K. 172
biblical prohibition 156
Big Hero 6 (2014) 198-201
biocybernetic reproduction 189
biomechanical engineering 237
biopolitics 15, 211, 213, 222, 228-9, 255-6, 261-2
 in *Blade Runner* (1982) 215
 in *Do Androids Dream of Electric Sheep?* (Dick) 213
 figuration of the androids 213
 intra-species justice 222
 Law of Artificial Memory of 2101 215
 non-human characters 218
 Radical Replicant Movement 217
 and relationship with non-human creations 212-13
 in *Star Trek: The Next Generation* (1987) 218
 in *Tears in Rain* (Montero) 211-23
 and technohumans 215, 218-21
 teleportation technology 217
 ultra-Darwinists 216
 in *Weight of the Heart* (2016) 216
biotechnology and posthumanism
 dis/abled reflections (*see* dis/ability)
 experience of disability 234
 genetic normalization 239-42 (*see also* self-governance and genetic normalization)
 perspective on disability as suffering 235
 prosthetics and assistive devices 236-8
 technological optimism 233-4
 technomedicine and vital politics (*see* technomedicine)
Biro, Andrew 89-90
The Black Dahlia (2006) 190
Black Lives Matter 254
Blade Runner (1982) 213-15, 218
Bloodsworth-Lugo, Mary K. 45
Bodies That Matter (Butler) 53
body without organs (BwO) 42, 112, 114, 117-18, 255-6
Boyhood (2014) 140

BPO industries   177–8
Brahe, Tycho   108
Braidotti, Rosi   30, 130, 134, 138, 172–5, 189–90, 193, 196, 211, 217–20, 222, 230, 237–8
   affirmation   23–36, 243
   materiality   44–5
   neo-materialisms   23–36
   nomadic ethics   44, 218
Brison, Susan J.   51–2
Broken Earth Trilogy (Jemisin)   259
Brown, William   189, 191, 198, 200
Bryant, Levi R.   133–8
Buber, Martin   14, 147, 150, 157–9, 161
Buchanan, Ian   251
Burroughs, William S.   48
Butler, Judith   51–4
Butler, Samuel   113

Caillois, Roger   189, 196–7
Cameron, James   201
Canguilhem, Georges   26, 227
capitalism   2, 25–7, 30, 33, 36, 89, 155, 171–2, 211, 238, 253, 256, 260, 265
   contemporary capitalism   36
Captain America: The Winter Soldier (2014)   191, 195
Card, Orson Scott   199
Carr, Nicholas   193
cartographies   24, 32, 35
Cavarero, Adriana   51–2
Césaire, Aimé   252
CHAPPiE (2015)   170
   cast and characters in   180
   description of   178–9
   Postcolonial science fiction   178–81
   transhumanist fantasy in   178–80
Chastain, Jessica   131
Ciangottini, Valeria   154
cinema, posthuman
   and anti-anthropocentric potentialities   129
   de-hierarchization in   132, 134–5
   and Deleuze's transcendental empiricism (*see* transcendental empiricism)
   field of experience   136
   and philosophy of immanence   133

   and principle of determinability   132, 135
   representation and identity of   133
   and tenets of human exceptionalism   138
   and time-image   131
   transcendental empiricism and life   137–8
   transitions to images in   131
Cinema 1 (Deleuze)   147–8, 152
Cinema 2 (Deleuze)   117, 147–8, 156, 188
cinematic realisms   154, 157
Cisney, Vernon W.   141
The City We Became (Jemisin)   259
Clare, Eli   234–5, 237, 243
classicism   114
climate change   6, 41, 89–90, 220, 223
close-up and the face
   classical close-up   150
   'faceicity'   151
   'faceification,' process of   151
   'faceified'   152
   identification   151
   inauthentic 'mask' and authentic 'face'   152
   photoplay   151
   'selfie'   150
   state of Entity   151
Coates, Paul   147–8, 150–4, 157
Cognitive Behavioural Therapy (CBT)   88
Colebrook, Claire   45, 47, 53, 142
collaborative morality   24
colonialism   4, 25, 171–2, 174, 274
Comet (Stockhausen)   115
common notions/common sense ideas   64, 67–70, 75–9
composition and decomposition   67, 69
confession   17, 273–4
The Conformist (1970)   154
consciousness   4–5, 29, 33, 42–3, 49, 51, 136–7, 159, 175, 179, 189, 191, 202, 216, 222, 234, 259
constitutive anti-Blackness   250–2
Copernicus, Nicolaus   107–9
Cosmic Pulse (Stockhausen)   115
cosmological resonance   106

cosmology   13, 110–14, 117, 119–20
   and pseudo-cosmology   117
cosmology and Deleuze
   cosmic art   114–15
   cosmic earth   115
   geophilosophy *vs.* cosmo-
      philosophy   113–14
   Musica universalis, Pythagorian
      idea   115
   neologism 'chaosmology'   112
   supraearthly transcendence   113
cosmos   13–14, 107, 112, 114–15,
      118–20, 131, 136–8, 140–2,
      251–2, 263
   universe-cosmos   115
*The Crisis of European Sciences and
   Transcendental Phenomenology*
   (Husserl)   107–8
   heliocentric system   107
   objective perceptions   108
   science as *teoria*   107
   subjective perceptions   108
   telos of science   108
CRISPR-Cas9 system   241
Cuarón, Alfonso   141
cultural values   222
The Curious Case of Benjamin Button
   (2009)   198
cybernetic Nazism   191
cyberstars   195
cyborg   5, 172–6, 180–1
Cyborg Manifesto (Haraway)   172

Dabashi, Hamid   174
Damasio, Antonio   63
Darwin, Charles   108
Daybreak (2019)   48–9
Days of Heaven (1978)   140–1
de-hierarchization   132, 134–5, 138
Deleuze, Gilles, *see individual entries*
De Palma, Brian   190
Depp, Johnny   202
Derrida, Jacques   3, 148–9, 156, 271–2
desires
   active   30, 33, 77
   humanizing   219, 257
   irrational   67
   obsessive   71
   passion   66–7

rational   67
subjective   260
utopian and exotic   273
de Sousa, Ronald   63, 74
deterritorialization   10, 95, 113–14,
      116–17, 120, 131, 215, 231, 252,
      262–3, 277
Dick, Philip K.   15, 213–14, 217, 222
Diderot, Denis   26
Difference and Repetition (Deleuze)   32
differentiation, structure of   32
The Digital Film Event (Minh-ha)   173
dis/ability
   affirmation-confrontation paradox
      in   231
   and Deleuzian becoming-
      minoritarian   232
   and dis/humanism   232
   dis/human manifesto   230–1
   fallacy of equivocation   232
   and new materialisms   230
   a priori status   230
   as suffering, perspective of   235
Discipline and Punish (Foucault)   211,
      254, 261
dis/humanism   232
dis/human manifesto   230–1
Do Androids Dream of Electric Sheep?
   (Dick)   15, 213
Doane, Mary Ann   147, 150, 155
Douglas, Michael   198
Doyle, Conan   114
Driver, Dorothy   272
D3D (Digital 3D)   190, 201
Dussel, Enrique   174

egocentrism   110
Einstein, Albert   108, 112
Elysium (2013)   175
embryogenesis   95–8
emotions   65, 73–5, 150
   and affect   74–5, 149–50
   and goals   74
   impact of   274
   negative   74–5
Ender's Game (2013)   198–9, 201–2
Enlightenment   2, 5, 108, 148, 212
enlightenment humanity   212
Enter the Void (2010)   200

Enthiran/The Robot (2010)   14–15, 170, 181–3
  description and cast   181
  'masala' aesthetics in   182
  and proper posthumanist conception   183
  time- and movement-image in   182–3
ethics of affirmation   23–4, 28, 32–3, 236, 243
ethics of the image   160
E.T.: The Extra-Terrestrial (1982)   178
Eurocentrism   15, 170, 172–3, 183
European humanism   25
euthanasia   90
Ex Machina (2015)   175, 182
extra-terrestrials   114, 117, 120, 217

faceification process   151
'faceified'   152, 155
Fanon, Frantz   16, 250, 252, 254, 256, 259, 264
Fechner, Gustav   114
feminism   5, 12, 35, 41, 54, 172–3, 229–30
feminist epistemology   24
Fichte, Johann Gottlieb   65
field of experience   14, 130–8, 141–2, 233
fields of tension   47, 49
Fight Club (1999)   200
Flaxman, Gregory   189
Fleming, David H.   14–15
Floyd, George   261
Flusser, Vilém   189, 191, 193–5
Forbidden Planet (1956)   140
forgiveness   271–2, 278
Foucault, Michel   16, 25, 27–8, 32, 211–12, 216–17, 227, 232–3, 254–5, 260–1, 273
frantic consumerism   30
Frijda, Nico   63, 75–6
Fukuyama, Frances   3
Furstenau, Marc   140–2

Gabilondo, Joseba   175
Galilei, Galileo   107
genetics
  reverse genetics   241
  screening and manipulation   226, 228, 240, 243

genetic technologies   241–2
genuine actions   66
geocentrism   110
geophilosophy *vs.* cosmo-philosophy   113–14
Ghost in the Shell (2017)   191, 195, 199
Girl with a Pearl Earring (2003)   190
Giving an Account of Oneself (Butler)   51
globalized film industry   177–8
Global South and science fiction cinema   170
Goggin, Gerard   242
good encounters
  association in mind   71–2
  common notions   75–8
  emotions   65
  external circumstances   65
  joyful passions   63–4
  obsessive desires   71
  passive sorrows   66
  problems   63–6, 72
  rational explanation   76
  stages for becoming-active, Deleuze's proposal   66–70
  'titillation'   70
  vacillation and ambivalence   71–3
Goodley, Dan   230–2, 234, 240
Govil, Nitin   177
Gramsci, Antonio   173
gravity   96, 110–11, 115, 117–18, 138, 159, 197
Gravity (2013)   141, 200
Great Ape Animal Project   91–2
The Great Train Robbery (1903)   150, 153
Greenspan, Anna   193
Greenspan, Patricia   74
Grusin, Richard   152
Guattari, Félix, *see individual entries*

habit   276–7
Hadot, Pierre   113
haecceities   10, 43
Hail Caesar (2016)   190
Halsema, Annemie   52
Haraway, Donna J.   11, 15, 172–5, 180
Hayles, Katherine N.   3, 15, 172–3, 175, 193, 195
heliocentric system   107–8, 116
Her (2013)   175, 191

Herbrechter, Stefan 3
hermeneutic new realism 94
historical trauma 17, 271
The History of Sexuality (Foucault) 273
Hitchcock (2012) 191
Hollywood Renaissance, 1970s 148
Holocaust 25
Holst, Gustav 115
Howard, Ron 141
How We Became Posthuman (Hayles) 3, 172
Hughes, Bill 227
Hughes, Joe 44
human exceptionalism 2, 4–5, 14, 23, 30, 41, 135, 138, 142, 251, 261
Human Genome Project 240
human rights 212
Hume, David 27
Huntington's disease 239
Husserl, Edmund 13, 106–12
   and anthropo/Euro-centric pseudo-cosmology 117
   deterritorialization of perceptions 117
   earth as an originary Ark *(Ur-Archè)* 108–10
   eidetic variations 109
   geostatism 116
   gravity 117–18
   'logic of the earth' 118–19
   and modern scholasticism 118
   perceptions 109
   pheno-cosmological view 109
   phenomenological functionaries 118
   pseudo-cosmology 117

I and Thou (Buber) 157
impairment of spatial perception (ISP) 110–11
incorporeal transformations in truth and reconciliation, *see* assemblage; truth commissions
Inhuman Conditions: On Cosmopolitanism and Human Rights (Pheng Cheah) 212
Insect Media (2010) 196
interaction between bodies 68–9
interobjectivity or intercorporeality 47
Interstellar (2014) 140

intra-activity 45–6
intra-species justice 222
ipse 50–1
Irigaray, Luce 57, 258
Islam, Monirul 174, 178
The Island (2005) 191
IT industry 177–8

Jemisin, N. K. 259
Johansson, Scarlett 15, 190–8, 202–3, *see also* science fiction films
   beings and identity, notions of 192
   cybernetic Nazism 191
   and dividuality 190
   liquid topology 193–4
   'media archaeology' perspective 190
   non-linear models of 191–2
   post-human or inhuman roles in fictions 191
   racialized and sexualized image 191
   science fictive-themed films 191
Jonze, Spike 198
Joy
   active 12, 63–8, 77–9
   definition 63
   partial 71–2
   passive 13, 63–4, 66–8, 72–3, 75–9
joyful passions 63–8, 71, 73, 75–9
Jurassic Park (1993) 131

Kafka, Franz 118
Kant, Emmanuel 9, 116, 255
Kearney, Richard 156
Kierkegaard, Søren 65
Kieslowski, Krzysztof 151
Klee, Paul 115, 252
Knee, Adam 190
Kubrick, Stanley 140, 189
Kurzweil, Ray 5

La Dolce Vita (1960) 154
Law of Artificial Memory of 2101 215
Lawrence, D. H. 252
Lazarus, Richard 63, 75
LBGTQ+ 30
Léaud, Jean-Pierre 153
Le Doeuff, Michèle 47
Leibniz, Gottfried Wilhelm 27
Leigh, Janet 191

Lenoir, Tim 202
Levi, Primo 25, 99
Levinas, Emmanuel 14, 92, 149, 155–7, 253
Lewis, Bradley E. 226
life as *zoe* 33–4
Linklater, Richard 140
liquid bio-aesthetics 195
liquid topology 193–4
Location of Culture (Bhabha) 173
'logic of the earth' 118–19
Lowood, Henry 202
Lucas, George 140
Lucy (2014) 191

McFarlane, Colin 275
Macherey, Pierre 12, 63–6, 72–3, 75, 77–8
machinic autopoiesis, notion of 31
Malick, Terrence and cinema of life
  exploration of cosmos 140
  Malick's aesthetic 141
  narrative concentrations in science fiction 141
  principle of indiscernibility 140
  space-as-immanence 142–3
  space explored by humans 140–1
Mallarmé, Stéphane 118
Martin-Jones, David 182–3
Marxism 28, 33
Massumi, Brian 50, 53, 149–50, 152, 160–1
Match Point (2005) 191
material feminism 5, 41–2, 54
materialist ontology 29–30
materiality
  Alaimo's view of material self 45
  Barad's intra-activity 46
  Bennett's concept of vibrant matter 46–7
  Braidotti's views on nomadic subjects 44
  viscosity and fluidity 45
material science 237
Matheson, Richard 200
Matrix (2014) 176
Méliès, Georges 140
Mendeleev, Dmitri 108
Mendieta, Eduardo 211

Metamorphoses: Towards a Materialist Theory of Becoming (Braidotti) 189
Metropolis (1929) 175
micro-technologies 199
Mitchell, William J. T. 189
modern scholasticism 118
Monroe, Marilyn 191
Montero, Rosa 15, 213, 215–19, 222–3
Moravec, Hans 175
morphogenesis 85–7, 95–6
Morton, Samantha 198
Morton, Timothy 90
Mulvey, Laura 129
Münsterberg, Hugo 151
Musica universalis, Pythagorean idea 115
mutation 47, 85, 87, 93, 98, 222, 226–8, 269, 277

Naked Lunch (Burroughs) 48
Narendra, Divya 178
narrative identity 52
NASSCOM 177
naturecultures 30–1
nature-culture-media ecologies
  notion of machinic autopoiesis 31
  principle of autopoiesis 31
  radical neo-materialism 31
  and Spinozism 30
  transversality 31
  vital materialist understanding of 'life' 30
Nayar, Pramod K 3, 5
negative emotions 74–5
neoliberal individual formation, tenets of 33
neoliberalism 2, 89, 214, 227, 229, 236, 239, 254–5, 261
neo-materialism 12, 23, 25, 31–4
  radical neo-materialism 31
neo-realism 31
Newell, Christopher 242
new materialism 5, 41, 230
Ng, Jenna 198
Nietzsche, Friedrich 3, 7–8, 12, 25, 27, 41–2, 44, 48–9, 72, 113, 119–20, 148
Nolan, Christopher 140

nomadic subjects, Braidotti's views 44
Noys, Benjamin 32
Nussbaum, Martha 63

obsessive desires 71
Of Gods and Men (2010) 14, 147, 157–8, 160
  Christological metaphorization 160
  communion as 'dialogue' 160–1
  scenes 157–9
Orientalism (Saïd) 173
Orwell, George 216

Pandora's Box (1929) 148, 152
Parikka, Jussi 193, 196
Parthasarathy, Balaji 177
passion-desires 66–7
The Passion of Joan of Arc (1928) 154, 160
Patel, Dev 179–81
pathologization 227
patriarchy 4, 172
patterning and stabilization
  morphogenesis 85–6
Pepperell, Robert 175
perception-image 152–3, 160
perceptions 88, 108–10, 117, 132–3, 136, 153, 197
Persona (1966) 154
pessimism 16, 250–3, 255, 257, 259–65
pheno-cosmological view 110
phenomenological functionaries 118–19
philosophy of immanence 24, 27, 133
photoplay 151
Pisters, Patricia 193, 197
Pistorius, Oscar 236–7, 243
plant
  architecture 96
  bodies and living 95–6
  ethics 13, 87, 92–3
Plate, Brent S. 153, 155
poison and toxicity, concept of 68
polyps 12, 48–9
  and body without organs (BwO) 42
  haecceities 43
  ipse-identity 50–1
  and material inscription of trauma in body 51–2
  and materiality 44–7

and narrative identity 52
as processes of subjectivation 42–3
Ricoeurian notion of narrative self 51
transjectivity 49–50
Porter, Edwin S. 150–1
posthuman, *see also individual entries*
  as conceptual persona 12, 23–5
  assemblage 24
  cartographies 24
  collaborative morality 24
  feminist epistemology 24
  Guattari's ecologies 24
  neo-materialist posthuman philosophy 25
  posthumanism and post-anthropocentrism 23
  subject-formation 24
  subjectivity 24–5
  zoe-centred egalitarianism 25
and Deleuze
  analysis of capitalism as schizophrenia 26
  European humanism 25
  'life as surplus' 27
  Primo Levi – colonialism and despotic power 25
  thinking 27
  vital materialism 27
  zoe 27
The Posthuman (Braidotti) 129, 172
posthuman ethical pathways 54–5
posthumanism
  and AI 175–6
  and barbarian philosophy of liberation 174
  contemporary posthumanism 261
  cyborg and 172
  description of 171–2
  and neo-colonialism 174
  and post-anthropocentrism 23
  and postcolonial theory 172–3
  and subaltern theory 173–4
power-formations 34
primordial and ancestral 109
'primordial history' *(Urgeschichte)* 120
'primordial home' *(Urheimat)* 120
'primordial people' *(Urfolk)* 120
'primordial territory' *(Urgebiet)* 120
principle of determinability 132

principle of indeterminability   131, 135
principle of indiscernibility   140
problems of ambivalence   72
Process and Reality. An Essay in Cosmology (Whitehead)   112
productive 'eco-sophical' approach   29
prosthetics and assistive devices   234, 236–8, 242
   music editing software   236
   prosthetic limbs   236–7
   robotic/cybernetic limbs   238
'psychasthenia'   196
Puig de la Bellacasa, María   11
'pure becoming'   86–8

qualities of vegetality   94

racial delirium   255–6
racism   30, 256, 260–1, 263–4
radial concentricity   88
Radical Replicant Movement   217
RAM (the 'root apical meristem')   96
Ray, Satyajit   177
realism   46, 154, 157
refrain, concept of   276
The Republic (Plato)   171
Ricoeur, Paul   42, 50–1
   notion of narrative self   51
right-left bilaterality   88
Riley, Snorton, C.   250
Rivera, Alex   170
RoboCop (2014)   176
robotic/cybernetic limbs   238
romanticism   115
Rose, Nikolas   228, 239, 241–2
Runswick-Cole, Katherine   232, 279

sadness, effects of   68–9
Saïd, Edward W.   172
SAM (the 'shoot apical meristem')   96
schizoanalysis   258, 262–4
science as *teoria*   107
science fiction films
   artificial intelligence (AI)   202
   bad cinema hallmarks of   203
   and becoming-digital-insect   196–8
   D3D technologies   201
   evil militaristic and corporate themes   201–2
   human bodies and digital technologies   199
   micro-technologies   199
   molecular resonances and reflections   201
   narrative conventions   202
   'psychasthenia'   196
   Pym gas technofantasy   199–200
   space-image   200
sci phi category   189
Scoop (2006)   191
Screening the Face (Coates)   147
Scully, Jackie Leach   235, 237, 243
Sedgwick, Eve Kosovsky   149
self
   self-constitution   42, 46, 49–50, 52–4
   'self-imposed eugenics'   240
   self-labelled 'neuro-atypicals'   241
   self- (relation) to self (identity)   53–4
   violence to   51
self-governance and genetic normalization
   CRISPR-Cas9 system   241
   genetic technologies   242
   IVF births   241
   'self-imposed eugenics'   240
   self-labelled 'neuro-atypicals'   241
   Transcription Activator-Like Effector-Based Nucleases (TALENs)   240
   Zinc Finger Nuclease (ZFN)   240
'selfie'   150
sentimental humanism   261
Sexton, Jared   250
Shaviro, Steven   149, 193, 196
Sheerin, Declan   53
shoot indeterminacy   97
Short Circuit (1986)   170, 175–7
   animals as equals in   176
   posthumanist discourse in   175–7
   story and characters of   176
   and transhumanism   175
Short Circuit 2 (1988)   177
Silicon Valley   177
Simondon, Gilbert   26
slavery   64, 171, 250–1, 262–4
Slumdog Millionaire (2008)   178–9
Smith, Daniel W.   9
social constructivism   46
social-medical interventions   227
The Social Network (2010)   178

Sources of the Self (Taylor) 52
South African Truth and Reconciliation
  Commission 268–9, 279
Soviet cinema 151
space-as-immanence 142–3
space-image 200
spatial mechanics and significance
  adaxial-abaxial axis 98–9
  apical-basal axis 96
  axes of asymmetry 99
  development within embryo 97
  plant architecture 96
  RAM (the 'root apical meristem') 96
  SAM (the 'shoot apical meristem') 96
  shoot indeterminacy 97
species equality 30
Spielberg, Steven 131
Spinoza, Benedict de 3, 7–8, 12–13,
  27–8, 32, 41, 44, 46, 50, 63–79,
  172, *see also* good encounters;
  vital materialism
  ars vivendi 73
  common notions as 'adequate
    ideas' 64, 67, 76
  criticism of Spinoza 28
  monism 7–8
  and nature-culture-media
    ecologies 30
  Spinozian-esque model of mind and
    body parallelism 194
Spinozism 28–30, 64
  critical Spinozism 28
  'Spinozist legacy' 28–9
Spivak, Gayatri Chakravorty 173–4
Star Trek: The Next Generation
  (1987) 218
Star Wars (1977) 140
state of Entity 151
The Stepford Wives (1975) 175
Stockhausen, Karlheinz 115
Stoicism 66
'subaltern' theory 173–4
subject-formation 24, 34
subjectivity and body 42–4
  body without organs (BwO) 42
  haecceities 43
  'me' or 'we' 43
  processes of subjectivation 42–3
  process-oriented vision of 35

supraearthly transcendence 113
The Swan Book (Wright) 258
Swan Lake (1875) 159
symmetry and asymmetry, conceptual and
  morphological formations
  and adaxial-abaxial axis 98–9
  as animalesque nature of thought's
    body 89
  and apical-basal axis 96
  and axes of asymmetry 99
  of becoming-plant 94–5
  and care about plants 92
  and climate change 89–90
  and Cognitive Behavioural
    Therapy 88
  and condition, description 89
  of development within embryo 97
  and embryogenesis 95–6
  and evolution, deformation,
    growth 86–8
  and formal characteristics 88
  and front-to-back split 88
  and morphogenesis 85–6, 95–6
  and mutation 93
  as 'pure becoming' 86–8
  as radial concentricity 88
  and RAM (the 'root apical
    meristem') 96
  and right-left bilaterality 88
  and SAM (the 'shoot apical
    meristem') 96
  as shoot indeterminacy 97
  of stable up and downness 88
  and styles of thinking 86

Taylor, Charles 52
Tears in Rain (Montero) 211–23
technohumans 215, 218–21
technological optimism 233–4
technomedicine 15, 233, 238–43
  and disability 226–7
  genetic screening and
    manipulation 228
  medicine's relationship to body
    226–7
  pathologization 227
  social-medical interventions 227
  vital information 228
teleportation technology 217

telos of science   108
Terminator (1984)   176
territorialization and deterritorialization   262
Theory of the Heavens (Kant)   116
thinking
  -as-animal-thinking   88
  efficacy of   268–71
    assemblages   269
    global assemblages   269–70
    structures of determinism   269
    transitional justice   270–1
    truth commissions   268–9
  styles of   86–7
The Thin Red Line (1998)   140–1
A Thousand Plateaus (Deleuze and Guattari)   8, 16, 94, 112, 117, 148, 155, 252–3, 255, 258, 260, 263, 276–8
Thus Spoke Zarathustra (Nietzsche)   119
Timaeus (Plato)   114, 116
'time image'   147
'titillation'   70
Transcendence (2014)   8–9, 15, 26, 35, 113, 149, 155, 176, 198, 202, 211, 223
transcendence of negativity   26, 35
transcendence of representation   149
transcendental empiricism   14, 129–30, 132–4, 136–9, 141–3
  consciousness   136–7
  definition   132
  de-hierarchization   132, 134–5
  field of experience   136
  and life   137–8
  philosophy of immanence   133
  principle of indeterminability   135
  representation and identity   133
  tenets of human exceptionalism   138
'transcendental' film style, theory of   154
Transcription Activator-Like Effector-Based Nucleases (TALENs)   240
transformations   16, 26, 30, 33, 35, 41, 117, 147–8, 191–4, 197, 220, 235, 257, 269–70, 272–4, 277–80
The Transformers (2007)   178
transhumanism and posthumanism, distinction   175

transjectivity, concept of   12, 41, 44, 47
transversality   31
The Tree of Life (2011)   129
  principle of determinability   132
  time-image   131
  transitions to images   131
Tremain, Shelley   229
Trinh, T. Minh-ha   172–3
A Trip to the Moon (1902)   140
TRON: Legacy (2010)   175
truth commissions   16–17, 268–73, 275–9
  apology   273–5
  confession   273
  cultural dimensions   279
  forgiveness   271–2
  as global assemblage   270
  global modality of assemblage   269
  historical trauma   271
  procedures of transformation   273
Tuana, Nancy   45
2001: A Space Odyssey (1968)   140, 189

Uexküll, Jakob von   94
Ullmann, Liv   154
ultra-Darwinists   216
Under the Skin (2013)   191, 195–6
universe-cosmos   115, 118
univocity   32, 254, 258
  radical affirmation of   254

vacillation and ambivalence
  association in the mind, one thing with another   71–2
  obsessive desires   71
  problems of ambivalence   72
  'titillation'   70
Vampyroteuthis Infernalis: A Treatise, with a Report by the Institut Scientifique de Recherche Paranaturaliste (Bec and Flusser)   194
  biophilosophical treatise   194
  cyberstars   195
  liquid bio-aesthetics   195
  post-coital cannibalism   195
  vamp becoming Vampyroteuthis   194–6
vegetality   94

vibrant matter, Bennett's concept
    of 46–7
Vicky Christina Barcelona (2008) 191
violence to self 51
vital materialism 26–30
    critical Spinozism 28
    criticism of Spinoza 28
    materialist ontology 30
    productive 'eco-sophical'
        approach 29
    species equality 30
    'Spinozist legacy' 28–9
Viveiros de Castro, Eduardi 253

Warren, Calvin 250, 252
'we' as collective assemblage 34–5
Weight of the Heart (2016) 216
What Is Philosophy? (Deleuze and
    Guattari) 1, 13, 43, 85, 106,
    112, 115–16, 251, 257

Wilcox, Fred 140
Wilderson, Frank B. 250
Wolfe, Cary 3, 175
Woolf, Virginia 252
Wright, Alexis 258–9
Wright, Wendy M. 158

xenophobia 30

Zajonc, Robert 63
zero-gravity environment 110
Zinc Finger Nuclease (ZFN) 240
zoe 25, 27, 31, 33–5, 189, 212, 218–20
    Braidotti on 220
    'living matter' as *zoe*-centred
        process 25, 31
    zoe-power 25
zoe-centred egalitarianism 25, 31
Z-screen and IMAX D3D (and 4D)
    formats 200